THE AFRO-AMERICAN FAMILY

ASSESSMENT, TREATMENT, AND RESEARCH ISSUES

SEMINARS IN PSYCHIATRY

Series Editor

Milton Greenblatt, M.D.

Director, Neuropsychiatric Institute Hospital and Clinics

Professor and Executive Vice Chairman
Department of Psychiatry and Biobehavioral Sciences
University of California at Los Angeles
Los Angeles, California

Other Books in Series:

Psychiatric Aspects of Neurologic Disease, edited by D. Frank Benson, M.D., and Dietrich Blumer, M.D.
Borderline States in Psychiatry, edited by John E. Mack, M.D.
Topics in Psychoendocrinology, edited by Edward J. Sachar, M.D.
Consultation-Liaison Psychiatry, edited by Robert O. Pasnau, M.D.
Drugs in Combination with Other Therapies, edited by Milton Greenblatt, M.D.
Suicidology: Contemporary Developments, edited by Edwin S. Shneidman, Ph.D.
Alcoholism Problems in Women and Children, edited by Milton Greenblatt, M.D., and Marc A. Schuckit, M.D.
Ethological Psychiatry: Psychopathology in the Context of Evolutionary Biology, edited by Michael T. McGuire, M.D., and Lynn A. Fairbanks, Ph.D.
The Family in Mourning: A Guide for Health Professionals, edited by Charles E. Hollingsworth, M.D., and Robert O. Pasnau, M.D.
Clinical Aspects of the Rapist, edited by Richard T. Rada, M.D.
Sex Education for the Professional: A Curriculum Guide, edited by Norman Rosenzweig, M.D., and F. Paul Pearsall, Ph.D.
Psychopharmacology Update: New and Neglected Areas, edited by John M. Davis, M.D., and David Greenblatt, M.D.
Methods of Biobehavioral Research, edited by E. A. Serafetinides, M.D., Ph.D.
Alcohol and Old Age, by Brian L. Mishara, Ph.D., and Robert Kastenbaum, Ph.D.
Psychiatric Research in Practice: Biobehavioral Themes, edited by E. A. Serafetinides, M.D., Ph.D.
Family Therapy and Major Psychopathology, edited by Melvin R. Lansky, M.D.
Mental Health and Hispanic Americans: Clinical Perspectives, edited by Rosina M. Becerra, Ph.D., Marvin Karno, M.D., and Javier I. Escobar, M.D.

THE AFRO-AMERICAN FAMILY
ASSESSMENT, TREATMENT, AND RESEARCH ISSUES

Edited by

Barbara Ann Bass, M.S.W.
Lecturer in Social Work
Department of Psychiatry
Neuropsychiatric Institute
UCLA Center for the Health Sciences
Los Angeles, California

Gail Elizabeth Wyatt, Ph.D.
Assistant Professor of Psychiatry
Neuropsychiatric Institute
UCLA Center for the Health Sciences
Los Angeles, California

Gloria Johnson Powell, M.D.
Associate Professor of Psychiatry and
Director, Child Psychiatric Outpatient Department
Neuropsychiatric Institute
UCLA Center for the Health Sciences
Los Angeles, California

GRUNE & STRATTON
A Subsidiary of Harcourt Brace Jovanovich, Publishers
New York London
Paris San Diego San Francisco São Paulo
Sydney Tokyo Toronto

Library of Congress Cataloging in Publication Data
Main entry under title:

The Afro-American family: assessment, treatment, and research issues.

(Seminars in psychiatry)
Papers presented at a series of seminars organized by the Neuropsychiatric Institute, UCLA Center for the Health Sciences, beginning in 1974.
Includes bibliographical references and index.
1. Afro-Americans—Mental health—Congresses.
2. Afro-Americans—Mental health services—Congresses.
3. Afro-American families—Mental health—Congresses.
I. Bass, Barbara Ann. II. Wyatt, Gail Elizabeth.
III. Powell, Gloria J. IV. University of California, Los Angeles. Neuropsychiatric Institute. V. Series: Seminars in psychiatry (Grune & Stratton) [DNLM: 1. Blacks—Psychology. 2. Cross-cultural comparison. 3. Psychotherapy. 4. Socioeconomic factors. WA 305 A846]
RC451.5.N4A77 616.89'008996073 81-13267
ISBN 0-8089-1377-8 AACR2

Grune & Stratton, Inc.
111 Fifth Avenue
New York, New York 10003

Distributed in the United Kingdom by
Academic Press Inc. (London) Ltd.
24/28 Oval Road, London NW1

Library of Congress Catalog Number 81-13267
International Standard Book Number 0-8089-1377-8
Printed in the United States of America

In appreciation to my parents, my husband Dick and to my daughter Stephanie for their support, love, and encouragement.

Barbara Ann Bass

To Lewis, Lance, and Lacey, who have strongly encouraged my professional growth and lovingly nurtured my self-confidence.

Gail Elizabeth Wyatt

For April, Allison, and Daniel in appreciation of their patience and understanding.

Gloria Johnson Powell

Dedicated to the memory of Ralph Geeenson, M.D., who was a source of inspiration to all of us.

Contents

Acknowledgments

This collection of works is an achievement beyond just that of the editors and represents the efforts of countless individuals without whom this project never could have reached fruition. From the outset, we have had the continuing moral and financial support as well as the dedicated commitment to the goals of the seminar and the book from our chairman of the Department of Psychiatry, Dr. Louis J. West. We were all junior faculty when the idea was born and in his usual pioneering spirit Dr. West encouraged, inspired, and urged us on. It was not an idea whose time had come, and we had to face the initial skepticism of those who felt that such a project had no place in an academic research center like the Neuropsychiatric Institute. Dr. West continued to support the course at the time when there were no other courses of this nature in any of the medical schools or psychiatry departments in the country.*

As the child psychiatry program expanded and the numbers of Afro-American families seeking services at the NPI increased, Dr. James Q. Simmons III, Director of the Mental Retardation/Child Psychiatry Division, felt the urgency to have the child inpatient and outpatient staff trained in this area. The course has been based within the MR/CP Division with generous support of staff time, space, and financial support. Needless to say, without such support the seminar with the research that it has generated, the training it has provided, and this book it has produced would have been difficult goals to accomplish.

We also wish to express our sincere appreciation to Dr. Milton Greenblatt, the series editor, and to our publisher, Grune & Stratton, whose continued enthusiasm regarding the book has served as a tremendous reinforcement to the editors. In addition, Dr. Chester Pierce has served as our mentor and has encouraged us to pursue our efforts to redefine techniques for the mental health care of Afro-American people; we are greatly indebted to him for his continued support. Linda Itson and Perry Lim have worked tirelessly with the initial manuscript, some of which required complicated transcription. Susan Haynes was also very helpful in organizing the chapters prior to publication. And, finally, we wish to extend our special thanks to Annelisa Romero, whose expert suggestions helped to refine much of the material in the book.

*Wyatt, G.E., Bass, B., and Powell, G.J.: A Survey of Ethnic and Sociocultural Issues in Medical School Education, J Med Ed 53: 627–632, 1978.

Foreword

For some time, Americans have upheld the ideal of providing health services to all citizens as an inalienable right. The growth of private insurance coverage for many persons in the middle and lower classes and the great strides made in thinking and planning for a national health insurance program gave heart to this great dream. The reader will recall that the 1978 Presidential Commission on Mental Health assigned very high priority to programs for the poor, the underserved, and minority groups. Twenty years before, an earlier Joint Commission on Mental Illness and Health had stressed the need for substituting a community-based program for a primarily hospital-based program, with the expectation that the former would come face to face with community values, traditions, and belief systems. In fact, these expectations have come to fruition in a very large sense. We have learned that service delivery systems to minority peoples and to the impoverished cannot succeed unless they close the language, tradition, and culture gaps. And so a challenge of major proportions has been set before the clinical establishment: how to reach and serve those who are culturally different or even culturally alien.

The problems of "outreach" will not be settled merely by sitting in an office and wishing that a few minority people would straggle in. Neither will it be settled by an injection of massive funds into a national health program and then letting natural social events have their way. To make a significant change, several crucial forces must be encouraged and strongly supported: (1) The national conscience must be further awakened to the obligation to serve those who have for so long been neglected. This implies, in particular, a shift in the commitment of professional caregivers from an individual to a public health orientation, especially as it applies to the mental health populations. (2) Much more research must be directed to the epidemiology of mental illness and to the development of effective service delivery systems. (3) Caregivers must learn how to bridge the gap between majority ideology, values, and beliefs and those of minorities and the poor. (4) Health-seeking pathways and health utilization patterns of minorities must be defined and understood so that the tendency for minority people and the poor to turn away from distant, culturally irrelevant establishment services can be fully corrected.

I think relatively few of our mental health leaders today see this as our central task and recognize the enormity of the problems that lie ahead. Perhaps fewer have developed plans for solving the problem, and even fewer have taken any practical steps in this direction. But many Afro-Americans, Hispanics, Asians, and many, many poor people know what it is all about and are willing to tell us if we will listen. There is no alternative but for leaders and professionals with intelligence and a social conscience to listen and learn what our minority colleagues are telling us and join with them in local and national plans and actions to ensure their inalienable rights to health and happiness.

This book, edited by Barbara Bass, Gail Wyatt, and Gloria Powell, three distinguished Afro-American women colleagues, updates the clinical knowledge and research information that our field now possesses about treating the Afro-American individual and his or her family. I found it highly informative, even inspirational.

As series editor, it is my great pleasure to welcome this book into the family of *Seminars in Psychiatry*.

Milton Greenblatt, M.D.

Preface

There has been a growing awareness among many mental health professionals and trainees treating Afro-Americans in psychotherapy that their interpretations of patient–therapist dialogues might be viewed from a culturally different perspective if they understood more about the culture and life experiences of Afro-Americans. Because few training programs for mental health professionals have provided the needed training in ethnopsychiatry and the delivery of mental health services to minority group people, and because of countless requests over the years for consultations and presentations on this subject, the editors, a multidisciplinary team of Afro-American mental health professionals, decided to formally organize a course to meet the demand for such training. Consequently, in 1974 a seminar entitled "The Assessment and Treatment of Afro-American Families" was developed in the Department of Psychiatry at the Neuropsychiatric Institute, UCLA Center for the Health Sciences, for the purpose of offering lectures and a clinical experience in the assessment and treatment of Afro-American patients. Our past experience as minority group faculty members convinced us that most professionals and trainees needed to learn to identify aspects of the evaluation and treatment process with Afro-Americans that should be approached from the patients' cultural and psychosocial perspectives. The seminar was not only sorely needed, but extremely popular among trainees and staff from the Neuropsychiatric Institute as well as from other universities, colleges, and mental health centers ranging as far south as San Diego and as far north as Berkeley. This book highlights the information presented in that seminar over a period of five years.

Included here are selected lectures and research papers from scholars who are highly respected in their fields and are considered to be specialists in the areas in which they have written.

Because we represent a multidisciplinary mental health team, this book is written for mental health practitioners of all disciplines. We have also attempted to maintain a research perspective for each topic, and the contributors have organized their discussions to include, whenever possible, the most recent empirical investigations. The editors are hopeful that the book will also prove useful to those conducting clinical research with

Afro-Americans as well as to academicians in training institutions and clinicians in private practice.

We wish to make special note that, whenever possible, the term *Afro-American* is used instead of *black* when referring to the cultural and national diversity of the ethnic group about which this book is written. The emphasis will be on examining those aspects of the peoples' African heritage as they interface with American values, economics, language, and culture rather than on skin color as the only determinant that influences every aspect of a people's existence.

Like the seminar, this book was created from a growing need to offer information to mental health professionals about the assessment and psychiatric treatment of Afro-Americans and relevant research issues. It is hoped that it will reach an even wider audience.

Contributors

Barbara Ann Bass, M.S.W.
Lecturer in Social Work
Department of Psychiatry
Neuropsychiatric Institute
UCLA Center for the Health Sciences
Los Angeles, California

Gordon L. Berry, Ed.D.
Professor of Education
Graduate School of Education
University of California
Los Angeles, California

Yvonne B. Ferguson, M.D.
Assistant Professor
Department of Psychiatry
Neuropsychiatric Institute
UCLA Center for the Health Sciences
Los Angeles, California

Ralph Greenson, M.D. (*deceased*)
Clinical Professor of Psychiatry
Department of Psychiatry
Neuropsychiatric Institute
UCLA Center for the Health Sciences
Los Angeles, California

Joan E. Johnson, M.S.W.
Lecturer in Social Work
Department of Psychiatry
Neuropsychiatric Institute
UCLA Center for the Health Services
Los Angeles, California

Lewis M. King, Ph.D.
Assistant Professor of Psychology and
Director, Fanon Research and Development Center
Charles R. Drew Postgraduate Medical School
Inglewood, California

Perry Lim, B.A.
Graduate Student
California State University
Los Angeles, California

Helen A. Mendes, D.S.W.
Associate Professor, School of Social Work
University of Southern California
Los Angeles, California

Claudia Mitchell-Kernan, Ph.D.
Associate Professor of Anthropology and
Director, Center for Afro-American Studies
University of California
Los Angeles, California

Hector F. Myers, Ph.D.
Associate Professor of Psychology
Department of Psychology
University of California
Los Angeles, California

Gloria Johnson Powell, M.D.
Associate Professor of Psychiatry and
Director of Child Psychiatric Outpatient Department
Neuropsychiatric Institute
UCLA Center for the Health Sciences
Los Angeles, California

Annelisa Romero
Senior Editor
Department of Psychiatry and Biobehavioral Sciences
Neuropsychiatric Institute
University of California
Los Angeles, California

Barbara Bryant Solomon, D.S.W.
Professor, School of Social Work
University of Southern California
Los Angeles, California

Ellis E. Toney, M.D.
Professor of Psychiatry
Charles R. Drew Postgraduate Medical School
Los Angeles, California

Kayvonne Wright, R.N., M.N.
Lecturer in Nursing
Neurosychiatric Institute
UCLA Center for the Health Sciences
Los Angeles, California

Gail Elizabeth Wyatt, Ph.D.
Assistant Professor of Psychiatry
Neuropsychiatric Institute
UCLA Center for the Health Sciences
Los Angeles, California

PART I

Sociocultural Variables and General Background Issues

EDITOR'S INTRODUCTION

The five chapters in Part I provide background information such as social and cultural patterns, some of which are African in origin, that can stil be observed in the lifestyles of Afro-American families today. The chapter by Joan Johnson, "The Afro-American Family: A Historical Overview," describes the early history and family structures adopted during and after slavery.

In "The Validity of Sociocultural Factors in the Assessment and Treatment of Afro-American Families," Barbara Bass identifies contemporary sociocultural variables and their relationship to mental health issues. Black English is one aspect of the Afro-American culture that is receiving attention in research and clinical practice. Claudia Mitchell-Kernan describes the history and linguistic structure of Black English and the controversies around its use in educational and mental health settings in the chapter "Linguistic Diversity in the Service Delivery Setting: The Case of Black English." The manner in which Afro-American families have been studied from a social science research perspective is reviewed by Hector Myers in his chapter, "Research on the Afro-American Family: A Critical Review." "The Survey of Afro-American Behavior: Its Development and Use in Research," written by the editors, provides an extensive review of research regarding mental health professionals' knowledge of and racial attitudes towards Afro-Americans that may influence the services provided and the treatment outcome.

Joan E. Johnson

1

The Afro-American Family: A Historical Overview

The Afro-American family, with its "unique" structure, functioning, flexibility of roles, and strong religious orientation, has been an area of interest to dominant societies since the arrival of the first African to the North American continent some 350 years ago. The mere survival of Africans and their descendants is phenomenal, given the infamously dehumanizing manner with which they were abducted and transported. While enslaved, Africans were stripped of their rights as human beings. The slave, determined to survive, preserved many of the African customs, folklores and cultural practices, which continue to have a strong influence on the structure of the Afro-American family today. It is this African influence that has set the Afro-American family apart from the dominant group and that has been the focus of repeated analyses and comparisons by social scientists over the decades. All conceivable attempts have been made to demean, discredit, and label as weak and ineffective the adaptive features of this group which have been essential to the survival of Africans and their descendants. This chapter offers evidence that Afro-American family units have successfully struggled to maintain their continuity and strength despite the onslaught of slavery and its aftermath.

THE AFRO-AMERICAN FAMILY UNDER SLAVERY

Survival for the first Africans arriving in North America did not have the same significance in 1619 as it did for those arriving in the latter part of that century.[1] The Africans arriving in that year were brought to Jamestown, Virginia, and sold to a merchant as servants. They entered as unfree persons into a society in which large numbers of people were similarly unfree. Their status was similar to that of many Indians and other European immigrants. Africans also had rights, during that time, similar to the rights of indentured servants; that is, they were required to serve their masters for a period of seven years, after which they became free persons.

However, the need for an abundance of free labor grew as the Colonies expanded. The number of European immigrants was insufficient to meet the needs of the mushrooming cotton industry; those American Indians who were enslaved frequently escaped or physically succumbed to the adverse climate of the South. Plantation owners found that the African was able to withstand the hot, humid conditions of the South and proved to be the best source of labor available. As the number of Africans increased, their status gradually changed from servant to slave and in 1661, Virginia passed the first laws making them formally and legally slaves for the duration of their lives.

Slavery in the American Colonies took on a peculiar form in that the African was denied all human rights and labeled "subhuman." To maintain the African in this subhuman category, slave owners systematically segregated those slaves coming from the same tribe or clan. The denial of contact or communication between relatives, friends, or slaves speaking the same regional language was one of the most devestating blows that could be inflicted upon a group of people whose daily life, prior to enslavement, was centered around a strong family structure. Marriage and family life for the African was entrenched in centuries of tradition, ritual, custom, and law. Marriage was not just the uniting of two people, but the union of two families, each with an extended network, each having considerable influence and responsibility for the new family's development of well-being. In essence, African family life was highly articulated within the rest of society. The family, through its ties with wider kinship circles, was an economic, religious, and political unit. Family life was strong and viable; it was the center of African civilization.[2]

Unlike the diffused, almost hidden manner in which African practices are found among Afro-Americans, in the South American regions and islands of the Caribbean, tribal customs and practices of African descendants are more pronounced and identifiable. Historian Frank Tannebaum speculates that the Catholic Church played an important role in the preservation of the African culture because in all areas where Catholicism was the dominant religion, the church demanded that all slaves be offered religious instruction.[3] Teaching them to read in the native language increased the ease with which they adapted to their new and hostile environment.

How slaves adapted and ultimately established their family structures was thought by historians E. Franklin Frazier, Kenneth Stamps, and Stanley Elkins to depend solely upon the direct influence the slave had with those families of the dominant group or on the contact some slaves may have had with members of the free Afro-American community.[4–6] John Hope Franklin and E. Franklin Frazier in their historical writings suggest that those slaves who worked as field hands or lived on plantations where they were isolated from contact with their masters suffered the most and had no values or mores to guide them, whereas those who lived in close proximity to their masters or worked as house servants were more advanced with cultural values and mores similar to the dominant group.[4,7] Gutman proved through his examination of various plantation records that a common tie could be found among slave families, whether they had resident or absentee owners.[8] In the examination of a single South Carolina slave birth register, Gutman found that slave families lived in close proximity over many generations, thus allowing them to pass on common sexual, marital, familial, and social choices. The slave child was socialized through the close union with parents and the close extended bond of the slave community. Adult slaves who were able to maintain long marriages were able to provide role models for the young slave couple. It appears that young slaves learned more about family life from those families visibly accessible, as opposed to acquiring family life values from outside groups.

Systems for survival were apparently well established and functional for the family and slave community. Yet slave owners felt that slaves had no rights to be respected; when two slaves sought to marry, they were required to engage in a meaningless marriage ceremony carrying no legal sanction. The master or preacher would read a few lines from a bible or have the slave couple simply jump over a broom to sanction their union. Lacking respect for the slave union, the master felt free to sexually exploit slave women, knowing slave men were generally powerless to protect them. However, it is important to recognize that not all slave men relinquished their families and culture without resistance. Just as there were almost daily mass slave insurrections, whenever possible men would defend their families against the cruel and massive assaults of the slave system.[1] The following is an account of a man who described the humiliating and cruel experiences of his father while attempting to defend his mother:[4, p.48]

> His right ear had been cut off close to the head, and he had received a hundred lashes on his back. He had beaten the overseer for a brutal assault on my mother,

and this was his punishment. Furious at such treatment, my father became a different man, and was so morose, disobedient and intractable, that Mr. N. decided to sell him. He accordingly parted with him, not long after, to his son who lived in Alabama, and neither mother nor I ever heard from him again.

Another blow both physically and psychologically to the slave family was the separation of children from their parents. The literature has frequently tried to represent the slave mother as indifferent to her own children and as the devoted, caring, foster-mother of her master's children. There is an abundance of evidence, however, demonstrating the slave mothers developed deep and permanent bonds with their children, often defying their masters and enduring suffering to prevent separation from their young. Josiah Henson in his book, *Father Henson's Story of His Own Life*, recalled the anguish his mother suffered when he and his brother and sisters were being sold. He described his mother as being "paralyzed with grief" as she watched her children sold one by one. She was also violently beaten as she clung to her master "entreating him to buy her baby as well as herself, and spare to her at least one of her little ones."[9] Even the children of hated white fathers were cherished as Frederick Douglass described his close relations with his grandmother and the devotation his mother felt toward him even though she only saw him a few times because she had been sold to another slave master. He recalled:[10, pp. 24–25]

I never saw my mother, to know her as such, more than four or five times in my life, and each of these times was very short in duration, and at night. She would travel the whole distance of twleve miles by foot. She would lie down with me, and get me to sleep, but long before I waked she was gone.

Separation of family members was inevitable. The most common occurrence was the sale of men. In their attempts to establish some form of continuity, families commonly named male children after their fathers. Gutman states, "naming a child for its father therefore confirmed the dyadic tie and gave it an assured historical continuity that complemented the close contact that bound the child to its mother."[8]

Social scientist Jessie Bernard surmised in her writings that the female slave was able to develop a stronger and more superior position than the male slave because she was allowed to perform her role more adequately than he was.[11] The subservient role of the female slave was not too far out of line with the western world's definition of a "woman's place." She was also strategically better off than a man because of her usefulness as a breeder as well as a worker. Nonetheless, she was not exempt from whippings, and frequently risked floggings by attacking the master or overseer for brutalizing her children.

While the institution of slavery generally restricted conventional family functioning in the slave population, there was a sizable population of free Afro-Americans whose family systems were able to acquire an institutional character. The greatest population increase of free Afro-Americans occurred during the seventeenth and early eighteenth centuries. Estimates vary, but historians generally agree that during the early 1700s, out of nearly a half-million African slaves, about one in eight were free persons.[7] However, as slavery became more oppressive and the demand for more slave labor increased by the latter part of that century, only a relatively smaller percentage had gained their freedom. The legal status of the free Afro-American was never certain. Obviously they were not true slaves and yet, it was continually made clear to them that neither were they the equals of Anglo-Americans.

The free population initially consisted of indentured servants who had gained their freedom after having served their stipulated terms. Freedom from slavery for others was obtained a number of different ways. One was through manumission—the freeing of slaves by their masters (most often, old slaves were released so that their masters would not have to support them in their unproductive years).[12] Some were also reportedly freed after long and meritorious service, because of a particular act of heroism, or because the master had promised them freedom. Many slaves who served in the American Revolution were also granted their freedom, as were children from various interracial unions. Children born of African men, whether slave or free, and Anglo women, were considered free because the child inherited the status of the mother. However, the children of slave women gained their freedom most often because their wealthy Anglo fathers released them when they reached maturity.[7]

As previously mentioned, a somewhat stable family life was possible among the free Afro-American population partly because they had more of a secure economic foundation, especially in the Southern cities. Their family structure was similar to that of the slave holders: it was partriarchal in organization and the status of women was similar to that of women among the dominant Anglo group. These free communities established schools, churches, literary societies, and organizations for mutual aid. Not only did these families support institutional life, but they were supported by institutions in their communities.[7]

THE AFRO-AMERICAN FAMILY IN FREEDOM

Following the collapse of the slave regime, the roles of the father and mother varied according to the circumstances of slave family organization. Those families that had managed to establish a fair degree of family organization during slavery made the transition to a patriarchal household without much disturbance in their regular routine of living.[8] Gutman found in North Carolina that ex-slaves, in seventeen counties, registered slave marriages with county clerks and justices of the peace.[8] In a condition of freedom, the father's authority was firmly established and in most cases the role of mother and wife fit the pattern of a patriarchal household. The loose ties that had held men and women together in nominal marriages during slavery broke easily during the crises of emancipation.[12] Those men, and in some cases women, without children wandered about the country in search of work and new experience. But more often the woman with family ties, whether she had been with a husband during slavery or had been deserted when freedom came, became responsible for the maintenance of the family group. It was this group that emerged as what Frazier called the "maternal family." This family organization was most common in the rural South and on the plantation. It was thus under the "maternal family" pattern that the term matriarch was first used to describe these households. It was not the mother, but the grandmother who was the head of the household and the guardian of the generations. The grandmother had acquired a prestigious position during slavery among both Anglos and slaves. She was usually the midwife for both, and became the repository of slave folklore and superstitions. The grandmother was also very important because it was usually only through the maternal ancestors that family linkage could be traced.

During the period following the Emancipation and the Reconstruction, masculine authority and the family was firmly established. The Afro-American man began to assert himself in politics, he purchased land, established independent churches and organizations, and participated freely in the overall social structure of the society. However, this progress was short-lived, because as the federal government withdrew and Jim Crow laws in the South were enacted, Afro-American men were once again denied the opportunity to provide adequately for their families.[7] This was accomplished by maintaining a high level of unemployment, by immobilization, and ultimately by spiritual and physical demoralization. Afro-Americans subsequently began to look to the North with its increased industrialization. During World War I, many Afro-American men saw, in the North, their chance to share more fully in the promise of the "American Dream." They moved to many northern cities in order to better provide for their families. However, they soon learned they were not to share in that dream, because the job opportunities denied them during slavery and in the South continued to be denied them in the North.

The mass migration of Afro-Americans to the North during and after the two World Wars had a tremendous impact on the quality of family life.

With the move to the North came the emergence of ghettoes, and with the ghettoes, the spawning of new life styles and family patterns. Survival of the family system demanded the assignment of new roles within the family unit, and these unique adaptive features have been termed negative and maladaptive by many social scientists. Stanley Elkin termed them "ineffective,"[6] and Patrick Moynihan called them "disorganized." Moynihan summed up his analysis by stating, "in essence, the Negro community has been forced into a matriarchal structure which, because it is so out of line with the rest of American society, seriously retards the progress of the group as a whole, imposes a crushing burden on the Negro male and, in consequence, on a great many Negro women as well."[13, p. 75] By focusing on such negative analyses and connotations, the dominant society could thus justifiably blame the Afro-American family itself for all of the many social, economic, legal, and educational problems with which it was confronted.

Within the Afro-American community today, there is no one monogamous family type, but a variety of family structures which are found at all levels of the socio-economic strata. The Afro-American community is much more complex and highly stratified than is generally appreciated. Andrew Billingsley describes three basic social class groupings. According to Billingsley, about 10 percent of Afro-American families may be considered upper class, 40 percent are middle class, and about half of all families are located in the lower classes. It is within the latter group that about one quarter of the families are classified as the "nonworking poor." This group is peopled by men and women who are unemployed or intermittently employed, rely upon support from family and friends, or receive assistance from public welfare.[2] This is group about which the most information appears in the literature and in the public press.

Afro-American structure today varies within the socio-economic strata. Billingsley described three such structures: nuclear families, extended families, and augmented families. Roughly two-thirds of all Afro-American families are nuclear and consist of husband and wife and their children. Extended families constitute about one quarter and consist of relatives or in-laws of the family head, sharing the same household with the nuclear family members. A tenth are augmented families, which include members not related to the family who share the same household living arrangements with the nuclear family.[2]

African kinship patterns continue to influence Afro-American kinship patterns today, regardless of socio-economic status or family structure. Social science research with families at poverty and working class levels show that these families were helped substantially by their kin, who took care of young children and frequently shared meals and money.[14] In the first empirical study of the Afro-American middle class since Frazier's study in the 1930s and 1940s, Harriette Pipes McAdoo found that today's Afro-American middle class families have retained an important part of their heritage.[14] They have maintained their present status with the support of mutually helpful family and friends who aided them in their rise to current levels of achievement. Her research revealed that these families kept in close touch with their parents, brothers and sisters, and other kin. They gave and received substantial kinds of assistance with finances, child care, and with discussions of personal problems. In short, kin networks that are an enormous strength for poor and working class Afro-American families seem to persist in prosperity as well.

SUMMARY AND CONCLUSIONS

Stemming from an African marriage and family life which was entrenched in centuries of tradition, ritual, custom, and law, Afro-Americans have evidenced an enduring history of maintaining family ties wherever and whenever possible. This emphasis on kith and kin survived their enormous traumatization as "subhuman" slaves whose family members were sold as market commodities and whose marriage "rites" most often consisted of jumping over a broom to sanctify the matrimony. In an attempt to maintain family continuity, for example, male slave children were routinely named after their fathers. An examination of plantation records demonstrated that common ties could be found among some groups of slave families who lived in close proximity over many genertions. Finally, when freed, either from slavery by manumission or from indentured service, Afro-Americans established stable family and community lives complete with schools, churches, literary societies, and organizations.

Following the formal abolition of slavery, families that had managed to establish a fair degree of organization during slavery made relatively smooth transitions to a family lifestyle which was characteristically patriarchal. The much-maligned matriarchal family phenomenon of Afro-Americans surfaced when post-slavery single or abandoned women became responsible for the maintenance of the family group. In fact, it was the grandmother, not the mother, who headed the household and who became the guardian of generations.

Seeking better conditions under which to support their families, Afro-American men migrated in large numbers with kin to the North during and after the two World Wars. However, the job opportunities denied them in the South continued to elude them in the North. Ghettos emerged, creating new transitional lifestyles and family patterns. Unique adaptive features of Afro-Americans struggling to survive against most often overwhelming odds have been termed, by some researchers, "pathological," ineffective," and "disorganized." Thus, by focussing on negative analyses and interpretations, the dominant society found a rationale for blaming Afro-Americans themselves for their many social, economic, legal, and educational problems.

Today, Afro-Americans constitute more diverse and complex socioeconomic class groupings than are generally known and appreciated. For example, 40 percent of Afro-American families are middle class, 10 percent are upper class,and about half of all families are located in the lower classes. Approximately one quarter of the latter group are classified as "nonworking poor," and it is with these subjects that the preponderance of research studies on Afro-American family life have been conducted, purporting to represent most Afro-Americans. Roughly two-thirds of all Afro-American families today are nuclear, consisting of father, mother, and their children.

The influence of African kinship patterns reaching back hundreds of years is still operative in Afro-American families today. Poverty level and working class families are helped substantially by their kin. Middle class Afro-American families maintain their ties with relatives, who have often helped them in rising to their current levels of achievement. Such strengths of Afro-Americans as their kinship networks, which have survived and served them in poverty and prosperity alike, merit further systematic study as mechanisms enhancing and preserving the family unit. These networks are not unique to Afro-Americans. They are found to be operating among a variety of minority groups, and thus may constitute a basic feature of survival for oppressed groups.

REFERENCES

1. Bennet L, Jr.: Before the Mayflower: A History of the Negro in America 1619–1964. New York, Rev. ed., 1978
2. Billingsley A: Black Families in White America. Englewood Cliffs, N.J., Prentice Hall, 1968
3. Tannebaum F: Slave and Citizen: The Negro in the Americas. New York, Random House, 1946
4. Frazier EF: The Negro Family in the United States. Chicago, University of Chicago Press, 1966 edition
5. Stampp KM: The Peculiar Institution: Slavery in the Ante-bellum South. New York, Knopf, 1956
6. Elkins S: Slavery: A Problem in American Institutional and Intellectual Life. Chicago, University of Chicago Press, 1963

7. Franklin JH: From Slavery to Freedom. New York, Alfred A. Knopf, 1956
8. Gutman HG: The Black Family in Slavery and Freedom 1750–1925. New York, Vintage Books, 1976
9. Henson J: Father Henson's Story of His Own Life. New York, Corinth Books, 1962, p. 1213
10. Quarles B (ed): Narrative of the Life of Frederick Douglas, An American Slave, Written by Himself. Cambridge, Harvard University Press, 1960, p. 24–25
11. Bernard J: Marriage and Family among Negroes. Englewood Cliffs, N.J., Prentice Hall, 1966, p 68
12. Frazier EF: The Free Negro Family. Nashville, Fisk University Press, 1932
13. Moynihan DP: The Moynihan Report and Politics of Controversy. Cambridge, M.I.T. Press, 1967
14. McAdoo HP: Black Kinship. Psychology Today, May, 1979

Gail Elizabeth Wyatt
Gloria Johnson Powell
Barbara Ann Bass

2

The Survey of Afro-American Behavior: Its Development and Use in Research

This chapter will describe research that examines the impact that prejudicial attitudes have upon societies' perception of minority group people and how these attitudes can influence the self-concept of individuals of ethnic minority groups. The racial attitudes of mental health professionals are of particular concern because Afro-Americans and other minority group people are continually seeking mental health services. Mental health professionals can mirror and reinforce societies' values, attitudes, and beliefs about their patients in a therapeutic relationship. Therapists' understanding and acceptance of cultural differences can be a key element of success to their clients' self-acceptance and to understanding mental health issues which are influenced by virtue of minority group status.

It was because of this concern that the Survey of Afro-American Behavior was developed to assess cognitive information and attitudes of mental health professionals regarding Afro-American people. This assessment offers to professionals and those in training programs some specific information regarding the areas in which the professional or trainee would require additional training in order to adequately provide psychiatric services to Afro-American people. However, before the Survey is described along with the research which demonstrates its usefulness, a review of the literature which provides a historical perspective to research regarding racial prejudice and assessment techniques that have been developed will better illustrate the necessity for measures like the Survey of Afro-American Behavior.

HISTORY OF RESEARCH ON RACIAL ATTITUDES

The research regarding racial attitudes has taken many interesting and oftentimes diverse paths which have not always led to changes in social policy. In his astute review of trends in research on racial discrimination, Pettigrew makes several pertinent observations.[1] Research on racial attitudes, discrimination, and ethnocentrism has remained in Pettigrew's opinion in "an insulated domain within social science." The field has been considered with disdain, resulting in low status and minimal fundings for research. Through the 1920s the race relations literature was openly anti-black. Following the depression, some significant studies emerged such as Klineberg's study of intelligence among Afro-Americans[2] and Gunnar Myrdal's *An American Dilemma*,[3] which received more attention than any other social science research on racial discrimination.

The Stauffer, Schuman, DeVinney, Star, and Williams study, *The American Soldier*,[4] was a departure from the descriptive studies of Davis et al.[5] and Dollard,[6] and heralded in a series of social psychological experimental studies. However, such publications were limited in their distribution and were published only in the *Journal of Social Issues*. With the publication of *The Authoritarian Personality*,[7] the emphasis shifted to the study of racism and discrimination on a personality level. The authoritarianism or "F" scale, the ethnocentrism or "E" scale, the anti-Semitism scale, and the politico-economic conservatism scale were widely used by many social scientists. Bettelheim and Janowitz's *Dynamics of Prejudice*[8] and Ackerman and Jahoda's *Anti-Semitism and Emotional Disorder*[9] were also noteworthy contributions and illustrative of the era when the thrust was on persuading racists to accept minority group individuals through the various methods of interracial contacts and human relations programs.

The field of race relations was profoundly affected by the 1954 U.S. Supreme Court ruling on segregation in the public schools and catapulted issues regarding race to the forefront of the nation's attention.

By the mid 1950s, survey research data on racial attitudes began to appear. In 1956, Hyman and Sheatsley published their study comparing racial attitudes of 1942 and 1944 with those in 1956.[10] The subsequent studies in 1964[11] and in 1971[12] noted the continued improvement in whites' attitudes towards blacks. Similar trends were noted among blacks.[13,14] However, it should be noted that during the late 1960s, the rate of improvement in white attitudes began to decrease considerably and many young blacks began to consider alternatives other than integration.[1] Indeed, because of the more recent decrease in the progress of curtailing racism, future research in this area will have to depend on what Pettigrew[1] calls process research on institutional change, the importance of which cannot be underscored for the elimination of institutional racism.

Any review of the literature on racial attitudes and stereotypes is incomplete without a review of the work of Gordon Allport, one of the most noted social psychologists in the area of race relations and attitudes. In his well-known book, *The Nature of Prejudice*, Allport defines stereotypes as "primarily images within a category invoked by the individual to justify either love-prejudice or hate-prejudice" (p. 189).[15] Allport further elucidates certain other aspects of stereotypes that may add insight to this discussion. They are that a stereotype: (1) may sometimes grow in defiance of all evidence, (2) may be totally unsupported by facts, (3) may develop from a sharpening and over generalization of facts, (4) acts both as a justificatory device for categorical acceptance or rejection of a group and to simplify perception and thinking, making both processes less complex, (5) is sustained by selective perception and selective forgettings, and (6) changes in time.

This last characteristic of stereotypes is especially interesting and, of course, invites the immediate question of whether negative stereotypes of a minority-group people are decreasing over time. One such study by Gilbert in 1951 showed a "fading effect" of stereotypes for ten national and ethnic groups between 1932 and 1950.[6] However, Allport maintained that although all minority groups in America suffer from the same state of marginality to a considerable degree, for the Afro-American it is always there, and changes little over a period of time as compared with other minority groups.[15] "The marginality for the minority-group person has," says Allport, "its haunting consequences of insecurities, conflict, and irritation." Especially for Afro-Americans, efforts to achieve "relatedness" are almost always likely to be rebuffed. They are never, ever, really part of the "in group."

There have been many treatises on the psychology of prejudice. Time and space do not allow a comprehensive recapitulation of the many studies and theories about prejudice here, but Bettelheim and Janowitz[17] have offered a thorough review of the subject that encompasses the causal problems within the perpetrator, as well as the consequences for the victim.

In their earlier work on stereotyping the minority, Bettelheim and Janowitz found that when there were two or more ethnic minorities, there was a tendency for the prejudiced person to separate the stereotypes into two sets and to assign each of them to one minority group. In their study of prejudice toward Afro-Americans and Jews in the Army, they found that the intolerant soldier selected the Jew for projection of those characteristics rejected by the superego and the Afro-American for those id desires which represented greater irrationality. They also found that when the two minority groups were diffused in physical characteristics such as skin color, the minority group having the greater physical difference was used for projecting the anxieties about dirt and sexual desires, while the minority group with more physical similarities was a target for the anxieties about overpowering control.

The stereotyping used to characterize Afro-Americans in the 1950 study were that Afro-Americans: (1) were sloppy and dirty, (2) depreciated property, (3) were taking over and forcing out the whites, (4) were lazy and avoided work, and (5) were immoral.[8] The tendency for there to be a preponderance of id stereotypes about blacks, Chicanos, and darker skinned people still persists, as more current reviews of stereotypes and ethnocentrism demonstrate.

The reported changes in racial attitudes over the past 20 to 30 years toward a more tolerant and positive point of view do not mean all is well in racial America. Allport noted that:[15, p.224]

> Heterogeneity and the urge toward upward mobility thus make for ferments in society and are likely to bring ethnic prejudice in their wake. But the process seems to be speeded up in times of crisis . . .
>
> Whenever anxiety increases, accompanied by a loss of predictability in life, people tend to define their deteriorated situation in terms of scapegoats.

According to Bettelheim and Janowitz, ethnic hostility is a symptom of the individual's effort to "maintain a balance in his psychic economy," and the expression of prejudice helps protect his or her individuality.[8] The same authors also note that "as a person develops his need for securing his identity, this need may feed ethnic hostility and prejudice."[17, p.57] The impact of racial prejudice leaves an impression on the perpetrator as well as the target of racial hostility and indeed has far-reaching effects on every individual in that society.

Stereotypes do not always become more extensive but they do become more sophisticated and elaborate in form and less direct in intent. They, then, are more specifically defined as "ethnocentric attitudes" because they often describe the individual's preferences for one ethnic group over another because of racial attitudes towards the least preferred groups.

As a social institution within this country, the mental health profession has not been invulnerable to the percepts of racism. Needless to say, in the field of mental health it is particularly germaine that the practitioner and the client be aware of their ethnocentric attitudes and the ways such attitudes may function to delay or distort the therapeutic process. Thus, an assessment of ethnocentrism and stereotypic attitudes among mental health professionals is initial to the quality of the delivery of mental health services to minority group people.

In order to gain a perspective on the knowledge base of most health care professionals about Afro-Americans and the information formally taught in training programs, Wyatt, Bass, and Powell reviewed the literature regarding the curricula of graduate and medical school programs.[18] They found that since the 1960s, courses including information on sociocultural issues were only to be found in Black Studies Departments and those courses taught in medical schools did not include the supervised experiential training of psychotherapy with Afro-American children and adults. Curriculum materials have recently become available for incorporation into training programs within the last five to ten years. Some monitoring of how the information learned is incorporated into the therapeutic process still appears to be minimal to nonexistent. Information regarding the lifestyles of Afro-American people which highlights sociocultural differences in the family has not been included as a requirement in most graduate training programs. Thus, a large variance in the knowledge base of mental health professionals regarding Afro-American life would be expected, but has yet to be documented empirically. Additionally, because of the influence of prejudicial attitudes toward minority groups and the perpetuation of ethnic stereotypes in this society, the racial attitudes of these professionals towards Afro-Americans is another important dimension to assess. The following is a review of the literature regarding assessment tools that have been developed to measure racial or ethnocentric attitudes in lay and mental health professional groups. This review underscores the rationale for developing The Survey of Afro-American Behavior.

THE ASSESSMENT OF ETHNOCENTRIC ATTITUDES

Ethnocentric attitudes and preferences which are manifested in adult behavior have not been clearly defined in the literature due to the complexities of: (1) defining the concepts to be studied; (2) developing assessment tools which can accurately measure those concepts; and (3) obtaining representative populations from which inferences can be drawn.

The greatest area of controversy is in defining attitudes and stereotypes and concepts which have been postulated to be determinants of behavior toward ethnic group members. Brigham's review of the literature in this area defines and describes the characteristics of stereotypes and the tendency to use them as generalizations regarding groups or individuals.[19]

Though stereotypes often are characterized as having negative attributes, Fishman states that one cannot always assume that stereotypes are false and unfavorable.[20] Stereotypes have some positive value in that they are convenient, time-saving generalizations that can provide information without an individual having to weigh every specific reaction of every person for their meaning and value. The more essential aspect of why stereotypes persist is not to be found by questioning their degree of accuracy, because national normative behavioral baseline data that could be used to prove or disprove stereotypic statements is nonexistent. The key element to understanding stereotypes is not only their content (i.e., what is said or believed) but the process by which they are derived (i.e., the hasty weighing of evidence with a bare minimum of defining, distinguishing, and inducing). Stereotypes are derived from judgments or conclusions from which the higher mental processes are minimally used. The short-circuiting or blocking of higher mental processes is what Fishman terms as an "inferior process" used in stereotyping, which is apart from the traditional "faulty content" viewpoint.[20]

Research examining attitudes and behavior has been equally as controversial because of the difficulty in predicting the relationship between these concepts.[21–24] Most researchers agree that attitudes are learned predispositions to respond to an object or class of objects in a consistently favorable or unfavorable way. However, the use of this unidimensional conceptualization of attitudes is perceived to contribute strongly to the reason why the relationship between attitudes and behavior is such a tenuous one. The dimension that has gained too little attention is the qualitative nature of attitudes which would allow two people to have the same degree of affect and differ qualitatively in their attitudes.

The optimal conceptualization of an attitude is one that recognizes its several components: affective, cognitive, and conative. Research that measures racial attitudes and ethnic stereotypes tends to focus on one or two of these components, namely the affective and conative rather than the cognitive.

ATTITUDE TESTS

The majority of empirical studies utilize discrimination or semantic differential tests to measure ethnic attitudes of children, and their simplicity renders them inappropriate for studies with adults.[25–28] Assessment tools for adults have included:

1. Semantic differential tests[27]
2. the Negro Attitude Test (NAT)[29]
3. check-lists of trait attributes of ethnic groups[30]
4. the Multifactor Racial Attitude Inventory (MRAI)[19,31–33]
5. hypothetical test situations wherein evaluations of specific ethnic groups are related to behavioral intentions[19,34,35]
6. the Bogardus Social Distance Scale which measures social desirability[35–38]
7. the Attitude Behavior Scale: Blacks toward Whites and Whites toward Negroes (ABS:BW/WN), a multi-dimensional test which constructs items by a systematic a priori method[39, 40]
8. the Likert-type test which measures anti-Negro attitudes[41]

With the exception of the Attitude Behavioral Scale, these instruments are designed for college students or lay populations and tend to be too obvious in their ethnocentricity and intent for use with more sophisticated groups, such as mental health professionals.[19,27,29,30,32–34, 36,39,41–44]

Another criticism leveled at most of these scales is that they are unidimensional and fail to identify specific areas of child-rearing, sexuality, and cognitive functioning in which ethnic attitudes are held. The Attitude Behavior Scale (ABS:BW/WN) is an example of a well-constructed measure which specifies areas in which the attitudes are held and presents results by ethnic group, religion, and sex of subjects. However, the measure has limited utility for use with lay groups or mental health professionals. The seven attitude content areas were derived from the Report of the National Advisory Commission on Civil Disorders[45] and from suggestions from personnel working with Afro-American adults who had not completed high school. The selection of items presented unique sampling problems because they focussed upon the lifestyle of Afro-Americans of limited education and income, living in the nation's urban areas where employment, education and housing are major problems. These items limit their applicability to Afro-Americans who range widely in economic, education and life experiences. Additionally, items on such attitude scales as the ABS:BW/WN tend to force compliance to existing traits or statements. They also may present a hypothetical situation which has little congruence to broad real-life situations and are often blatantly ethnocentric.[32,39] For example, subjects are asked to respond on six levels of interaction, ranging from how they personally would respond, to how others of their ethnic group would respond, to items such as "Can Negroes be trusted with money?"

Research regarding mental health professionals' ethnocentric attitudes towards Afro-Americans appears to be more clear-cut in establishing a relationship between attitudes and behavior. The ethnocentricity of mental health professionals is of increasing concern due to the fact that Afro-Americans are significantly less often recipients of individual or group psychotherapy, spend less time in the hospital, and often are discharged without referral despite pathology and diagnoses similar to white patients.[37,46] The ethnocentricity of mental health professionals, particularly therapists, has been found to influence the length and type of services and treatment received by Afro-Americans. Yamamoto, James, Bloombaum, and Hattem found that mental health professionals' selections of patients are influenced by their stereotypes and racial biases as well as a lack of knowledge and exposure to sociocultural issues which enter into the therapeutic relationship with the minority group patient.[38]

However, the attitude tests used in the preceding study measured social distance or desirability of the ethnic group in the subjects' social interactions. Some important questions left unanswered are whether the measurement of social distance is comparable to the acceptability of an Afro-American as a candidate for psychotherapy, and whether the measurement reveals the kind of information upon which the therapists will base their assumptions and understanding of the behavior exhibited in therapy. The use of social distance scales to measure mental health professionals' knowledge and attitudes fails to generate information to address these questions adequately.

This chapter will describe an attempt to develop a more sophisticated, objective assessment tool for mental health professionals to examine their attitudes and to identify the areas in which these attitudes are held. In order to view attitudes and stereotypes using a multi-dimensional approach, the Survey of Afro-American Behavior was devised to assess the affective component of attitudes by positive (favorable) and negative (unfavorable) statements regarding Afro-American behavior and the cognitive component of attitudes by stereotypic and factual statements in seven areas. In light of the controversy about the relationship of ethnic attitudes to behavior, the conative or behavioral component was not included as a dimension of this assessment device. The identification of deficits in the knowledge base of mental health professionals, the adherence to stereotypes about a range of Afro-American behaviors, and the overall response to positive (favorable) and negative (unfavorable) statements was established as a priority. The results can provide graduate and post-graduate training programs with specific information that should be disseminated to mental health professionals of all disciplines who interact with Afro-Americans, and particularly those involved in therapeutic relationships.

A secondary purpose for the development of the Survey of Afro-American Behavior was to devise an instrument based upon the kinds of information that mental health professionals tend to have about Afro-American people, which is based not only on their experiential background and perceptions of social desirability of ethnic group members but also upon their professional contacts and knowledge of the social science literature regarding Afro-Americans. In light of the research documenting the ethnocentricity of lay groups and mental health professionals, this study will re-examine those attitudes and focus on their cognitive and affective aspects.

According to some researchers, Afro-American therapists tend to have more knowledge and more positive affect regarding the Afro-American subculture due to their common ethnic identity when compared to Anglo-American therapists whose social contact with Afro-Americans may be limited and whose knowledge may be based on viewing the Afro-American family solely within a deficit model. Thus, the following trends were hypothesized:

1. Afro-American therapists will agree more with positive statements regarding Afro-American people than white therapists
2. Afro-American therapists will agree more with factual statements regarding Afro-American people than their white peers
3. Afro-American therapists will disagree more with negative stereotypes than their white counterparts
4. Afro-American therapists will agree more with negative factual statements about Afro-American people than their white peers
5. White therapists will agree more with positive stereotypes regarding Afro-American behavior than their Afro-American counterparts

METHOD

Development of the Study

In order to obtain a variety of statements for use in the Survey of Afro-American Behavior, 125 mental health professionals and scholars in Southern California were asked to list statements which were factual, stereotypic, negative (unfavorable) or positive (favorable) regarding Afro-American behavior or performance. Over 500 statements were obtained, including some that were extracted from the literature over the past 25 years, in the following areas: school achievement; superego, impulse-control functions; child rearing practices; intellectual and cognitive functioning; social interactions; family life; and sexual values and behavior.

The Survey consisted of 116 statements selected from the orginal 500 items. The criteria for selection of items included those statements that were clearly and concisely worded, ranging in ethnocentricity from those that were mild to strong in terms of racist content, i.e., "Black people are lazy and shiftless." We defined positive (favorable) statements as those that described the favorable outcome of events or that generally affirmed positive aspects of Afro-American behavior. An example of such a statement was

> The Afro-American family regardless of class or status, inspires and supports their children toward achievement.

Negative (unfavorable) statements were those that described an unfavorable outcome of events, an absence of acceptable characteristics or concentration on pathological features of Afro-American behavior. An example of such a statement was

> Afro-American parents subject their children to harsh and conservative upbringing which restricts development of free and open personalities.

The factual statements were derived from reviews of the literature and were assumed to have credibility in that they were excerpted from articles by noted Afro-American social scientists and were published in refereed social science journals most likely to be read by mental health professionals. It should be noted, however, that factual statements were not always based upon empirical observations or data. An example of a factual statement was

> Afro-American children become sensitive to skin color at an earlier age than their white peers.

Stereotypic statements were defined as generalizations made about Afro-Americans based upon trait attributions, aspects of daily behavior, and cultural norms which are considered to be non-factual or unjustified by empirical observation. These stereotypic statements were considered to be assumptions, factually incorrect, and to imply rigidity or rationalizations of prejudicial attitudes.[33] An example of a stereotypic statement was

> Afro-Americans are better in their affective than cognitive functions.

The items were also cross-categorized to measure the cognitive-affective dimension of mental health professionals' attitudes. The item category combinations were: positive factual, positive stereotypic, negative factual, and negative stereotypic. Subjects were asked to rate each of the 116 statements on a Likert-type scale with 1 representing strong agreement and 5 representing strong disagreement. For the purposes of the analysis, the ratings of positive (favorable) statements were reversed in order to coincide with the ratings of negative (unfavorable) ratings.

Subjects

The subjects were volunteers from mental health facilities whose participation was solicited in weekly staff meetings. The mental health professionals and trainees were told that their participation would help to refine an attitude scale that would be used in future studies with mental health professionals, and they were assured of anonymity. The questionnaires and return address envelopes were given to each staff member or trainee to avoid visible participation or nonparticipation. Of the 493 mental health professionals from 13 facilities, 201 volunteered to participate. The nonparticipant group consisted of those who did not attend that meeting during which their participation was requested as well as those who elected not to participate. Not all subjects completed demographic information on all Survey items; consequently, the number of subjects was reduced to 172. The subjects were 151 staff and 17 trainees from 13 mental health facilities in Southern California and consisted of 55 white males; 62 white females; 20 Afro-American males; and 35 Afro-American females. Four subjects failed to list their discipline. There were 81 subjects under 35 years of age, 46 subjects ranging in age from 35 to 45, and 45 subjects over the age of 45. Additional demographic information regarding the disciplines of the subjects is presented in Table 1.

We attempted to obtain a selection of county, state, federal, and privately funded mental health facilities which served heterogeneous populations, whose staff was multi-disciplined and multi-ethnic and would have varying degrees of expertise in providing service to Afro-American families. One mental health center received county and state funds exclusively; four centers received county, federal and state funds; one center with two sites was a large health maintenance organization (HMO) and received no public funds; one center was a non-profit organization and received no ancillary funds; and five centers were non-profit organizations and received ancillary funds designated for county mental health facilities.

It was anticipated that because mental health professionals tend to maintain hectic schedules at work, they would find it difficult to complete the Survey in its entirety. We found that the support of the administrator or director of the agencies participating, acknowledging the length of the questionnaire and allowing for volunteers to take between one-half to one hour to complete all items, increased the number of participants, as well as questionnaires that supplied complete data.

Table 1
Frequencies and Percentages of White and Afro-American Mental Health Professionals Responding to the Survey of Afro-American Behavior by Discipline

	Ethnicity			
	white (n = 117)		Afro-American (n = 55)	
Discipline	Frequencies	% of Total	Frequencies	% of Total
Psychiatry	10	6.33	2	1.27
Psychology	39	24.68	16	10.13
Social Work	41	25.95	16	10.13
Nursing	3	1.90	1	0.63
Child Psychiatry Fellows	1	0.63	0	0.00
Medical Residents	1	0.63	0	0.00
Educational Consultants	1	0.63	1	0.63
Mental Health Practitioners	2	1.27	9	5.70
Behavior Modification Workers	3	1.90	1	0.63
Administrators	2	1.27	2	1.27
Teachers	2	1.27	1	0.00
Occupational Therapists	2	1.27	0	0.00
Discipline Unclear	1	0.63	1	0.63
Missing	9	7.69	5	4.27
Total		**68.35**		**31.65**

Because of past experience, we also anticipated that some individuals would be hesitant to participate, even though they would do so anonymously, because they would not wish to reveal their level of knowledge of or their attitudes towards Afro-American people. The comments made by fewer than five participants were regarding the wording and contents of the statements. These individuals tended to write one or more comments about the items on their questionnaires. The following are examples.

"I found the questions frustrating and difficult to answer because of the generalizations."

"Unclear, lousy statements!"

Other participants had difficulty with comparative statements.

"Afro-American children who are reared in the inner city are more aggressive and have violent outbursts."

Comment: "More aggressive than whom?"

Finally, a few participants objected to the entire questionnaire.

"This is the most biased survey in which I have ever participated."

One participant wrote that she had been an "active participant of the Civil Rights Movement" and refused to complete the questionnaire.

These responses indicated that the statements on the Survey elicited a range of responses: those that focused on the content of certain items which were broad statements, often suggesting but not directly requiring comparisons between Afro-Americans and whites; and those that illustrated the discomfort that subjects experienced in being requested to respond to statements, some of which were blatantly racist. They might have sensed the need to offer additional information to add credibility to their responses, should they be found to be in agreement with the more negative and stereotypic items.

Needless to say, the sensitivity of the subject matter was a major factor in the decision to use caution in collecting data on the subjects reported in this chapter. The goal was to maximize the participation and cooperation of as many subjects as possible, rather than to elicit the cooperation of additional mental health agencies and risk being less available to answer questions about the purpose and usefulness of the study. The value of spending time to obtain the completed Surveys was reflected in the results of the study.

RESULTS

T-tests were used to evaluate differences in arithmetic means of white and Afro-American subjects on positive, negative, factual, stereotypic, and all combinations of the item categories (i.e., positive factual, negative factual, positive stereotypic, negative stereotypic). For the present report, the data were analyzed only with ethnicity as a factor on the model.[47] The General Linear Model (GLM) procedure of the Statistical Analysis System for unbalanced data was used.[48]

An analysis of the mean scores for the positive (favorable) statements lent support to the first hypothesis and showed significant differences between the white and Afro-American respondents. The Afro-American respondents scored significantly higher than the white respondents in terms of agreeing more frequently with the positive (favorable) statements overall (p = 0.008), particularly in the specific areas of child rearing practices (p = 0.001), and sexual values and behavior (p = 0.006) (see Table 2). The differences between groups on total negative (unfavorable) statements were not statistically significant.

In support of the second hypothesis, the difference between the means of the total factual scores of the white and Afro-American

Table 2
Means and Standard Deviations of White and Afro-American Responses to Varying Statements on the Survey of Afro-American Behavior

Type of Statement	White Scores (n = 118)		Afro-American Scores (n = 57)		Probability*
	Mean	S.D.	Mean	S.D.	
POSITIVE (favorable)					
Total	3.388	0.480	3.582	0.380	0.008
Child-Rearing	3.666	0.573	4.060	0.626	0.001
Sexual Values and Behavior	3.358	0.763	3.684	0.460	0.006
FACTUAL					
Total	3.932	0.172	3.057	0.161	0.001
Child-Rearing	3.171	0.333	3.441	0.385	0.001
Family Life	3.161	0.351	3.310	0.310	0.007
Sexual Values and Behavior	2.966	0.320	3.166	0.261	0.001
STEREOTYPIC					
Sexual Values and Behavior	3.504	0.602	3.749	0.604	0.013
POSITIVE FACTUAL (favorable)					
Total	3.430	0.476	3.615	0.391	0.0115
Impulse Control	2.790	0.726	3.118	0.605	0.004
Child-Rearing	3.666	0.573	4.060	0.626	0.001
Sexual Values and Behavior	3.436	0.764	3.719	0.502	0.004

*Significant at .01.

respondents was statistically significant ($p = 0.001$), with the Afro-American respondents showing more agreement with the factual statements than their white counterparts. Among the factual statements on child-rearing practices ($p = 0.001$), family life ($p = 0.007$), and sexuality ($p = 0.001$), Afro-American respondents showed significantly more agreement than the white respondents (see Table 2).

Contrary to the third and fourth hypothesis, Afro-Americans agreed more with stereotypic statements than whites, but the difference between the means of the total scores was not statistically significant. However, it was interesting to note that the Afro-American respondents agreed more with the sterotypic statements about sexuality than the white respondents, and the difference was significant at the .01 level (see Table 2).

When the factual statements were analyzed regarding positive (favorable) statements and negative (unfavorable) statements, some significant differences emerged. The mean score of the Afro-American respondents on the total positive (favorable) factual statements was somewhat higher than the mean score for the white respondents ($p = .0115$). The means of the subscores for impulse control, sexuality, and for child-rearing were significantly higher for the Afro-Americans indicating more agreement with the positive (favorable) factual content than the whites (see Table 2).

The data did not support the fifth hypothesis, i.e., that Afro-American therapists agreed more with negative (unfavorable) factual statements than white therapists: the differences between the mean scores were not significant.

Although there were no significant differences between white and Afro-American respondents on any of the stereotype mean scores, Afro-American respondents agreed more with the statements about sexuality and family life that conveyed negative (unfavorable) stereotypes.

DISCUSSION

There has been national recognition of the need for the expansion of mental health services to Afro-Americans. However, mental health professionals have not responded in sufficient numbers to this need by including in clinical training programs important didactic and experiential programs regarding sociocultural variables related to the assessment and treatment of Afro-American patients. Despite the training programs that have been created in some professional schools,[18,49,50] there remains a great need for the inclusion of such courses in the curricula of professional schools, and research to determine how the delivery of mental health services to minority group patients is affected.

The professional literature contains some discussion of the problems of the Afro-American therapist with the white client and the general problems of Afro-Americans in America.[51–54] An insufficient number of studies have centered on the problems of the self-image, racial and social class of Afro-Americans, and their handling of anger towards whites.[53–57] The notable fact, however, is the reluctance of therapists and the professional literature to discuss the impact of racial attitudes on the therapeutic process. The importance of these themes has not been emphasized enough and they must be acknowledged and dealt with in the psychotherapy of patients whether the therapist is black or white.

One of the primary problems is that few therapists know much about Afro-American culture, much less about the impulse control of Afro-American clients for whom social, cultural, and environmental factors mediate behavior and interpersonal interactions. Inasmuch as the field of mental health deals with human behavior, the providers of services must be knowledgeable about the behavior of the clients. The professional's lack of knowledge may well influence the course of treatment.

Most mental health professionals have had little experience with the poor and/or minority groups.[58] Chester Pierce has noted that most therapy, at least with the most severely ill Afro-Americans, is provided by foreign medical graduates who are neither white nor Afro-American;[59] the implications of this fact are far-reaching. Unfortunately, many Afro-American mental health professionals have failed to appreciate and utilize their unique knowledge of their ethnic background and have aped traditional white-oriented perceptions of the behavior of Afro-Americans.[60,61]

This is not to say that Afro-American therapists should not evaluate and treat patients of their own ethnic group. On the contrary, it would seem more appropriate for those Afro-American therapists who have the knowledge and sensitivity to do so in order to enhance their patients' self-concept and ethnic identity. There is some research which points in the direction of Afro-American mental health professionals having more success with Afro-American patients than do white therapists.[44,62–64] However, there are insufficient numbers of Afro-American mental health professionals to serve the population of Afro-Americans seeking mental health services, especially in the fields of psychiatry.[65] Of greater significance are the findings in recent studies which indicate that Afro-American patients do not have strong perferences for Afro-American professionals, which may be due to the fact that they believe that Afro-American middle class professionals have the same stereotypic views as do white professionals.[54,55,58,66,67]

It is significant that, of the original 500 statements obtained from the

125 Afro-American and white mental health professionals and scholars and the literature, only three positive stereotypic statements were elicited. This suggests that most stereotypes about Afro-Americans are decidedly negative or unfavorable. Most positive (favorable) stereotypes seem to be held about Asian-Americans and Jews than about Afro-Americans or most other minority groups in the United States.[68] A large proportion of the literature on racial attitudes concerns Afro-Americans because of the negative attitudes held about them by the general society. The results of the present study bear this out, especially in the areas of sexual values and behavior.

The hypothesis that Afro-Americans would tend to agree more with positive (favorable) statements about the Afro-American family life was supported, perhaps due to their positive affect regarding their culture and people. However, white therapists disagreed with positive (favorable) statements, and therapists of both ethnic groups had comparable levels of agreement on negative (unfavorable) statements. These findings demonstrate that the negative sentiment regarding Afro-Americans still exists, even in the 1980s. It appears that both groups can be characterized as ethnocentric; the Afro-Americans for validating the positive aspects of their culture, and whites for disagreeing with them. Perhaps mental health professionals are more sophisticated in their racial attitudes and, while they may not adhere to the blatant attitudes of the lay population, they remain ethnocentric in their own right. While Afro-American therapists may be supportive of their culture, they may also appear to be defensive or protective by agreeing with positive statements in an effort to "go on the record" as attesting to the strengths of Afro-Americans.

On the cognitive level, Afro-American therapists do seem to have more factual information, particularly in the areas of family life, child-rearing, and impulse control functions, where just as much literature can be found to focus on deficits as it can be found to delineate strengths of families.[69–72] Afro-American mental health professionals may be more likely to participate in courses in which sociocultural issues related to the delivery of mental health services to Afro-Americans are provided. The Afro-American respondents in our study may, therefore, be a select group. Such courses offering didactic and experiential components should be required of all mental health professionals. White therapists may adhere to the reports in the scientific literature of the deficit model for the Afro-American culture rather than recognizing the strengths.

One of the most significant findings in this study centers around mental health professionals' views of Afro-Americans' sexual values and behaviors. The Afro-American therapists' adherence to factual and stereotypic items attests to the need for empirical research which identifies and describes sexual values and behaviors within a cultural perspective and does not label differences as deficits. Secondly, it appears that white therapists, and no doubt others as well, need to be the recipients of this information if therapists are to be expected to offer clients an education and understanding regarding Afro-American sexuality.

Finally, the strength of the Survey of Afro-American Behavior is in its identification of affective and cognitive dimensions of attitudes. We know that work remains to be done in the area of therapists' attitude change that perhaps cannot be accomplished without social contact and interpersonal involvements with Afro-Americans. However, graduate and professional schools may need to reorient or reemphasize their training programs to include child-rearing practices, sexual values and behavior, impulse control, and family life, particularly for white therapists. Without knowledge and awarenes of these issues in supervised practice or internships, Afro-American and white supervisors may be of limited help in suggesting approaches to other professionals and trainees to understand when sociocultural issues are factors in the therapeutic relationship and process.

The sample in this study is relatively small, highly stratified, and not representative of the number of mental health professionals in the Southern California area. Further analysis of the cognitive and affective dimensions of the Survey is needed in order to measure the consistency of the responses among both groups. Though there were no overall differences found by profession, discipline, sex, or mental health facility, some of the mean differences were age-related in some of the seven areas of the Survey. A more detailed analysis of age as a variable may shed more insight into the attitudes of these mental health professionals. However, the Survey has utility in identifying aspects of mental health professionals' attitudes towards Afro-Americans that can inhibit or enhance the therapeutic process and influence the treatment of the growing numbers of Afro-Americans seeking services.

It becomes quite clear that the inclusion of ethnopsychiatry courses in the curricula of the professional training programs would serve to increase the knowledge base and reduce the negative stereotypes, myths, and attitudes held by mental health professionals and may lead to the provision of more effective mental health services.

REFERENCES

1. Pettigrew T: Racial Discrimination in the United States. New York, Harper & Row, 1975

2. Klineberg O: Prejudice: The concept, in International Encyclopedia of the Social Sciences. Macmillan and the Free Press, 1968
3. Myrdal G: An American Dilemma. New York, Harper & Row, 1944
4. Stouffer SA, Schuman EA, De Vinney LE, et al: Studies in social psychology in World War II. Vol 1, The American Soldier: Adjustment During Army Life. Princeton, N.J., Princeton University Press, 1949
5. Davis AW, Gardner BB, Gardner MR: Deep South. Chicago, University of Chicago Press, 1941
6. Dollard J: Caste and Class in a Southern Town. New Haven, Yale University Press, 1937
7. Adorno TW, Frenkel-Brunswick E, Levinson DJ, et al: The Authoritarian Personality. New York, Harper & Row, 1950
8. Bettelheim B, Janowitz M: Dynamics of Prejudice. New York, Harper, 1950
9. Ackerman NW, Jahoda M: Anti-Semitism and Emotional Disorder. New York, Harper & Row, 1950
10. Hyman H, Sheatsley P: Attitudes towards desegregation. Scientific Amer 195:35–39, 1956
11. Hyman H, Sheatsley P: Attitudes towards desegregation. Scientific Amer 211:16–23, 1964
12. Greeley A, Sheatsley P: Attitudes toward racial integration. Scientific Amer 225:13–19, 1971
13. Brink W, Harris L: The Negro Revolution in America. New York, Simon & Schuster, 1964
14. Brink W, Harris L: Black and White. New York, Simon & Schuster, 1967
15. Allport G: The Nature of Prejudice. New York, Addison-Wesley, 1954
16. Gilbert G: Stereotype persistence and change among college students. J Abnor Soc Psychol 46:245–54, 1951
17. Bettelheim B, Janowitz M: Social Change and Prejudice. New York, Free Press, 1964
18. Wyatt GE, Bass B, Powell GJ: A survey of ethnic and sociocultural issues in medical school education. J Med Educ 53:627–632, 1978
19. Brigham J: Racial stereotypes, attitudes and evaluations of and behavioral intentions towards Negroes and whites. Sociometry 34:360–380, 1971
20. Fishman JA: An examination of the process and function of social stereotyping. J Soc Psychol 43:27–64, 1956
21. Beckman L, Kamzan A: The effect of race and need on helping behavior. J Soc Psychol 89:73–77, 1973
22. Ehrlich HJ: Attitudes, behavior, and the intervening variables. Amer Soc 4:29–34, 1969
23. Fishbein M: Attitude and prediction of behavior, in Fishbein M (ed): Readings in Attitude Theory and Measurement. New York, Wiley, 1967, pp 477–492
24. Schuman H: Attitudes vs. actions versus attitudes vs. attitudes. Pub Open Quartly 36:347–354, 1972
25. Stevenson H, Steward E: A developmental study of racial awareness in young children. Child Developm 29:399–409, 1958
26. Katz, PA: Stimulus predifferentiation and modification of children's racial attitudes. Child Developm 44:232–237, 1973
27. Williams J: Connotations of color names among Negroes and Caucasians. Percep Mot Skills 18:721–731, 1964
28. Farber R, Schmeidler G: Race differences in children's responses to "black" and "white." Percep Mot skills 33:359–363, 1971

29. Caffrey B, Anderson II S, Garnson J: Change in racial attitudes of white southerners after exposure to the atmosphere of a southern university. Psychol Rep 25:555–558, 1969
30. Katz D, Braly K: Racial stereotypes of one hundred college students. J Abnorm Soc Psychol 28:280–290, 1933
31. Woodmansee JJ, Cook SW: Dimensions of verbal racial attitudes: Their identification and measurement. J Pers Soc Psychol 7:240–250, 1967
32. Brigham J: Racial stereotypes: Measurement variables and the stereotype-attitude relationship. J Appl Soc Psychol 2:63–76, 1972
33. Brigham J: Ethnic stereotypes and attitudes: A different mode of analysis. J Person 41:206–223, 1973
34. Word C, Zanna M, Cooper J: The non-verbal mediation of self-fulfilling prophecies in interracial interactions. J Exper Soc Psychol 10:109–120, 1974
35. Bloombaum M, Yamamoto J, James Q: Cultural stereotyping among psychotherapists. J Consult Clin Psychol 32:894–900, 1968
36. Bogardus E: Racial distance changes in the United States during the past thirty years. Social Soc Res 43:127–135, 1958
37. Yamamoto J, Dixon F, Bloombaum M: White therapists and Negro patients. J Med Educ 54:312–316, 1972
38. Yamamoto J, James QC, Bloombaum M, et al: Racial factors in patient selection. Amer J Psychiat 124:630–636, 1967
39. Hamersma R, Paige J, Jordon J: Construction of a guttman facet designed cross cultural attitude behavior scale toward racial-ethnic interaction. Educ Psychol Meas 33:565–576, 1973
40. Dell Orto A, Jordon J: A multivariate analysis of racial attitudes, structure, content and determinants. Rehab Psychol 20:126–135, 1973
41. Tarter D: Toward prediction and attitude-action discrepancy. Soc Forces 47:398–405, 1969
42. Clark, K: Dark Ghetto. New York, Harper & Row, 1965
43. Gottlieb D: Teaching and students: The views of Negro and white teachers, in Webster SW (ed): The Disadvantaged Learner. San Francisco, Chandler, 1964
44. Katz I, Henchy T, Allen H: Effects of task difficulty, race of administrator, and instructions on digit symbol performance of Negroes. J Person Soc Psychol 5:53–59, 1965
45. Report of the National Advisory Commission on Civil Disorders. New York, Bantam Books, 1968
46. Mayo JA: The significance of sociocultural variables in the psychiatric treatment of black outpatients. Comp Psychiatr 15:471–482, 1974
47. Graybill FA: An Introduction to Linear Statistical Models. New York, McGraw-Hill, 1961
48. Barr AJ, Goodnight JH, Sall JP, et al: SAS User's Guide 1979 Edition. Raleigh, N.C., SAS Institute, 1979
49. Hicks L, Ridley S: Black studies in psychology. Amer Psychol 34:597–602, 1979
50. Norton DG: The Dual Perspective: Inclusion of Ethnic Minority Content in the Social Work Curriculum. New York, Council on Social Work Education, 1978
51. Curry A: Myth, transference and the black psychotherapist. Psychoanal Rev 51:7–14, 1964
52. Grier W: When the therapist is Negro: Some effects on the treatment process. Amer J Psychiatr 123:1587–1591, 1967
53. Lindsay I: Race as a factor in establishing a casework relationship. Soc Casework 28:101–107, 1947

54. Silberman C: Crises in black and white. New York, Random House, 1964
55. Frazier E: Black Bourgeousie. New York, Free Press, 1957
56. Grier W, Cobbs P: Black Rage. New York, Basic Books, 1968
57. Wyatt GE, Strayer R, Lobitz C: Issues in the treatment of sexually dysfunctioning couples of Afro-American descent. Psychother Theo Res Prac 13:44–49, 1976
58. Jones E: Social class and psychotherapy: A critical review of research. Psychiat 37:307–320, 1974
59. Pierce CM: Manpower: The need for Negro psychiatrists. J Nat Med Assoc 60:30–33, 1968
60. Calnek M: Racial factors in the countertransference: The black therapist and the black client. Amer J Orthopsychiat 40:39–46, 1970
61. Wilson A: Developmental Psychology of the Black Child. New York, Africana Research Publications, 1978
62. Baratz S: Effect of race of experimenter, instructions, and comparison population upon level of reported anxiety in Negro subjects. J Pers Soc Psychol 7:194–196, 1967
63. Katz I, Henchy T, Allen H: Effects of race of tester, approval-disapproval and need on Negro children's learning. J Pers Soc Psychol 8:38–42, 1968
64. Katz I, Greenbaum C: Effects of anxiety, threat, and racial environment on task performance of Negro college students. J Abnor Soc Psychol 63:562–567, 1963
65. American Medical Association Council on Medical Education. Seventy-Sixth Annual Report on Medical Education. J Amer Med Assoc 236:2960–2964, 1976
66. Billingsley A: Black Families in White America. Englewood Cliffs, N.J., Prentice-Hall, 1968
67. Dubey SN: Blacks' preference for black professionals, businessmen, and religious leaders. Pub Opin Quartly 34:113–116, 1970
68. Abbott KA, Abbott EL: Juvenile delinquency in San Francisco's Chinese-American community: 1961–1966, in Sue S & Wagner N (eds): Asian Americans: Psychological Perspectives. Ben Lomond, Calf., Science and Behavior Books, 1968, pp. 171–180
69. Hill R: The Strengths of Black Families: A National Urban League Research Study. New York, Emerson Hall 1972
70. Gutman H: The Black Family in Slavery and Freedom: 1750–1925. New York, Pantheon Books, 1976
71. Nobles WW: The Black Family and Its Children: The Survival of Humaneness. Black Books Bulletin (in press)
72. Staples, R: The Black Family: Essays and Studies. Belmont, Calif, Wadsworth 1970

Hector F. Myers

3

Research on the Afro-American Family: A Critical Review

> *"The family is a creature of the society. And the greatest problems facing black families are problems which emanate from . . . [a] society which places higher priorities on putting white men on the moon than putting black men on their feet on this earth." (Billingsley, 1970, p. 130).*

Over the past 75 years, we have witnessed a growing body of research focusing on the struggles of the Afro-American family as a social institution. From the earliest classic studies,[1–4] the debate has raged as to the viability of the institution as a vehicle for the socialization of effective citizens. A majority of the earlier, more frequently quoted writers expressed the belief that the Afro-American family is a system in crisis and decay. Externally, it is burdened by the forces of poverty and discrimination. Among the lower class, the Afro-American family is torn apart by internal conflicts, instability, and a poverty of values, skills, and resources. Only those Afro-American families that are able to assimilate into the mainstream of society and culture are viable and nonpathological. In more recent years, Afro-American scholars have challenged this earlier conceptualization of the Afro-American family and have begun to define and

This chapter was developed from a series of lectures entitled "A Historical Overview of Black Family Research," given by Hector Myers in 1979–1980, at the Neuropsychiatric Institute, UCLA.

describe it as a complex, varied, and dynamic entity with distinct strengths and resources.[5–15] These scholars challenge the majority cultural perspective and assimilationist agenda of earlier writers and assert the need to view the Afro-American family in its own right, rather than as a darker facsimile of the white American family.

In this chapter, we propose to selectively review the extensive body of literature of the Afro-American family, and to highlight and elaborate on process-oriented formulations and measurements of families over time, on researchers studying the Afro-American family who are still engaged in cross-sectional analysis (e.g., single parent vs. bi-parental families) and on single time measurements of discrete family attributes (e.g., dominance, role fulfillment, etc.). Generic family researchers have long since dropped the idea of a single, model American family. Researchers on the Afro-American family, however, are still trying to prove that there are as many different familial forms among Afro-Americans as there are different Afro-American experiential and phenomenal realities.

This dichotomy within the field of family theory and research is not unique, however. As the author has pointed out, there is a distinct dual tradition in the field of social science research—a "generic" theory and methodology developed on and used in the study of white behavior, and an "applied comparative" theory and methodology used to address issues in non-white groups.[16] For example, the field of child development is based on systematic research performed largely on white middle-class children which is assumed (or defined as) normative and generic to all children. The behaviors and patterns of development in non-white children are then viewed comparatively against this "norm" and defined as "exceptions" or "deviations from the norm." Then, such deviations are attributed to either the characteristics (i.e., deficiencies) of the individual, or to inadequacies and deprivations in the environment.

While we cannot, and perhaps should not, deny the inherent value of comparative studies, we must recognize that there are serious scientific and social consequences of the assumptions underlying this dual tradition. The notion of white behavior as superior and normative is not a scientific fact, but is rather a cultural and political phenomena (i.e., "cultural arrogance"). In order for a pattern of behavior to be considered normative, that is, applicable to all, it requires the specification of, or at least the attempt to explore, the full range of behavioral experience and the "normative" range of variability of that pattern of behavior as a function of the interrelationship of the factors operative within the context studied. Therefore, factors such as social class, family structure, self-esteem, socio-political status, sex, race, etc., that are so frequently studied as sources of variance in non-white behavior should be integral to any generic model of behavior. These factors affect the behavior of all people to a greater or lesser degree.

Additionally, by relying almost exclusively on direct or indirect comparisons as the major research paradigm in non-white research, the behaviors of Afro-Americans and other similar groups are only seen through "white glasses." Therefore, by definition, Afro-American behavior achieves the status of a legitimate scientific phenomena only if it is evaluated from the perspective of the majority culture and viewed against white norms and standards of behavior. For further elaboration on this point, please see Nobles,[9,10,17] Clark, [18,19] and Akbar.[20]

It is not surprising, then, that we see years of creative and purposive energies dissipated in inane and nonsensical debates about the difference and uniqueness of Afro-American behavior vis-à-vis the behavior of majority groups. This is, in fact, a moot question not answerable by science, for science is not independent of the cultural context in which it develops. As Mannheim[21] reminds us, ideas are the products of a context. What is known affects what is knowable—it affects the questions to be asked and the answers to be obtained. Therefore, given the social and political history of the United States in relation to Afro-Americans, and the record of American social science as an extension of that historical relationship, it is doubtful whether social science is capable of fully recognizing and accepting the true fundamental uniqueness of Afro-American behavior.

In order to avoid the conceptual incarceration of culture-bound perspectives, the productive scientific question to be addressed should not be whether the behavior patterns of subgroups are different and unique from those of the majority group, but rather what are the patterns of relationship between the key factors known to account for the behaviors seen across and within groups when these groups are catergorized by salient demographic characteristics, such as race, sex, socioeconomic status, age, etc. To answer such a question, we would need to elaborate a complex conceptual matrix which includes all of the principal variables known and suspected to affect the behavior(s) in question for all of the population groups to be studied.

The Family as a Social Product

Applying the notion of a generic conceptual matrix to the study of the family, we would have to begin with a theoretical perspective that allowed for such an analysis. One such perspective views the family, and all families, across all groups and social conditions as social systems that are the products of society. The distinct familial forms and dynamics that emerge in this context are functions of the dialetic between the groups in the various social niches and the larger society. Thus, along the dimension of race, the familial patterns present result from the unique and differential nature of the transaction between each racial or ethnic grouping, and the society at large. White familial forms would be expected to emerge as different from non-white familial forms to the degree that the dialectic between whites and the larger society differs in meaningful and relevant ways from that of non-white group families. One important variable in this race-differential dialetic would be economic and occupational history. White-Americans as a group have differential access to higher-paying, higher-status, and more stable occupations than do non-whites. To the extent that income and occupational stability and status are related to family structure and dynamics, we would expect differences between white and non-white families. However, to the extent that whites and non-whites do not differ significantly as racial groups on variables meaningful to familial structure and dynamics, differences in the families of these groups should not be expected (e.g., two-parent, employed, middle-class Afro-American and white-American families).

Similarly, along the dimension of socio-economic status, the pattern of families extant in socioeconomic status (SES) groups should be related to the unique relationships that each SES group has with the larger social structure. To the extent that these group differ in access to family-relevant resources, differences in families across SES groups should be expected.[2–5,22–24]

A note of caution regarding social class is appropriate at this juncture. There is still debate about the number of meaningful categories of social class that should be made, especially at the lower end of the spectrum.[23–28] There is also the question of whether the same social class and status criteria should be used in defining social classes for whites and for Afro-Americans.[29,30] This issue will be discussed in greater detail later in this chapter.

Taking the analysis in this matrix one step further, and looking at the intersection of these two dimensions of race and class, we approach a more complex level of analysis. At this intersection, the issue is not simply what is the differential contribution that race and class bestow on variability in family systems, but rather, what is the combined (i.e., race $\times$ class) effect of these two dimensions on familial variability? In other words, are there aspects of family functioning that are better and more comprehensively explained by the combined effects of race and social class than can be explained by either variable by itself? One example that approaches this formulation is the role of the father in Afro-American and white-American families across SES. The literature suggests that white low SES fathers are clearly more authoritarian, while white middle SES fathers are more egalitarian. Afro-American low SES and middle SES fathers, on the other hand, tend to be more egalitarian in their role functions, but the low SES Afro-American father has a more inconsistent status than his middle SES peer.[31–33]

Looking from this perspective at the research on the family, and specifically on the Afro-American family, clearly demonstrates that there is no valid basis for the frequently reported myths about the Afro-American family. In fact, there are several types of Afro-American families, a great deal of whom have many characteristics in common with white families. It is also clear that the nature of Afro-American familial structure and functioning differs from white families mainly on the basis of differences in the historical relationship between groups and the larger society created by the race of the members. This fact is undeniable. As the dynamics of color, race, sex, and age vary; as society differentially values, reinforces, facilitates, and supports the strivings of its members on the basis of these factors; we would expect that individual behaviors, family structures and functioning, social institutions, and communities should evolve differentially, consistent with their particular realities and resources.

The Afro-American Family: Models and Perspectives

In recent years, several Afro-American scholars have asserted that the existing theoretical and conceptual framework for the study of Afro-American families is ill-suited to the study of these families.[5,10,13–15,17,34] The existing models seriously distort and restrict our understanding of the complexity of the Afro-American family because they introduce ethocentric biases and distortions into the analysis. These scholars all agree on the need for the elaboration of new models of analysis of the Afro-American family, but disagree on the perspective and focus the new models should take. To shed light on this subject, we shall review and discuss major research assumptions, ideologies, and models in Afro-American family research, treating each as a distinct issue. We recognize, of course, that considerable overlap and cross-influencing exist among these issues (i.e., the assumptions made affect the ideology ascribed to, which, in turn, affects the research model used). First, we will discuss the principal assumptions and conceptual errors underlying this research. Second, we will review historical changes in the locus of emphasis extant in the literature. Next, we shall discuss the subjective ideological perspectives underlying the various schools of thought. Finally, we will discuss the formal research models presented, and the types of studies that fit each of these approaches.

PRINCIPAL ASSUMPTIONS

Research on Afro-American family life has been severely criticized by several investigators because of problems inherent with the assumptions that remain implicit in many studies. Principal among these are three erroneous assumptions: (1) the assumption of the equivalence of culture, color, and class, (2) the assumption of the homogeneity of Afro-Americans and of their communities, and (3) the assumption of general cultural equivalence.

As noted by Lewis, the term culture is often confounded with class and with color in the analysis of Afro-American behavior.[22] Many researchers, both Afro-American and white, have consistently argued for an Afro-American lower class subculture and assume this group's pattern of rules, values, and standards to be normative and representative of generic Afro-American culture. In fact, as a group, Afro-Americans have evolved a rather complex set of beliefs, attitudes, values, and standards of behavior that are distinct from those of the majority culture as a result of the historical experiences of Afro-Americans in accessing majority culture. Further, and despite opinions to the contrary, these beliefs, attitudes, etc. at the core of Afro-American behavior and institutions, are remnants of African cultural contributions. They are seen throughout the black diaspora, and cannot be entirely attributed to the common experiences of slavery, colonization, and racial discrimination.[9,10,17,20] The pattern of behavior frequently referred to as "black culture", namely, the behavioral characteristics of low income ghetto community members, should probably best be characterized as part of a larger black culture and not as the culture itself. Ghetto behavior, as demonstrated by Lewis[22] is not unique to Afro-American communities, but rather is present among the urban poor of all dispossessed ethnic groups. Race adds a unique quality or rhythm to the generic "poor life style" to make it uniquely black. However, social class and the exigencies of life under poverty conditions probably account for much, if not most, of the behavior commonly ascribed to low income Afro-American groups.

Finally, culture is not a stable phenomenon reflected in superficial trappings and symbols. Rather, it is dynamic, evolving, and ever-changing. It includes private meanings and symbols, general guidelines for behaviors, as well as ranges of acceptable behaviors under defined circumstances. Culture also incorporates the ideology, mythology, beliefs, and hopes of a people. These change as the condition of a people changes, and as the nature of the interaction betwen the entire Afro-American society, or segments thereof, and the larger society changes. Therefore, the behavior of middle and lower SES Afro-Americans, the patterns of attenuated and bi-parental families, the behavior and values of the disenfranchised and the more affluent, are all part of the larger organic whole. No segment represents or is normative of the whole.

A second frequent source of difficulty in research on Afro-American family life is the common error of assuming that Afro-Americans constitute a homogeneous group and that their neighborhoods and communities are homogeneous entities. Few studies of Afro-American life take into account the various subgroups that are included in the larger Afro-American nation. Important differences are due to geographic location of residence, as well to location of origin (i.e., south versus north, east versus west, rural versus urban, specific states, and even sections within states). While generic experiences related to color may be held in common, patterns of behavior, expectations, even religious and mythological beliefs may be different. Other important sources of variability are nationality (e.g., multinational blacks), ethnocultural (e.g., French and Spanish blacks), language, and, of course, socioeconomic status. More recently, important work by Harriet McAdoo[35,36] on cross-generational mobility and its implications for occupational and educational achievement is noteworthy. She points out that recent arrivals into the Afro-American middle class often demonstrate greater achievement-striving than those who have been middle class for several generations. The same is true for the first generation out of poverty into the working class. Thus, for Afro-Americans, it is not sufficient to simply characterize someone as a member of a specific social class. Familial history of mobility may have important implications, at least for present achievement behavior.

The flaw in the homogeneity assumption is even more evident with respect to Afro-American communities. While it may be reasonable to assume homogeneity of social class in most other neighborhoods, in Afro-American neighborhoods discriminatory real estate practices have often required that working and middle class Afro-Americans live in the same block. Therefore, even if a particular neighborhood or block appears to be lower class, one cannot randomly select any Afro-American household on the block and assume it fits the neighborhood social class norm. Parker and Kleiner[29] and TenHouten[30] have illustrated the need to carefully specify and measure actual SES in Afro-Americans, as well as to control for SES variability in Afro-American neighborhoods.

Finally, the third and perhaps most difficult assumption under debate is the error of assumed general cultural equivalence (i.e., that Afro-Americans and whites share the same basic culture). Its central premise is that the behaviors of both groups are essentially equivalent and can be legitimately compared against a single normative set of standards. Again, we must return to the notion of culture. Nobles[10] defines culture as

> A montage of specific ways of thinking, feeling, acting, which is peculiar to the members of a particular group. In its combined form, the dominant 'tone' or unique 'rhythm' of a particular cultural montage distinguishes it from other cultural montages (p. 602).

Further, Merton[37] argues for differential access to specific cultural information which affects differentially the ability to understand the insider relative to an outsider. Thus, the outsider who denies and disregards the cultural integrity of the foreign group and mistakenly assumes a substantive equivalency of his or her culture to that of the other group is prone to committing what VonLue[38] refers to as a "trans-substantive error:" meanings, beliefs, values, and behaviors of one culture are erroneously transformed, defined, and interpreted into the substance of another. Unwittingly, or perhaps arrogantly, many researchers of Afro-American family life have made transsubstantive errors.

Collectively, these three faulty assumptions have served to perpetuate many myths and have severely retarded the legitimate scientific study of Afro-American family life.

RESEARCH EMPHASES: THE HISTORICITY OF DATA

Historically, five distinct emphases in Afro-American family research are evident. These emphases seem to parallel loosely the nature of the race relations climate in the country and related themes in the general social sciences. These periods, as suggested by Staples[15] include the poverty/acculturation period (pre-1950s), the pathology period (1950s, early 1960s), the reactive apology period (late 1960s), the black nationalist period (middle–late 1960s, early 1970s), and the proactive-revisionism period (middle–late 1970s). The differences in these emphases were not so much in the basic picture of the Afro-American family presented but rather in the direction of the causal attributions made.

Early classic studies by Dubois[1] and Frazier[2–4,39] can be categoried into the first phase of *poverty/acculturation*. They were the first to focus on the Afro-American family as a legitimate area of research activity. Consistent with the racial and social policy climate of their times, the emphasis in their research was on the detrimental effects of poverty and discrimination. Central to their thinking was the notion that Afro-Americans were more successful and healthier to the degree that they were successful in acculturating to the norms, values, and standards of white middle-class society. Familial disorganization (i.e. Afro-American matriarchal structure) and pathology seen in lower class Afro-American families were described as products of slavery, racism, and poverty that established and reinforced lifestyles and patterns of behavior inimical to effective acculturation. In contrast, the Afro-American middle-class was presented as evidence of Afro-American familial stability, achievement, and success, due to its acculturative prowess. Frazier,[4] however, noted that Afro-Americans paid a high price in this acculturation to middle-class American society. Individualistic pursuit of material possessions in the face of racist obstacles served to condemn many newly arrived Afro-American middle-class families to a state of anomie and insecurity; stresses were created that undermined the stability of families, and servered ties with kinship networks which had been critical in the survival and upward mobility of these families.

Direct byproducts and elaborators of the poverty/acculturation focus of the early 1930s and 1940s were the pathologists of the 1950s and 1960s. Elaborating principally on Frazier's notion of the Afro-American matriarchy and emphasizing the dilemma and consequences of urban poverty on the Afro-American family, pathologists like Moynihan,[34] Aldous,[40] Clark,[41] Bernard,[42] Rainwater,[23,24,28] and Hess[70,71] presented empirical evidence associating the degree of familial disorganization with personality, cognitive, and social deficits in Afro-American children. Moynihan went one step further, reversing the direction of attributed causes for familial disorganization and its consequences toward the Afro-American individual.[34] His now infamous report proposed the thesis that the deterioration of the Afro-American family was at the root of the deterioration of the Afro-American community. For the first time, the Afro-American family as victim became characterized as the agent of its own oppression. Rainwater was later to modify this theme and to propose his reciprocal "tangle of pathology" thesis, wherein oppression creates a "culture of poverty" which, although an effective survival strategy, ultimately restricts the upward mobility of the lower classes.[23,24]

It is not without merit to note the political climate surrounding this change in perspective. The emphasis on Afro-American pathology came at the time when blacks were mobilizing in a national movement against institutionalized racism, and making important gains in the area of civil rights.

Almost as a direct reaction to the pathologists, both white and Afro-American scholars began a series of studies directly challenging the pathology notion. These studies argued that Afro-American families were essentially the same as white families except for the experiences of racism, discrimination and poverty. The work of Scanzoni,[43] Liebow,[44] and Willie[45] can be so characterized. These works sought to demonstrate that

Afro-white familial differences were not substantive but mainly due to economic and social status differences. The Afro-American family was essentially a victimized and less fortunate darker version of the white family.

As the Civil Rights Movement began to lose ground, its leadership decimated by either violence or complicity, the radical black nationalist orientation began to gain validity and credibility. The notion that "Black is Beautiful", and that black culture is unique and legitimate as a byproduct of its African cultural roots, became the hue and cry of the black masses. Afro-American scholars of this era began to challenge many of the previously unstated assumptions about Afro-American behavior. The notion of an autonomous Afro-American culture, and the notion of Afro-American familial forms both as elaborations of survival strategies to deal with the oppressive reality of America as well as elaborations of African cultural themes, began to permeate the literature. Emphasis on strengths and competencies replaced attention to pathology and deficiency. Previous deficits (e.g., family structure) were redefined as strengths (e.g., the extended kinship support system). Afro-American families were no longer viewed as homogeneous, non-white entities, but rather as complex multi-structured phenomena. The work of Billingsley,[5] Ladner,[8] Hill,[7] Jeffers,[46] Stack,[11] Staples,[12–14] and more recently Nobles,[9,10,17] fall into this category.

In addition to initiating a conceptual shift, these scholars also introduced and extended the use of more complex, although not especially precise, methodology into the study of Afro-American families. The issue of social class differences within these families was more firmly acknowledged, and greater utilization of balanced designs and within-group comparisons were substituted for the earlier reliance on class-confounded, cross-racial comparison designs.

During the mid to late 1970s, we have seen a less clearly defined emphasis developing. For lack of a better term, these trends can best be characterized as *proactive revisionism*. Old questions are being restated and reconceptualized in a more precise and scientific fashion. Popularly accepted "facts" are being subjected to more precise and empirical testing, and more qualified statements about Afro-American families are beginning to appear. With this strategy, a more complex and a perhaps more realistic picture of Afro-American family life is emerging. No single notion can easily be used to characterize this family system, and old stereotypes and myths are slowly being laid to rest. This group includes, among many, TenHouten,[30] Allen,[47] McAdoo,[35,36] Hays and Mindel,[48]

Williams & Stockton,[49] Babchuck and Ballweg,[50] and a host of new scholars emerging in the field with enlightening dissertations.

IDEOLOGICAL PERSPECTIVES: YOU SEE WHAT YOU EXPECT TO SEE

Inherent in our historical overview of changes in the foci of attention in Afro-American family research over the last 75 years were distinct differences in the ideological perspectives of the investigators. These ideological perspectives are based not on scientific objectivity but rather on subjective value premises with which the investigator approaches the subject matter. These perspectives not only influenced the questions asked and the answers obtained (or perhaps preperceived), but also affected interpretations. It is very common in the literature to see separate investigators who used similar methodologies, used comparable samples, and addressed the same question produce completely contradictory findings and conclusions. For example, Rainwater,[23] Ladner,[8] Frazier,[3] and Scanzoni[43] applied similar conceptual frameworks and in some cases similar methodologies, yet emerged with radicaly different conclusions about Afro-American families. These differences appear to relate to differences in the theoretical perspectives influencing the researchers' initial conceptualizations of the phenomena studied and coloring their interpretations of the results.

In an interesting conceptual article, Allen offers a typology of subjective perspectives in which the major figures in Afro-American family research can be grouped. He suggests three principal groupings on the basis of their perspectives on Afro-American culture. These include the *cultural equivalent* perspective, the *cultural deviant* perspective, and the *cultural variant* perspective. The cultural equivalent perspective essentially assumes that Afro-American culture is, for all intents and purposes, American, and therefore functionally equivalent to white American culture. What differences exist are superficial artifacts created by structural obstacles to full access and participation in the mainstream culture.[47] The works of Frazier,[3] Bernard,[42] and Scanzoni[43] would fall into this group.

The related cultural deviant perspective assumes from the outset that Afro-American culture, with its institutions and social norms is a deviation from the majority culture. Deviations result either from adaptations to a hostile reality, or more likely, as products of the deficiencies of individuals and of their life styles. The Afro-American family, therefore, to the degree that it is different from the normative structure of the white middle-class nuclear family, is deviant and pathological. Frazier,[3] Moynihan,[34] Rainwater,[23,24,28] Schultz,[51] and others approach their research from this perspective. It is noteworthy that few of these investigators were able to identify or appreciate any legitimate strengths in the Afro-American families they studied.

Finally, and most recently, there has been an elaboration of a cultural variant or cultural autonomy perspective. This view starts with the assumption that Afro-American culture is different from white culture because of its original African roots and/or because it evolved out of completely different existential and phenomenal realities. Billingsley,[5] Stack,[11] Rodman,[52] Ladner,[8] and Hill[7] generally subscribe to the idea of a distinct, adaptive Afro-American culture that spawns Afro-American familial forms possessing distinct strengths. Staples[13,14] and Nobles[9,10,17] assume a more dynamic, transactional perspective based on the dual contributions of distinct African cultural origins modified by a peculiar historical interaction with American culture and society. Nobles notes:

> . . . we suggest that the black family system should be thought of as African in nature and American in nurture[10, p.684]

Staples[14] further divides Allen's[47] cultural variant perspective into two distinct suborientations: the Nobles perspective, based on the concept of Africanity as central to Afro-American culture, which Staples labels *Pan-African*, and his own developing perspective, which he calls *domestic colonialism*. He distinguishes the latter as evolving from a historical materialist base with an emphasis on the political and economic exploitation of races. Principal notions of the "racially priviledged" and the "racially subordinate" are used to define the basis for differences in life style, culture and functioning of social institutions, such as the family, in each of the status groups. Afro-Americans function as domestic colonial subjects whose resources, talents, and lives are controlled by the same economic and political forces that maintain their subordinate status.

COMPETING CONCEPTUAL MODELS:

Finally, in addition to differences in emphases and in theoretical perspectives, studies on the Afro-American family also differ in terms of the conceptual models used. Unfortunately, most researchers in the field do not specify their conceptual models but rather tacitly employ concepts, assumptions, and orientations consistent with one or more conceptual models. Nevertheless, we can identify at least three principal models. Allen[47] labels them (1) the structural/functional model, (2) the interactional/situational model, and (3) the developmental/life-cycle model.

The *structural/functional* model is the most popular and versatile of the models used in Afro-American family research. It emphasizes the importance of familial structure in the fulfillment of socially defined instrumental and affective functions. The model assumes, perhaps somewhat erroneously, that from a knowledge of familial structure, inferences can be drawn about the equilibrium or disequilibrium in the system, as well as about the functional or dysfunctional nature of the system. Starting with the value perspective of the nuclear family as ideally balanced and functional, family structures that deviate from that norm, either towards attenuation (i.e., broken) or towards augmentation (i.e., extended), are therefore unbalanced and viewed as most likely to be dysfunctional. Studies falling into this category would include Frazier's classic early studies[2–4] and later studies by others relating socioeconomic status and sexuality,[28] child-rearing practices,[53] marital dissolution,[54] and family attitudes.[52] Studies on the relationships and functioning of different family structures by Billingsley[5,6] and extended kinship networks[11,48,55] also utilize this approach. Finally, studies on conjugal roles, specifically, studies on the popular notion of the Afro-American matriarchy[3,20,34] and more recent studies on the egalitarian Afro-American family[7,13,30,32,51,56–59] are primarily functional/structural studies.

Although very popular and useful for empirical research, the structural/functional model is limited in that it infers functioning of a family from its structure, and approaches the family as a static, discrete entity rather than as a dynamic, changing system.

The *interactional/situational* model is described by Allen as focusing attention principally on the internal dynamics of the family, on the individual traits of the members, or on both.[47] Principally, studies such as Rainwater,[23,24,28] Ladner,[8] Stack,[11] Lewis,[22] and Jeffers,[46] that utilize participant-observation or intensive interview strategies concentrating on the actual dynamics in the family, employ this approach. Issues about the process of decision-making, child-rearing and socialization, communication patterns, the use of extended kinship, and primary affiliation patterns are addressed by this model. In general, it is a more dynamic and rich approach to the study of the Afro-American family. However, because of the complexity of the task and the volume of data generated, only very limited issues can be addressed by this model. Nevertheless, it is the approach most commonly and effectively used by family therapists, anthropologists and sociologists who are interested in getting to know a few families very intimately.

Finally, the least known and least applied model to the study of the Afro-American family life is the *developmental/life-cycle* model. No studies have been found in the literature that use this longitudinal approach with Afro-American families. Such a model would highlight the stagelike, dynamic nature of family functioning and negate the static, structural, single-time assessment of families. Obviously, the cost in time, the volume of data to be collected, reduced, and summarized, and the limited sample size makes this approach extremely costly and not feasible for most research efforts. However, in the case of Afro-American families, the total absence of such studies in the published literature at this time leaves important lacunae in our knowledge base.

Some investigators, such as Staples[15] and McAdoo,[35,36] use family evolution histories and cross-sectional and life-stage variants of the developmental model to discuss issues such as sexuality, and the relationship between extended kinship and cross-generational mobility.

In sum, it appears, on the basis of historical changes in emphases, differences in basic theoretical perspectives, and differences inherent in conceptual models used in Afro-American family research, that considerable imprecision, contradiction, and downright distortions are normative for the field. It is not surprising that old issues continue to be debated, that demonstrated falsehoods and myths continue to be perpetuated, and that resulting social policies designed to improve the lot of low-income Afro-American families are misguided and useless. The need for a sound and unified theory is imperative, and removal of the dichotomy in the quality of methodology used in studying Afro-American and non-Afro-American families is essential.

Methodological Issues In Afro-American Family Research

Research on Afro-American family life is not only conceptually flawed but also suffers from important methodological weaknesses. Principal among these are: (1) the confounding of race and class in unbalanced designs, (2) the problem of small and nonrepresentative samples, and (3) the problems of measures and sources of data of questionable reliability and validity.

RACE AND CLASS AS PREDICTORS

The major methodological (and for that matter conceptual) criticism that can be levied on the literature on Afro-American families is the consistent tendency of early empirical studies to use unbalanced designs where race and class effects are confounded. Typically, these studies compare low socioeconomic status (SES) Afro-American families with middle class white families, and attribute the differences obtained to race. In addition, the conceptualization of class, especially at the lower end of the spectrum, is rather naive and simplistic. The tendency is to sample from the lowest SES levels (i.e., the chronically unemployed or unemployable, multiproblem families, ones most likely to be single-parent families, etc.) and to use them as representative of the lower class. In reality, as Billingsley[5] and Rainwater[23,24] point out, we can identify at least three qualitatively different groups in the lowest SES levels. They suggest a categorization of the *working nonpoor*, the *working poor*, and the *underclass*. The first group, the working non-poor, include those generally employed regularly in the industrialized sector of the economy (i.e., factory workers, truck drivers, etc.). The stability of their status is tied to fluctuations in industry and in the economy. The second group, the working poor, are those who work hard and regularly at their jobs but don't make enough to escape the poverty line. Included are janitors, busboys, some porters, unskilled factory workers, service workers, etc. These are the ones typically last hired and first fired. Job instability and low income keeps them in a marginal status. These two categories include a large number of employed Afro-American women. The third category, the underclass (i.e., the chronically unemployed), also referred to as "the disreputable poor"[60] is at the very bottom of the scale and constitutes the group generally used as representative of the Afro-American lower class.

Miller[27] suggests an even more meaningful typology of the poor based on their level of economic security and degree of family stability. This typology was designed to recognize that among even the very poor, families have been found to show considerable resiliency, ingenuity, and stability. These families may be economically depressed, but their members enjoy a strong sense of cohesiveness and stability. He suggests, on this basis, four types of poor: (1) the *stable poor* (secure economics and stable family), (2) the *strained poor* (secure economics, but unstable family), (3) the *coping poor* (insecure economics, but stable family), and (4) the *unstable poor* (insecurity and instability on both dimensions).

Both of these typologies reinforce the problem in Afro-American family research of sampling from the Afro-American underclass and inferring that the behaviors typically found in that group are representative of all of the poor.

SAMPLE SIZE AND REPRESENTATIVENESS

Related to the previous problem is the common error in the majority of studies on Afro-American families of using small samples for convenience, and then generalizing the findings to all Afro-Americans. Volumes have been written on the problems of using small, nonrandom and nonrepresentative samples: we need not belabor the point here. Suffice it to say that this methodological weakness raises serious doubts about the value of much of what is reported in the literature on the Afro-American family. The fact that so many studies have been conducted and published with such glaring technical errors further reinforces the need for more carefully designed and sound research in the field.

DATA SOURCE ERROR

Considerable controversy has been raised about the appropriateness of using research tools standardized on majority populations to assess comparable behaviors in nonmajority populations. This is especially true in the area of intelligence testing. However, even more severe criticisms have been levied against personality measures, interview procedures, and the use of non-standardized instruments (see Chapter 6). It is interesting to note, then, that not only is it common for measures of unknown reliability and validity to be used in the study of Afro-American families, but often the investigators do not even take the basic precaution of pretesting their measures to insure that the language used is understandable to the respondents.

Further, as Frazier[2] and Moynihan[34] demonstrated, it is not uncommon for unreliable data sources such as historical documents and the census to be used as data to support particular hypotheses. While these data are useful sources of impressions and trends and are valuable sources from which to generate testable hypotheses, they are not adequate to support precise scientific statements.

Other methods used, such as participant observation and case studies, are useful techniques. They are, however, vulnerable to investigator bias and cannot be assumed to be generalizable to a nonobserved sample.

In sum, this brief overview of the major theoretical and methodological criticisms that can be levied against the literature on Afro-American family life suggests quite clearly the need to critically evaluate reported findings. Biased ideological perspectives and faulty conceptualizations have led to the perpetuation of myths about Afro-American families. Flawed methodologies have allowed those myths to be taken as scientific facts. Therefore, as we proceed to highlight the major content issues and to discuss the major findings in the field, the concerns raised about theory and methodology should be kept in mind.

PRINCIPAL RESEARCH ISSUES AND THEMES IN THE LITERATURE

The Afro-American family has been intensively and extensively studied over the past 75 years. Hundreds of articles and books have been written about aspects of the Afro-American family. Studies have been conducted on issues of family structure, stability, role, and functioning of women and men in the family, the effects of poverty on family functioning and the socialization of Afro-American children, the effects of maternal employment, issues of dominance and power, the role of extended kinship networks, etc. Several review articles, books of readings, and bibliographies have been published that give a more detailed overview of this voluminous literature than is possible here. We recommend to the reader Robert Staples' *The Black Family: Essays and Studies*(1971),[13] Charles V. Willie's *The Family Life of Black People* (1970),[45] and Lynwood Davis' *The Black Family in the United States: A Selected Bibliography* (1978) as excellent sources of original articles and bibliographic sources. We also recommend to the reader the original classics in the field which are frequently cited, such as E.F. Frazier's *The Negro Family in the United States* (1939),[3] and *Black Bourgeoisie: The Rise of a New Middle Class in the United States* (1957);[4] Andrew Billingsley's *Black Families in White America (1968);*[5] Joyce Aschenbrenner's *Lifelines: Black Families in Chicago* (1975);[55] Jerold Heiss' *The Case of the Black Family: A Sociological Inquiry* (1975);[57] Joyce Ladner's *Tomorrow's Tomorrow: The Black Woman* (1971);[8] and Carol Stack's *All Our Kin: Strategies for Survival in a Black Community* (1974).[11]

In this section, we shall focus our attention on the empirical literature in five major areas of research on Afro-American family life. These include research on: (1) the structure, functioning and stability of Afro-American families, (2) the effect of single-parent, low-income Afro-American family structure on the achievement and sex-role socialization of Afro-American children, (3) parental role and power in two-parent Afro-American families, and (4) the role of Afro-American kinship networks and support systems.

The Structure, Functioning and Stability of Afro-American Families

The most controversial issue and popular myth in the Afro-American family literature is the notion of the Afro-American family as essentially a matriarchal[2,34] or a matrifocal family.[24] Reasoning on the basis of the cumulative effect of a history of slavery, the great northern migrations, and poverty and discrimination on Afro-American families, Frazier proposed that the Afro-American low-income family was functionally condemned to being a matriarchy.[2,3] Women are often the sole parents and heads of these families, and the fathers are generally either absent, or ineffectual and tangential in the actual running of the home. Frazier argued that this picture of disorganization and marital instability which is said to characterize the Afro-American lower classes was the product of social structural practices that emasculated the male.[3] Subsequent researchers, such as Clark,[41] Rainwater,[23,24,28] Moynihan,[34] Bernard,[42] and Aldous[40] found support for this hypothesis, principally by relying on the evidence of a greater incidence of female-headed families among Afro-Americans than among whites, as well as in empirical studies of low-income, single-parent families. Clark[41] and Rainwater[23,24] attributed the reported instability and matriarchal structure of Afro-American families principally to the effects of economic and social deprivation. Restricted access to and exclusion from stable, high status employment, and restriction from equal access to and participation in the majority culture resulted in undermining the very fabric of the Afro-American family. This disorganized, less competent family in turn inculcated in its members attitudes, behaviors, and values that, although realistic survival reactions to abject poverty, served to restrict their ability to be upwardly mobile and to ever effectively adapt to the general society (i.e., Rainwater's *Tangle of Pathology* thesis).[23,24]

The most powerful statement in favor of the "black matriarchy" hypothesis was perhaps best stated by Moynihan,[34] and later supported by Aldous[40] and others. Relying on data from the 1960 United States census and crime statistics, Moynihan in his now infamous report concluded that on the basis of the number of female-headed families, divorce rates, percentage of families on Aid to Families with Dependent Children (AFDC), illegitimacy rates, juvenile crime and delinquency statistics, etc., that the Afro-American family was an inadequate, pathological, and dysfunctional social institution. Furthermore, it is this pathological state of the Afro-American family that is at the very root of the disorganization of Afro-American neighborhoods.

Later researchers, such as Billingsley,[5] Staples,[14] Heiss,[56,57] and Leslie[61] argued against the matriarchal thesis both by challenging the validity of the Moynihan et al. data, as well as by challenging the notion of a matriarchy itself. Their essential argument is that while there are more Afro-American female-headed families than there are white, (e.g., recent estimates are 37% for Afro-Americans and 11 percent for whites),[62] and while Afro-American divorce rates continue to exceed that of whites (about 40 percent for Afro-Americans and 15 percent for whites), the majority of Afro-American families are bi-parental. Furthermore, the Afro-white differential in family stability, and hence in structure, was more directly a function of greater Afro-American vulnerability to economic fluctuations and to the operation of institutional racism. Therefore, differences in social class distribution by race account for most of this Afro-white differential in marital stability.

They also note, as do subsequent researchers, that the notion of an Afro-American matriarchy assumes incorrectly that Afro-American males are in fact absent in reported female-headed families; that when present in poor families, the men are tangential and uninvolved in the decision making processes in these families; and thirdly, that in two-parent Afro-American families, the woman exercises inordinate power and influence. More recent studies have submitted the competing sides of this debate to more direct empirical tests and demonstrate that there is, in fact, no evidence to support the notion of an Afro-American matriarchy. In fact, Hyman and Reed in a secondary analysis of three national surveys, found that there is a pattern of maternal influence even in intact families that is characteristic of American families generally, and not specifically of Afro-American families.[63]

In his classic 1968 book, Billingsley proposes an alternative structural formulation for the Afro-American family. He suggested a structural model consisting of three basic forms—nuclear (couple), extended (relatives in the home), and augmented families (nonrelatives in the home). Adding the dimensions of incipient, simple, and attenuated to account for whether the family was developing with no children (incipient), as stable (simple) or as uniparental (attenuated), Billingsley proposed a 12 category typology which he felt was a more accurate depiction of the structural complexity of Afro-American families.[5] In a more recent test and revision of this structural typology, Williams and Stockton suggested the need to modify these categories to allow for the inclusion of parent-surrogates, individuals who are heads of Afro-American households but who are neither married, parents, nor surrogate parents, and individuals living alone or with unrelated others.[49]

An additional issue in the study of Afro-American familial structure is the issue of the extended family. Billingsley,[5] Staples,[14] Hill,[7] Stack,[11] Ladner,[8] Nobles,[9,10,17] and several more recent writers have all argued for the legitimacy of the extended kinship network as a viable and essential part of the Afro-American family. These investigators view this feature as a unique evolutionary and adaptive component which may well be a cultural extension of original African family systems and ethos. The differences in meaning, dependence, and value that this extended kinship network has for Afro-Americans as compared to whites suggest that this is a key feature differenciating Afro-American culture from majority culture in both the definition and the structuring of families.[35,36,48,50,64]

It appears, on the basis of this cursory review of the literature, that several important points can be made about the structure, stability, and functioning of the Afro-American family. First, while the model Afro-American family appears to be the simple nuclear family, there are a wide variety of structural variations in the Afro-American family, many of which are not commonly found among majority families. Therefore, simplistic statements about the structure of Afro-American families or the notion of a singular, monolithic Afro-American family are incorrect and should be avoided. Second, the stability and functioning of these families seem to be affected disproportionately by economic and social forces influencing the employment status of both Afro-American men and women. The latter are frequently at risk of being abandoned, separated, or divorced, and left with the responsibility of the children. Third, the status and authority of the male in the Afro-American family probably varies considerably as a function of his employment status, his personal role definition, and the personal characteristics of both spouses. Fourth, extended kinship, para-kin, and support networks are important and integral parts of the definition and functioning of Afro-American families.

The Single-Parent Afro-American Family: Dynamics and Effects

As a direct consequence of national concern over poverty and discrimination and their effects on the personality, cognitive, and social development of children and youth, an extensive body of literature has emerged dealing specifically with single-parent Afro-American families, especially those of the underclass. The majority of these studies were conducted with the initial hypothesis that the female-headed family was ill-equiped to effectively fulfill its primary socialization function. Therefore, the frequently reported poor intellectual and cognitive development, low self-esteem, poor academic achievement, confused sex-role identification, and juvenile delinquency problems among dispossessed Afro-American youth were attributed to the weaknesses of the family. In a recent compilation of 50 years of published research in the social sciences on Afro-American child development, we found this to be the central theme of the majority of the 1274 studies cited (see Myers et al.[65]).

Research on the female-headed, single-parent Afro-American family is rather complex. Several major studies of poverty-stricken families[23,24,40,42,51,66–68] consistently reported that female-headed low-income Afro-American families can be characterized as living in environments where mistrust, displaced anger, and hatred are the norm;[51] where children display negative self-images[28,69] and confused sex-roles;[23,24,28] where masculine models are either absent or ineffectual and boys learn to compensate for feelings of inadequacy via super-masculine posturing, violence, and delinquency,[41,62] where language deficiency and inadequate socialization leads to retardation in cognitive, affective, and intellectual development;[38,39,72–74] and where sexuality develops early and is expressed without moral restraint.[24,41,75]

This picture of unredeeming and abject pathology popularized in the 1960s has been challenged by other studies which suggest that a more balanced and complex picture of female-headed, low-income Afro-American families is probably more accurate. Billingsley reviews and discusses a series of studies that addresses various aspects of the functioning of these families even under the worst conditions and does not find a standard pattern of pathology.[6] Rather, the studies report that in the case of child abuse, for example, low-income, female-headed Afro-American families are significantly less likely to abuse or neglect their children than a comparable sample of white families.[76,77] When low-income Afro-American families are compared among themselves, different patterns of child-caring emerge. Some parents care effectively for their children, some express great concern but appear unable to provide consistently for their children, and a third group appeared to be completely unconcerned and ineffective in their child-caring activities.[22,46,78] In a comparison study to the major Rainwater participant-observation study in a St. Louis housing project, Ladner[8] described the pattern of early psychosexual development and behavior of low-income Afro-American adolescents as a healthy reaction to real environmental constraints and a healthy avoidance of the neurotic and dishonest dual-system sexuality of the middle-classes. This perspective is further supported by Staples,[12–15] even though he recognizes the double-bind and the very high price that such an adaptation entails.

With respect to the presence of men in female-headed, Afro-American homes, Schultz described a seven-category typology of male status based on the degree of marginality of the men in the families.[51,67] Included in this typology were four types of "boyfriends" in order of increasing marginality: the quasifather, the supportive biological father, the supportive companion, and the pimp. Schultz noted that the latter, which epitomizes the stereotyped exploitative character attributed to low SES Afro-American male-female relationships, was extremely rare. The majority of the boyfriends involved with these families appeared to spend most of their time bargaining for a familial relationship as a quasifather (i.e., intimately involved with the women and her children). Their ability to succeed at this task was tied to their occupational status and income, their willingness to assume parental responsibility, and the women's confidence in their abilities and sincerity.

In three more recent studies, different conceptual strategies were used to study Afro-American single-parent families. In a study of successful products of "broken homes," Morris[79] reported that these Afro-American individuals generally came from female-headed households, yet did not perceive their families as "broken." Their fathers, although absent from the home, continued to play an important part in their lives. Third, their communities and kinship networks offered important paternal substitutes and support to their families.

In a similar study comparing Afro-American and white, single-parent, low-income families to distinguish familial features associated with antisocial adolescent behavior, Thompson found that, across racial groups, antisocial boys perceived their mothers as more powerful than the mothers saw themselves; the mothers perceived the boys as more immature and dependent than did the controls; and the antisocial boys had more siblings, and fewer mothers that graduated from high school or who were employed.[80]

Finally, in a large survey study on 200 Afro-American parent-absent families, Savage et al. assessed a variety of different types of single-parent families on their attitudes and feelings about family role structure, family cohesion and parent-child relationships. The families were divided into five groups: male-headed parent; and four female-headed families—husband incarcerated, separated, divorced, and widowed. Results showed important differences in the functioning of the groups in the various areas studied. Overall, it appears that the divorced and male-headed families were more stable and effective across the board. This may in part be due to the fact that these parents were generally employed the longest, had higher paying jobs and a better education. The separated group reflected qualities of instability related to the crisis of separation. The least competent and most vulnerable families overall were the husband-incarcerated group. The women in these families had the lowest income, the least amount of education, and were more likely to be unemployed. They were also more likely to receive assistance from agencies and from kin.[81]

In sum, these studies suggest that the frequently reported negative effects of single-parent families on Afro-Americans are probably due not as much to the existence of single parents, as they are to a list of other factors. Principal among these are socioeconomic, educational, and personal resources of the remaining parent, and the availability of positive support from kinship and community resources. Further, we must recognize that single parents are frequently not "alone". The companion(s) plays an important, even if indirect, role in the quality and effectiveness of the functioning of these families. To the extent that employment status, stability, and income of the parent is low and to the extent that education and other personal resources are limited, the risk of being overwhelmed by the task of being a single parent is great, and the likelihood of producing maladaptive individuals is high. Among Afro-Americans, the quality and availability of resources and supports from the kinship network and from the general community serve as very important mediators of the risks of single parenthood.

Parental Role and Power in Afro-American Two-Parent Families

Several major questions have been addressed or are implied in the research reviewed in this section. First, the principally debated question is, are Afro-American women generally more powerful and influential in their families than Afro-American males, or are Afro-American biparental families egalitarian? This is a corollary to the "black matriarchy" debate, which implies that if the matriarchy hypothesis is in fact true, then Afro-American women should rule the roost even when the "rooster" is present. The second, and perhaps more important question is, what is the pattern of influence of Afro-American males and females within the family? Realistically, in most modern American families, the pattern of authority and power is differentially assumed by husband and wife in different areas, with different issues, and at different times. Third and finally is the developmental question, namely, what are the changes in the pattern of influence and power between the conjugal pair at different stages of familial development?

In the past ten years we have seen increased attention paid to the study of the internal dynamics of the Afro-American family, especially to the question of dominance and power. This shift away from purely structural analyses has resulted in the refutation of several stereotypes and the reaffirmation of these families as neither inherently matriarchal nor pathological.

The task of assessing dominance required a shift of attention away from single-parent families to two-parent families, encouraged both within and between group comparisons across social classes, and forced investigators to conceptualize more carefully and precisely the phenomena of dominance and power in families.

In a recent review of what they termed four "classic" studies of power relations in Afro-American families, Willie and Greenblatt[38] offered empirical evidence to refute the hypothesis of the "powerful black female". The first study reviewed was the Middleton and Putney[82] study comparing 40 Afro-American and white families matched on SES (i.e., working class and middle class), number of years married, and mean age of each spouse. Using a 15-item questionnaire dealing with child care, purchases and living standards, and recreation and role attitudes, they found quite unexpectedly that (1) most families, both Afro-American and white, were egalitarian, (2) that more Afro-American families across SES were egalitarian than white families, and (3) that Afro-American middle-class families were the most egalitarian of all the families studied. The expected pattern of matriarchal dominance was found in only two of the ten working class Afro-American families.

In a similar study that was first reported in 1971 in *Psychology Today* and subsequently published in 1978, Delores Mack conducted a study of 80 Afro-American and white couples matched by SES (i.e., working class and middle class). The couples were asked to participate in three tasks: (1) fill out a questionnaire on family decision-making separately, then (2) jointly, and finally, (3) participate in a role-play situation as "salesperson" and "customer" in an African boutique. The variables of interest were level of authority, influence, and degree of persuasibiilty of the husband. The results showed that all four groups saw the wife as slightly more powerful and influential overall than the husband. The wife had the least power and influence in the Afro-American working class family and the most influence in the white middle-class family. In the case of conflict resolution (i.e. joint questionnaire responses), no significant differences were found between the sexes across the four groups. However, the working-class husbands were slightly more powerful than the middle-class husbands. Mack contends that these results suggest that social class is a more important predictor of sex-role influence than is race.[58]

In a more complex and elaborately designed survey study, TenHouten compared 550 Afro-American and white low-SES and middle-SES biparental families on *conjugal power* (i.e., male dominance ideology, conjugal decision-making power and conjugal power structure) and *parental power* (i.e., mother's parental power, mother's and father's parent-child decision power, and parental control).[86] Results showed that on male dominance ideology, Afro-American males and low-SES males reported greater dominance than whites or the middle class. On conjugal decision power, there were no consistent Afro-white differences, but a weak race/SES interaction was obtained. There were no differences in male dominance across social classes. However, among whites, there was a slight difference in male dominance in favor of the lower class white male. In terms of conjugal power structure, families could be described as patriarchal (male), matriarchal (female) egalitarian-autonomic (equal and harmonious) or egalitarian-conflictual. Results showed that wife-dominated families were generally infrequent, and were least frequent in Afro-American lower class families. Lower class white families were least likely to have an egalitarian-autonomic family and most likely to have a father-dominant family. The other famiies were mostly egalitarian-autonomic in nature. In terms of parental power, there were distinct social class effects for maternal power (i.e., low-SES mothers were more powerful); no significant race differences in male-female parental decision power, although Afro-American women were slightly more powerful than white women and Afro-American men; and most families (75 percent) were egalitarian on parental control.

These results are largely supported by the case studies by Willie,[92] Hyman & Reed,[63] Grisby,[83] Cromwell and Cromwell,[31] and Hammond and Enoch.[84] These latter studies suggest, in addition, that Afro-American male-female dominance in biparental families is curvilinear, related to the man's employment status. The higher the man's status, the greater his influence. However, at the higher status levels, the relationship tends to become more egalitarian.[84] Cromwell and Cromwell also note that in the area of conflict resolution, most of the couples studied—Afro-American, Mexican-American, and white-American—were egalitarian-conflictual in that the majority of the conflicts remained unresolved.[31] This finding has important implications for the stability and level of satisfaction extant in most American families.

A final note on the question of power and dominance: in a descriptive typological study, Schultz describes three types of father roles in the biparental, low-income Afro-American family—the indiscreet free man (i.e., obviously "playing around"), the discreet free man (i.e., "playing" discreetly), and the monogamous father. Schultz noted that in the low-income Afro-American family, the father's status and authority were dependent on his ability to earn a living, his willingness to share that living with his family, the degree of adherence to a monogamous marriage, his ability to cope with the harsh realities of ghetto life and poverty, and his relationship with the children.[51]

It appears, in sum, that the stereotypical notion of the Afro-American matriarchal structure of the family is not a tenable hypothesis, at least not for the majority of these families. However, as Hare,[85] Staples,[15] and Nobles[10] note, this does not mean that these families don't face serious obstacles and that some don't clearly fail in their survival and socialization tasks. In fact, many do. However, the nature of Afro-American family structure and its dynamics are far more complex than was heretofore recognized. Many factors, both personal and external, contribute to the success or failure of these families. As our conceptualizations and research designs improve, we will become better equipped to fully capture and appreciate the richness and strengths of this social institution.

The Role of Afro-American Kinship Networks

In many of the studies reported in the earlier sections of this chapter, the issue of the supportive kinship network was raised. The importance and uniqueness of this feature of Afro-American family life deserve more specific attention. Hill,[7] Nobles,[9,10,17] and Staples[14] all acknowledged the value of this familial feature, often tracing its origin either to African historical cultural roots[10,17] or viewing it as an adaptation to the unique experiences of Afro-Americans in the United States.[5,7,11,55] These two apparently conflicted explanations of the origins of the Afro-American kinship system are not, in fact, mutually exclusive. The African conception of family as extending horizontally to include all members of the tribe and lineage, and vertically to include all members living, dead, and yet-to-be-born, provides the most basic and fundamental grounding for the system of Afro-American kinship.[86] The specific nature and character of this system as manifested throughout history in the United States, however, must also have been influenced and shaped by the peculiar historical forces extant in Afro-American experiences. Thus, compared to most white families, Afro-American families are most intimately connected to a kinship network.[48,50,64] However, it is also important to recognize that other groups experiencing the ravages of discrimination and poverty also maintain connections in a kinship network (e.g., Asians, Hispanics, Jews, Italians, etc.). Thus, the value of the network is not simply cultural, or unique to Afro-Americans, but rather may have a more universal foundation in the dynamics of excluded groups banding together and developing networks of communication, resource sharing, and supports for survival.

The research on Afro-American networks is fraught with debate. Some researchers believe that many Afro-American poor must break their kinship ties in order to facilitate their own mobility and growth.[11,12,87] Others believe most Afro-American families continue their network connections during periods of mobility and, in fact, use these networks as social mobility conduits.[35,36,59] Probably neither of these two positions is entirely incorrect. Family networks can be both potentially supportive and potentially destructive. As Williams and Stockton[12] and McAdoo[35] suggest, the value of the extended family network may be determined by the resources available to match the need, and the stage of development and mobility of the target family unit. McAdoo suggests that before mobility, Afro-American families may maintain very close and frequent contact with their kin.[35] This contact may be either maintained or drastically reduced during the period of mobility and then either reduced or reestablished after the new social status has been achieved. (See McAdoo,[35] page 765 for a more detailed exploration of this sequential pattern).

In sum, then, it appears that extended kinship networks and community support systems play a significant role in the survival, viability, and progress of Afro-American families. More research is needed to clarify when, under what conditions, and for whom this network is useful, and under what circumstances it is injurious. Staples,[15] Nobles,[10] and others have expressed grave concern about the apparent decreasing importance of the extended family among contemporary urban Afro-Americans. The evidence seems to suggest that a very important resource in the survival arsenal will be lost if the extended Afro-American family is allowed to disappear and Afro-Americans accept the isolated, nuclear family model that predominates in white America.

SOME EMERGING AFRO-AMERICAN FAMILIAL FORMS

Most of the research reviewed and discussed here deals principally with issues of social class and family structure and functioning, mainly as they apply to single- versus two-parent Afro-American families. Not enough attention, however, is being placed on emerging familial forms in Afro-American communities and their implications for the future directions of Afro-American families. Three principal forms are worth noting: the adolescent family, the nonprocreating family, and the cohabitating family. All three of these forms are not unique to Afro-Americans, but rather reflect some general trends in American society.[40,96] Nevertheless, a historical analysis of research on the Afro-American family would be incomplete without some attempt to project the lessons of history into the future.

The Afro-American Adolescent Family

A recent director of the Department of Health, Education and Welfare (J. Califano, 1978) described present trends in teen pregnancy as a national epidemic which the federal government must address. The thrust of his proposed public policy was to increase access to contraceptives by teenagers. Unfortunately, Mr. Califano's assessment of the situation was only partially correct, and his proposed strategy for intervention somewhat nearsighted. For Afro-Americans, especially those of low income, adolescent pregnancy is not an epidemic but an endemic problem. In fact, a recent National Institute of Child Health and Development (NICHD) report suggested that while the number of teen births among Afro-Americans continues to exceed that of whites by almost four to one, there is a noticeable drop in the Afro-American teen fertility rate, and a dramatic increase in the fertility rates of white females ages 14–15.[88] These data suggest that the problem of early pregnancy and parenting which has historically plagued Afro-Americans is beginning to spread throughout the entire society. A problem usually ascribed to the poor, the ignorant, and the immoral is now beginning to touch the priviledged, both white and Afro-American. Perhaps now there will be a serious and concerted effort to study, understand, and deal with this problem.

We are increasingly seeing, especially among the poorer segments of our communities, the emergence of "families within families" (i.e., the teen mother and her infant living within the home of her family of origin). This trend has been described by many as healthy in that these families do not reject their own despite whatever feelings, disappointments, and added burdens they must face with this new addition.[15] Nevertheless, what we must be conscious of is the fact than an increasing percentage of Afro-American children are growing up in families with one parent (or two or more same-sexed, multi-generational parents) and are living below the poverty line.[87] Similarly, we must recognize the fact that teen mothers run the greatest risk for birth defects and premature births, due to inadequate prenatal care and, for the youngest teens, limited physical ability to give birth. Similarly, a substantial majority of these youngsters do not complete high school; they often do not subsequently become employed, or when they do, they must accept low status, low pay, and unstable employment; they often end up on Aid for Families with Dependent Children (AFDC) rolls and are ill-equipped to make any future substantial progress in their lives. Many of these girls are 15 and 16 years of age and are assuming the responsibility of parenting a child at an age when their own parenting is incomplete. It is important, then, that students and scholars of the Afro-American family begin to focus some careful attention on the needs, dynamics, and resources of these "new families" so that adequate and sensitive public policy can be designed to accurately meet their needs.

Nonprocreating and Cohabitating Families

Increasingly, we find among the Afro-American middle class a trend towards fewer children and towards nonprocreation.[14] These couples are further complemented by the increasing number of those who have chosen alternative arrangements to marriage and traditional familial structures. While only preliminary data are available on these two groups, the author believes it is important that Afro-American family researchers begin to recognize these trends and focus some attention on them. Perhaps we are witnessing the development of a group of highly educated, upwardly-mobile Afro-Americans who, like their white counterparts, are chosing a childless, nontraditional existence. Before premature judgements and opinions are passed, it would be useful to initiate careful study of this phenomena so as to obtain a more honest and complete picture of Afro-American family life in America.

SUMMARY AND RECOMMENDATIONS FOR FUTURE RESEARCH

In summary, the field of Afro-American family research has been fraught with controversy, conflict, and confusion. Much of the controversy is centered around conceptualization of the structure and dynamics of these families and political and social implications of the various perspectives presented. Is the Afro-American family a broken and pathology-ridden institution, contributory to the failures of Afro-American people? Or, is it the victim of sociostructural processes of racism and discrimination that systematically impose excessive burdens and restrict its effective functioning? Or is the reality somewhere between these contradictory victim-victimizer views? In reality, Afro-American families are varied and complex. Depending on socioeconomic class, some of these families are stable, adaptable, and effective socialization vehicles. Others are marginal and seem to operate close to the limits of their resources and capabilities. A third group of Afro-American families, mainly located at the lowest end of the SES scale, are clearly ravaged by poverty and limited resources. These families fit many of the stereotyped characteristics generally attributed to the Afro-American family.

The studies we have reviewed suggest that there are no simple structural "truths" about Afro-American family life. Economics and social status seem to play important roles in the structure and stability of these families. However, even in the presence of stable and adequate financial resources, many Afro-American families, despite comfortable incomes and high social status, appear to be unstable and ineffective.

Research on the internal dynamics of Afro-American families generally suggests that they are more likely to be egalitarian and that the popular conception of a matriarchal structure is not substantiated by careful research. Finally, we see several additional familial forms emerging which should be studied. The teenage family within a family, nonprocreating and cohabitating Afro-American families are emerging as important familial trends at different ends of the socioeconomic ladder.

Two major criticisms can generally be levied against much of the research in this field. The majority of studies suffers from simplistic and ill-informed conceptualizations of the Afro-American family, and a significant number are methodologically flawed to a point where the utility and validity of their results can be seriously questioned. Future reseach efforts in the field, therefore, need to be clearly grounded in a sound theoretical base. Such a theory must recognize that Afro-American families are complex social systems with idiosyncratic internal dynamics and important external connections to communities, kinship networks, and the larger society. Researchers need to incorporate into their conceptual models and methodologies the peculiar duality of Afro-American life and institutions. On the one hand, Afro-American institutions such as the family share many, if not all, of the features of other families and can thus be understood in terms of generic principles applicable to all family systems. On the other hand, given the peculiar historical status of Afro-Americans in America, the very quality of being black adds a unique feature to the family that underscores and permeates the structure and functioning of that family. The conceptual synthesis of this fundamental dualism is the major task facing all students of Afro-American life.

Methodologically, researchers need to avoid the common error of unbalanced designs that fail to control for social class. They need to recognize that Afro-Americans are distributed along the full range of SES categories, but disproportionately grouped in the lower classes. However, meaningful use of the SES variable requires greater precision in the specification of which social class category best fits the families studied. The admonition of several sociologists that the lower class is a heterogeneous grouping consisting of at least three distinct levels is of particular significance in the study of Afro-Americans. The field would benefit from studies that make a deliberate effort to insure the representation of families from all of the major classes and levels within classes. Additionally, sample size, representativeness of the sample on the basis of geography, degree of urbanization, and neighborhood characteristics are important considerations. Finally, there is a clear need for studies of the Afro-American family to utilize developmental strategies that assess the evolution and functioning of these families over time. Questions about child-rearing, spousal dominance, decision making, social mobility, and stability have been generally addressed as static, single-time measurement phenomena. In reality, they are all processes that change and evolve over time. It is important, then, for serious researchers in the field to begin to study Afro-American family life as a dynamic and evolving system with distinct patterns and stages. Perhaps in this manner more precise answers can be derived about which combination of factors over time best accounts for and predicts the outcomes of Afro-American family systems.

REFERENCES

1. Dubois, W.E.B: The Negro American Family. Atlanta, Atlanta University Press, 1908

2. Frazier EF: The Negro Family in Chicago. Chicago, University of Chicago Press, 1932
3. Frazier EF: The Negro Family in United States. Chicago, University of Chicago Press, 1939
4. Frazier EF: Black Bourgeoise: The Rise of a New Middle-Class in the United States. New York, Free Press, 1957
5. Billingsley A: Black Families in White America. Englewood Cliffs, N.J., Prentice-Hall, 1968
6. Billingsley A: Family functioning in the low-income Black community. Soc. Casework 50:563–572, 1969
7. Hill RB: The Strengths of Black Families. New York, Emerson Hall Publishers, 1972
8. Ladner JA: Tomorrow's Tomorrow: The Black Woman. Garden City, N.Y. Doubleday, 1971
9. Nobles WW: African Root and American Fruit: The Black Family. J Soc Behav Sciences 20:52–63, 1974
10. Nobles WW: Toward an empirical and theoretical framework for defining Black families. J Marriage and the Family 40:679–688, 1978
11. Stack CB: All Our Kin: Strategies for Survival in a Black Community, New York, Harper & Row, 1974
12. Staples R: Towards a sociology of the Black family: A theoretical and methodological assessment. J Marriage and the Family 33:119–138, 1971
13. Staples RE: The Black Family: Essays and Studies. Belmont, Wadsworth Publishing, 1971
14. Staples R: The Black Family Revisited: A Review and a Preview. J Soc. Beh Science 20:65–78, 1974
15. Staples RE: Black family life and development, in Gary LE (Ed): Mental Health: A Challenge to the Black Community. Philadelphia, Dorrance, 1978, pp.73–94
16. Myers HF: Stress, ethnicity and social class: A model for research with black populations, in Jones E, Korchin S (Eds): Minority Mental Health. New York, Holt, Rhinehart & Winston. (in press)
17. Nobles WW: Africanity: Its role in black families. The Black Scholar 5:10–17, 1974
18. Clark X, C: Frames of reference in the evaluation of Black families. Paper presented at Charles R. Drew Postgraduate Medical School Conference on the Black Family, Laguna, California, November 18, 1972
19. Clark X, C: Black studies on the study of Black people, in Jones R (Ed): Black Psychology. New York, Harper & Row, 1972
20. Akbar N: Rhythmic patterns in African personality. In King L, Dixon V, Nobles W (Eds): Assumptions and Pardigms For Research On Black People. Proceedings from the First Annual J. Alfred Cannon Research Series Conference, Los Angeles, April, 1975
21. Mannheim K: Ideologia and Utopia. New York, Harcourt, Brace and World, 1936
22. Lewis H: Culture Class and Poverty. Three papers from the Child-Rearing Study of Low Income District of Columbia Families (CROSSTELL), Health and Welfare Council of the National Capital Area, Washington, D.C., February 1967
23. Rainwater L: The Problem of Low-Class Culture. J Soc Issues 26:133–148, 1970
24. Rainwater L: Behind the Ghetto Walls: Black Families in a Federal Slum. Chicago, Aldine Publishing, 1970
25. Allen VL: Personality correlates of poverty, in Allen VL (Ed): Psychological Factors in Poverty. Institute for Research on Poverty monograph series. Chicago, Markham Publishing, 1970, pp. 242–266
26. Allen VL: Theoretical issues in poverty research. J Soc Issues 26:149–167, 1970

27. Miller SM: The American lower classes: A typological approach, in Glasser, Glasser (Eds): Families in Crisis. New York, Harper & Row, 1970, pp. 38–55
28. Rainwater L: Crucible of identity: The Negro low-class family. Daedalus 95:172–316 1966
29. Parker S, Kleiner RJ: Mental Illness in the Urban Negro Community. New York, Free Press, 1966
30. TenHouten WD: The Black Family: Myth and Reality. Psychiatry 33:145–173, 1970
31. Cromwell VL, Cromwell RE: Perceived dominance in decision-making and conflict resolution among Anglo, Black and Chicano couples. J Marriage and the Family 40:749–759, 1978
32. Mack DE: Where the Black-matriarchy theorists went wrong. Psychology Today January 1971, pp. 24, 86–87
33. Weisman CS: An analysis of female dominance in urban Black families. Dissertation Abstracts International 34:440, 1973
34. Moynihan, DP: The Negro Family: The Case For National Action. Office of Policy Planning and Research, U.S. Department of Labor, 1965
35. McAdoo HP: Factors related to stability in upwardly mobile Black families. J Marriage and the Family 40:761–776, 1978
36. McAdoo, HP: Black Kinship. Psychology Today, May 1979, pp. 67–70, 79, 110
37. Merton RK: The Sociology of Science. Chicago, The University of Chicago Press, 1973
38. Von Lue T: Transubstantiation in the study of African reality. African Affairs 1975, 74, pp. 401–419
39. Glasser, PH, Glasser LN (Eds): Families in Crisis. New York, Harper & Row, 1970, Introduction, pp. 3–12
40. Aldous J: Wife's employment status and lower-class men as husbands: Support for the Moynihan Thesis. J Marriage and the Family 31:469–476, 1969
41. Clark K: Dark Ghetto. New York, Harper & Row, 1965
42. Bernard J: Marriage and Family Among Negroes. Englewood Cliffs, N.J. Prentice-Hall, 1966
43. Scanzoni JH: The Black Family in Modern Society. Boston, Allyn & Bacon, 1971
44. Liebow E: Tally's Corner. Boston, Little, Brown & Co., 1967
45. Willie CV (Ed): The Family Life of Black People. Columbus, Ohio, Charles E. Merrill, 1970
46. Jeffers C: Living poor: A participant observer study of priorities and choices, in Glasser PH, Glasser LN (Eds): Families in Crisis. New York, Harper & Row, 1970, pp. 18–29
47. Allen WR: The search for applicable theories of Black family life. J Marriage and the Family 40:117–129, 1978
48. Hays WC, Mindel CH: Extended kinship relations in Black and white families. J Marriage and the Family 35:51–57, 1973
49. Williams JA, Stockton R: Black family structures and functions: An empirical examination of some suggestions made by Billingsley. J Marriage and the Family 35:39–49, 1973
50. Babchuck N, Ballweg JA: Black family structure and primary relations. Phylon 28:334–347, 1967
51. Schultz DA: Coming Up Black: Patterns of Ghetto Socialization. Englewood Cliffs, N.J., Prentice-Hall, 1969
52. Rodman H: Lower class attitudes toward deviant family patterns: A cross-cultural study. J Marriage and the Family 31:315–321, 1969

53. Davis WA, Havighurst RJ: Social class and color difference in child-rearing. Am Sociol Rev 11:698–710, 1964
54. Goode WJ: Family disorganization, in Merton RK, Nisbet RA (Eds): Contemporary Social Problems. New York, Harcourt, Brace & World, 1961, 467–544
55. Aschenbrenner J: Lifelines: Black Families in Chicago. New York, Holt, Rinehart & Winston, 1975
56. Heiss J: On the Transmission of Marital Instability in Black Families. Am Sociol Rev 37:82–92, 1972
57. Heiss J: The Case of the Black Family: A Sociological Inquiry. New York, Columbia University Press, 1975
58. Mack DE: The power relationship in Black families and white families, in Staples R (Ed): The Black Family: Essays and Studies, (2nd ed). Belmont, Ca., Wadsworth Publishing, 1978, pp. 144–149
59. Willie DV, Greenblatt SL: Four "classic" studies of power relationships in Black families: A review and look to the future. J Marriage and the Family 40:691–693, 1978
60. Matza D: The disreputable poor, in Reinhard B, Lipret S (Eds): Class, Status and Power. New York, Free Press, 1966
61. Leslie GR: Black Families, in Leslie GR (ed): The Family in Social Context. New York, Oxford University Press, 1976, pp. 263–285
62. DHEW: *The Mental Health of Urban America*: The Urban Programs of the National Institute of Mental Health, April, 1969
63. Hyman HH, Reed JS: Black matriarchy reconsidered: Evidence from secondary analysis of sample surveys. Public Opinion Quarterly, 33:346–354, 1969
64. Elmer MP: A descriptive analysis of the Black extended family: Toward a new perspective of Black family life in America. Dissertation Abstracts Int 36:6313-6314, 1976
65. Myers HF, Rana PG, Harris M: Black Child Development in America, 1927–1977: An Annotated Bibliography. Westport, Conn., Greenwood Press, 1979
66. Peters MF: Nine Black Families: A study of household management and child-rearing in Black families with working mothers. Dissertation Abstracts Int 37:4648-4649, 1977
67. Schultz DA: Variations in Complete and Incomplete Families of the Negro Lower-Class. Unpublished doctoral dissertation. Washington University, 1968, 29/01-A, pp. 339
68. Deutsch MP, Katz I, Jensen AR: Social Class, Race and Psychological Development. New York, Holt, Rinehart and Winston, 1968
69. Proshansky H, Newton P: The Nature and Meaning of Negro Self-identity, in Deutsch, Katz, Jensen (Eds): Social Class, Race and Psychological Development. New York, Holt, Rhinehart & Winston, 1968, pp. 178–218
70. Hess RD, Shipman VC: Early experience and the socialization of cognitive modes in children. Child Devel 36:868–886, 1965
71. Hess RD: The transmission of cognitive strategies in poor families: The socialization of apathy and underachievement, in Allen VL (Ed): Psychological Factors in Poverty. Chicago, Markham Publishing, 1970, pp. 73–92
72. Jensen AR: Social class and verbal learning, in Deutsch, M, Katz I, Jensen A (Eds): Social Class, Race, and Psychological Development. New York, Holt, Rinehart & Winston, 1968, 115–174
73. Olim EG, Hess RD, Shipman VC: Role of mothers' language styles in mediating their preschool children's cognitive development. School Rev 75:414–424, 1967

74. Whiteman M, Deutsch M: Social disadvantages as related to intellective and language development. In Deutsch M, Katz I, Jensen A (Eds): Social Class, Race and Psychological Development. New York, Holt, Rhinehart & Winston, 1968, pp.66–114
75. Etzkowitz H, Schaflander GM: Ghetto Crisis: Riots or Reconciliation? Boston, Little, Brown & Co., 1969
76. Griswold B, Billingsley A: Personality and social characteristics of low-income mothers who neglect or abuse their children. Unpublished manuscript, 1967
77. Young LR: The behavioral syndromes of parents who neglect and abuse their children. Unpublished doctoral dissertation, Columbia University School of Social Work, 1963
78. Samuels MR: A Study of Maternal Role Performance in One-Parent Negro Families. Unpublished doctoral dissertation, Columbia University, 1970
79. Morris RB: Strengths of the Black community: An investigation of the Black community and broken homes. Dissertation Abstracts Int 38:1960, 1977
80. Thompson CL: Perceptions of intrafamilial relationships in single parent lower-class families and male adolescent antisocial behavior. Dissertation Abstracts Int 39:1968 1978
81. Savage JE, Adair AV, Friedman P: Community-social variables related to Black parent-absent families. J Marriage and the Family 40:779–785, 1978
82. Middleton R, Putney S: Dominance in decisions in the family: Race and class differences. Am J Sociol 65:605–609, 1960
83. Grisby B: Family structure and family behavior: A consideration of Black working-class and middle-class families. Dissertation Abstracts Int 34:882–883, 1973
84. Hammond J, Enoch JR: Conjugal power relations among Black working-class families. J Black Studies 7:107–127, 1976
85. Hare N: What Black intellectuals misunderstand about the Black family. Black World, 20:4–14, 1976
86. Mbiti JS: African Religion and Philosophy. New York, Anchor Books, 1970
87. McQueen A: Incipient social mobility among poor Black urban families. Paper presented at the Howard University Research Seminar, Spring, 1971
88. Baldwin WH: Adolescent pregnancy and child bearing: Growing concerns for Americans. Population Bulletin 31:3–36, 1977
89. The Status of Black Americans, National Urban League Report, Wash., D.C., 1978

Barbara Ann Bass

4

The Validity of Sociocultural Factors in the Assessment and Treatment of Afro-Americans

Afro-Americans have been looked upon as strangers, as a foreign element, in American society. Middle class America has never known quite how to deal with black people in any capacity. There is a great need for more information and research on the variety of Afro-American family life-styles, and more familiarity with existing research. In the area of assessment and treatment, mental health professionals need to become aware of, acknowledge, and discuss the issue of similarities and differences in race, class, and culture, and how to discuss them in the therapeutic relationship.

It is hoped that these feelings or attitudes will be changed by becoming acquainted with Afro-American culture and the differences which have been and still are seen as deficits in comparison to the white or mainstream culture. Skin color is a major issue here and to believe that color does not matter is no virtue if it means denial of differences in the experience, culture, and psychology of Afro-Americans—and other Americans. To ignore the formative influence of substantial differences in history and social existence is a monumental error.

It is somewhat difficult to find a precise definition or description of Afro-American culture. Past and contemporary textbooks in sociology and psychiatry either overlook completely or give only a glancing reference to black people and their special problems in American society. Sociocultural factors are omitted from the traditional medical model that may be important in diagnosis and treatment. The mental health professional's failure to appreciate and capitalize on sociocultural factors, adaptations, and survival skills may reflect a simple lack of understanding and concern or a hypersensitive concern not to be discriminating or prejudiced.

CULTURAL PATTERNS

All societies develop rules and procedures that provide general guidelines for appropriate behavior. Such rules and procedures are called norms. Their importance to a society lies in the fact that they are learned and shared by the members. Without some structure of norms, interaction between individuals would be very difficult.

The norms in every society vary in their characteristics. For example, norms differ in their degree of specificity and applicability to various situations. Some are more important than others and become formalized into laws. Many norms, commonly referred to as institutional norms, are arranged in complex networks that specify behavior concerning important societal activities such as the distribution of power or the bearing and care of children.

Societies also develop values and beliefs, which often define important societal goals. They usually become embodied in legends and traditions, supplementing and supporting the norms of a society. These are major components of culture, which can be defined as collective methods or patterns of social adaptation.

The ingredients of a culture can be seen as being interwoven in a consistent and integrated fashion. Cultural patterns may undergo changes, however, because of the introduction of innovations, or because of the efforts of groups to modify important norms and values, or for a variety of other reasons. And within complex societies the ingredients of a culture may exhibit a wide range of variation and diversity for the simple reason that large groups of people may act and think somewhat differently from one another. These groups often have their own partially developed systems of norms, values and beliefs. Their members follow some of the patterns of the general culture and also some alternative patterns that are peculiar to their own group. Such groups are usually designated as having subcultures.

Racial and ethnic groups often have significant subcultures. In America such groups voluntarily immigrated from other societies, establishing their own communities and following many of the patterns of their parent culture. Although some groups eventually gave up their distinct way of life, others continue to persist.

Afro-Americans are an outstanding exception to this process. Black people were brought to this country in bondage and were worked as slaves; almost all of the elements of their former African cultures were erased. It is generally believed that Afro-Americans have never had a distinct subculture, that they have always followed the general cultural patterns of American society. From the works of Gutman[1] and Bennett[2] we have evidence that indeed there were patterns carried over from the African cultures.

White people are frequently given to drawing parallels between the American experiences of black people and other immigrant groups. Afro-Americans are reminded that the Irish, Italians and Poles came to these shores of opportunity and "made something of themselves" as a result of hard work and frugality. The implication, of course, is that if Afro-Americans had worked harder, their fate would have been different. Generations of Americans were reared to believe the idea that through personal effort one could go from rags to riches. Stokely Carmichael has repeatedly stated that if hard work was the key to advancement "Black people would be the richest people in the country."[3]

Afro-American people resent such comparisons. No group ever worked harder in the service of building America. For all but the fairest blacks, the possibility of "melting" in the great American ethnic pot simply did not exist. Black people could never get lost in the crowd, thus the slave stigma stuck. A Pole could change his name from Marcieszewski to Muskie and become the father of a Presidential hopeful. As yet, there are no bleaching agents strong enough to make a Jesse Jackson an Andrew Jackson.[4]

Afro-Americans have endured a unique set of experiences from slavery up through the present forms of discrimination and oppression. Since they have always been segregated from the rest of society, Afro-Americans have shared in these experiences together as a group. Such a process has led to the development of some cultural patterns that differ from those commonly found in American society.

It may be argued that these patterns are not sufficient to receive recognition as a subculture. It might also be argued that they are merely a variation of the subcultural patterns characteristic of impoverished people in the lower class. A further complication is that there are differences in these patterns within the black community; all black people do not follow the same norms, values and beliefs. However, it is clear that distinct cultural elements do characterize at least some portions of the black community. This milieu may be defined not only by its different styles of living, but also by the significant products that it has developed and contributed to American society, especially in the areas of literature and music. This milieu also provides the base upon which Afro-Americans are attempting to rediscover their former African heritage.

Members of a subculture often have some sense of group consciousness and identification. They are aware of those things that they share in common and are conscious of the differences between themselves and others. For many Afro-Americans such an awareness is reflected in the meaning of the term "soul."

Language often takes on certain distinct forms in a subculture, as it has in portions of the black community. Black culture is an "oral culture" in which traditions are maintained orally. Vocabulary and speech patterns have often been described as well as the heavy reliance upon certain kinds of verbal communication to control and manipulate situations.

Afro-American culture has been viewed and defined in many different ways, by different people both black and white. It is very difficult, if not impossible, to understand the life-styles of Afro-American people using the traditional theories developed by white psychologists to explain white people. When these theories are applied to the lives of Afro-Americans many incorrect, weakness dominated, and inferiority-oriented conclusions come about.[3] Listed below are a few of the major definitions used to explain or describe Afro-American culture:

culturally deprived
culturally disadvantaged
culturally deficient
culturally different
underprivileged
socially deprived

Andrew Billingsley has depicted the black community as an ethnic sub-society.[5] His conceptual model makes use of three social dimensions on which members within an ethnic group vary, namely, social class, rural or urban residence, and region of the country lived in. Therefore, not only are black people compared or contrasted with whites, they also may be upper class, middle class, or lower class, with northern, southern, or western residence, with urban or rural backgrounds, and significantly, may be meaningfully compared and contrasted with each other.

Even though Afro-Americans in this country are viewed as a group apart from other people and as showing common intra-group attributes, behaviors, and conditions, great variations are also obvious. Billingsley offers the concept "ethnic sub-society" as a means of capturing this duality.[5]

With members of other groups, Afro-Americans may share political participation, occupational relationships, common civic enterprise, perhaps even an occasional warm friendship, but in a very special way, which history has decreed, Afro-Americans share a sense of indissoluble and intimate identity with their group and not that group within the larger society and the world.

This reflects the duality of the existence of Afro-Americans. It also reflects the growing black consciousness or awareness of a peoplehood, which has evolved at a rapid rate in black communities throughout the country. While we are one, as members of a color caste system and by virtue of our common peoplehood, we are not a homogeneous mass. An ethnic group is a relatively large configuration of people with a "shared feeling of peoplehood." In this society such groups are organized around race, religion, national origin, or some combination of these.

Most psychologists and social scientists take the point of view that Afro-Americans are culturally deprived and psychologically maladjusted. The environment in which they were reared as children and in which they continue to rear their own children lacks the necessary early experiences to prepare them for excellence in school, appropriate sex role behavior, and, generally speaking, achievement within a white middle-class frame of reference.[3] In short, we are culturally and psychologically deprived because our experiential background provides us with inferior preparation to move effectively within the dominant white culture.

According to White, a simple journey with the white researcher into the black home can provide some insight into how such conclusions are reached. He depicts the journey as follows:

> During this visit, the researcher may not find familiar aspects of the white culture such as Book of the Month selections, records of Broadway plays, classics, magazines such as *Harper's*, the *Atlantic Monthly*, or the *New York Review of Books*. He also might observe a high noise level, continuously reinforced by inputs from rhythm-and-blues radio stations, TV programs, and several sets of conversations going at once. This type of observation leads one to assume that the homes of black children are very weak in intellectual stimulation that might be provided by informative rapping or the local black newspapers and national magazines such as *Jet*, *Ebony*, *Sepia*, and the Motown sound. Black children in these same homes who supposedly cannot read, even preschoolers, can sing several rock and blues tunes from memory and correctly identify the songs of popular entertainers. These same researchers or educational psychologists listening to black speech assume that our use of non-standard oral English is an example of bad grammar without recognizing the possibility that we have valid, legitimate, alternate dialect.[3, p. 43]

With regard to the use of language, the oral tradition with its heavy rap, folk tales, blues, spirituals, and down home sermons has a vital impact within the black experience. Historically speaking, any discussion of the black experience with language is further complicated by the fact that words were used to express and conceal at the same time. Certain ideas had to be hidden from the white man.

For example, the slaveowners in the antebellum South listening to the field "nigras" sing "Steal Away, Steal Away to Jesus, Steal Away Home" were deceived into believing the slaves were thinking about heaven. The real message was about fleeing to the North to freedom.

As White points out, a poem like the "Signifying Monkey" confuses even the most hip revolutionary white person,[3] yet black people who cannot read or write know exactly what the poem means—it is foolish, if not suicidal, to fight a powerful enemy on its own ground and to neutralize obvious advantages. The monkey engages in effective trickery, deceit, and a black form of psychological warfare known as "signifying," playin' the dozens, woofing, marking or capping. A lot is lost in the translation because these words and idioms are accompanied by a very rich background of gestures, body motions, and voice changes. Mitchell-Kernan defines signifying as "a tactic employed in verbal dueling which is engaged in as an end in itself as well as a way of encoding messages or meanings which involves, in most cases, an element of misdirection."[6] According to Abrahams, signifying

> can mean any number of things; in the case of the toast, 'The Signifying Monkey and the Lion,' it certainly refers to the monkey's ability to talk with great innuendo, to carp, cajole, needle and lie. It can mean in other instances the propensity to talk around a subject, never quite coming to the point. It can mean "making fun" of a person or a situation. Also it can denote speaking with the hands and eyes, and in this respect encompasses a whole complex of expressions and gestures . . . [7, p. 54]

What then is "soul?" As the concept has come to be used in urban ghettos over the last number of years, it stands for what is the "essence of blackness." The question whether a middle-class, white collar suburban black also has "soul" is often met with consternation. In fact, "soul" seems to be a folk conception of the lower class urban black's own "national character."[8] Modes of action, personal attributes, and certain artifacts are given the "soul" label. Typically, in conversations, one hears statements such as "man, he's got a lot of soul." This appreciative opinion may be given concerning anybody in the ghetto, but more often by younger adults or adolescents about others of their own categories. In particular, speaking in terms of "soul" is common among younger men. There are many definitions presented in Kochman's work such as "the ability to survive" or "having the spirit in slavery to sing in order to overcome the monotony."[8]

The choice of the term "soul" is in itself noteworthy. First of all, it shows the influence of religion on lower-class Afro-Americans, even those who are not themselves active church members—expressions of religious derivation such as "Lord, have mercy!" are frequent in everyday speech among many Afro-American people of all class, age, and sex categories, and in all contexts. Some fields are particularly "soulful":

1. Music, particularly the field of progresive jazz and rock and roll. Excellence in musical expression is indeed a part of the lower class Afro-American self-concept
2. A second area of widespread "soul" symbolism is that of food. The dishes that are now "soul food" were once—and are still to some extent—referred to simply as "southern cooking," but in the Northern ghettos they come to stand for race rather than region.

There are foods such as chitterlings, hog maws, ham hocks, black-eyed peas, red beans and rice, collard greens, cornbread and grits. Typically, they were the poor man's food in the rural South. In the urban North, they may still be so to some extent. They have come to stand as signs of ethnicity. Some middle class Afro-Americans would refuse to eat such foods once they had so-called "made it."

"Soul" is used among younger Afro-American ghetto dwellers to designate, in a highly approving manner, the experiences and characteristics which are essentially black. It is part of a vocabulary that is used within the group.

CHARACTERISTICS OF AFRO-AMERICAN FAMILIES

General Life Style and Social Classes

There is a lack of valid research on Afro-American families and, therefore, there is a limited understanding of the variety of Afro-American life that exists in the United States, and the tendency is to overstereotype and to assume there is a singular Afro-American family life-style.

Recent Afro-American social scientists such as Andrew Billingsley[5] and Robert Hill[9] have written about the diversity of family life-styles. Hill identifies and analyzes five characteristics (strengths) which lead toward survival, advancement, and stablility of Afro-American families. They are (1) adaptability of family roles; (2) strong kinship bonds; (3) strong work orientation; (4) strong achievement orientation; and (5) strong religious orientation. These characteristics are very similar to those of importance for achievement in the white community as well.

Just as in the mainstream culture, Afro-Americans can be divided into three main classes: upper, middle, and lower despite the fact that more has been written about the Afro-American lower class, leading many to assume that all Afro-Americans are of the lower class.

The indices of social class which have been developed in social science research are relatively more reliable when used within white ethnic groups, where they were developed, than when used unmodified with Afro-American groups. For example, a school principal and his family in the white community would be considered middle class. However, in some black communities, a black school principal and his family—in all probability—would be considered upper class.[5] Factors such as respectability and community activity loom large in the attributions of social status as well as education, income, and occupation.

A number of social scientists hold that middle class blacks are more akin to middle class whites than to either blacks or whites of lower socioeconomic status. It is important to stress, however, that social class does not obliterate the differences between blacks and whites, not even on so simple a dimension as income. Perhaps most important is the fact that even when the two groups are in the same income range, they do not have the same incomes. Middle class Afro-American families do not have the resources available to them that middle class white families do. For example, Afro-American physicians earn three times less than white physicians. White families earn three to five times more than Afro-American families.[10] For Afro-American families to maintain middle class status it requires that both father and mother work, and family supports (extended family members) be available to help care for the children.

Lower class Afro-American families are considerably poorer than lower class white families. Afro-American families earning above $3000 for example, will have considerably lower average-earnings than white families in the same range. Afro-American families will cluster toward the lower end of the range and white families toward the upper end.[5] In a similar manner, levels of education, occupational security, and opportunity are not equal for middle class Afro-Americans and whites. The same is true at the lower class levels. There are more Afro-American fathers with college educations in the lower class levels than the white high income group.[11] Even with comparable education, Afro-Americans do not have the same occupational opportunities, and even with similar occupations, they do not have the same incomes, and even if they could be equated on all these measures, they have different statuses and histories in this country.

For Afro-American families, the higher the social class status, the greater access its members have to the resources of the wider community, and the greater the level of supports they receive from the wider community. Consequently, the family's ability to meet the requirements of society and needs of its members will be greater.

In the Joint Commission on Mental Health of Children's report on minority group children, there was overwhelming evidence of the relationship between poverty and minority group status. The report also noted that the unemployment, underemployment, and low wages were more prevalent for minority groups; that education does not always provide the upward mobility for minorities as it does for the majority; and that "among the multiple causes of poverty are racist policies and attitudes."[12]

The intent here is not to deny the many problems that Afro-American children and their families face in American society but rather to show that the economic, political, and social forces of the larger society determine the conditions for the substance of Afro-American family lifestyles.

About 10 percent of Afro-American families may be considered upper class in the sense that they are headed by men who are highly educated (often with advanced degrees beyond college) who are in the high income brackets, who have secure occupations in which advancement is possible, and who live in adequate and comfortable housing.[5]

Afro-American middle class families account for perhaps 40 percent of all Afro-American families. Within this group, however, there are three distinct groupings: upper middle class, solid middle class, and the precarious middle class. These are distinguished by education, income, occupational achievement, and by the security of their hold on middle class status.

Finally, there are the lower classes, where perhaps half of all Afro-American families are located. Again, however, there are several groupings which may be distinguished by the occupational history and security of their heads as well as by education, income and the like. Starting from the top of the lower class, the groupings are: "working nonpoor," "working poor," and the "nonworking poor." The first group is comprised of heads of families who are likely to be semiskilled or who have a stable and secure niche in the unionized industrial sector of the economy. The largest group of lower class families, however, is the working poor whose family heads work in unskilled and service occupations with marginal incomes. The final group of lower class families is the one about which most information appears in the literature and public press. Comprising about a quarter of all lower class Afro-American families, it is largely peopled by men and women who are employed or intermittently employed, supported by relatives and friends or by public welfare.[5]

Some lower class Afro-American families live a "middle class life-style," placing emphasis upon decorous public behavior, general respectability, insisting that their children "get an education" and "make something of themselves." They prize family stability, and an unwed mother is something more serious than "just a girl who had an accident"; premarital and extramarital relationships, if indulged in at all, must be discreet. For this type of family, social life is organized around churches, volunteer associations of all types, and, for women, "the cult of clothes" is so important that fashion shows are a popular fund raising activity even in churches. For both men and women, owning a home and going into business are highly desired goals, the former often being a realistic one, the latter a mere fantasy.[13]

Within the same income range, and not always at the lower margin of it, other Afro-American families live an "organized lower-class life-style." The "organized" lower class is oriented primarily around churches whose preachers, often semiliterate, exhort them to "be in the 'world' but not of it." Conventional middle-class morality is preached, although a general attitude of "the spirit is willing but the flesh is weak" prevails except among a minority fully committed in the Pentecostal sects.[13]

In the "organized lower class," young people with talent find wide scope for expressing it in choirs, quartets, etc., which travel from church to church and sometimes city to city. Adults as well as young people find satisfaction and indeed prestige in serving as ushers and deacons, "mothers," Sunday School teachers, and choir leaders.

At the lowest income levels, an "unorganized" lower class exists whose members tend to be involved in gambling, excessive drinking, the use of narcotics, and sexual promiscuity. For this group, violent interpersonal relations reflect an ethos of suspicion and resentment. It is within this milieu that criminal and semicriminal activities burgeon.[13]

Valentine stresses the need to distinguish between cultural values and situational or circumstantial adaptations.[14] It is a misconception that people live the way they do because they prefer their actual mode of existence and its consequences. In a highly stratified social system like that of the United States, poor people have a narrow margin of choice as to how they live. It is risky to infer a group's preferences and potentialities from adaptations forced upon them by their conditions of existence.[15]

Numerous studies have examined the prevalence of psychopathology relative to class.[16–18] The studies were in keeping with trends explored by Dohrenwend & Dohrenwend that there is an inverse relationship betwen low socioeconomic status and mental illness.[19] The reason for this trend is not clear. The overrepresentation of one class has perhaps many levels of explanation. The class variables are not at all well defined in the literature.

One is not sure if the cause is exclusively an economic reality or the sum total of varying social conditions or status relative to other groups. The issue of prevalence is complicated by an almost exclusive preoccupation with, and overrepresentation of, the lowest class in research. Is this because they are more readily accessible or exploitable than any other class? Embedded in this question, in fact, may be the primary diagnosis to be made about the group—not that they are mentally ill, but that they are oppressed.[20]

King reviewed several studies which looked at cultural issues or specific cultural groups and which failed to examine the parameters of culture and instead focused on prevalence within the culture as a whole.[21]

Self-Identity and Skin Color

Afro-American class distinctions began in slavery. When the white slave owners had children by black females, these mulatto children were generally favored by the owners and the mothers, and given special treatment.[5] Those children became what was called "the house slaves" while the other slaves were referred to as "the field slaves." Slave owners more often than not saw to it that his half-white children received an education, which led to the development of the "educated elite" among the blacks. It also led to discrimination and intraracial conflict among black people based on skin color alone. Skin color and hair texture became a preoccupation.

Throughout the years and up to the Black Nationalist Movement, Afro-Americans tried to become as much like white people as possible, attempting to modify their physical as well as body image by, for example, processing or straightening the hair, pinching the nose to make it pointed, tightening the lips to make them smaller, and lightening the skin with commercial cosmetics. Obviously, these attempts were to no avail in trying to look as much as possible unlike the stereotype of kinky hair, wide nose, big lips and dark skin.

Concerns about hair—more specifically being ashamed of kinky or wooly hair—was a big issue. It may also explain why today there are few Afro-American aquarians. Afro-American mothers did not encourage their children, especially the females, to swim because swimming "messed up" the hair. The mother would have to "hot comb" their daughter's hair daily. Add this to the fact that pools were not always accessible to Afro-American people.

Wearing a "natural" or Afro hairstyle which came with the Black Pride movement of the late 60's represented liberation of the mind from white brainwashing, i.e., only straight hair is attractive, and functioned as a public display of conscious racial pride. Now it is also seen as a personal preference and an opportunity for variety in the ways Afro-Americans can wear their hair—both men and women.

Jeanne Spurlock has shown that Afro-American children who felt most secure about themselves identified with being Afro-American.[22] Those who felt the least secure made more of an out-group identification and also had more hostility toward whites.

Family instability, on the other hand, only compounds the racial identity problems for other Afro-American children. Spurlock also notes that although some Afro-American children proclaim "black is beautiful," they may still harbor negative feelings about their racial identity.[22] This is particularly characteristic among children from lower socioeconomic groups who may be exposed to more racist and rejecting experiences than those from more sheltered kinds of backgrounds. Skin color is an important issue here because the darker the skin, the more problems one encounters.

COMMUNITY NETWORK

Afro-Americans have exhibited a strong humanistic quality which portrays a sense of brotherhood. The friendly speech patterns demonstrated by black people toward each other on campus and in public gatherings show to some extent this brotherhood. In fact, when one black person fails to return the greetings to another, the question arises: "Why is he so stuck up?" or "Who does he think he is, somebody special?"

Afro-American families have placed hevy emphasis and reliance on interactions with both relatives and nonrelatives outside the immediate nuclear family. Therefore, people of importance in the community, e.g., elders, the minister, teachers, or other responsible adults, have always been called upon to help the family socialize its children. Many Afro-American men and women can point to a member of the community who made the difference between success and potential failure.[5]

There are several ways in which community members supplement the efforts of the family. They may serve as extensions of the family and parents, and may instruct, discipline, assist, and otherwise guide the young of a given family. They may serve as role models and show an interest in the young people. As advocates, they may actively intercede with major segments of society to help young Afro-Americans find opportunities which might otherwise have been closed to them. As supportive figures, they may simply inquire about the progress of the young and take a special interest in them. In the formal role of teachers, leader, elder, etc., they serve youth generally as a part of their general role or occupation.

CONCEPT OF TIME

Afro-Americans have been characterized as always late for appointments and events. The phrase "CP" or Colored People's Time has been used to define this stereotype. Being late could be interpreted as resistance in therapy, but it can also be a way of controlling the situation, expressing self-importance, or a passive-aggressive reaction to being powerless. It is important to find out what is operating in such cases. One's sense of time is derived from one's place in the social structure and one's lived experience.[8] Some people who live outside the constraints of industrial work-time don't have a fast-paced life or adhere to schedules. The attitude may be one of "nothing's going to happen anyway" or "it can be done tomorrow if it doesn't get done today."

Kochman further defines CPT as "uncertain predictability" and stresses that it is not some special trait of Afro-Americans—instead, it is clearly a street and class phenomena.[8] In the street, one has to be ready to move at a moment's notice to where the action is.

SUMMARY

In order to judge what is healthy or morbid in an individual's psychological functioning, one must be aware of what is appropriate and effective within his or her specific cultural milieu. Social scientists and mental health professionals must learn that overt behavior patterns may mean different things to people from culturally different backgrounds, just as psychiatrists should come to realize that they cannot explain away all deviant behaviors as a normal and justified reaction to an oppressive environment. For mental health professionals involved with patients whose cultural and experiential backgrounds may be different from theirs, this becomes crucial to the delivery of effective psychiatric services.

Sociocultral factors are often omitted from the traditional medical model, on which many therapeutic approaches are based, that may be important in the diagnosis and treatment of minority group patients. Overt behavior patterns may have different meanings for people of culturally different backgrounds. The mental health professional's failure to appreciate and capitalize on sociocultural factors, adaptations, and survival skills may reflect a simple lack of understanding and concern or a hypersensitive concern not to be discriminating or prejudiced.

With regard to treatment of the Afro-American patient—or any patients—each patient should be considered on an individual basis and generalizations should be avoided as there is great variation within all normal groups of people and in all classes regarding life-styles, behavior, attitudes, expectations, and values.

REFERENCES

1. Gutman H: The Black Family in Slavery and Freedom: 1750–1925. New York, Pantheon, 1976
2. Bennett L: Before the Mayflower: A History of the Negro in America: 1619–1964 (Revised Edition). Baltimore, Penquin Books, 1966
3. White J: Toward a black psychology, in Jones R. (ed): Black Psychology. New York, Harper and Row, 1972, p 43
4. Grier WH, Cobbs PM: Black Rage. New York, Basic Books, 1968
5. Billingsley A: Black Families in White America. Englewood Cliffs, N.J., Prentice Hall, 1968
6. Mitchell-Kernan C: Signifying, loud-talking and marking, in Kochman T. (ed): Rappin' and Stylin' Out. Chicago, University of Illinois Press, 1972, p 315
7. Abrahams RD: Deep Down in the Jungle. Hatboro, Pa., Folklore Associates, 1968, p 54
8. Kochman, T: Rappin' and Stylin' Out: Communication in Urban Black America. Chicago, University of Illinois Press, 1972
9. Hill R: The Strengths of Black Families: A National Urgan League Research Study. New York, Emerson Hall, 1972
10. Smythe M, Smythe H (eds): Afro-American Reference Book. Englewood Cliffs, N.J., Prentice-Hall, 1976
11. Langer TS, Gersten J, Green EI, et al: Treatment of psychological disorders among urban children. J Consult Clin Psychol 42:170–179, 1974
12. Joint Commission on Mental Health of Children: Crises in Child Mental Health. New York, Harper and Row, 1970
13. Drake SC: The social and economic status of the Negro in the United States, in Endo R, Strawbridge W (eds): Perspectives on Black America. Englewood Cliffs, NJ, Prentice-Hall, 1970
14. Valentine CA: Culture and Poverty: Critique and Counter-Proposals. Chicago, University of Chicago Press, 1968
15. Ryan W: Blaming the Victim. New York, Pantheon, 1971
16. Dunham HW: Society culture and mental disorder. Arch Gen Psychiatry 33:147–156, 1976
17. Havighurst RJ: The relative importance of social class and ethnicity in human development. Human Development 19:56–64, 1976
18. Srole L: Measurement and classification in sociopsychiatric epidemiology: Midtown

Manhattan study (1954) and Midtown restudy (1974). J Health and Soc Beh 16:347–364,1975
19. Dohrenwend, BP, Dohrenwend, BS: Social and cultural influences on psychopathology. Annual Rev of Psychol 25:417–452, 1975
20. King LM, Dixon V, Nobles W: African Philosophy: Assumptions and Paradigms of Research on Black Persons. Los Angeles, Fanon Center Publications, 1976
21. King, LM: Social and cultural influences on psychopathology. Annual Rev of Psychol 29:405–433, 1978
22. Spurlock J: Some consequences of racism for children, in Willie CV, Kramer BM, Brown BS (eds): Racism and Mental Health: Essays. Pittsburg, University of Pittsburg Press, 1973, p 147

Claudia Mitchell-Kernan

5

Linguistic Diversity in the Service Delivery Setting: The Case of Black English

Interest in the study of intralanguage variation in speech has been heightened in recent years as such variation has been demonstrated to overlap with features of social structure.[1–3] Sociolinguists employing innovative methodologies and analytic techniques have presented convincing evidence of the existence of linguistic correlates of features of social stratification within our own society. In a series of articles that served to rekindle interest in the study of language among social scientists, linguist William Labov has shown how certain features of pronunciation and grammar correlate significantly with ethnic and social class divisions in New York City.[4–7]

It is a fact of practical importance, as well as sociological and historical interest, that there are widespread differences in speech between many Afro-Americans in the United States and their conationals of other ethnic derivations. In the first section of this paper a linguistic and historical overview of the dialect referred to as *Black English* (BE) will be presented. A brief definition of BE will be offered in conjunction with a discussion of dialect differentiation within single languages. A summary of the linguistic features of BE is beyond the scope of the present paper since such an undertaking would require a technical elaboration that would be article length in and of itself. It is recommended that readers interested in the linguistic features of the dialect consult Burling's *English in Black and White* for an excellent descriptive treatment written for the non-specialist.[8] The second section of the paper is broadly concerned with the practical implications of dialect differences in clinical and other service delivery settings where the adequacy of communication between service provider and client is an important determinant of the quality of the service provided. Topics to be considered in this section include communication failures and their sources in the lack of match between the communication systems of service provider and client. The potential of stereotypes to impinge on communication between clinician and client will also be explored. Attention will be devoted to how stereotypes may involve attributions about each other by both client and service provider that may both impede communication and involve misinterpretations of semantic intent. Finally, I wish to draw attention to some semantic and psychosocial dimensions of dialect choice and dialect allegiance which, if properly researched and understood, have the potential to yield information of clinical value.

LINGUISTIC AND HISTORICAL OVERVIEW

Empirical research conducted over the last fifteen years has provided substantial evidence that varieties of English spoken by Afro-Americans show certain features of pronunciation, grammar, and syntax in common that differentiate them from other varieties of English and from *Standard English* (SE), the dialect elevated and institutionalized in the United States as the correct form of English. The linguistic features that serve to define BE have been observed in such widely separate geographic areas as New York City,[5] Detroit,[9] and the San Francisco Bay area,[10] and are sufficiently distinctive to warrant the treatment of BE as a separate dialect of English. It is inaccurate, however, to think of BE as a single dialect since it is characterized by both regional and social variations.

While it is not uncommon for English speakers to conceive of their language as a single entity, most people are aware that English as it is spoken in different parts of the United States and in different parts of the world, such as Australia, Great Britain, and Canada, differs in pronunciation, grammar, vocabulary, and idiom. Englishmen take the *lift* to travel to the fifth floor; English scientists work in a *la-'bor-a-to-ry* while we in the United States take *elevators* and refer to rooms where one finds test tubes and microscopes as *'lab-or-ra-to-ries*.

All widespread languages spoken in the world today vary in their spoken forms from region to region.[8] Boundaries between dialects of a single language are not easily drawn since dialects quite commonly shade off gradually one into another. An accumulation of features of pronunciation and grammar lead most people in the United States to readily identify Southern and New England accents in the speech of others. While most people tend to think of others as speaking dialects, the term dialect is properly used to refer to all differentiable spoken varieties of a language.[8] Dialects of a language may differ at all levels of linguistic structure, embracing contrastive features of pronunciation, grammar, and vocabulary. There are, for example, alternative words for the referent soft drink throughout the country, among them, *soda* and *pop*. Some of the features that linguists note are characteristic of BE are also shared by other dialects of English. There is, for example, a tendency for speakers of BE to pronounce the initial *th* in words such as *the*, and *them* as *d*, producing "de" and "dem," and this feature is shared with other dialects of English. Some features of the dialect, however, are not widespread among English dialects. Among these is the phenomenon of copula deletion, a term used to refer to the tendency of BE speakers to omit conjugated forms of the verb *to be* in certain syntactic environments. A BE speaker may say: "He walking." or "She at home." whereas speakers of other dialects follow obligatory grammatical rules that cause these same sentences to be realized as "He is walking." and "She is at home." Similarly, BE is distinctive in making grammatically nonobligatory the use of the possessive suffix. It is thus possible to say in BE "John book." and "Richard dog bit me." BE speakers may also use the unconjugated form of the verb *to be* in sentence environments where speakers of other dialects would use conjugated forms. It is possible to say in BE "She be at home." Unlike the other examples offered, the latter usage does have a somewhat different meaning than "She is at home." To convey the same meaning, a SE speaker must do so through the addition of an adverbial phrase such as "She is at home most of the time." or "She is usually at home."

Change is a process that all languages experience and is central in the formation of different dialects of a language. When dialect differences emerge from the separation of people in geographic space, the resulting varieties are referred to as *regional* or *geographic* dialects. All dialect differences however, do not have their origin in the separation of people in geographic space. Dialect differences may also emerge when groups of people are separated in social space by such factors as social class and ethnicity. Features of social stratification alter the frequency and nature of intercommunication between groups and serve to promote the genesis of different linguistic norms among groups separated socially, as well as geographically. When social separation figures in the origin and maintenance of a particular dialect, such a dialect is generally called a *social* dialect.

The Origins of Dialect Differences Between Afro-Americans and Non-blacks

There are two current theories of the origins of dialect differences between Afro-Americans and non-blacks in the United States. Some scholars argue that BE is a lineal descendant of regional dialects spoken in Great Britain and imported to the United States during the seventeenth, eighteenth and nineteenth centuries.[11,12] Scholars belonging to this school of thought, occasionally referred to as the *archaist school*, have reasoned that BE shows some common features with other nonstandard dialects of English and has preserved, for various social reasons, some features that have for the most part disappeared from other dialects of English spoken in the United States. There has been speculation that such vectors of linguistic change as formal education and urbanization differentially influenced blacks as a result of their social separation and political and economic subordination in the United States. A second view of the origins of BE that has gained increasing support is referred to as the *Creole hypothesis*.

The forcible removal of Africans from their homelands to various parts of the New World and their incorporation into new societies as chattel slaves was economic in motivation. These immigrants supplied the labor to build colonial societies throughout the New World dominated by plantation economies. Linguists speculate that these political-economic developments beginning in the 16th century led to the development of new language systems through complex sociolinguistic processes that are labelled *pidginization* and *creolization*. It should be remembered that plantation society at its inception was characterized by considerable linguistic diversity and an initial absence of a common language that could serve as the vehicle through which the societies could function. It is argued that the challenge of this situation involved the mobilization of universal human cognitive capacities and the language resources of the groups in contact. Pidginization involves a restructuring of the grammars of languages in contact. In the New World the languages in contact were a variety of Indo-European languages, including Spanish, Portuguese, English, French, and Dutch, as well as numerous African languages. If as a result of pidginization new grammars became stabilized, the resulting linguistic issue is referred to as pidgin language.[13]

Pidgin languages are not spoken as native tongues by any group, and tend to be simple in grammar and limited in vocabulary. Typically, in speech communities where they are in currency, they are used for limited purposes, such as trade and other task oriented activities. When and if they become the native language of some group they experience internal expansion and extension in use. If they undergo stabilization, they achieve the status of a creole language. A number of creole languages did develop in the New World and are still spoken today.[13,14]

The view has gained adherents that the varieties of English spoken by Afro-Americans in the United States are related to varieties spoken by blacks in the English-speaking Caribbean region, and are the present day legacy of the processes of linguistic evolution referred to above. The precise details of the evolution of English-based creole languages are not known. Many efforts to render the "peculiarities" of black speech in the United States in the 17th, 18th, and 19th centuries are little more than caricatures contaminated by language prejudices and distorted by linguistic naivete. We do find, however, in the United States and in the Caribbean, a continuum of dialects from the most- to the least-differentiated from SE that show a number of features in common. The presence of this continuum given support to the Creole hypothesis as a theory of the origin of dialect differences that exist between Afro-Americans and whites in the United States today.

LINGUISTIC DIVERSITY AND PROBLEMS OF INTER-CULTURAL COMMUNICATION

That the United States is a nation of immigrants is a fact too well known and widely acknowledged to belabor. It will suffice for the present purpose to note that while the diverse origins of the groups who comprise our nation have sometimes been celebrated as a source of the vitality of American culture, historically our society has not been altogether hospitable to cultural and linguistic diversity.

During the colonial period, the English, French, and Spanish languages enjoyed official status in large areas of our country. There were additional enclaves where German, Ukranian, and Chinese were used as languages of instruction in primary schools. The period following World War I, however, witnessed the development of a nationalistic fervor which was so hostile to bilingualism and bilingual education, that laws were enacted against the use of languages other than English as the medium of instruction in schools.[15,16]

Prejudice against linguistic diversity has not only figured in American attitudes toward foreign languages, it also figures in the subordination of some dialects of English and in the elevation of the dialects of social and politically dominant groups as the correct form of English.

The antiracist and egalitarian zeitgeist of the 1960s witnessed a rearticulation of the strengths of cultural and linguistic diversity, and the growth of well meant but often poorly conceived efforts to nurture this diversity. Attempts were made to give greater recognition to the contributions of American minorities to the economic development and cultural vitality of American society. The rapid establishment of ethnic studies departments and programs in American institutions of higher learning, bilingual programs in elementary schools, and attempts to rewrite American history to include neglected minority groups, are all notable tokens of a patchwork of remedies fashioned to respond to centuries of neglect and the social and cultural subordination of dispossessed minority groups.

Concern with the practical implications of linguistic and cultural diversity was a feature of much scholarly research conducted among ethnic minorities in the past two decades. New knowledge was sought as a basis for devising a more enlightened social policy and for the development of improved strategies to deal with the myriad of social problems attributed to groups such as Afro-Americans.

Indeed, a major stimulus for research on dialect diversity in the United States, and for much of the research conducted among Afro-Americans, was a fear that dialect differences might be implicated in the widespread problems many Afro-American children experienced in acquiring literacy.[17,18] As a result of research stimulated by questions of applied social science, there are now available a number of grammars of BE vernaculars that are of pedagogical value. The attention BE received during this period also served to promote a more enlightened conception of and appreciation for this dialect, at least in some circles. While BE had not gone unnoticed in the past, it was not until the mid-1960s that BE came to be regarded as a systematic dialect. Until that time BE was regarded by most people as a degenerate form of English. As linguists began to carefully describe and analyze the speech of black children and adults, they could find no evidence that their dialect was less systematic and rule-governed than other dialects. The grammatical and phonological rules of the dialect, it was concluded, were different but no less complex than those of SE; and the grammatical system was certainly not structurally underdeveloped as had been assumed by some educators.

Communication Failures

Communication failures between speakers of different dialects may have a variety of sources. Some failures may result from differences in pronunciation, grammar, and vocabulary that create intellibility problems.

In the case of different dialects of a language, the actual linguistic differences may be minor, but they may nevertheless be implicated in difficulties in communication and in misunderstandings. Speakers of different dialects may find that they must listen more carefully to their interlocutor than is the case when they converse with someone with whom they share a dialect. The flow of conversation may have to be interrupted by requests for clarification of the meanings of words and idioms along with requests for repetitions. Such difficulties in communication may in turn impinge on the establishment of rapport between service provider and client, and may attenuate the free exchange of information between them.

In recent years, as social scientists have begun to focus on the description and analysis of speech as a communication system,[19] it has become clear that social norms, and not just grammatical rules, operate to influence the communication process. Building on the notion of *linguistic competence*, a concept used to describe a native speakers ability to produce and interpret novel utterances in his own language, anthropologist Dell Hymes coined the term *communicative competence* to highlight the fact that in actual social interaction, competent speakers of a language do not simply go about producing grammatical utterances. They are also constrained to produce speech relevant and appropriate to the context and to use speech in socially conventional ways.[20] It is important to emphasize that such social constraints on speech are culturally organized and vary from culture to culture and from subculture to subculture. Competent speakers of a language must observe a wide range of sociocultural norms in verbal interaction. They must know, for example, when it is appropriate to use title and last name versus first name to an addressee; they must make vocabulary choices appropriate for their addressees and the social situation; they must know how to phrase requests without violating rules of etiquette.[21] In many cases it is the violation of such norms, rather than grammatical norms per se, that are at the source of communication failures.

Black Americans, for example, not infrequently report that they resent the use of their first names by service providers such as doctors and nurses and consider it a presumptuous practice. This may come as a surprise to a white nurse for whom the choice of first name is intended to create informality and friendliness. The resentment of blacks toward this practice must be understood against a background of conventions that developed in the southern United States. Custom in that area called for the obligatory use of first names or kin titles such as Uncle or Aunty to all blacks regardless of age or social status. In this system Afro-Americans were never accorded the respect of the title and last name.

It is frequently the case that people who share a basic code such as

English, assume that they share other social conventions with regard to language use. Different subcultural expectations about appropriate linguistic etiquette have a tremendous potential to create antagonism, suspicion, and mistrust between members of different social groups since the violation of such rules is typically assigned a meaning. To inappropriately address someone by their first name who expects to be accorded their title and last name, may not be interpreted as a mistake, but taken as an insult.

So integral is speech to the conduct of human affairs, and so subconsciously do we employ norms of usage we acquire in our own communities, that we seldom become aware of how the ways in which things are said shape their interpretation—that is, unless our norms are violated. We all send and receive far more information via the verbal channel than is strictly referentially encoded. We gain impressions of peoples' social status, personality, and psychological states through linguistic cues. A person may impress another as furtive-open, friendly-unfriendly, warm-cold, intelligent-unintelligent, not simply on the basis of the semantic content of their message, but also on the basis of the social conventions they employ when speaking—on the way they say what they say, on the way they respond to questions, and so forth.

The clinical setting, as well as other service delivery settings, is one in which many people may experience what they feel are violations of their privacy. Compound this with subcultural differences in beliefs about what is considered private, and therefore must be approached carefully and sensitively, and it is easy to envision the barriers of self-defense that clients may erect that block the flow of information necessary for optimal service delivery.

The impact of dialect diversity between service provider and client may be even more subtle than the instances noted above, and the communication problems they face may often be more attitudinal in source than linguistic. As linguists attempted to counteract popularly held views of BE, it became apparent that a good deal of prejudice against dialect diversity exists in the United States, particularly against dialects such as BE and other varieties spoken by lower- and working-class groups.

Dialect Stratification and Stereotyping

It is commonly the case in speech communities where more than one language or dialect is spoken, that one language or variety of a single language is elevated and preferred over others coexisting within the community. In such speech communities the convention may arise that the subordinate language or dialect becomes restricted to familial and informal settings and the superordinate variety becomes "de rigeur"' for formal and public settings and achieves the status of lingua franca in intergroup communication.

When dialects or languages become stratified in a society or local community, the normative conventions with regard to language use typically reflect power relations between the groups who speak the different languages or varieties as native tongues. Such stratification also creates a situation in which speakers of minority dialects or languages are forced to acquire a second dialect or language, in other words, to become bilingual or bidialectal. Bilingualism and bidialectism have a number of features in common sociopolitically.

The practice and requirement of switching from one language or dialect to another can become, in situations of intergroup conflict, a potent symbol of power relations between groups. When a minority group which also speaks a minority language or dialect asserts itself against the political, social, and economic domination of a superordinate group, language issues can emerge at the center of social movements. The right to retain and socially elevate a minority language or dialect may be asserted as a political demand.

In situations of intergroup competition and conflict, dominant group attitudes and prejudices toward a subordinate group very often correspond closely to attitudes held by dominant group members toward the dialect or language of the subordinate group. Indeed they seem inextricably interwoven.

In attempting to understand the stereotyping of different languages and dialects, it is helpful to draw attention to functions of language apart from the strictly instrumental function of conveying referential information. A common language seems to be an important factor creating consciousness of kind within groups. People who speak the same language seem to be united by this very fact. The propensity of a common language to create and symbolize esprit de corps is a social function of language sometimes referred to as *unifying*.[2] The unifying function of language appears to exist on the dialect level as well as the language level. This unifying function of language is, however, only one side of the picture. As a common language or dialect welds its speakers, it serves to differentiate them from speakers of other languages and dialects. As a common language is an important symbol of the social unity of a group, it can be a equally potent symbol of their separation from groups who speak different language is an important symbol of the social unity of a group, it can be an socially centrifugal force is often discussed as the *separatist* function of language. Language differences can be a factor in suspicion and misunderstanding between groups and can be a basis for social prejudice, discrimination, and segregation as well as a source of cultural, social, and political antagonism. As people take pride in and are loyal to their own language or dialect, they are often very ethnocentric in their attitudes toward the languages and dialects of other groups.

So subtlely can prejudice centered on language be instilled, that the dialects spoken by the middle and upper classes in the United States are thought of by most people as "the correct form" of English. As noted earlier, it has only been in recent years that dialects that differ from SE have even been recognized as dialects in their own right with their own internal linguistic structure and rules. Rather they were viewed as poor and deviant English, and invidious distinctions were typically made between groups who speak English "correctly" and those who do not.

That speech can be an object of stereotyping has been well demonstrated in a number of recent sociolinguistic studies that have focused on attitudes toward particular dialects and languages. One procedure that has been used in these studies is the subjective reaction test. In experimental settings, subjects are presented with a series of speech samples and then are requested to evaluate the personalities or social characteristics of the speaker. Subjects may rate a speaker on intelligence, occupation, and even sometimes personal appearance. These studies have shown that people not uncommonly hold stereotypes of particular speech features. The use of particular grammatical constructions and pronunciations and even specific languages may set in motion a whole range of unflattering characterizations of the person who uses them.

One of the most interesting studies of this kind was done by the Canadian sociolinguist Wallace Lambert, who studied attitudes toward English and French in Canada. In this research, speech samples were produced by a group of Canadians fully bilingual in both French and English. Lambert demonstrated that the same speaker, when speaking English rather than French, was rated very differently along a number of dimensions. The English guises were judged as more intelligent, better looking, taller, more dependable, kinder, more ambitious, and as having more character than the French guises. Significantly, Lambert used both French and English judges in his experiments and discovered that many of the French speakers had internalized the prejudices of the English speakers toward their own language. In their evaluations they also rated the English guises more favorably and showed similar biases toward the French guises.[22]

Although invidious distinctions may be made between different languages and dialects on social, cognitive, and aesthetic grounds, which dialects or languages are elevated to prestige status and which are stigmatized is a matter of historical and political fact, not linguistic fact.

Language prejudice does however exist, and such prejudices may have profound consequences for those who speak stigmatized and socially devalued dialects as native tongues. The differential social value accorded BE in contrast to SE is a factor that has served to encourage bidialectism among many Afro-Americans, and a compartmentalization of the contexts in which it is appropriate to use the vernacular versus the standard. Depending on their level of mastery of SE, BE speakers may feel very insecure in situations they feel call for SE. On the one hand, BE speakers have had to come to terms with the fact that SE is important in social and occupational mobility. On the other hand, BE seems to serve a kind of unifying function within black communities, and its preservation may be a factor in the maintenance of group identity.

Because stereotypes can be elicited in experimental settings, our understanding of stereotypes as belief structures surpasses our knowledge of their actual relation to behavior. That stereotypes may serve as a catalyst for discriminatory practices is, however, a source of concern. To the extent that people hold beliefs that some dialects are inferior to others and are structurally deficient for conveying logical thought, and believe that the use of some dialects is a sign of the ignorance of the speaker, it is likely that these beliefs will influence the flow of communication essential to the effective accomplishment of clinical tasks.

BILINGUALISM AND BIDIALECTISM IN PSYCHOLOGICAL PERSPECTIVE

It was noted earlier that bilingualism and bidialectism share certain sociopolitical features. Bilingual and bidialectal patterns of usage also evidence so many similarities that sociolinguists have argued for the use of a single theoretical model to handle both bidialectal and bilingual code variation.[23] Anthropologist Dell Hymes has noted that "No normal person, and no normal community is limited in repertoire to a single variety of code, to an unchanging monotony which would preclude the possibility of indicating respect, insolence, mock seriousness, humor, role distance, etc., by switching from one code variety to another."[24] It appears that bilingual and bidialectal speakers may switch from one language or dialect to another for the same purposes that monolingual speakers may make stylistic shifts. What is important about such switching in clinical settings is that its expressive semantic weight may be unintelligible to the service provider whose verbal repertoire differs from that of the client. It is also often the case that bidialectal and bilingual individuals do not possess symmetrical competence in the two languages or dialects they speak. This seems to derive from the acquisition of different varieties and their customary use of different social settings.[25] For example, an Afro-American may ordinarily use BE in familial settings and with close friends who are also black. It is in such settings that an individual is more likely to discuss private matters and emotionally laden topics such as family problems and other personal matters. The clinical setting is one in which clients are likely to feel it proper to use the SE variety shared with the service provider. This situation presents somewhat of a dilemma. The client may switch to a variety of BE that may create intelligibility problems for the clinician, and risk the possibility of creating an unfavorable impression because of the stereotypes many people hold of BE. Clients, on the other hand, may use SE and find that through this choice, they have rendered themselves inarticulate.

Dialect and language shifting serves important expressive functions and there is some evidence that shifts between different languages and dialects may also invoke different cultural frames of reference and attitudinal dispositions. One of the more provocative studies raising this possibility was undertaken by Ervin-Tripp. Her research was aimed at investigating the acquisition of English by Japanese women and in the course of her analysis she identified relations between language, culture, and cognition. Using word association and sentence completion tasks with first generation and second generation Japanese women, Ervin-Tripp discovered that the content of the first-generation womens' word associations and sentence completions shifted toward American norms when their responses were in English as opposed to Japanese. For example, when responding in Japanese the women might complete the sentences "What I want most in life—is peace," or "When I am with men I—am uncomfortable." Whereas when speaking English they would shift to American norms and respond "What I want most in life—is happiness" and "When I am with men I—am content"[26]

While the psychological dimensions of bilingualism and bidialectism have not been well studied, MacNamara in his introduction to *Problems in Bilingualism* alerts us to the psychological complexity of this phenomenon. For the psychologist, he notes, issues are raised " . . . about the use of two sets of language skills by a single individual and problems about the sometimes conflicting emotions and attitudes associated by the individual with his two languages . . . "[23]

SUMMARY

It is clear that we are only on the threshold of understanding the ways in which linguistic diversity may exert influence in different types of service delivery settings. Problems of linguistic diversity are interrelated with problems of cultural diversity. We have, however, reached a milestone in acknowledging cultural and linguistic diversity as factors of importance in the delivery of mental health and other services in heterogenous societies such as our own. Dialect diversity can create problems that are linguistic in nature, that is, intelligibilty problems. It may create problems that are attitudinal in source. Further, the psychological complexities of dialect shifting raise the possibility that bilingual and bidialectal persons may in some service delivery settings be conveying information about a culturally embedded self rather than a self which transcends the two cultures to which the individual belongs. An individual who says to the clinician that in situations of interpersonal conflict she generally attempts to discuss the problem with the person with whom she is having difficulties may be describing her behavior at work where she operates in terms of one set of sociocultural norms. Her behavior at home, where she operates with different norms, may differ and she may withdraw into hostile silence.

In the case of Afro-Americans, service delivery settings not only frequently involve differences between service provider and client in verbal repertoire and dialect, they also involve differences in socioeconomic status, power relations, and racial group membership. It is precisely in these circumstances that speakers of BE are likely to feel that it is appropriate to use SE, a dialect in which they may not be fully fluent. There are many tensions attendant to this situation since clients may experience a great deal of linguistic insecurity and have difficulties in expressing themelves. Clients may be laconic under such circumstances and sometimes even become hostile in the face of the tensions evoked by this setting and its requirements. The result may be communication failures that undermine the possibility of effective service delivery.

REFERENCES

1. Gumperz J, Hymes D: The ethnography of communication. American Anthropologist 66:6, 1964
2. Hertzler J: A Sociology of Language. New York, Random House, 1965
3. Grimshaw AD: Language as obstacle and as data in sociological research. Social Science Research Council, Items 23(2):17–21, 1969
4. Labov W: The Social Stratification of English in New York City. Washington D.C. Center for Applied Linguistics, 1966
5. Labov W, Cohen P, Robins C, et al: A Study of the Non-Standard English of Negro and Puerto Rican Speakers in New York City. Cooperative Research Project No. 3288, Office of Education, U.S. Department of Health Education and Welfare. Final Report OE-6-10-059. 2 Volumes. New York, Columbia University, 1968

6. Labov W: Language in the Inner City. Philadelphia, University of Pennsylvania Press, 1972
7. Labov W: Sociolinguistic Patterns. Philadephia, University of Pennsylvania Press, 1972
8. Burling R: English in Black and White. New York, Holt, Rinehart, and Winston, 1973
9. Wolfram WA: A Sociolinguistic Description of Detroit Negro Speech. Washington D.C Center for Applied Linguistics, 1969
10. Mitchell-Kernan C: Language Behavior in a Black Urban Community. Language Behavior Research Laboratory Monograph No. 2. Berkeley, University of California, 1971
11. Brooks, C: The Relation of the Alabama-Georgia Dialect to the Provincial Dialects of Great Britain. Baton Rouge, Louisiana, Louisiana State University Press, 1935
12. McDavid R, McDavid V: The relationship of the speech of American Negroes to the speech of whites. American Speech 26:3–16, 1951
13. Hymes D: Preface, in Hymes D (ed): Pidginization and Creolization of Languages. New York, Cambridge University Press, 1971 p 3–11
14. Turner LD: Africanisms in the Gullah Dialect. Chicago, University of Chicago Press, 1949
15. Fishman J: Language Loyalty in the United States. Mouton, The Hague, 1966
16. Haugen E: Bilingualism: A Research and Bibliographical Guide. Publication of the American Dialect Society, University of Ala Press, 26:159, 1956
17. Stewart WA: Urban Negro speech: Sociolinguistic factors affecting English teaching, in Shuy R (ed): Social Dialects and Language Learning, NCTC, 1964
18. Stewart WA: Sociolinguistic factors in the history of American Negro dialects. Flordia Foreign Language Reporter 5 (Spring): 2–4
19. Gumperz JJ, Hymes D (eds): Directions in Sociolinguistics: The Ethnography of Communication. New York, Holt, Rinehart and Winston, 1972
20. Hymes D: On communication competence, in Pride JB and Holmes J (eds): Sociolinguistics, Harmondsworth, Penguin, 1972
21. Ervin-Tripp S: Is Sybil there? The structure of some American English directives. Language in Society 5:25–66, 1976
22. Lambert WE, Hodgson RC, Gardner RC, et al: Evaluational reactions to spoken languages. J Abn Soc Psychol 60:44–51, 1960
23. MacNamara J: Bilingualism in the modern world, in Macnamara J (ed): Journal of Social Issues, 5:1–7, 1967
24. Hymes D: Modeling the interaction of language and social setting, in Macramara J (ed): Problems of Bilingualism, The Journal of social Issues, 23:8–28, 1967
25. Mitchell-Kernan C, Kernan KT: A sociolinguistic approach to the relations between language, society, and the individual, in Nader L, Maretski T (eds): Cultural Illness & Health: Essays in Human Adaptation. Washington, D.C., American Anthropological Association, 1973, pp 104–114
26. Ervin-Tripp S: An Issei learns English, in Macnamara J (ed): Problems of Bilingualism, The Journal of Social Issues, 23:78–90, 1967

PART II

The Assessment of Afro-American Children and Adults: Aspects of Their Subcultural Experience

EDITORS' INTRODUCTION

In Module II, the assessment of sociocultural factors and the accompanying knowledge base needed regarding Afro-American cultural experiences is discussed in the following three chapters: Lewis King in "The Assessment of Afro-American Families: Issues in Search of Theory" outlines a framework for understanding and developing specific techniques in the assessment of the Afro-American family; "Alternatives to the Use of Standardized Tests with Afro-American Children" and "Sociocultural Assessment of Home and School Visits in Psychiatric Evaluations of Afro-American Children and Families", Gail Elizabeth Wyatt provides a brief overview of the history of psychological testing and describes traditional and alternative tests that can be utilized to obtain a more comprehensive perspective regarding the Afro-American child's and adolescent's cognitive, social, and emotional development. Techniques that can be used in assessing the strengths of the Afro-American home and community in a psychiatric evaluation are described as critical aspects of this comprehensive perspective which are often overlooked by mental health professionals.

Lewis M. King

6

The "Assessment" of Afro-American Families: Issues In Search of Theory

> *Because it is a systematic negation of the [family] and a furious determination to deny the [family] all attributes of humanity, colonialism forces the people it dominates to ask themselves the question constantly, "In reality, who am I?"*[1]

Fanon's statement, above, is an accurate assessment of the social context of colonialism, and it raises a central question: what is the relationship between the force of domination and the people it dominates? This relationship and its consequences are at the heart of Fanon's concern. They are the primary concerns of this chapter as well. The term *assessment* is placed in quotation marks in this chapter's title because the word is itself a compelling example of this same relationship and its consequences. Assessment techniques should not be misunderstood as mere tests. They are processes for observing selected variables, and are necessarily influenced by the assessor's assumptions, implicit or explicit, about human families and about the variables selected for study. If investigators claim, for example, as so many do, "that mental illness, particularly depression, is increasing among blacks as protective cultural features are disrupted or lost in the vigorous movement from isolated, reasonable homogenous communities to the melee of the ghetto,"[2] then why do we bother to assess, and what critical issues are left in the specification of how to assess?

It is the thesis of this chapter that, in the specification of techniques in the assessment of Afro-American families, we must at least explore answers to the following question: (1) Why do we assess? An answer to the question rests on the assessor's value premises and beliefs about human enterprise, the theory that this generates, and the outcomes which are derived; (2) What do we assess? An answer to this question ought to define the variables that the assessor selects in making a determination or scientific decision on the lives of humans. What the assessor does not select to assess is as important as what he or she does select; (3) How do we assess? An answer to this question ought to specify both a design and a practice consistent with the responses to the "why" and "what" questions. We treat all these questions as critical to any formulation regarding techniques. This chapter will begin with an exposition of the premises that support our analysis.

First, the family is the institution that perpetuates cosmological ideas of society through family rituals and rites.[3] It is not only the basic unit of human social organization, but also the most accessible for prevention and therapeutic intervention.[4]

Second, the family is more than the sum of its members and is the principal mediating agent between the individual member and society. Through its teachings, sanctions, and examples, children are socialized into the culture of the family. A Nobel peace prize chemist said that water consists of two parts hydrogen, one part oxygen, and "something else, but we don't know what that is." So it is with family—that "something else" that makes it a family is central to our considerations.

Third, Afro-American families reflect essential similarities with and, simultaneously, fundamental differences from every other family. The Afro-American family, for instance, can be viewed as a unit of social organization,[5] but the family's American presence does not negate its African essence. The Afro-American family is African by nature but American by nurture.[6] This implies that these families possess value systems, meanings, life styles, and world views forged out of a condition that is the source of their essence, and which must be truly represented.

Fourth, Afro-American families do not represent a monolithic group using structural or functional parameters as points of departure. The monolithic entity is not in the families but in their common "systematic-negation" historically, their exploitation, and their undermining as a unit of social organization.[7]

Fifth, assessment of these families in the field of mental health is not a social act or a psychological act, but fundamentally a political act. Mental health is not a fact of life; it is based on the values of particular societies and particular times. The decision to assess is a decision that is fraught with political consequences.

Finally, assessment is a dynamic process to be distinguished from testing, which is a static exercise in the service of assessment.

This chapter will be concerned specifially with a clinical investigation in the area of mental health functioning, addressing itself to process and techniques only as related to the chapter's stated thesis. It is intened to be used in clinical investigation in the service of family transformation and change.

WHY DO WE ASSESS

Do we assess because we already know that Afro-American families have problems, or do we assess the problems these families have? Do we learn more about specific problems Afro-American families have because we assess them, or do we already know about the specific problems of the Afro-American families we assess? Why do we assess?

Too often, we assess because we are following an unexamined, routinized, historical tradition in which assessment is a central vehicle to keep the Afro-American family under seige. Assessment has become a sacred cow, enshrined in a mystique, with superstitious beliefs associated with its worship.[8] We cannot do justice to the Afro-American family in this society unless we recognize and resolve the contradictions inherent in the internal structure of our assessment enterprise. These contradictions are not defined by issues of good versus bad science, and objective versus unobjective people, as we have debated historically. The central issues are ones of *social* science and *political* people.[9]

We have overlooked too often both social and political issues in the assumption that our actions are objective and scientific and therefore value-free. Good science and objective people continue to be undermined by social and political issues embedded in the deep structure of our assessment undertaking. This deep structure is a ruling ideology of fixed beliefs, expectations, and practices contained in the history and tradition of assessment. In its most constructive sense, it is the history and tradition of the industrial and technological revolution over the last three centuries. In its most destructive sense, it is the history and tradition of imperialism and racism over the same period. It is this past which contains its own philosophy and its own reason that must be understood and transformed.

This particular history and tradition have provided a vocabulary and a set of concepts that rationalized and helped justify the value system upon which the ideas of family assessment now rest in American thought.[10] Both Haller[10] and Graham,[11] in definitive works in the field of the history of American science, have traced, for example, the links between particular political ideologies and specific biological theories of human heredity. In a short pamphlet published in 1891, Brinton assessed the psychology of white families and Afro-American families for signs of inferiority. On examination, he found a complete absence of acute alcoholism among the Afro-Americans. He argued, "The Negro's seeming immunity was attributable to his general physiological inferiority and in particular to the inferior susceptibility of his nervous system.[12]

This subversion of true science to politics, which began in the 1820s with the developement of theories of race, reached its pinnacle 100 years later when race delusion, in the form of eugenics, conquered European and American science, When Van Ervie wrote in 1868 that "the Negro's family tendency toward race extension is directly related to the freedoms thrust upon them,"[13] he was engrained in that tradition; when Simons wrote in 1902 "it is doubly easy for the Negro family to imitate the culture of the Caucasian, since they possess no transmitted culture of their own to act as barriers to the adoption of a new life,"[14] she was invested in that tradition; when Monyihan wrote about "the tangle of pathology"[15] in the Afro-American family, he too was steeped in this tradition. It is a fundamental contradiction to believe that within the shape of this deep structure, the master's intent in assessing his slave is to remedy the ills resulting from labeling and segregation or from nonrecognition and nonintervention. In fact, assessment serves to maintain the master. As Nash writes:[16]

> No group of men is able systematically to subordinate or deprive another group of men without appeal to a body or values which makes the exploitation, the disprivilege, the expropriation, and the degradation of human beings a "moral" act.

This deep structure maintains its supremacy because it has become accepted as a fact of nature. Under the guise of finding general laws of nature operating in both the social and biological organism, it has developed the essence of a strategy to precode what Afro-American families ought to be.[10] It would have us believe that science is an absolute objective tool engaged in reflecting the truth of the universe.[17] We all tend to forget that science is only an entrenched idea that incorporates the subjective prejudices and assumptions of the ruling class about themselves and others.

This critique is not intended to raise a false conscious question between assessment and no assessment. The central issue is, why do we assess? Is it to validate tradition and maintain the status quo; is it to satisfy our need for "supporting data" for our "publish or perish" pursuits; or is it because we wish to help transform the quality of life for the Afro-American family?

WHAT DO WE ASSESS: INTENT AND DIRECTION

We take, as our point of departure, assessment for social transformation in which Afro-American families are participants in improving the quality of their lives. The Afro-American family has historically been under seige. There is clear evidence for this over the past four centuries.[18,19] In the last two decades, president after president of the United States has called the treatment of the Afro-American family an American tragedy and has then proceeded to ignore the problems in setting forth social policy and legislation. "Life on the run" (migration, intra-city migration) has become a common feature of existence for Afro-American families in the United States. Their long history of stress under racist laws and economic exploitation has been a source of violent flare-ups as well as dysfunction and severe disruption in this basic social instituion—the family.[20,21] Professionals who wish to engage in clinical intervention into the dynamic conditions experienced by the Afro-American family in order to assist them in transforming the quality of their lives, need to consider some critical issues.

First, what has been the historical role and function of family in society? Historically, the family as a unit of human social organization provided for both the instrumental and expressive needs of its members and provided a social environment for the natural development and fulfillment of all who lived within its ambience.[4] A brief history of this function is useful.

The family moved from hunting to settled agriculture and became the bare unit of food production. This laid the foundation for population increase, but intensive land use created hazards and epidemic deseases. As the family in agricultural communities seemed to become self-sustaining in food resources, its power in societal matters began to decline with the growth of strong centralized authority, war, invasion, or brute force. The family was forced to adapt to this new dislocation of its power and resources.

In feudal states, and indeed in slavery, the relationship between production in the family unit and the landlord or slavemaster nearly removed all the values and powers that had developed in the family institution. The master thrived on exploiting the family in a wide range of ways—from the debasement of rape, to forcing them to beg for the barest necessities. Families were used to produce surplus to meet the food requirments of the master and his class. These conditions transformed agricultural communities based on the family/village unit into peasant-slave societies.

In the industrial society, the structure of the family was reduced almost to the basic minimum and its roles were taken over completely by the state—from education to child care. National ideology and values were stressed rather than cultural or familial values.[3] As we consider the family today, we must be aware of the difficulty in attempting to analyze the family independent of the trends of the society in which it functions. Nevertheless, we can still develop measures of family functioning. The degree to which the family is able or allowed to meet its responsibilities and needs, given the historical reality, is a measure of family functioning.

Parsons and Bales,[22] and later Billingsley,[5] defined the instrumental, expressive, and instrumental-expressive roles. The instrumental functions serve to maintain the basic physical and social integrity of the family and include the provision of food, clothing, shelter, and health care. Chief among the instrumental functions is the economic function. The expressive functions are designed to maintain socioemotional relationships and feelings among the family and include the sharing of love and affection, the provision of security, and the creation of an atmosphere for the development of self-awareness, self-worth and dignity. Roles which are both instrumental and expressive in nature include the issues of sex, reproduction, and child-rearing, i.e., joint issues in family development.

The roles are all interrelated, although it is possible to speak of them as specific subentities serving specific purposes. The point of ennumerating the functions is to indicate that the role of the family as the lay unit of social organization has undergone major changes over the past centuries as a function of the changes in the society. This is particularly true for the Afro-American family, which has gone through a history of uprooting from its economic base and cosmological space, enslavement, racism, and economic and psychological genocide in the context of the "soft guillotine" of United States society.[1]

One manifestation of this changed relationship between family and society is the change in the structure of the family from traditional extended, in which interdependent extended family networks provided the vast nexus of help exchanges of mutual aid, to growing numbers of single-person households with increased alienation in which society-defined nonfamily institutions (e.g., day care centers, single's bars) provide the aid exchange. Another level of change is the cultural movement from a way of relating to nature and humans to that of becoming what many authors have defined as a "culture of poverty," or culture of oppression.

Instrumental and expressive roles describe events within the family in relation to the society. Family functioning, however, is at least two dimensional: (1) *within* the family, i.e., internal role consistency among family members; consistency of family roles and norms with actual role performance; meeting the psychological needs of the family; and (2) *between* the family and the community, i.e., compatability of family roles and norms with community norms; the ability of the family group to respond to change.[23] It is this "between" dimension that has often been overlooked in family assessment. Geismar and Ayres define three issues critical to family functioning in this regard: (1) the family integrative role, i.e., its ability to provide security, love, and social and intellectual stimulation, and to meet some instrumental needs; we call this, in our formulation, the development of *identity*; (2) family autonomy, i.e., its ability to act as a provider and to create family solidarity and power; we call this the development of *status*, or power; and (3) family viability, i.e., its capacity for creating change, overcoming social, emotional, and economic crises, and for promoting its movement; we call this *viability*, or growth potential.[24]

We can chart these issues into a matrix which highlights the issues raised by the question, What do we assess? (See Table 6-1.) Contained in this matrix are the relations between two parameters, internal roles and external roles. The external (Community Role Relations) parameter is divided into Identity, Status, and Internal Viability. The viability column in the Internal Role Relations parameter difines potential outcome: Instrumental and Expressive (or the potential for internal growth) and Viability in the Community (or the potential for social input or impact). The labeled boxes of the matrix (A–D) contain possible variables which ought to be considered in assessment of the family.

Note the suggested outcomes in the viability dimensions of each interaction. Instrumental roles should lead to problem solving; expressive roles should lead to psychic security. Where there is identity, there should be a feeling of continuity; where there is status, there should be a feeling of participation. There is no relative or absolute weighting of the variables at this time. All that is being suggested is that in evaluating family functioning, this whole matrix of events must at least be considered. The importance of each will depend on another set of relationships having to do with the social context of reality.

These factors or variables interact, in the most ideal of situations, with social forces and the community to produce family and social transformation. We assume that assessment must define the potential for the Afro-American family to accurately represent (internal role relation) and reconstruct (community role relation) its reality. What this matrix allows us to do is simply to generate more specific "assessment for what?" questions in the context of responses to the larger question and direction. As examples, one may assess a migrant family from Haiti for social integration into a new Florida community; one might assess a family in

Table 6-1
Family Function Criteria Variables in the Assessment of Afro-American Familes

	Internal Role Relations		
Community Role Relations	*Instrumental*	*Expressive*	*Viability in Community*
Identity, Security	A. Health, welfare, nutrition Life cycle customs; birth; death Care and protection of child Family roles Clothing, shelter	B. Intimacy, companionship Ideology; world view Language; religion; history Values; beliefs Time/space orientation	Continuity Creative Work Family representation
Status, Power	C. Economic organization Resource allocation Vocation, employment Education, works Network/social support	D. Social organization Role, responsibility in community Autonomy, cohesion Communication Leisure time	Movement Action Participation
Internal Viability, Growth	Decision making Problem solving Productivity	Psychic security Marriage, sexual service	Potential for family and social transformation

Watts for its worsening transportation problems given new gasoline costs; one might assess a family in Harlem for adjustment to a father with lung cancer. All these represent one level of specificity. Even more specific than these are the variables that one must ferret out to answer these questions. We suggest that this matrix, which is by no means complete, will aid that process. Whatever the nature of the specific "what" question, however, we are suggesting that in principal one should never lose sight of the ultimate issue—assessment—to give the family a functional role in the transformation of itself and society.

One other point becomes critical. This assessment of the potential of Afro-American families to participate in action and transformation is not independent of the society. We must therefore, as professionals, at least be able to obtain the sociological data that gives an assessment of the social context of reality. This must include assessment on: oppression; stress in the community (see Chapter 3, Research on the Afro-American Family: A Critical Review); responsiveness of social/community institutions; the ecology of the living environment to include issues of transportation, recreation, access to goods and services, and other families; and history and tradition of the society in relation to the Afro-American family (e.g., racism and class exploitation). It is the relationship between the family and society that one finds the essence of family formation and mental health.

HOW DO WE ASSESS

The Search For Designs

The discussion above raised questions regarding the intent and direction of assessment. We considered it the second critical issue in developing techniques, the first being an examination of the deep structure of our knowledge production. This section will explore issues relevant to assessment designs or general strategies. Of concern here is the first part of the "how to assess" question. Do we approach the family as the sum of its individual members, or do we address "that something else?" It will be useful to outline some principles.

This discussion will be limited to techniques employed by clinicians, counselors, and educators in working with particular families. The first principle is that there is no point in trying to understand family problems in isolation from the wider society which gives meaning and significance to what happens to families. The social and cultural demands of the society impinge on family functioning, and it is a mistake to treat the family as a psychogenically closed system which society activates, but does not structure. The social structure both activates and structures the family. The problem is one of discovering relationships between this structure and the family.[25] One relationship, for example, is the family as a social support system in the consideration of the empirical relationship between stress and mental illness; another approaches the family as a deviance-amplifying system. It is a mistake to assume that if you understand one or two family members, you begin to understand the family; this is especially true for the extended family. Third, the family is not just a small group but a socioeconomic and psychological entity - a social unit embedded in culture. The small group process is an inadequate mode to use when addressing, for example, power differentials and the place of women and children in the group.

Hill identifies five conceptual frameworks utilized in family assessment and study. They are:[26]

1. The *interactional* framework, which views the family as a unity of interacting persons, each with an assigned role. This approach focuses on internal aspects of family such as status, communication, problem solving, and stress reaction.
2. The *structure-function* framework, which views the family as a social system best studied for the functions it performs in society. Structure is seen as a boundary maintenance system and encompasses the interplay between family and collateral systems outside the family and transactions between the family and subgroups within it.
3. The *situational* framework, which views the family as a social situation for behavior, which is purposive, and which attempts to resolve a problem posed by particular situation. The focus is on situations within the family such as rituals, child rearing and crisis.
4. The *institutional* framework, which views the family as one component that helps to support society as a whole. The focus is on descriptive studies of the family as a social unit organized according to cultural principles.
5. The *developmental* framework, which views the family as a series of stages in a family life cycle, each with its own peculiar sources of conflict and solidarity. The focus is on role expectations of parents, children, and developmental tasks which flow from cultural imperatives at each stage of growth.

The time has come for us to view the family in a sixth way—as a political social unit—which sees the family as a unit of social and economic power. The family also has a social reality that is based on values, beliefs, and expectations, and is ideologically contradictory to the mainstream of society. We can understand the family only if we examine the contradictions of the family in relation to society as a political reality; furthermore, change is dependent on resolution of these contradictions. The history of the family, briefly outlined above, gives a clear message about the extent to which the family has changed in relation to the political reality. Both Capitalists and Marxists alike see the family as a threat to their conception of the social state when in fact the opposite appears to be true. The political manipulation has particularly affected Afro-American families who have been the first to be uprooted from the cosmological and ecological realities and then turned into a commodity on the capitalist's markets.

It is this systematic and increasing attempt by political powers to destroy the Afro-American family that we consider one of the essential elements to be faced in understanding the Afro-American family. First, there is a clear message of the strength of this family and the viability of the family given its extreme historical reality.[18] But at the same time, we must consider the consequences of "life on the run": oppression, unemployment, overcrowding, poor housing, educational system failure, ecological demise, powelessness, and racism.

We must begin to understand the family as a political unit of activity, meaning first (internally), its understanding of its internal power, its class position, its political structure as a small party cell as defined by it unity, cohesion, stability, and its continued ability to be the basic unit of mental health and health care in general; second (externally), its understanding of its relation to the social community, and, how social events impact on family functioning. For example, how does unemployment "break up" the family, produce migration, or limit the family in performing its roles; how does the family continue to be a buffer against the dehumanizing features of the society?[27]

In looking at the family politically, we are taking direct aim at the issue of power, i.e., the power of the family to represent itself, the power to reconstruct reality, and, the power to participate in the transformation of itself and society. This means that the assessment must be one of the family as both a political institution and a political process, simultaneously; as a political formation concurrently prescribed and capable of permutations; as a political body that convention and collective ideals fix in a basic mold but that can be flexibly maneuvered to serve its goals.[28]

One political issue that must be understood is central to the very existence of the Afro-American family, yet almost never addressed in traditional assessment practice. This issue is the effect of migration and the resultant uprooting from organic ties, social and family supports, and family networks. It is important to understand not only the meaning of the historical uprooting from the motherland, but the rural–urban migration process and the intra-city migration. In migration to the city, the domestic group yields its traditional functions to state-sanctioned professionals who regulate the legal, educational, housing, health, and welfare bureaucracies.[29] The new political order may disrupt the balance of social relations. In the rural setting, the sharecropper and laborer family are bound by economic contractual agreements with a wealthy landowner in a feudal patronage system. The family, local political leaders, and landowners form a patron-dependent relationship which orders the nature of power and exchange in the small community.[30] In migration to the city the migrant family becomes independent of the former nexus: the relationship of dependence now is transferred to an impersonal goverance structure and bureaucracy.

Family political redefinition—affiliations, obligations, and reciprocal exchange—must now begin in order to develop mutual aid and emotional support during life crises. Through cooperative approaches to child rearing and the creation of new strong social networks for the provision of necessary goods and services, the family bond may be extended to include trusted non-kin. The family becomes augmented. It has become a new political unit in its struggle for social integration, cultural assimilation, and its own continuity.

The Search For Practice

This chapter has deliberately emphasized the connectedness of technique specification to theory of technique development. "Why" and "What" were the first questions. Given and understanding of this, we have approached the first segment of a question of "How" through an examination of designs. Within designs, there are procedures or practices to which we now address our final analyses.

Practice is the place where too many clinicians only begin to consider the assessment of the Afro-American family. Indeed, the point at which our education begins is the university. The model is as follows: the Afro-American family walks into the clinic—what instruments or tests do we use to test the family, ostensibly for the purpose of intervention? Our very structure has already determined who shall come to the clinic, how many family members will be present with what kind of verbal facility, and with what kind of transportation. Our predetermined process of test instruments has already defined the problem as something exclusively internal to individual members of the family, as historical, noninteractive with the social community and indeed, not related to their world views or value orientations.

There is perhaps one overall technique that may prove helpful in understanding the family as a social system. It is a general systems theory technique that views the interrelationships between components within a given or particular system and the interchange of this system with related strategy:

1. The *cybernetic* model is a receptor-center/effector-feedback model; the technique can be employed in examining how the family gets attacked, how it processes attack, how it acts on the attack, and how the consequences are fed back. An example of this is the placement by the school system of a family member into an Educable Mentally Retarded (EMR) class. Is the family aware of this as an attack? How does this attack come to be recognized by the family? How is this data processed by the family? How is it acted upon and followed-up? A West Indian migrant family would view this as a grave attack on its stability and would demonstrate greater overt crisis than many other families, although the crisis may be the same.
2. The *information* model is an encoding/noise decoding model; it is used to examine how the family receives information, how it filters out the extraneous, keeps the essential, and transmits the key message. An example of this is the growing silence and alienation of one family member. Does the family pick up information related perhaps to sex problems, drug use, communication breakdown, or some other problem? If so, how does it get the key message from this individual member, and how does the key message get transmitted to the whole?
3. The *decision* model involves the analysis of events to arrive at a choice; one can look at problem solving or decision making in the family and between the family and the community. An example of this is police aggression in the black community. The family is in crisis over shootings and, a lack of security. A decision has to be made: how does the family proceed?
4. The *behavioral* model is a functional analysis between behavior and environment. The environment to which the family is responding becomes the stimulis.
5. The *behavioral-analytic* model places emphasis on both familial and environmental units. The influence is more reciprocal. The therapist makes an analysis of the impact of family or family members on the environment and in turn, the environment's impact on the family, e.g., the sick role of an identified member.

6. In the *epidemiological* model the therapist looks at the frequency of the occurrence of the events among families in the community and seeks a more community-based explanation for the manifestations. This is particularly useful in studying prevention strategies, e.g., alcoholism, drug abuse, or child abuse.
7. In the *ecological* model the therapist looks at the family environment interaction not in fragmented ways, but as an interrelationship between psychological phenomena and the environments in which they occur, e.g., the relationship between existing family mental health services and other family support services.
8. In the *anthropological/archeological* model the therapist looks at historical records (as in *Roots*), household arrangements, artifacts and rituals, e.g., disposal of the dead, loss, abandonment, possession, and birth.

Within these eight strategies, one can utilize more specific techniques on more specific elements of the family social system, being careful to heed a warning that the family is more that the sum of its elements. There is real danger in approaching the family in parts, although the data generated may be useful. Most current techniques are designed for use with individuals and focus on traits or assumed inherent characteristics of individuals using structured devices such as the Minnesota Multi-Phasic Inventory (MMPI), semistructured devices such as projective tests, or unstructured devices such as the Rorschach.

More useful approaches include conjoint family assessment, in which the emphasis is on discovering the social learning contexts in which problem behaviors, internal to the family, are instigated and maintained. This technique is distinguished by its evaluation of interaction patterns of whole and partial families as systems.[32] It requires focus on interactions, transactions, and decision making. Its aim is to discover the process of relations. It should be emphasized that this technique does not introduce the community into the social context of reality and thus is limited in resolutions associated with this critical interaction. This is particularly important to keep in mind, especially in dealing with Afro-American families at the lower end of the social spectrum or of the working class. These families have a more collective orientation to nonfamily relations as well as family ones.

The consequence of this is that the focus of conflict is different for the middle class, and so is the balance of values. For the working class, conflict arises in nonfamilial social relations, for example, in dealing with teachers or employers, where contradictory ideas and values are encountered. Conjoint principles will have limited utility for this working-class group.

Another valuable technique is the audio-visual feedback strategy. This technique is very useful because of the power of the media and their ability to reflect and represent images. This "representation assistance" allows the family to place alternative constructions on its reality and find ways to reconstruct or change it.

Self-report inventories, checklists, verbal analysis, and observer ratings are still other techniques that can be utilized in the context of the frame of reference outlined. The critical question, then, is not so much the technique but the nature and validity of the instrument, given what our political agenda happens to be. This focus does not preclude psychiatric diagnosis of the family atmosphere; it simply continuously stresses the need for the assessor to use his or her technique as an advocate of the family and not as a classifier for some large social institution.

Most recently, a much neglected area in family assessment has been given some attention among clinicians—assessing the Afro-American family. Both the over-emphasis on the nuclear family and the assumption that this is the standard against which to judge family life have undermined the development of network techniques. The use of family, friends, and other members is especially important in the psychiatric help-seeking process. What the clinician needs to assess is the role of different family structures; the relationship of family interactions to the extent and type of help-seeking from this network; the different types of assistance from different sectors of the network; ways to augment and strengthen this network; and the role of other social institutions to this social network. The techniques for undertaking this very critical task are still being developed.

CONCLUSION

Family functioning is a frequently neglected but most important variable in family studies relating to mental health. This chapter has outlined a framework for both understanding and developing specific techniques in the assessment of the Afro-American family. We have emphasized that families must have an advocate in the therapist, a person who will facilitate the family's participation in the transormation of itself as well as society. Families must not be studied only in terms of their history and their present, but must also be considered in terms of their future—their anticipations, desires, and expectation for family growth and stability in a just and humane society.

REFERENCES

1. Fanon F: Wretched of the Earth. New York, Grove, Press, 1963, p203
2. Schwab F: A review of the Black rural land owner—endangered species: Social, political and economic implications by Leo McGee and Robert Boone (ed). Annals of American Academy of Political and Social Science. 448, 198, 1980
3. Ndeti K: Future of the Family: A cross cultural perspective. International Cultural Foundation, San Francisco, 1978
4. McEwan PJ: The social approach to family health studies. Soc Sci Med (Med Psychol Med Social) 8:487–493, 1974
5. Billingsley A: Black Families in White America. Englewood Cliffs NJ, Prentice-Hall, 1968
6. Nobles W: African root and American fruit: The Black Family. Journal of Social and Behavioral Science, 20:1974
7. King LM: Social and Cultural Influences in Psychopathology. Annual Review of Psychology 29:405–433, 1978
8. Staples R: The Black Family. Wadsworth Publications, N.Y., 1971
9. King LM: Race, Reason, Research: An Analysis of Violence in Black Communities. National Medical Association, Washington, D.C., 1979
10. Haller J: Outcast From Evolution. University of Illinois Press Chicago, 1971
11. Graham MA: Impact of Slavery on the Black Family: Social Political and Economic. Journal of Afro-American Issues. 3:4 p 343-356, 1975
12. Brinton G: Negroes. Lectures on Science of Ethnology Phil., 1891
13. Van Ervie JH: White Supremacy and Negro Subordination. N.y. 1868
14. Simons JL: Liberalism, Alienation and Personal Disturbance. Am J Socio 49:7, p 456–464, 1902
15. Moynihan DP: The Negro Family: The Case for National Action. Office of Policy Planning and Research, United States Department of Labor, March, 1965
16. Nathanson CA: Moving Preferences and Plans Among Urban Black Families. Journal of American Institute of Planners 40:5, p 353–359, 1974
17. Phillips CJ: Children from Socially Disadvantaged Families and Special Education. Research in Ed., p 22–24, 1974
18. Hill R: Strength of Black Families. National Urban League, 1971
19. Gutman R: The Black Family in Slavery and Freedom. Patheon Press New York, p 1750–1925, 1967
20. Beckman PL: Life Stress and Pschological Well Being. J Health Soc Behav 12:35–45. 1971
21. Fullilive CA: A Review of Minority Issues in Mental Health by W.D. Smith, A.K. Burlew, M.H. Mosley, Contemporary Psychology. 25:5,381 1980
22. Parsons T, Bales R: Family, Socialization, and Interaction Process. New York, Free Press 1955
23. Glasser PH: Families in Crisis. Harper and Row, N.Y., 1970

24. Geismar LL, Ayres B: Measuring Family Functioning - A manual on a Method, New York, 1970
25. Turner RH: Family Interaction. New York: John Wilen and Sons, Inc. 1970
26. Hill R: Methodological Issues in Family Development Real Family Process 3, 186–204, 1960
27. Lewis H: Child rearing Practices Among Low Income Families in the District of Columbia. Paper presented at the National Conference on Social Welfare, Minneapolis Minnesota, May 1961
28. Jackson KA: The Family Entity and Famine Among the 19th Century Akamha of Kenya: Social Responses to Environmental Stress. J Fam History 1:192, 1976
29. Garofalo J: Social Structure and Rates of Imprisonment: A research note. The Justice System Journal 5:229, 1980
30. Wolf E, Hansen E: The Human Condition in Latin America. New York Perquin Publications, 1972
31. Berkhoffer RF: A Behavioral Approach to Historical Analysis. The Free Press, N.Y., 1971
32. Satir V: Peoplemaking. San Francisco, California Science and Behavior Books, 1972

Gail Elizabeth Wyatt

7

Alternatives to the Use of Standardized Tests with Afro-American Children

Standardized tests are used today to identify the amount of information children have acquired in school-related environments, and to evaluate their thinking processes and performances under stress. For some, standardized tests are used to determine intelligence regardless of the controversy that surrounds the idea that intelligence can be measured by IQ tests. In this chapter, standardized test results will be viewed as only one aspect of a comprehensive psychological assessment, which in totality offers a broad scope of information including cognitive, emotional, perceptual, language, and adaptive skills and behaviors of children.

Psychological evaluations are usually static assessments of the child's abilities based upon one or two data gathering sessions. They can be only as valuable as the psychologist who compiles the test data, together with information gathered from alternative sources if the psychologist is skillful. The psychologist should know the uses and limitations of psychological tests and how to administer and score them, as well as how to make interpretations based on the norms upon which the test is standardized. The psychologist should be able to identify children that differ from the standardization group and should have a repertoire of assessment skills to obtain information beyond that generated from norm referenced tests. Most importantly, the psychologist should be motivated and committed to obtaining additional information to make a pluralistic assesment, which reflects many dimensions of a child's functioning. If psychologists do not meet these criteria, their expertise in making interpretations about the test protocols should be seriously questioned by lay and professional groups.

The purpose of this chapter, therefore, is to educate psychologists or mental health professionals who consult with psychologists about the uses and limitations of standardized tests and to describe alternatives to tests for children under 18 years of age.

A CHRONOLOGY OF THE TESTING MOVEMENT

In order to provide the reader with background information regarding the rationale for the use of standardized tests, a chronological history of the testing movement will be reviewed. Historical aspects of psychological testing have been thoroughly reviewed elsewhere,[1] but the major issues influencing the philosophy behind psychological tests as measures of intelligence will be briefly outlined.

The historical timeline for psychological testing began before the nineteenth century in America, when scholars, philosophers, and scientists were attempting to develop an approach which would identify both those who had the ability to achieve and those who did not. Their intent was to eliminate the traditional European use of heredity or lineage as a criterion for achievement and to identify a method that would be based upon more objective standards.

A significant contribution to the development of theory behind the concept of intelligence as measured by a test began in England at the beginning of the nineteenth century, when science and technology first provided objective data to support the concept of racial supremacy. Adolph Quetelet introduced the concept of the "average man," which demonstrated that measurements of the human body were normally distributed. Sir Francis Galton adapted this mathematical concept to psychological traits in individuals, explaining that these traits fell within a normal distribution as well. Charles Sperman proposed a two-factor theory of intelligence, in which any intellectual activity must have two attributes: the first specific to the particular activity, and the second common to all activities, labelled as general intelligence or "g".

This was the first genuinely scientific effort to establish a foundation for test items that reflect intellectual activity. Sir Cyril Burt established the concept of "g" into an innate general cognitive ability. Though much of his research has been discredited, Burt initially attempted to prove that the contributions of heredity were stonger than those of environment in test performance.

In summary, the following concepts were established by the London line of scientists before the 19th century:

1. Intelligence is normally distributed
2. Intellectual activities are similar to each other in intellectual attributes
3. Hereditary influences on intellectual activities outweigh those contributed by the environment

In 1905, Alfred Binet and his colleague, T. Simon, developed the Binet-Simon Intelligence Test in France. This was basically an atheoretical and practical diagnostic tool to identify students whose academic aptitudes required special training. However, when psychologists Lewis Terman and Maude Merril of Stanford University adapted the test for the United States population, rather than using the atheoretical French rationale as a basis for psychological tests, they chose to employ the British concepts of intelligence, based mainly on heredity influences.

Yerkes, Goddard, and Thorndike, the fathers of American psychology, were instrumental in shaping the use of psychological tests in the United States. They, along with Sir Francis Galton, were also proponents of the eugenics movement, a movement to insure the breeding of the most intelligent races, and to limit the reproduction of undesireable people. Assumptions prevalent during this period (1885) about people with lower intelligence being more susceptible to poverty, mental illness, and criminality had a later impact on sterilization laws in the United States between 1907 and 1927. Immigration laws which limited the influx of ethnic groups known to score poorly on standardized tests were also instituted.

Intelligence testing on a large scale was first conducted in the United States during World War II, and provided the first evidence that Afro-Americans scored lower on standardized tests than did their white peers. Immigrants from the southeastern parts of Europe were also found to perform poorly.

Another major development in the historical timeline was initiated by Carl Brigham, who compiled test data collected in the United States Army and concluded that immigrants from Great Britain, Scandinavia, and Germany scored higher on intelligence tests than those from the Alpine and Meditteranean areas. He was subsequently hired by the College Entrance Examination Board and developed the Scholastic Aptitude Test. This was dramatic evidence that both intelligence and achievement tests were developed by some of the same individuals and were based upon similar lines of thought.

In summary, the most immediate consequence of the development of other standardized tests for purposes of screening and selection into educational institutions was that it had an impact on immigration quotas. Those who resided in areas of Europe where quotas were low during World War II were denied entrance into the United States. The focus of research on racial differences in intelligence shifted dramatically from genetic differences to the effects of the environment on children's intelligence. This was an attempt to draw attention away from the eugenics movement and the devastating effects of that philosophy upon Jewish people under Nazism.

Increasing support for standardized tests was demonstrated with the establishment of the Educational Testing Service in 1947. On the other hand, with the 1960s and the Civil Rights Movement came programs such as Head Start, founded by the government to ameliorate deficiencies in the environment of the poor and minority groups. This and other programs exemplified committment and concern with environmental factors contributing to the development of intellectual abilities.

In 1968, the nature-nurture controversy surfaced again with Arthur Jensen's research documenting quantitative and qualitative differences between blacks and whites on intelligence tests.[2] The differences between groups were attributed to hereditary factors, and Jensen cited the limited problem-solving and abstraction abilities of the Afro-American samples utilized as contributing to these differences. The publication of Jensen's article was followed by controversy over the next ten years, resulting in a moratorium against the use of standardized tests with minority group children in California. An overabundance of Afro-American children were found in classes for the mentally retarded, because their performance on standardized tests suggested that they were retarded. Finally, as recently as 1978, the California Supreme Court set the example for other states, and banned the exclusive use of standardized tests to assess the intelligence of minority group children. This is one example of the growing trend to use standardized tests with extreme caution in making determinations regarding the intelligence of children who are not equitably represented in the standardization groups of norm referenced tests.

The history of the testing movement describes the uses of one type of test. However, there are other tests which have been administered to Afro-American children with varied results.

A DESCRIPTION OF PSYCHOLOGICAL TESTS

In order to gain an appreciation for the kinds of psychological tests that are available, they will be described in terms of their development and purpose.

Norm Referenced Tests

Norm referenced tests are standardized on a population whose demographic characteristics are expected to be somewhat representative of those persons to whom the tests will be administered. These tests are to be administered under similar circumstances. For example, if children of one age group are administered a test, it must be administered to each child with the same instructions and time limitations, and it must be scored by the same criteria. An individual's scores on a test are compared to some standard which represents an average performance. The childrens' scores indicate their level of performance as compared with other children of comparable age in the standardization group. However, the score does not offer information regarding the child's achievement on a specific type of task. The following are examples of norm referenced tests:

Cognitive Tests. The Weschsler Intelligence Scale for Children - Revised (WISC-R); Stanford-Binet Intelligence Test; the Wechsler Intelligence Scale for Children; the Wechsler Pre-school and Primary School of Intelligence (WPPSI).

Language Tests. The Illinois Test of Psycholinguistic Abilities Test; The Peabody Picture Vocabulary Test.

Personality Tests. Personality Inventory for Children.

PROBLEMS

The standardization groups fail to represent the population at large, and are especially limited in their ethnic minority group representation. The test developers do not specify in their manuals the limitations of interpretations made about test scores of children that are poorly represented in or absent from standardization groups.

Some standardization efforts frequently combine all minority children in one group category, entitled "nonwhite children", without regard to experiential, cultural, language, or dialect differences.

The comparison of a child's test scores with those of the standardization group does not offer information as to how well the child can perform on a particular task in comparison to others outside of the standardization group.

The performance of minority children on the WISC-R, especially those from within lower socioeconomic levels, can be influenced by several factors:

- Misunderstanding words that may more often be heard with the consonant dropped at the end of the word. Question (WISC-R Vocabulary Subtest): "What does join mean?" Noncredited response:

"You smoke it." Credited response: "To go into something you haven't been in before; like you join hands to play a game."

- Misunderstanding the use of words based upon the experiential background of the child. Question (WISC-R Information Subtest): "Where is the continent of Chile?" Noncredited response: "In a can." Credited response: "In South America."
- Failing to understand where the "missing part" is, as defined by the WISC-R test. Question (Picture Completion Subtest): "Point to what is missing." Noncredited response: "Nothing is missing." Credited response: "There is a leg missing on a table." This noncredited response is frequently given by children who have seen tables with three legs, pushed against a wall, and the table functioning quite adequately. Therefore, a missing leg, the credited response, is not perceived as essential.
- Perceiving socially-appropriate situations differently, as related to other socially-appropriate values.
  1. Question (Comprehensive Subtest): "What is the thing to do if a boy/girl smaller than yourself starts to fight with you?" Noncredited response: "Fight back." Credited response: "Walk away; ignore the kid."
  2. Question (Comprehensive Subtest): "What should you do if you find someone's wallet or pocketbook on the street?" Noncredited response: "Keep it." Credited response: "Turn it in to the police; try to find the owner."
  3. Question (Comprehensive Subtest): "What is the thing to do if you lose a ball that belongs to one of your friends?" Noncredited response: "Say I'm sorry." Credited response: "Give them one of mine; try to find it." Some children of low socioeconomic status (SES) could not afford to replace a lost ball.
- Lack of exposure to the environmental experiences which might provide the child with the specific information required on the test.
  1. Question (Information Subtest): "How many things make a dozen?" Noncredited response: "I don't know." Credited response: "Twelve." Most children would be able to respond appropriately to this answer, based upon their early childhood experience of buying eggs in a carton of a dozen. However, those children who go to the store to buy one or two eggs at a time may not have the opportunity to learn the concept of 12 without directly being taught at home or at the school.
  2. Question (Information Subtest): "What are the four seasons of the year?" Non-credited response: "Basketball, football, track, and baseball." Credited response: "Summer, Fall, Winter, and

Spring." This response is based upon a specific interest rather than the expected knowledge.

3. Question (Information Subtest): "What does the stomach do?" Noncredited response: "It growls." Credited response: "It digests food; turns foods to juices." This is another example of a specific incident more relevant to the child's personal experience that is not credited.
4. Question (Comprehension Subtest): "What are some reasons why we need policemen?" Noncredited response: "To kill you or put you in jail." Credited response: "To guard and protect the streets; to stop fights; to help us find our way home."

Criterion Referenced Tests

Criterion referenced tests are measures of achievement of educational tasks using a criterion standard of performance, rather than a norm group. When the objectives of learning are outlined, students are taught the necessary information and tested to see if they have met the criteria based upon age or grade level expectancy. This is considered to be the most objective approach to learning, and the most objective assessment tool.

PROBLEMS

There have been some criticisms of this test because the approach is only as objective as the person setting the criteria for learning. If the test items do not always reflect the criteria, then the assessment is inaccurate.[3] See Table 7-1.

Table 7–1
A Criterion Referenced Test of a Sixth-Grader

	Grade Level Achieved	Curriculum Section
The student was able to:		
Choose a word to complete a sentence that compares persons	7th Grade	17(a)
The student needs to review:		
Choosing syllables in a three syllable word.	5th Grade	52B
The student needs to learn how to:		
Find the antonym for a word	4th Grade	37A

The students are given printouts of skills that they have mastered and the grade levels that they have achieved, those in which their responses were erratic, indicating that a review is necessary, and those that the students are still required to learn. When the students have mastered all concepts necessary at that grade level, they would be advanced to the next grade level and subsequent learning material. The variety of teaching modalities used to teach these concepts would be the teacher's responsibility.

Learning Potential Tests

Learning potential tests are also called ability tests. They are used to measure the extent to which a subject learns with teaching, and are usually focused on the learning of a specific concept. The learning potential is defined as the subject's ability to profit from what is taught. Pretesting is important in order to obtain a baseline of the child's knowledge. Coaching is provided and then posttesting is obtained to measure the extent of learning. The pretest familiarizes the subject with the task and what is expected, the coaching includes problem solving strategies for task reasoning, and the posttest measures the subject's initial ability and the effects of learning. Budhoff experimented with this approach using non-verbal reasoning tasks similar to ones found in the Davis-Eells Games.[4]

Dialect Fair Tests

Dialect Fair Tests of any kind are administered in the tone and vernacular of black dialect, to accommodate those children who are accustomed to speaking and hearing dialect. These tests can also be administered to children living in Appalacia or in other regional areas that speak specific dialects. There has been some documentation that test instruction in standard English penalizes an Afro-American child.[5] When the language of the tests is placed in familiar terms without training or coaching, the child's performance tends to improve. Examples of Dialect Fair items:

1. What do the stomach do?
2. From what animal does we get milk?

PROBLEMS

Since there are no tests that have been standardized upon children who were administered tests in a dialect, the child's scores on these modified tests are compared with the scores of children whose test instruction and test items were administered in standard English. Comparisons of this type limit the ability of the interpretation of results. Additionally, some children are accustomed to hearing dialect, but speak standard English. Tests would probably have to be administered in both dialect and standard English to observe the differences in the test performance.

Culture Fair or Culture Free Tests

Culture fair or culture free tests were developed in an effort to measure general abilities, as described in Charles Spearmen's concept of "g". More specifically, these general abilities should not be influenced by dialect, language, culture, or economic level of the subject, but should measure perceptual experiences or skills that are common in the United States. The culture free tests that have been developed—the Porteus Mazes, Raven's Progressive Matrices, the Davis-Eells Games, and the Cattell Culture Free Test—are a few examples that have been standardized for children. The tests rely on perceptual skills and involve neither reading nor reference to culturally bound pictures, originating from extensive research such as that of Cattell[6] and Raven.[7]

The following exemplifies a Culture Fair Test question: "Listen to what I say: Take the eraser and walk over and open the door. Shut the door and put the eraser on the table. Now do what I say."

PROBLEMS

Research comparing the scores of children on culture free and norm referenced tests has not shown that minority group children of lower socioeconomic status score higher on the particular matrices used.[8] In reality, this finding is not surprising. It is difficult to select a number of experiences which are common to all individuals and are uncontaminated or uninfluenced by culture, economics, or experiential background. Secondly, these tests do not include tasks which measure the scholastic aptitude of the subject and the subjects potential to achieve in school. Therefore, they offer little information that is useful in evaluating school performance.

Culture Specific Tests

Culture specific tests are intended to accentuate the knowledge and experience of a particular subcultural group. Robert Williams has developed the Black Intelligence Tests of Cultural Homogeneity (BITCH), and Adrian Dove devised the Dove Counterbalance Intelligent Test. These tests assess aspects of the cultural experience of Afro-American people.

They include words and phrases which are used in the Afro-American vernacular and names of people or events familiar to their historical experience. These are not intelligence tests, and the items are highly influenced by the subject's cultural diversity, regional background, and knowledge of the Afro-American vernacular. The following are samples from Culture Specific Tests.

Example No. 1 (BITCH Test) "What is an alley apple?"

Multiple choice response:
a) brick
b) piece of fruit
c) dog
d) horse

(The correct answer is [a]).

Example No. 2 (Dove's Test) "Money don't get everything it's true__________."

Multiple choice response:
a) But I don't have none and I'm so blue.
b) But what it don't get, I can't use.
c) So make with what you've got.
d) But I don't know that, and neither do you.

(The correct answer is [b]).

ALTERNATIVE TESTS

The previous section dramatizes the uses and limitations of psychological tests and their utility with Afro-American children. This section describes alternate techniques that can be used to conduct a pluralistic assessment of the child and family and to obtain information that might otherwise be overlooked. A few of these assessment techniques are discussed below.

The System of Multicultural Pluralistic Assessment (SOMPA)

The SOMPA was developed by Jane Mercer and collaborators.[9] The need for this approach to assessment grew from the premise that IQ tests are not appropriate when used with many minority group persons who do not have the same cultural experiences as those of the dominant culture. The disproportionate numbers of minority group children found in classes for the mentally retarded in the public schools of Riverside, California served as a major impetus to develop measures that included an assessment of adaptive behaviors in terms of social roles that individuals assume. Additionally, information relating to the cultural experience, acculturation into the dominant culture, a health history, and assessment of perceptual motor development are also included. (See Table 7-2).

Mercer's contention is that the WISC-R measures what a child has learned about the dominant white culture, and is a good measure of the child's current functioning level in relation to the culture of the traditional public school. Therefore, the child's score is not perceived as a measure of biological or genetic potential. The SOMPA uses multiple regression equations to estimate the child's learning potential from sociocultural scales and the WISC-R full scale, verbal, and performance scores. The

Table 7–2
System of Multicultural Pluralistic Assessment

INFORMATION OBTAINED FROM THE *MOTHER/GUARDIAN*	
Sociocultural Scales	Urban acculturation
	Family structure
	Social-economic status
	Family size
Adaptive Behavior Inventory (ABI)	Family roles
	Peer group roles
	Community roles
	Non-academic school roles
	Earner-consumer roles
	Self-maintenance roles
	Total ABI score
Health History Inventories	Pre-postnatal inventories
	Trauma inventory
	Pathologies and diseases
	Vision inventory
	Hearing Inventory
INFORMATION OBTAINED FROM THE *CHILD*	
WISC-R	placement
Physical dexterity tests	ambulation
Bender	involuntary movements
Height and weight	fine motor sequence
Visual acuity	equilibrium
Auditory acuity	finger-thumb dexterity

resulting score is the average IQ score expected for a child from that ethnic background. This method attempts to control for sociocultural differences and offers a better estimate of the child's learning potential than the traditional comparison of the child's scores with standardized norms.

The SOMPA attempts to incorporate aspects of the cultural experience that is otherwise not included in tests which are standardized upon individuals who, for the most part, do not share that experience. It is a compromise approach which recognizes the short-comings of the present norm referenced tests. However, the WISC-R is still a part of the assessment approach and the knowledge base, language, or dialect differences, and styles of encoding and decoding information that are seldom assessed in Afro-American children are not included in this assessment.

Culture Specific Tests

Robert Williams has pioneered in developing tests which elicit information and knowledge from Afro-American subjects that is specific to their cultural experience. These tests can be especially useful in assessing the children's ethnic awareness, and their feelings about their ethnic group. For example, the Themes of Black Awareness (TOBA) is a 40-item test which requires that the subject complete a sentence relating to ethnic issues. The responses can demonstrate the subject's openness to disclosing feelings about these issues. Three methods of scoring can be used to identify different dimensions of the Afro-American personality. A profile of the response style of the subject can also be generated as a visual illustration. In Table 7-3 can be seen examples of TOBA responses from two Afro-American teenagers, a $14\frac{1}{2}$ year old girl and a 13 year old boy.

Table 7–3
Sample Resonses to Themes of Black Awareness (TOBA)

Item #1:	Girl:	*The black woman* "is sometimes fierce."
	Boy:	*The black woman* "gave away her cookies."
Item #12:	Girl:	*White people* "sometimes are more sophisticated than some blacks."
	Boy:	*White people* "are O.K."
Item #16:	Girl:	*Uncle Toms* "are blacks that act white."
	Boy:	*Uncle Toms* "are at home."
Item #24:	Girl:	*The white man* "sometimes doesn't like blacks."
	Boy:	*The white man* "is o.k., too."

The ethnic consciousness and awareness of social nuances between the two ethnic groups appear to be more obvious in the girl's responses than in those of the boy. Additional clinical information revealed that the adolescent boy had been raised in communities where his family was racially isolated. His socialization experiences were exclusively with white children and his parents did not stress the importance of ethnic consciousnes, friendships with peers of his minority group, or knowledge about Afro-American life.

The *Themes Concerning Blacks* (TCB) is a projective test consisting of a series of 15 charcoal drawings about which the subject is asked to make up a story. Williams also included structured questions in the test manual that can be used with youngsters who might experience difficulty in completing a story. However, the TCB can also be administered with a free association approach. The difference between the Thematic Apperception Test (TAT) and TCB is that the main characters in the TCB are Afro-American, the characters on the cards are more contemporary, and the pictures reflect both an urban and rural life style.

In response to card #12, an 11-year-old Afro-American boy told a story of a policeman harrassing two Afro-American boys because the officer "liked to make trouble." The subject described in detail the young boy's resentment of this authority figure's abuse of power and control over their lives. The content of the story lent insight as to how this subject perceived authority figures and why he experienced problems in complying with expectations of those adults in positions of control.

Some of the culturally specific tests by Robert Williams are best administered to subjects in their late teens and early adulthood, or to the parents of the child being evaluated.[10] The Black Personality Questionnaire (BPQ) consists of 50 items designed to identify the subject's personal convictions about topics such as black politics, culture, economy and religion. These six response sets form the basis of the statements: prowhite, antiwhite, antiblack, problack, Pan Africanism and Third World. The *Black Preference Inventory* (BPI) includes 22 items and was designed to determine cultural, political, social, educational and personal preferences of Afro-Americans. The *Black Opinion Scale* (BOS) contains 10 values which the subject is asked to rank according to the most to least important for Afro-American people. The BOS attempts to identify the subject's perceptions of their ethnic group's value system. These tests can enrich the protocol of the child in that they provide information regarding ethnic consciousness or that of the immediate family. Some sample items from these tests are given in Table 7-4.

The Thematic Apperception Test (TAT) is also a useful projective test with subjects who demonstrate the verbal and emotional maturity to

Table 7–4
Sample Items from Some of the Robert Williams' Culturally Specific Tests

The *Black Personality Questionnaire* (BPQ) consists of 50 items designed to identify the subject's personal convictions about topics such as black politics, culture, economy, and religion. These six response sets form the basis of the statements: prowhite, antiwhite, problack, antiblack, Pan Africanism and Third World.

	Agree	/Disagree	/Cannot Say
1. White doctors generally take good care of their black patients	_____	_____	_____

The *Black Preference Inventory* (BPI) includes 22 items and was designed to determine cultural, political, social, educational, and personal preferences of Afro-Americans.

(Circle one answer)
Where do you prefer to live?
a) all black community
b) a racially mixed community
c) does not matter
Comment:

The *Black Opinion Scale* (BOS) contains 10 values which the subject is asked to rank from the most to the least important for Afro-American people:

	Your Preferred Order
A. Unity (togetherness of black people)	_____
B. Power (economic and political influence)	_____

respond to the thematic material in the pictures. The life experience and value system of the subject can often be difficult to isolate from underlying motivations, as it was in this story by a 14-year-old Afro-American girl:

Card 7GF:	"She's 14 and had a baby."		
Examiner:	What happened before?	Subject:	"They had sex."
Examiner:	Who?	Subject:	"Wynette and Tony."
Examiner:	Did this really happen?	Subject:	"Yes"
Examiner:	How do they feel?	Subject:	"Happy"
Examiner:	How will they take care of the baby?	Subject:	"The county . . . she's on the county (welfare) and he works."

Examiner:	How old is he?	Subject:	"18"
Examiner:	How does it end?	Subject:	"They kept the baby."
Examiner:	Did they get married?	Subject:	"They want to."
Examiner:	Why don't they?	Subject:	"I think she's too young."

Becoming sexually active before marriage, having a baby, and yet, being too young to marry may seem to some people to be slightly out of order of socially desireable events. However, it is important to remember that this TAT story offers a wealth of information as to how this teenager perceives these events as occurring. Sexual intercourse, pregnancy, childbirth, the responsibility for a child's welfare and marriage are perceived as separate entities. While sex and pregnancy occur, they do not necessarily require total financial responsibility for the child, nor do they require marriage if it does not insure financial security. Additional questioning during clinical interviews can help to determine if the content of this TAT story is a reflection of a pattern of events that this teenager has observed through the behavior of peers or adults with which she associates, or if this is her personal perception of the course of events which she may wish to follow. It would be presumptuous for a clinician to assume that either of these possibilities is the case without obtaining additional information from the youngster that will clarify the meaning of the story in terms of her values regarding sex, marriage, and parenting responsibilities.

General Areas of Assessment

Regardless of the tests selected, the subjects' self-concept, awareness, and acceptance of their Afro-American heritage should be included in the data. The following are additional techniques that can be used to obtain this information:

- In addition to the traditional kinetic drawings, request that the child draw an Afro-American boy and girl on separate sheets of paper. Note the specific differences in hair style, i.e., "Afro" hair style or texture, skin color, or other details which the subjects perceive as characteristic of their ethnic drawing.
- Questions regarding subjects' first awareness of their ethnicity, differences in skin color, or hair as compared to family members, peers, or other persons, how these differences were explained to them and by whom, can sometimes reveal the positive or negative circumstances around ethnic awareness and identity that can influence the self-concept in later years.

- An assessment of how the subject copes with being "different" in dialect, cultural experiences, preferences for music or food, at school, in social situations, or with peers can indicate whether the subject is experiencing difficulties interfacing with the dominant culture on the one hand and subcultural values and practices on the other.

CONCLUSION

This chapter reviews the uses and limitations of tests utilized with Afro-American children and families from the perspective of the dominant culture. Some often-overlooked alternative measures that can broaden the assessment to include aspects of the Afro-American culture are described. Tests are not always the best devices to use in psychological assessments. However, they do provide a structure to follow and content areas to explore. As long as the areas of cognitive, perceptual, and emotional development, adaptive behaviors and self-acceptance are included, the examiners should create an assessment battery to fit their personal levels of expertise with Afro-American lifestyles to meet the needs, strengths and weaknesses of the child. However, assumptions and interpretations of the protocol should also include descriptive information as to how the data was obtained, its validity and reliability, and additional areas that need to be explored through additional testing or in the clinical interview.

REFERENCES

1. Padilla E, Wyatt GE: Academic achievement and IQ testing among minority group children, in Powell G, Yamamoto J, Morales A (eds): The Psycho-Social Development of Minority Group Children. New York: Brunner/Mazel, 1981. In press
2. Jensen A: How much can we boost IQ and scholastic achievement? Harvard Ed Rev 39:1–123, 1969
3. Bohem AE: Criteria-referenced assessment for the teacher. Teachers College Record 75:117–126, 1973
4. Budhoff M: Treasuring learning potential: An alternative to the traditional intelligence test, in Gredler GR (ed): Ethical and Legal Factors in the Practice of School Psychology. Proceedings of the First Annual Conference in School Psychology. Philadelphia, Temple University, 1972.
5. Williams RL, Rivers LW: The use of Standard and Non-Standard English in Testing Black Children. A Paper Presented at the Annual Meeting of the American Psychological Association, Honolulu, Hawaii, September, 1972
6. Cattell RB: Handbook for the Culture Fair Intelligence Test: A Measure of "g". Champaign, Ill., Institute for Personality and Ability Testing, 1959
7. Raven JC: Guide to the Progressive Matrices. London, Lewis, 1952

8. Higgins C, Silvers CH: A Comparison of Stanford-Binet and Colored Raven Progressive Matrices IQ's for Children with Low Socioeconomic Status. J Consult Psychol 22:465–468, 1958
9. Mercer JR: Labelling the Mentally Retarded. Berkeley, University of California Press, 1973
10. Wright BJ, Isenstein VR: Psychological Tests and Minorities. Mental Health Studies and Reports Branch, Division of Scientific and Public Information, National Institute of Mental Health, October, 1975

Gail Elizabeth Wyatt

8

Sociocultural Assessment of Home and School Visits in Psychiatric Evaluations of Afro-American Children and Families

One criticism of psychiatric evaluations is that they observe and address static behaviors based upon responses emitted in a clinic and tend to make judgments about the functioning of an individual without gaining additional information regarding whether these behaviors are consistent in other settings and are within the cultural perspective of the Afro-American child or adult. The purpose of this chapter is to describe the process of evaluating the home of an Afro-American child and family, the child's school placement, and their role in a psychiatric evaluation and treatment. This assessment is important because it involves observing a critical aspect of the Afro-American life experience and is particularly valuable in evaluating children and adolescents. Some of this information should also be obtained from adults in order to gain insight into their early home and school experience. The home and school visits will be examined, followed by a discussion of how this information should be incorporated into the evaluation or treatment process.

THE HOME VISIT

A Review of the Literature

Making a home visit to gain additional information regarding patients is not a new approach to a psychiatric evaluation. Although home visits were described in the literature in Europe as early as the late 1920s, descriptions of this sort were not published in the United States until the 1960s. While there are those who support the idea of mental health professionals visiting the home of the patient to at least gain a different perspective on psychiatric or physical problems, [1–4] most of the persons making the visits have been nonmedical professionals.[1,4] However, there have been a few descriptions of attempts to encourage medical students, physicians, and particularly child psychiatrists to make home visits.[2,5–7] Though there seems to be some controversy as to whether home visits make the best use of the time of the therapist with a medical background, the more salient issue seems to be who will assume the responsibility for making firsthand, and perhaps continuing, contact with the patient and family. The information gained can be provided by other professionals consulting with the primary therapist on these issues.

Traditionally, home visits for psychiatric evaluations appear to have been made to poor or minority group people or to urban areas of high density. One reason for this specific focus is because most mental health professionals are white and middle class and generally have had limited personal and professional contact with these groups.[8] Consequently, the likelihood may increase that they may tend to use stereotypes or generalizations in order to understand behavior.[8,9] In an attempt to minimize the resistance of professionals visiting these areas for the first time, one study attempted to dispel fears of physicians having to travel into so-called "black ghetto areas" for fear of personal injury or their property being stolen.[2] The need to assure therapists of their safety when travelling into these areas lends the impression that all low income or areas of high minority group density are dangerous and that special precautions are necessary. This approach is more likely to incite fear and to reinforce rather than to dispel stereotypes about the "dangers" of visiting predominantly Afro-American communities, and particularly those areas of high density and unemployment.

There has been considerable discussion regarding whether home visits are cost effective, generate new information, and cause discomfort for both therapist and family. However, most studies argue in favor of home visits for a variety of reasons. These visits are useful in obtaining information regarding the family that is frequently otherwise not available. For example, an assessment of the total family interaction including important or significant others in the community that may be helpful in the patient's adjustment can be obtained.[3,4] Some families feel alienated by coming to a clinic. The home visit serves as an effort to "meet them on their own turf," particularly for families who may tend not to seek psychiatric services or may be seeking them for the first time. They may also not be familiar with how agencies and institutions such as a mental health facility function.[4] A home visit allows the therapist to observe nonverbal cues that are transmitted within the family interaction, for example, the dynamics of the seating arrangements, which may reveal information regarding closeness or distancing mechanisms used by key family members, and other cues, including the absence of certain family members and their degree of interest or involvement in solving the presenting problems.[4] The home visit is excellent preparation for family therapy and can demonstrate the process and content of the therapeutic interaction, particularly for those families who are not psychiatrically oriented.[4] The cost of the home visit is frequently comparable to a clinic visit because the client is billed in the same manner. This point may be somewhat debatable in light of increasing gasoline costs and travel time required which often causes personnel to be away from the clinic for several hours.

However, home visits are generally not included as a standard practice of most clinics. Psychiatric clinics need to modify their approach to families who are not psychiatrically oriented or those who have strong reservations regarding coming to a clinic, particularly if the entire family is needed in order to understand the dynamics of the target patient's behavior. It is important to make the family comfortable, to educate them as to the psychiatric evaluation and treatment process, and to include family members or significant others who may not be able, for physical or transportational reasons, to make the journey to the psychiatric clinic.

Evaluating the Need for a Home Visit

Of the literature reviewed regarding home visits in the community, there was a lack of information regarding sociocultural aspects that should be noted by therapists who either have had no prior experience in the Afro-American community or may need to refamiliarize themselves with important concepts to consider prior to a home or school visit.

The first responsibility of the primary therapist is to develop a decision-making process as to when home visits are indicated. They may not be necessary for each family or child, but the guidelines explored below may help to facilitate the decision-making process.

When an Afro-American child is being evaluated, home visits can be very useful in understanding the physical, social and emotional environment of the Afro-American child or adolescent. Even when youngsters are to be returned to their home from residential treatment centers, it is important to know the quality and quantity of interactions of the people and situations in which the client may become involved again. This information can also be obtained through a tour through the community, meeting those important persons with which the child will interact. However, in the case of a child exhibiting extreme or bizarre behavior (e.g., a severely psychotic or autistic child, or one with specific learning disabilities), the advantages in specifically evaluating environmental influences would be negligible.

When multiple mothering figures or single-parent mother or father figures are involved in the caretaking or child rearing process, a home visit can often times help to determine the quality of parenting, the amount of time spent by the parent with the child, and the amount of time that the child may spend in caring for other children or may be left alone or unsupervised. Exercise caution in making any assumptions that multiple mothering or single parenting does not compare in quality to a two-parent child rearing situation. There are also affluent families whose members characterize the traditional family constellation and yet suffer from inadequate, uninvolved parenting and parents. An assessment of the support system of the parent or parents and the life-style that is adopted by the family that may influence the psychological, educational, and physical well-being of the child is the main consideration.

When family members, particularly those in the nuclear family or those involved in child-rearing, refuse to come to the clinic but show some concern and are known to have a strong influence on the functioning of the target child or adolescent, a home visit should be considered. On the other hand, mothers and fathers may refuse to become involved at the clinic but know that without their help it is impossible to make any headway with their youngster. In those cases, the therapist should make an effort to offer to visit the home at least once in order to develop some rapport with the family; it may result in the parents' later participation in the therapeutic process. When therapists extend themselves to the family and demonstrate concern about their total involvement, the family may reciprocate and make an extra effort in return. There is also a point at which a therapist must evaluate the family's level of motivation and efforts to manipulate the system for their own gains. This manipulation may sometimes be observed when therapists of other ethnic group affiliations deal with minority group families. In an attempt to offset limited experience with a minority group patient, the therapist may "bend over backwards" making assumptions about the family's transportation or financial problems. Services may be overextended to the home to facilitate the family's participation, while failing to require the family's involvement and understanding their ability to become involved. There is just as much disservice in these situations as there is when the therapist misunderstands the family's noninvolvement.

If there are reports that the child is "different" at home than in the school or in the clinic setting, a home visit is indicated in order to determine the differences or similarities in behavior or in the assessment of behavior. The child's pattern of functioning may be more inhibited in the home than when the child is in another setting like school. The child may be less inhibited due to permissive or dual value systems regarding certain behaviors. We frequently encounter the "9 a.m. to 5 p.m." mildly retarded youngster, who has difficulty in the clinic setting and in school, but has no difficulty functioning in their own community. These children are often socially sophisticated, have good peer relationships, and are supported and involved in family activities. They are often labeled as "functionally retarded" by the schools but they do not share that label in their communities. They also may have a great deal of what is termed "street knowledge" and exhibit the adaptive behaviors required in their communities, but have failed to develop "school knowledge" and the adaptive behaviors expected in the schools or in the larger community.

If there are reports that the youngster is having peer problems in school, it is also important to get an assessment of whether the child lives in an area of one predominant ethnic group composition and how the school situation may differ from that to which the child is most accustomed. For example, many Afro-American children are being bused to predominately white communities and schools, and have difficulty in developing and establishing peer relationships on the school ground and often in the classrooms. However, in their own communities, the children may not have these kinds of difficulties. It is valuable to assess the family's attitude toward same ethnic group and interracial socialization and to determine whether the youngster is experiencing the same pattern of socialization problems within his or her own ethnic group in the neighborhood or in other social situations. If this information can not be obtained accurately from the history taken from the family or in interviews with the child, a home visit can provide observations of the quality of neighborhood peer interactions.

Conducting a Home Visit in the Afro-American Community

The therapist who is anticipating making a visit into any neighborhood or area of the city in which he or she has had little prior experience needs to spend time attempting to identify misinformation or stereotypes that may serve as barriers to an effective evaluation or treatment and to develop a sensitivity to cultural and economic differences.

Until recently, however, there has been little information available regarding mental health professionals' attitudes toward the Afro-

American community or Afro-American people in general.[11] There is some documentation which demonstrates the influence of racial prejudice or ethnocentric attitudes upon the care and delivery of mental health services to Afro-American people.[8, 11] Consequently, there are behaviors and attitudes which can facilitate or serve as barriers to the level of comfort and the overall approach that a mental health professional utilizes with a family from a community which is alien to or different from that community in which the professional is most accustomed.[11] The following is an example of a child psychiatry trainee's difficulty in visiting a community known to be different from his own but similar to ones with which he was familiar in his youth:

A second year Child Psychiatry Fellow presented a case of an Afro-American adolescent female whose father was a very important person in her life but who refused to come to the clinic. At the end of the presentation, the psychiatry team members suggested that he make a home visit. There was too much missing information about this family that was judged to be necessary before diagnosis and treatment plans could be made. The Fellow admitted that he was "afraid" to go to the area of town in which this family lived. He went on to say that he had been around black people, but he remembered them in a "certain way" in West Virginia and didn't want to confront his fears. An Afro-American team member offered to accompany the Child Psychiatry Fellow and he agreed to make the visit "as long as he had a guide." However, two weeks later, the Fellow changed his mind, explaining that the family was "too resistant" and really didn't want to come to the clinic. His home visit would require him to miss certain seminars and scheduled patients. When he was confronted with his resistance, he admitted that he was "simply too afraid" and didn't anticipate treating many black families who lived in that part of town, anyway. Since home visits were at the discretion of the therapist, and the department in which he was a trainee did not see this kind of resistance and countertransference as a "problem" the home visit was not made, in spite of efforts by the Afro-American team member to the contrary.

These points should be considered when visiting a home:

1. After the decision has been made to make a home visit, it is important to discuss the possibility of a visit with the parent or adult who accompanies the child. Points in this discussion should include any resistance on the part of family members to allow the home visit so that resistance can be weighed and acknowledged or dispelled before the visit is made. If permission is secured before the visit, the family should be encouraged to communicate to other family members or to significant others the date and time of the visit and to request their presence. The time agreed upon should be when most family members will be present long enough to spend some time in talking with the primary therapist or whoever makes the visit.

2. Before the day of the home visit or on the morning of the visit, always call to confirm your arrival to ensure that all family members will be present or to give individuals a chance to leave prior to your arrival if they do not wish to be there. This minimizes the chances of "catching" individuals at home but also lessens the more embarrassing situation of family members walking out as you arrive.
3. Always identify yourself and the purpose of your visit when you meet the family members and emphasize that this is a routine part of a psychiatric evaluation. Point out that a home visit is not an attempt to identify or label a family as "sick," but often provides additional information regarding how the target patient functions within the home setting and around those individuals who are most familiar to them.
4. Assure family members about the confidentiality of all information obtained, even though it is obtained in the home.
5. Allow the family to arrange the seating because it can reveal important information regarding dyads or groups that are established within a family, and identify those members of the family who are excluded. Before leaving, encourage the family to candidly discuss how they felt about your visit. You might gain insight as to whether the visit has dispelled or developed future problems.
6. Taking notes during the visit often makes people feel uncomfortable, however, it is a good idea to take some notes when you return to your car. List some of the behaviors that you noted that were interesting or unusual and that you may want to observe again and compare with other reactions that are observed in the clinic.
7. Make sure to assess the family status in the community. This is traditionally determined by income, education, home ownership, and community involvement. Due to inequities in employment and educational opportunities, it is not alway possible to use these criteria with Afro-American families.[12] It is typical to find Afro-American parents overeducated and underpaid for their work as compared to white American familes of comparable income and education levels. Thus, status, visibility, and respectability must be derived through other means such as involvement in church, social, civic, and community organizations. This information can reveal the level of aspiration that the family may have for the target child, and the amount of community support that a family can utilize in the face of problems.

    Another important area to discuss is the family's overall values regarding education, employment, and the extended family members who may have established the same or different life-style due to education and income. This information lends insight into the continuity of values within the support system of the family, and the possible conflicts or support for the goals set by the family for the target child or adult.

8. Remember to make some positive remark regarding the family allowing you to visit with them in the home or in the nearby community. Assure the family that feedback regarding the visit will be made at particular points during the evaluation and treatment process; be sure to follow through and include observations made during the home visit in subsequent meetings with family members.
9. The family may want to obtain some personal information regarding you, not as a professional but as an individual. It is not unprofessional to disclose something about your personal life or information describing your family. This may be the family's attempt to determine the kind of person that you are outside of your professional realm and your level of comfort in social situations. Though this may be a very important process to accepting your professional opinions you need not reveal any strictly confidential or initimate information. However, it is important to be evaluated and accepted first as a person before you can be accepted and appreciated as a professional.
10. If the terminology used in the family visit appears to be unfamiliar, the best approach is to ask for a definition of these words or terms. Some of the family members may be speaking black dialect and quite a bit of the content of the conversation can be lost if you attempt to "catch on" to what is being said, rather than to admit that some of the conversation requires additional definition. There have been instances where dialect has been used to exclude or confuse the therapist who is reluctant to admit an ignorance of dialect used in coversation. Therapists of any ethnic group origin can make this mistake and lose rapport with a family who may be using dialect as a barrier to the therapeutic process or testing the honesty of the therapist. On the other hand, some clients may incorrectly assume that an Afro-American therapist understands the use of dialect. In either case, information can be lost when these assumptions are not dispelled.
11. Above all, be yourself. Family members may be observing your verbal and nonverbal behavior and level of comfort to determine if you find their home, and ultimately their family, acceptable. The family's acceptance of the therapist or home visitor can influence whether they will eventually reveal "family secrets" that can highlight family dynamics which often contribute to the presenting problems.

THE SCHOOL VISIT

Observing the child or adolescent in the school setting generates a wealth of information needed to complete a psychiatric evaluation. Traditionally, school visits have been made by nonmedical personnel such as psychologists and educational consultants, to evaluate the child or adolescent's functioning within the school. This section of the chapter is not intended to train professionals of other disciplines to make school visits. They should be conducted by those trained to identify and diagnose learning problems and to develop and discuss educational remediation of those problems with school personnel. The purpose of this section is to identify sociocultural factors that should be addressed when any professional either visits the school, consults with, or accompanies a professional who makes the visit.

It is more important to obtain necessary information regarding the school than to be concerned about the professional credentials of the person making the visit. School visits can offer vital information regarding the cognitive functioning of the child against the backdrop of other children, as well as the child's emotional or affective development and their influence on learning. These points are especially important for an Afro-American child because of the necessity of understanding the self-concept, the teacher's attitude towards the child, and the school's overall attitude, which can affect cognitive functioning and affective development. Points to be assessed in a school visit are discussed below.

An overall feel for the school setting and its relaxed or rigid approach to learning can often be assessed through a visit to the main office (sometimes called the personnel or attendance office). Note whether children are allowed to work behind the desk, and if minority group children have equal access to these and other "monitor" jobs. The children who attain these jobs often reflect the school's committment to involve all children in positions of leadership and visability.

The school principals are often key resources to gain information into their level of involvement in the daily ebb and flow of school activities. The principal who is always seated at the desk and who has very little interaction with the everyday functioning of the school may present a very different model from the principal who is on the school ground or in the cafeteria, relating with the children and interacting with the teachers both before, during, and after school. The principal can also indicate how much support the teachers or other children will have in bringing their problems to be resolved at that administrative level.

The classroom can generate important information at an elementary school level regarding the amount of flexibility for learning that is allowed. For example, if the seats are nailed to the floor the mobility of the classroom learning situation is somewhat set, versus the classroom where tables and chairs can be rearranged to facilitate the interaction of children in more than one setting. The classroom arrangement can contribute to the problems of high-activity level children who are easily overstimulated or those who would benefit from interacting socially with children on a small group basis.

The playground of an elementary, junior, or high school can provide rich information regarding social isolation, ethnic group or same-sex clusters, and the school's policy of diminishing or reconstituting these groups. Social groups can become especially intense at the junior and senior high school level where youngsters often cluster based upon multiple criteria of sex, ethnicity, socioeconomic or experiential background, and special interests (those who are in gangs, use drugs, or are sexually active often form cliques). Socialization is such a critical dimension to successful adjustment at this age and it can be especially difficult for Afro-American children. Research suggests that adolescent Afro-American girls from 11 to 14 tend to have lower self-concepts than Afro-American boys of their age group. The girls have more difficulty in being accepted into school activities which facilitate socializing and in other extracurricular activities, whereas Afro-American boys usually excel in sports and therefore tend to be more well known.[13] Knowledge of the target child's socializing patterns and in which of the social or special interest groups the child is involved or excluded can explain peer problems at school and can indirectly influence achievement or school attendance. Some administrators and counselors are sensitive to these problems and can be helpful in structuring a child's activities to lessen involvement in groups which may not be desirable. Parents of the target child often miss this dimension of their child's school experience and need to be informed of how they can foster desirable friendship clusters formed at school and minimize contact with youngsters in the least desirable clusters.

Note whether the school of a target child is desegregated, meaning that minority group children are in attendance, or is an integrated setting, meaning that all children have full access to the school's activities. For example, do children have the option to participate in before- and after-school clubs and organizations? This is a vital part of having full access to a school and suggests that all aspects of the school are integrated. When children live great distances from school, it becomes difficult to invite friends or to participate in a variety of activities without the cooperation of parents who may have to provide the necessary transportation to facilitate these friendships and activities. And yet, friends made at school can aid in the adjustment process, especially if a child is being bused a distance to school. Parents need to be made aware of the importance of a child having school and home community friends and the role that the parents play in facilitating these relationships.

Another point that can be shared with Afro-American parents, especially if both parents are working, is that they should inquire as to whether the school has or is willing to establish a foster family program. In this program, families of children of comparable ages or grades who live a great distance from the school are paired with families who live nearby. The families get to know one another and if a child becomes ill or has an emergency, the child has the option to call the foster family, who can often take responsibility for picking up the youngster or providing necessary parental supervision until the child's biological parents can take over. This program can be adopted not only by schools that bus youngsters, but by any school where parents are working and have difficulty leaving their work immediately to attend to the emergency of a child. These are the kinds of programs which can make adjustment for a youngster easier.

Information about the method of transportation, be it on foot, in a car pool, or by bus, provides information that can contribute to socialization problems in school. For the child who walks, passing through certain neighborhoods or walking on certain streets enroute to school can present physical threats if those neighborhood children are unfriendly. When a child refuses to go to school alone, parents and mental health professionals often fail to appreciate how it feels to be chased several blocks to or from school. Though this example may not be the case for all children, it is important to obtain the child's perception of the walk and the problems that are foreseen. Parents may need to walk that route on an unscheduled basis to observe the kinds of interactions that do take place and to be able to get a realistic assessment of some of the difficulties that their children experience when walking alone to school.

Children in a car pool are rarely selected to travel together because of their friendship networks or common interests. It is the parents who organize car pools, based upon their geographic proximity to each other and the shared desire to deliver their children to one destination. They arrange the entire system to fit their schedules, and seldom consider the personalities and needs of the children involved. Often there are children who have a great deal of difficulty getting along with others under these circumstances. Parents may observe constant fighting, teasing or bickering between children, in amazement, as if they were all expected to be friends. An assessment of the number of children in the car pool, the age range, length of ride and space in the car can help to explain why some children arrive at their destinations ready to fight, crying, or withdrawn, while others arrive smiling and eager to maintain their car pool friendships throughout the day.

Parents should be advised to listen to the interactions that take place during the drive. Children's conversations can often serve to gauge how others perceive and accept the target child, and the behaviors that may be resulting in problems at home or at school.

Some children resent having to share their parent with other children during an auto ride. This is frequently the only time when children can talk to parents on a one-to-one basis during the day, and the competition of the car pool crowd may be too much of a threat. Consequently, children having these feelings may constantly complain about other children or may act out in ways to initiate subtle conflicts between other children, in an attempt to increase the likelihood of their expulsion from the car pool. A therapist needs to interview both the child and parent separately to coordinate the perceptions of the car pool problem should this be the case.

Another dimension to consider in evaluating the target child's ability to adjust to the socialization group in a car pool is to assess if the minority group child is accepted or rejected in spite or because of ethnic group, dialect or other experiential differences. Afro-American children who live in suburban areas where there are limited numbers of families of their ethnic origin are often reminded of skin color or hair texture differences on a daily basis. These comments, though sometimes made in an innocent way, tend to have a cumulative effect upon a child's positive sense of self. Without supportive intervention from parents, teachers, or other ancillary adults, a child's minority status can be perceived as a negative attribute and can influence self- and family acceptance.

For the child who is bused, the experience can range from an extremely pleasant one, to a tense preamble to a long day at school. Of course, the length of the ride must be evaluated as it impacts each individual child. For some, the ride provides a time to listen to music and quietly socialize as well as to read, sleep, or do homework. For others, it can be chaotic and disruptive, providing too much sensory and visual stimulation before school and before homework must be completed. However, the other children who ride the bus should be viewed as another constituted peer group. The role that the child assumes with this group should be evaluated: do they "play the dozens," and does the target child end up being laughed at? Is the target child a clown or comic, often hanging from windows, throwing objects or fighting while eluding the controlling eye of the bus driver? The child may be the one by which no one wants to sit because of hygiene (some children have body odors, and particularly so after a long day); social reasons (they don't know how to "play the dozens" or they are shy or unpopular); or behavioral problems (they can't keep their hands to themselves and get other children in trouble as well). All of these factors contribute to or detract from the child's readiness to learn and to do homework upon returning from school.

Inquire about the rules of conduct for bused or out-of-district children and compare them with those children living in the district. Many schools have very strict disciplinary procedures for out-of-district children regarding theft, substance abuse, aggressive behavior, and underachievement that are much stricter than for children living in the district. If the target child has some of these problems, attendance at that particular school may be short and, in essence, an invitation to rejection and to being transferred to any school that will accept them. For example, in some California schools where minority children are bused, becoming involved in a fight or being caught with drugs constitutes an immediate expulsion with no second chance. Many times administrators of these schools have little tolerance to retain a youngster at school who is receiving psychotherapy but who still demonstrates some of these problems. They often prefer to return the child to their community school or to transfer the child to a less academically oriented school as a punishment for inappropriate or antisocial behavior. This policy is often different for within-district children, who sometimes experience the same problems and can be to have if they are attending a school with such a philosophy, and likelihood of such behaviors reoccurring. Some administrators feel that, because many minority parents would like their children to attend a school out of the district, if a child cannot abide by the school rules, they can be quickly replaced with another minority child that can. This system narrows the range of problems that an Afro-American child can "afford" to have if they are attending a school with such a philosophy, and reinforces the expectation that Afro-American children "must be better than the best" to attend that school. Needless to say, this may not be the best school for the target child with problems that a school is unwilling to try to manage.

SUMMARY

Home and school visits are particularly useful sources of information when there are aspects of the child or adolescent's presenting problems that are difficult to evaluate because of cultural, economic, or experiential factors relating to the overall life-style of the patient or specifically to the presenting problems. While information derived from home and school visits is useful in the psychiatric evaluation and treatment of any one of school age, and often for adults, professional time spent and transportation expenses frequently outweight their advantages. Consequently, careful consideration should be made as to if and when these visits are necessary and by whom they should be made. This chapter is not intended to suggest that home and school visits should be made for all Afro-American children being evaluated or treated in a psychiatric setting. However, there are some special issues related to their ethnicity, socioeconomic, and cultural background which should not be overlooked as important to the evaluation and treatment process, and which frequently cannot be adequately evaluated in a clinic setting. The time taken to observe the bicultural, bidialectical and sometimes dual value system of Afro-American children and adolescents, and the pressure that is brought to bear upon these children as they interface with their own subculture and that of the larger society, is often time well spent. This exposure places the therapist in the patient's shoes, facilitating the therapist's perceptions of the patient's point of view.

There is increasing recognition of sociocultural factors as a dimension in training programs for behavioral scientists that deserve more attention and study, particularly if mental health professionals are to consider themselves qualified to treat the so-called 'underserved groups,' i.e., children, adolescents, women, minority group people, the aged, and the poor. Training programs will have to carefully outline the didactic courses and experiential training that will constitute a training program specializing in the assessment and treatment of Afro-American children and families. Evaluating a family in a clinic setting is one necessary skill, but translating clinical skills into the community as part of the evaluation process and identifying how a child's sociocultural, language and economic background impacts upon their cognitive, social and emotional adjustment is quite another skill which too few professionals have refined. Making appropriate use of information gathered from visits to the home and school of the target patient should be considered as one of the necessary skills that professionals should be trained to demonstrate. However, we cannot afford to train only the small number of professionals specializing in treating those who historically have failed to receive equitable mental health service, to utilize these skills in their evaluation and treatment of Afro-American children and families. These are skills that should be required of any mental health professional, regardless of their area of specialization.

REFERENCES

1. Bloom ML: Usefulness of the home visit for diagnosis and treatment. Soc Casework 54:67–75, 1973
2. Chappel JN, Daniels RS: Home visiting in a black urban ghetto. Amer J Psychiat 126:99–104, 1970
3. Freeman RD: The home visit in child psychiatry: Its usefulness in diagnosis and training. Amer Academy Child Psychiat 6:276–294, 1967
4. Golner JH: Home family counseling. Soc Work 7:63–71, 1971
5. Brown BS: Home visiting by psychiatrists. Arch Gen Psychiat 7:98–107, 1962
6. Behrens MI: Brief home visits by the clinic therapist in the treatment of lower-class patients. Amer J Psychiat 124:127–131, 1967
7. Swartz D, Waldron R, Tidd, CW: Use of home visits for psychiatric evaluation: Clinical and teaching aspects. Arch Gen Psychiat 3:57–65, 1960
8. Mayo JA: The significance of sociocultural variables in the psychiatric treatment of black outpatients. Comp Psychiatr 15:471–482, 1974
9. Langner TS, Gersten J, Greene EL, et al: Treatment of psychology disorders among urban children. Consult Clin Psychology 42:170–179, 1974
10. Bloombaum M, Yamamoto J, James, Q: Cultural stereotyping among psychotherapists. J Consulting Clin Psychol 32:894–900, 1968
11. Wyatt G, Bass B, Powell G: A cognitive and affective assessment of mental health professionals' attitudes toward Afro-Americans. Grune & Stratton (in press)
12. Powell G, Fuller, M: The variables for positive self-concept in southern black adolescents. J Med Assoc 64:522–526, 1972

PART III

Psychotherapeutic Treatment Strategies and Issues

EDITORS' INTRODUCTION

Part III is comprised of seven chapters and begins with a review of the epidemiology of mental health of Afro-Americans in "Overview of Epidemiology of Mental Health Among Afro-Americans" by Gloria J. Powell. Barbara Bryant Solomon in "The Delivery of Mental Health Services to Afro-Americans and Their Families: Translating Theory into Practice" discusses inequities in the delivery of mental health services and describes aspects of the Afro-American culture that are frequently interpreted as pathological. Case studies are provided which include issues that arise in therapy for specific individuals, and Dr. Solomon evaluates and critiques the effectiveness of the therapist in identifying and adequately dealing with those issues in the therapeutic relationship.

We are most privileged to include the chapter, "Transference and Countertransference in Interracial Psychotherapy," which is a dialogue between two prominent psychoanalysts, Drs. Ralph Greenson (deceased) and Ellis Toney. In the dialogue, the two analysts (one white and one black), discuss their cultural differences that both interfered with and enhanced their therapeutic relationship.

The remaining four chapters discuss specific therapeutic and research strategies that can be used within the cultural context of Afro-American life. They are: "The Role of Religion in Psychotherapy with Afro-Americans" by Helen Mendes; "Improving Intervention Strategies with Adolescents" by Yvonne Ferguson; "Suicide from a 'Black Reality' Perspective" by Lewis King; and "Socio-Cultural Factors in Child Abuse" by Kayvonne Wright.

Gloria Johnson Powell

9

Overview of the Epidemiology of Mental Illness Among Afro-Americans

Within the constructs of this book, the subject of this chapter will be presented in a limited scope, focusing on well-known epidemiology studies that have included Afro-American subjects with any semblance of methodological soundness. Although inadequate methodology plagues most such studies, the problems in methodology, definition, criteria, and clinical practice will be addressed to elucidate the problem of determining incidence and prevalence of mental disorder among Afro-Americans. However, before we begin to discuss the technical problems of epidemiology, some sage references must be made about the observations of anthropologists regarding culture and mental disorder.

CULTURE, SOCIETY, THE INDIVIDUAL, AND MENTAL DISORDER

In selecting to talk about culture and normality, Linton begins by delineating the nature of culture. He aptly begins by reminding us that each society has its own culture. Society, on the one hand, is "an organized group of individuals;" culture, on the other hand, is "an organized group of ideas, habits, and conditional emotional responses shared by the members of a society."[1] Individuals participate in their society's culture to the degree that their participation is necessitated by their social roles. Within each culture there is a set of ideas, values, and behavioral norms which all members must eventually learn.

Linton divides the culture of any homogeneous society into three categories. First are the universals, which are the ideas, habits, and conditional emotional responses which are the same for all sane adult members. The second set of elements are called specialties which are shared by certain members of special categories. Alternatives represent different reactions to the same situations, or they may be different ways of achieving the same ends. Finally, individual peculiarities comprise the fourth category, consisting of habits, ideas, and conditioned emotional responses. Thus, individuals are shaped by their culture, and it is shaped by them. These concepts should be understood by the therapist who will be treating people of different cultural and ethnic backgrounds. The cultural context and backdrop against which the behavior is seen is crucial to understanding what is happening to that person.

Opler, in discussing the relationship of epidemiology and etiology in the study of mental illness, has observed that when western studies of epidemiology are reviewed critically, "the lack of articulation and significant connection between clinical studies on the one hand and sociocultural studies on the other" were particularly notable.[2] According to Opler, then, the effect of the sociocultural environment upon personality development must form the basis of the epidemiological end product. Yet as Diethelm noted, we have known that ethnic influences are important in psychopathology, yet they have never been studied.[3] Cultural attitudes have affected sexual life, and religion has played a role in suicide, but the interrelatedness of the sociocultural variables have been difficult to grasp in a technical scientific way.

THE SOCIOLOGY OF MENTAL DISORDERS

As the field of social psychiatry began to wane, and with it the anthropological influences that had helped to sustain it, psychiatric sociology or the sociology of mental disorders gained eminence. Weinberg defines psychiatric sociology as the study of mental disorders as social phenomena, e.g., social factors and social processes that contribute to mental disorders as forms of social deviance, the social facets of the treatment and care of disordered persons, and the social aspects of the prevention of mental disorders.[4] The proponents of this viewpoint consider the distribution of mental disorders in the socioeconomic structure as a step towards determining the relevant social indicators that may casually affect these disorders. Thus, in turn the social stresses affecting mental disorders can be investigated. The union of sociology and psychiatry has been helpful in moving the field of epidemiology of mental illness towards more clarity and definition.

AN URBAN STRESS MODEL

Myers, in an attempt to propose a model for understanding the relationship between stress factors and mental health of Afro-Americans, has created a useful pardigm. The paradigm is based on four parts, the first of which is "the antecendent stress state." In this state the level of stress operating is normal for the individual or group. The antecendent mediating factors are the factors outside and within the self that relieve or perpetuate the impact of the stressful factors on a person's life. Thirdly, the objective stressful social events are those that require adaptation in the usual level of performance. The coping process then is the complex physiological, cognitive, and affective response processes used to cope with the stressors. With several layers of stress the body's physiological processes become strained. Myers' model of urban stress takes into account (1) the greater the amount, intensity, and duration of the stress, the greater the chances of illness and a severe disorder, (2) the factors of social class and race increase the amount and severity of the impact of the stress, (3) the final outcome of the stress will be influenced by the person's social class and ethnic background, and (4) an individual's state of health is predicted on the basis of race and social stress dynamics.[5]

It is well known that individuals from low-income classes experience more stress in their lives and that such events are more disruptive for them than for the affluent.[6–8] The urgency is heard by King, who sees a significantly greater prevalence of serious psychiatric disdorders among the poor.

> Yet, while we have become aware of a mental illness trend among this group, we have sought to explain it from the perspective of "victim blaming." We explain the greater frequency of mental illness in the lower class, particularly the Afro-American poor, as a function of a downward drift of the weaker of the species who select the less competitive arena of society in which to function.[9]

Kramer, Rosen, and Willis come to the heart of the matter by stating forthrightly that the very fact that more Afro-Americans than whites are poor means that a higher proportion of Afro-Americans will be subject to those stresses which accompany poverty.[10] Indeed, racism has played a major part in beginning the conditions as well as the environments in which such stresses proliferate.

However, the data at hand on mental disorders among Afro-Americans is very problematic. As Kramer et al. note, there has never been any consistency in which studies have been reported by race.[10] This is only one of the major problems.

MENTAL HEALTH CONCEPTS BETWEEN AFRO-AMERICANS AND WHITES: A BRIEF REVIEW

In 1959, Crawford, Rollins, and Sutherland summarized the findings from several studies comparing mental illnesses among Afro-American and whites.[11] The findings included the following:

1. Northern Afro-Americans had higher incidences of mental illnesses than whites.
2. Reported admissions to state mental hospitals of Afro-Americans were at a higher rate than that for whites.
3. Afro-Americans received a lower quality of care while under treatment than white patients.
4. Proportionately fewer Afro-Americans were released from state mental hospitals than whites.
5. Once released, Afro-Americans remained in their communities at a higher rate than did whites.

In 1963 Pasamanick concluded that findings from community surveys, state, private, and VA hospitals showed nonwhites had higher rates for acute brain syndrome and mental deficiency, but that whites had higher rates for psychoses, psychoneuroses, and the psychophysiologic-visceral disorders.

In 1962 reports from the Monroe County case register showed an unadjusted prevalence rate of 7.38 per 1000 for nonwhites and 8.50 for whites.[13] The incidence rates for nonwhites was 10.17 compared to 8.46 for whites. However, Monroe County has a very small proportion of nonwhite citizens. There were only 185 nonwhites under care and 255 admissions, while there were 4773 whites under care and 4748 new cases. Thus, Crawford concluded that differences in diagnostic concepts, and interpretations in the population studied, the location, and research techniques "negate many valid comparisons and conclusions from study to study." Crawford also concluded that "adjusted incidence and prevalence rates of mental illness between Afro-Americans and whites are more similiar than different" and that Afro-American patients are proportionately more heavily concentrated among those who receive only limited care.[13] In short, as late as 1964 inequality in the kind and quantity of mental services still existed between Afro-Americans and whites.

One of the major mistakes made in the assessment of Afro-Americans' mental health status are such statements as made by Pasamanick in 1963 that "since the Negro population, relative to the white, is overwhelmingly lower class, it follows that non-whites will be proportionately over-institutionalized."[12] Afro-Americans are not a homogeneous group and the range of differences are as diverse as those found among whites.

In setting out to examine social status and psychological disorders, Dohrenwend and Dohrenwend begin by looking at the question of etiology, i.e., the role of poor heredity and the role of unfavorable etiology. In examing social status, they found that although it is easy to determine age and sex, the basic assignments to ethnic and class statuses were more complex.[7] The differences in the two variables determine differences in status situation and psychological disorder. Finally, it also has been assumed that the rate of untreated as well as the rate of treated psychological disorders in the general population would determine how social status is related to psychological disorders.

In a summary of the data on the frequency and severity of stress situations among social classes and races, the following findings were elicited:

1. That the evidence is inconsistent and does not clearly show that the rate of exposure to stressors varies with class.
2. Afro-Americans are exposed to a higher rate of stress than whites of their same class.
3. Internal mediating factors would also seem to indicate that lower class people are at a disadvantage compared to middle class whites.

The fourth level of analyses, however, showed that those of low socio-economic status (SES) are disadvantaged compared to middle SES; middle SES Afro-Americans are definitely disadvantaged compared to lower SES whites. Dohrenwend and Dohrenwend conclude:

> Thus the evidence for Afro-Americans as against whites seems to support our proposition concerning the experience of stress situations in disadvantaged and advantaged ethnic groups within the same socio-economic stratum, indicating that both the frequency and the severity of stress situations are greater for Afro-Americans than for white class counterparts.[7,p.149]

COMMUNITY SURVEYS OF MENTAL DISORDERS

The data reported in such studies cannot be compared because of the differences in the underlying purposes of the surveys. A review of a number of prevalence studies carried out in the United States between

1916 and 1952 specifically comparing Afro-Americans and whites found that there were no consistent differences between Afro-Americans and whites in the direction of rates.[7] Out of the seven studies, however, three studies showed that the rates for Afro-Americans were higher. In four studies the whites' rates were higher.[10]

Kramer et al. looked at the effect of racism on the composition of noninstitutional populations. For instance, the higher institutional rate for nonwhites in Baltimore was the result of the lower nonwhite noninstitutional rates.[10] At all levels of investigation one resounding theme rings out clearly, and that is that racist practices affect the composition and characteristics of the noninstitutional to the institutional setting at disproportionate rates.

In terms of an analysis of the patterns of use of psychiatric facilities, it is not possible to estimate the extent to which racism by itself accounts for differences between the races in patterns of use of services, because for many years the state hospital was the primary and only source for care and treatment.

In a review of six studies done between 1949 to 1964, the data were not reported in sufficient detail in each study so that a rate could be determined for a psychoses.[10] Separate rates for schizophrenia were reported showing higher rates for nonwhites in four of the six studies. Among the females the rates were higher for nonwhites in five of the six studies. Although it is well known that differences in incidence of mental disorders were dependent on local practices and racial prejudices, Kramer et al. point out that:

> "In addition, we are dealing with another variable that up to now has not been mentioned, namely, the consistency with which psychiatrists apply uniform criteria in determining presence or absence of mental disorders among Blacks, whites, and members of other minority groups and arriving at a diagnosis of schizophrenia, affective disorders, organic psychosis, neuroses, or personality disorder in persons of different racial origin."[10,p.393]

It is interesting to note that in 1969 close to one out of every one hundred nonwhite women between 35 to 45 years of age was admitted to either a public mental hospital or an outpatient psychiatric clinic with a diagnosis of schizophrenia. The racism glares through.

EPIDEMIOLOGY OF MENTAL DISORDERS: CLARITY OR MORE CONFUSION?

There have been a significant number of studies which have attempted to show a relationship between race and mental health. Thus far, the evidence weighs in the balance of there being significant differences between Afro-Americans and whites.[14] There are, however, still differences of opinion as to which group has the higher rates. It has been concluded that few definitive epidemiological patterns can be found. Indeed, the ambiguity is still reflected in current studies.[15] No recent research has determined true prevalence or incidence, and thus the question remains largely unanswered.

Many of the epidemiology studies have been extensively reviewed by Kramer, Rosen, and Willis[10] as well as by Warheit, Holzer, and Arey.[14]

The argument now advanced is that "the important research question centers on the balance between universal and cultural considerations in dealing with the mental health problems of Afro-Americans."[14] The real focus should be on cultural comparisons, for the mental health status of Afro-Americans consist of the following: in 1970 the rates of institutionalized Afro-Americans was 1412.7 per 100,00 population and 1004.3 for whites.[14] Included among the types of institutions were correctional institutions, mental hospitals, residential treatment centers, tuberculosis hospitals, chronic disease hospitals, homes for the aged, schools for the mentally handicapped, training schools for juvenile delinquents, detention homes, and homes for dependent and neglected children.

A review of the data from the President's Commission on Mental Health: Subpanel on Afro-Americans reveals the following:

1. Afro-American males show the highest rate of mental disorders, with the highest rates being for Afro-American males aged 18–34.
2. The treatment rates of Afro-American females is low until age 35, when their rates go up significantly.
3. Afro-Americans are admitted, committed, or sentenced for custodial care in mental institutions more often than whites.
4. Afro-American admissions to mental institutions are less likely to be voluntary, but Afro-Americans are less likely to be committed to mental institutions by a spouse or offspring.
5. The number of bed disability days per person is lower for whites than for Afro-Americans. For adults over 65, the number is twice as high for Afro-Americans as it is for whites.
6. Afro-Americans are twice as likely to be in mental institutions as whites, and twice as likely to suffer fatal consequences from psychoses and neuroses.
7. For Afro-Americans in mental health agencies, diagnoses are less accurate and disposition is more nonspecific.
8. Afro-Americans are more likely to be seen for diagnostic purposes and less likely to be selected for insight oriented therapy than whites.
9. Data show that mental illness is more prevalent among adults than young people.[14,p.102]

Myers, however, notes that there has been a recent increase in the use of psychiatric services for children under 18 years.[5] Shiloh and Selavan report the hospitalization rates for nonwhite males in New York City to be five times that of white males.[15]

Some significant recommendations, suggestions, and new ideologies emerged from the Subpanel on Afro-American Issues for the President's Commission on Mental Health. Thomas and Comer forcefully concluded for the group that the mental health of Afro-Americans must be conceived within the context of "the total cultural and societal system." The concept of mental health of Afro-Americans includes people's feelings of worth in the context of the total cultural and societal system as well as within the identifiable group to which they belong. Mental health encompasses the issue of the availability of the good life within a given social, political, and economic context . . . "the state of being mentally happy represents the possession of the ability to cope or function within society in an adaptive way."[14,p.99]

However, the statistics presented in the PCMH Report indicate that the status of Afro-Americans in relation to the institutions of health, education, and employment may be viewed as (1) indicators of the pervasiveness of institutional discrimination and (2) indicators of stressful life conditions which have long been recognized as major contributions to a variety of physical and mental illnesses.[14]

The most important recommendation arising out of the Subpanel's reports was that training programs be designed to help therapists develop the sensitivity to and understanding of these sociocultural issues as well as the manifestations and effects of racism on their patients. Secondly, the training received must then be a "backdrop" for the development of service delivery models. Only by such strategies can we establish the basic structure for the content and process of the various psychotherapies used with Afro-American patients.

REFERENCES

1. Linton R: Culture and Mental Illness. Springfield, IL, Charles C. Thomas, 1956, p. 4
2. Opler MK: Culture and Social Psychiatry. New York, Atherton Press, 1967
3. Diethelm O: Vide (Report of the Payne Whitney Psychiatric Clinic). New York Hospital, 1953, pp.11–12
4. Weinberg SK (Ed): The Sociology of Mental Disorders: Analysis and Readings in Psychiatric Sociology. Chicago, Aldine Publishing, 1967
5. Myers HF, King LM: Youth of the black underclass: Urban stress and mental health. Fanton Center J. 1:1–27, 1980
6. Srole L, Langner TS, Michael ST, et al: Mental Health in the Metropolitan: The Midtown Study No. 1. New York, McGraw-Hill, 1962

7. Dohrenwend BP, Dohrenwend BS: Social Status and Psychological Disorder: A Casual Inquiry. New York, Wiley-Interscience, 1969
8. Brown GW, Bhrolchain M, Harris T: Social class and psychiatric disturbance among women in an urban population. Sociology, 9:225–54, 1975
9. King L: The Future of Mental Health Research on the Black Population: Moves Toward a Creative Mental Health Model Part II. Fanon Research and Development Center Research Bulletin 1:1, 1980
10. Kramer M, Rosen M, Willis EM: Definition and distribution of mental disorders in a racist society, in Willie CV, Kramer BM, Brown BS (Eds): Racism and Mental Health. Pittsburgh, University of Pittsburgh, 1973
11. Crawford FR, Rollins GW, Sutherland RL: Variations between Negroes and whites in concepts of mental illness and its treatment. Annals NY Acad Sci 84:918–937, 1960
12. Pasamick B: A survey of mental disease in an urban population, in Grossock MM (Ed): Mental Health and Segregation. New York, Springer, 1963
13. Crawford FR: Variations between Negroes and whites in concepts of mental illness, its treatment and prevalence, in Peog SC, Edgerton RB (Eds): Changing Perspectives in Mental Illness. New York, Holt, Rinehart, and Winston, 1969
14. Task Panel Reports on the President's Commission of Mental Health: Reports of Special Populations Subpanel on Mental Health of Black Americans, vol III Appendix. Washington, D.C., U.S. Government Printing Office, 1978
15. Shiloh A, Selovan IC (Eds): Ethnic Groups in America: Their Morbidity, Mortality, and Behavior Disorders, Vol II of The Black Illnesses. Springfield, IL, Charles C. Thomas, 1974

Barbara Bryant Solomon

10

The Delivery of Mental Health Services to Afro-American Individuals and Families: Translating Theory into Practice

The author has described the United States as an ethnosystem: a collection of interdependent ethnic groups, each defined by unique historical and cultural ties but bound together by a common political system.[1] The white-American majority has sought to absorb most of these groups into its cultural sphere. This ethnocentrism was reflected in the mental health literature prior to the 1960s, a period during which the mental health professions were incredibly silent about the application of theories of practice to Afro-Americans experiencing mental health problems. In the past decade, however, this silence has finally been broken as a host of Afro-American and white-American scholars have called for interventive strategies that are nonracist, nonoppressive and more sensitive to Afro-American cultural values and lifestyles.

The behavioral science foundations of the core mental health professions are, unsurprisingly, similar in content. Psychiatrists, social workers, clinical psychologists, and psychiatric nurses have all been exposed in their professional training to Freudian psychoanalytic theory, learning theories, humanistic psychology, ego-psychology, etc. The theories of practice which have utilized one or more of these theories of behavior are also familiar to each discipline, e.g., psychoanalysis, behavior modification, Gestalt therapy, Transactional Analysis, and social casework. These practice strategies have met with varying degrees of success. Nowhere have they been more intensely criticized than within Afro-American communities. Consequently, mental health services are under-utilized by Afro-Americans.[2–4] Even when Afro-Americans have entered the mental health system, they have tended to be treated less often as outpatients, more often with drugs, less often with one-to-one modalities, and have dropped out earlier in the treatment process.[2,5,6]

It is the thesis of this chapter that our theories of human behavior and our theories of practice both have failed to take into consideration crucial variables that are relevant for Afro-American people. What is required are not new theories, but additional explanatory concepts which take into account the Afro-American experience in this society. These variables are primarily those that link microsystems and macrosystems, e.g., that link individual personality systems and organizational systems. The negative effects of complex social systems of Afro-Americans and other negatively valued groups in the ethnosystem has meant that their interaction is a more critical factor in the etiology and treatment of their mental health problems than in that of the white majority.

Ullman has suggested that power may be the key concept linking microsystem and macrosystem processes.[7] In fact, many people generally described as mentally ill may be perceived as persons deprived of adequate social solutions to the problem of individual growth and development. For those experiencing negative valuation from the wider society to an intense degree, powerlessness is a more virulent stressor than anxiety. Consequently, empowerment becomes a more important treatment goal than reduction of anxiety.

The following discussion will identify the basic assumptions which provide a framework for incorporating this added dimension into existing theoretical approaches to treatment. This will be followed by consideration of the impact of these assumptions on specific aspects of assessment and treatment: (1) etiology of problem behavior; (2) assessment of problem situations; (3) establishing treatment relationships; and (4) implementing treatment strategies.

BASIC ASSUMPTIONS

In our efforts to resolve or ameliorate the mental health problems of Afro-Americans and their families, the following assumptions provide a framework for assessment and treatment.

Afro-American people represent a stigmatized group in the ethnosystem. They are negatively valued. As a result they are subject to feelings of low self-esteem and powerlessness.

Self-esteem is not determined by forces inherent within the individual. It is dependent upon support and reinforcement from the external environment. Thus self-esteem is a function of the judgments of others who are often imbued with the prejudices and stereotypes which characterize a racist society. Afro-Americans learn that their ancestors in this country were slaves who were considered little better than domestic animals. Although slavery has been abolished, Afro-Americans still experience deficits in opportunities and resources that are not based on any individual attributes but on their membership in the stigmatized group. Colemen observed:

> . . . the phrase, freedom of social action, expresses the essential attribute of which the Negro, as a Negro, has been deprived in American society . . . It consists of all those constraints and strictures placed on the individual's action because his skin color categorizes him as a Negro: the lack of freedom to associate with whom he wants, the unavailability of certain jobs, the impossibility of joining certain clubs or organizations or of being served at certain places of business, discrimination of housing, and the enforced payment of deference by blacks to whites . . . Some of these deficits in freedom of action, or in civil rights, have been reduced in recent years, but many . . . remain.[8,p.7]

The fact that some deficits have been reduced does not mean that Afro-Americans will perceive themselves as correspondingly less negatively valued. On the contrary, the societal response to efforts to remove deficits in the lives of Afro-Americans, e.g., busing to achieve school integration, affirmative action programs in higher education and business, etc., have generated sometimes violent protest with racist overtones.

Assessment of the mental health problems of Afro-Americans should include exploration of relationships in the wider ethnosystem in order to determine the extent of exposure to negative valuation based on membership in the stigmatized group.

Not every Afro-American has had the same experience of negative valuation based on membership in the group. However, the more intense the experience, the more intense the feelings of powerlessness. There are some individuals or families whose exposure to negative valuations have been so intense that they accept these valuations as "right," or at least as inevitable, and therefore make no effort whatsoever to exert power. Power has been defined as "the ability to manage emotions, skills, knowledge, and/or material resources in a way that effective performance of valued social roles will lead to personal gratification."[1,p.16] Not all Afro-Americans are powerless. Many have been cushioned from the effects of negative valuations in the wider ethnosystem by strong family or group relationships. Therefore, an assessment of relationships between the person and the wider ethnosystem should not reinforce stereotyping by assuming low self-esteem and powerlessness, but should rather actually explore alternative sources when low self-esteem and powerlessness are observed.

Afro-Americans simultaneously share some characteristics with all other groups in the ethnosystem, some with certain other groups and some with no other groups at all.

Afro-American people like all others, are nourished in a prenatal environment before birth, develop both personal and social identities, learn to perform multiple social roles, and must face at some point the inevitability of death. Clearly, Afro-Americans experience the same risks and consequences of idiosyncratic family interactions as do others in the society. On the other hand, there are some experiences that they share with certain groups—usually stigmatized and negatively valued minorities like themselves—but not with members of the white majority. The experience of negative valuation is a common experience not only of Afro-Americans, but of Hispanics, Native Americans, and Asian Americans. Finally, however, Afro-Americans have their own unique experiences. No other group was brought to this country as slaves and had their ties to their original cultural roots so thoroughly broken. No other group experienced a massive migration from rural south, to urban north and east in less than a generation.

Given this simultaneous relatedness of Afro-Americans to all others in the ethnosystem, to some others, and to none at all, it is logical to assume that this is reflected in their mental health problems. Hence, there are problems experienced by Afro-Americans which are the same as those occurring in all groups in our society—depression, schizophrenia, adjustment reactions to illness, etc. The source of these problems may not be identical. Feelings of low self-esteem and powerlessness may play a greater etiological role with Afro-Americans than with whites experiencing the same problems, but more or less the same role with Hispanics or Native Americans experiencing the same problems. Some problems may be unique to Afro-Americans, such as dysfunctional male–female relationships created by a combination of the slavery experience, subsequent employment practices in the economic system, the ratio of Afro-American men to women, and the contemporary feminist movement. It follows that mental health services to Afro-American individuals and families must in many ways be no different from mental health services to anyone else; in other ways, these services must be similar to those provided to others who share minority group status; and finally, they must incorporate some additional features which address the uniqueness of the black experience.

Traditional models of mental health service delivery have not been sensitive to values, norms, beliefs, and attitudes of Afro-American people.

The primary basis of this assumption is the historical absence of attention to the mental health problems of Afro-Americans along with an absence of practitioners either of that ethnic origin, or having any significant exposure to Afro-American culture and lifestyles. Almost all mention of Afro-Americans in the early years of the mental health movement was found in statistics describing their presence in mental institutions.[9–12] This would lead one to believe that formal entry into the mental health system during its early history—for Afro-Americans as well as others—was at the point when one had "lost one's mind" or "gone crazy." Later, however, the mental health movement developed to include a wide range of out-patient as well as in-patient services, utilizing the medical model to generate large numbers of private practitioners with high fees. Neither the practitioners nor their patients were likely to be black. More important, theories of psychopathology and theories of practice were based on an experience that was almost exclusively white in its orientation.

Yet, there is considerable evidence that the stressful conditions under which disproportionately large numbers of Afro-Americans and other minorities live create emotional problems which may impair social relationships and reduce the capacity for effective social functioning. If services were available which demonstrated recognition of the values, lifestyles and unique pressures inherent in the black experience, they would be utilized. This would be a dramatic change from present circumstances in which the majority of persons who come for help to mental health agencies in Afro-American communities have been sent by agents of social control.

ETIOLOGY OF PROBLEM BEHAVIOR

The mental health problems presented by Afro-Americans cannot be considered entirely unique. Lerner, describing a representative sample of clients of a community mental health center in a poor, black urban neighborhood, writes:

> These forty-five clients are much too heterogeneous for any facile generalizations about typical problems. They include a Black Muslim incapacitated by an illness that had no physical basis, a suicidal prostitute, a welfare mother who abused her children, an unwed pregnant teenager who was withdrawn and hallucinating, a man trying to pick up the pieces of his life after his tenth hospitalization, a women who had struggled free of a crushing financial burden to pursue her lifetime ambition and then found herself paralyzed by depression, a child molester fearful of the police, a graduate student unable to finish his dissertation, a school teacher

struggling to establish a satisfactory heterosexual relationship, a factory worker who felt the people on TV were ridiculing him and broadcasting his deficiencies, a man who realized his lifetime ambition and then found that his achievement made his life a misery, and so on.*

Although these problems are not unique to Afro-Americans, in many instances the dynamic factors that generate, exacerbate, and/or maintain them may be different for Afro-Americans than for others in the ethnosystem. For example, the white suicidal prostitute may have been subjected to "sex is dirty" training and is therefore both incapable of entering sexual relations without being degraded by the partner, and overwhelmed with guilt when it occurs. The Afro-American suicidal prostitute may share etiological factors with a white-American suicidal prostitute, but could also be responding to overwhelming feelings of powerlessness stemming from the negative valuation of Afro-American women in the larger society.[14]

Current notions regarding the etiology of antisocial personality disorders reflect clearly the need to include the added dimension of societal explanations when identifying sources of problem behavior. Antisocial personality disorders (also referred to as psychopathic personality disorders or character disorders) are frequently encountered in mental health settings which accept referrals from the courts, the police, or other agents of social control. The incidence of Afro-Americans or members of other negatively valued minority groups is disproportionately high among those with this diagnosis. It has been suggested that persons with this diagnosis fail to experience anxiety as well as learn from their mistakes, because their autonomic nervous systems are deficient.[15] Research studies exploring the abilities of persons with antisocial personality disorder have revealed that they do not learn conditioned avoidance responses easily, but do learn as well as other subjects under conditions of positive reinforcement. This means that behavior which most of us learn out of fear may not be readily acquired by the antisocial personality. Yet, for many Afro-Americans, reinforcements that are positive are less likely to come from the environment than are punishment or other negative feedback.

It is also not surprising that Afro-Americans in the mental health system are disproportionately diagnosed as schizophrenic. This has been attributed to a tendency on the part of mental health practitioners to focus upon the most dramatic, unusual, and striking behaviors; as a result Afro-

*From Lerner B: Therapy in the Ghetto: Political Impotence and Personal Disintegration. Copyright 1972 by The Johns Hopkins University Press. Used with permission of the publisher.

Americans appear more pathological than whites who show the same behavior.[2,16] Researchers and clinicians have amassed large amounts of data to describe schizophrenia and to support multiple theories regarding the etiology of this puzzling disorder. A recent summary of the current knowledge is illuminating:

> We believe that people who are labeled "schizophrenic" begin life with an inherited predisposition to develop the disorder; this predisposition takes the form of a biochemical abnormality ultimately capable of affecting the functioning of the central nervous system. When these people experience the normal stresses of life with which nonpredisposed persons deal adequately (if not always happily), they begin to emit what are called schizophrenic behaviors . . . *

This suggests that the higher incidence of schizophrenia among Afro-Americans may be related to some extent to the more stressful environments in which they live. Although the advent of the phenothiazines have made it possible to control schizophrenic behaviors to the point that institutionalization can be avoided, research does suggest that drugs and therapy together are sometimes more successful than either drugs or therapy alone.[18] When the dimension of environmental stress is added as an etiological factor in schizophrenia, it implies that the therapy offered might well focus on transactions between the individual and other social systems, rather than on the intrapsychic life of the individual.

Clearly, Afro-Americans may present the same problem behaviors as others in the ethnosystem; not only prostitution, schizophrenia, or antisocial behavior but depression, alcoholism, somatization disorders, and a host of others as well. However, this group's more stressful transactions with complex social systems beyond the family—school, welfare departments, police, financial institutions, etc.—may make a unique contribution to the development and reinforcement of these problem behaviors. This is not to propose that all Afro-Americans will inevitably have mental health problems. Although the experience of negative valuation may be inevitable, overwhelming feelings of powerlessness may be avoided if some combination of genetic endowment, strong family relationships and strong group relationships have provided the sense of self-worth and the ego strengths needed to achieve gratifying personal and social goals.

CLINICAL JUDGMENTS

The emphasis in the preceding section has been on the need to include the consequences of negative valuation from the wider society as an

*From Nathan PE, Harris S: Psychopathology and Society. Copyright 1980, McGraw-Hill. Used with the permission of McGraw-Hill Book Company.

etiological factor in assessing the mental health problems of Afro-Americans. However, even after the mental health practitioner has developed an expanded view of etiological factors, the task of assessment has barely commenced. The multiple etiological factors will need to be weighed to determine their relative contribution to the problem situation. In addition, other factors which may not have been etiological, but which may now serve to reinforce the problem behavior, will have to be identified. Finally, some determination will have to be made of what desirable changes in the problem situation can occur, and by what means available to the practitioner. Thus, clinical judgments must be exercised.

In order for these clinical judgments to be accurate, the practitioner will need some depth of understanding of culturally specific aspects of the variables to be assessed. This knowledge has not always been included in the curricula of the mental health disciplines. For example, content on the nature and consequences of socialization processes may not have incorporated information regarding how Afro-American families socialize their children to deal with their blackness and its negative valuation in the wider society. Content on functional and dysfunctional male–female relationships may have ignored the impact of history and current social movements on relationships between Afro-American men and women, including their handling of the psychosocial crises of identity and intimacy. Content on the dynamics of small groups may not have contained data on the functioning of formal and informal groups in Afro-American communities, and the extent to which they generate or ameliorate mental health problems. The following case studies demonstrate how clinical judgments can be impaired without this kind of knowledge.

Case Study 1: James C., an 18-year-old Afro-American, contacted the university counseling center after failing most of his first semester courses. He had matriculated to this predominantly white, northern university after graduating from high school in a large southern city. He had been an honor student in high school and was active in basketball and swimming as well as captain of the debating team. His mother and father were a teacher and lawyer, respectively, and had been very proud when their only son had received a four-year university scholarship. James attributes his scholastic difficulties to his increasing fears that he may be homosexual. In high school, he had been "too busy" to date much, and had had little real interest in girls. Since coming to the university, he had many opportunities to ask girls to social activities but just seemed unable to do so. At the same time, several times he had found himself responding sexually to male dormitory residents whom he encountered in the game room or in "bull sessions" in his room. Both the homosexual feelings and the guilt had been increasing lately and he had found it impossible to concentrate on his studies. He had decided that he needed some kind of psychotherapy to "get rid of what's bothering me."

A skilled therapist would not fall into the trap of making a premature diagnosis of "ego-dystonic homosexuality," and would probably explore with James his understanding of "maleness" and "femaleness" existing simultaneously in both men and women. However, a therapist who is not sensitive to the nuances of socialization to acceptable sex objects in Afro-American families, may miss something of importance in the etiology of James' problem. In this instance, James had actually received mixed messages in his formative years. As the son of educated, middle-class parents, he had been imbued with the fact that race should be an irrelevant factor in judging individuals and their worth. Individuals should be judged on their own merits and not on the color of their skins. On the other hand, James' mother had unconsciously conveyed to her son that black men would only choose a white woman if they were rejecting their blackness—and especially if they were rejecting their mothers! Upon arrival at the university, James had met very few Afro-American female students but had been the recipient of considerable attention from several female white students. The resulting anxiety that he was experiencing had been defended against successfully by avoiding women of either race. Sexual feelings had been directed toward "safe" males but not without great, psychic cost.

Homosexual feelings and homosexuality are common among men when contact with the opposite sex is limited for any reason.[19] In this instance, lack of access was a function of the ambivalent attitudes incorporated into James' socialization and the underlying unconscious conflict this socialization had produced.

Case Study 2: Linda S., a 30-year-old Afro-American registered nurse, sought help from a psychotherapist after the end of her second marriage. She stated that she needed to know what "unconscious motivation" had led her to marry men "with less ambition and lower social status than I have." Her own parents had owned a small neighborhood drug store and it had always been understood that she would go to college. Her parents had wanted her to be a doctor "but I knew I didn't have what it takes to go through the pressures of medical school." After graduating with a Bachelor's degree in nursing, she had married her high school boyfriend who had not gone to college but was working in his father's catering business. "I guess after you graduate from college, you feel you'd better get married soon or it will be too late." However, the marriage lasted only two years. "He had no ambition except to have a nice apartment, have a good time on Saturday night, and get no hassles from his Dad on the job!"

A year after her divorce, Linda married her second husband, who was working as a travel agent at the time. He was attractive and a good conversationalist, and they had seemed compatible. However, after their marriage, Linda found that he was uncomfortable with her college graduate friends since he did not have a college degree. He described her friends as "uppity" and refused to participate in their social activities. Despite problems, Linda stated that she had tried to make the marriage work for almost five years. During that time her husband had held numerous jobs after notable lack of success as a travel agent. He had been an insurance salesman for a black-owned insurance company, a used car salesman, and a security guard for a department store. When Linda decided that she wanted to return to school for a Master's degree in order to qualify for a job in nursing administration, her husband had responded with hostility. He accused her of being a "women's libber" instead of a wife. Their relationship had deteriorated until separation and divorce had seemed the only solution. Linda does not regret her decision but is fearful that she must have "some unconscious need to get involved with these losers."

Linda may be right about the influence of some "unconscious motivation" operating in her interpersonal relationships. On the other hand, any assessment of those relationships should include consideration of some reality factors: for example, the fact that there are fewer black males than females in the 15 to 44 age range, which covers the years most marriages occur. More importantly for Linda, there are proportionately even fewer college educated men than college education women in that age range and ethnic group. Therefore, regardless of any effects of unconscious motives, her chances of marrying a man of the same or higher educational level are considerably less than excellent. Furthermore, her own attitudes regarding appropriate male and female behavior in the marital role may need some examination to determine whether they may not be rooted in models functional in other parts of the ethnosystem, but not in her own. This latter concern is crucial to accurate clinical judgment. For example, the reality of fewer Afro-American men for Afro-American women may be observed and accepted by the therapist, but the only issue perceived by the client is whether the woman will or will not be able to find a *suitable* mate. However, to question the definition of a suitable mate, i.e., to question whether what is considered a suitable mate from the perspective of the dominant culture is really functional for some ethnic subgroups, requires another kind of judgment. It is clinical judgment from an Afro-American perspective rather than from a white perspective.

ESTABLISHING TREATMENT RELATIONSHIPS

The probability that Afro-Americans experiencing emotional problems will perceive mental health services as potentially effective in solving their problems is low, with some exceptions. Unless Afro-Americans are located in systems where "counseling" is promoted as a resource for dealing with emotional difficulties (e.g., on a university campus), they are likely to present themselves only as a consequence of pressure from some agent of social control (e.g., the schools or the courts). In order to design effective strategies for connecting Afro-Americans with emotional problems to help sources in the mental health system, the practitioner must understand how to convince them that mental health services are efficacious in problem situations like their own.

In establishing a therapeutic relationship, it is necessary to understand on what basis individuals will give you permission to be an influence in their lives. Urban, middle-class individuals usually relate to others out of what sociologists have called a "gesellschaft" orientation, i.e., one which looks at the individual's place in the hierarchy of social statuses and determines what is appropriate behavior in relation to that status or position. Middle-class individuals are therefore concerned about the position of the practitioner as defined by credentials which sanction the helping roles in their lives. It is important for the practitioner to have framed degree certificates visible; the title of "doctor" is important. The location and decorative appointment of the office are also important. On the other hand, lower class and rural persons are much more likely to relate to others out of a "gemeinschaft" orientation, which is highly personalistic. The sanction for the role is given on the basis of personal attributes. Such clients may well ask whether you are married, how many children you have, or other personal questions which seek to identify you, not as a therapist or a mental health practitioner, but as a person.

Considering the difference in orientation of middle class and urban perons in contrast to lower class and rural, the delivery of mental health services in low income, Afro-American communities ought to reflect more often the involvement of the personal rather than the more traditional professional self of the practitioners. Perhaps the interviewing room should not be modeled after those utilized in traditional social or mental health agency settings: a room with a desk, behind which the mental health practitioner sits, with a rather stiff chair immediately in front of the desk. A more culturally sensitive room might be one with windows to the street, a kitchen table, a stove with a pot of coffee on, or a refrigerator from which one could extract a couple of beers.

Establishing rapport between client and practitioner is an important requirement in the initial stages of the helping relationship. It is particularly difficult when it is attempted across ethnic group boundaries. Yet, in order to be effective, the practitioner should be able to demonstrate familiarity with the communication patterns, lifestyles and life experiences of Afro-American people. Draper has suggested ways in which such familiarity may be achieved by nonblack practitioners:

> . . . the white worker must try to enter the life space of the black client. He/she must listen to the expressions of black language, its sounds and meaning. Read black literature and newspapers. Listen to black radio stations to get with the tempo and temper of blacks' feelings. Leave the office and walk around in black neighborhoods—look at the parts that are slums, but also acknowledge the blocks that are kept with pride. Look at the addict and pimp but also see those who carry themselves with dignity. Look at the hustler but also see the shopkeeper, the dentist, the doctor. Go with the black client to the hospital and the social service agency. Notice the very real differences in the way services are often given to black and white clients. Really listen and observe, and you will readily see that in the use of language blacks touch and feel, hurt, cry and laugh. Most of all learn to individualize. There is infinite variety among blacks whether in the metropolis or the small town."[20,p.279]

The personalistic, familiar approach to Afro-Americans entering mental health treatment, with keen sensitivity to the in-group diversity, may counteract real obstacles to the establishment of transracial therapeutic relationships. Pinderhughes has observed that psychotherapy methods which encourage discussion of thoughts, feelings, and problems in an open manner with a white person could not easily bypass a lifetime of conditioning in the opposite direction.[21] Instead of recognizing the resistance as an artifact of the relationship, it is often used as a basis for assessing the incapacity of Afro-Americans to make use of counseling services, or as justification for not engaging them in a counseling process.

The tendency for many Afro-Americans—even those clearly suffering from severe psychopathology—to present complex, concrete problems such as financial stress, inadequate housing, serious physical illness or disability, etc., has resulted in many practitioners assessing them as incapable of dealing more effectively with their emotional problems. The pessimism of the practitioner is often transmitted to clients. Instead of "hanging-in" to work simultaneously on their concrete problems *and* their emotional problems, they do not return, and thus create another instance of a self-fulfilling prophecy.

IMPLEMENTING THE TREATMENT PROCESS

There is a sometimes bewildering array of "therapies" aimed at helping persons with psychosocial problems. However, there are common underlying goals, such as a greater ability to cope with everyday affairs, a greater awareness of what one is doing and of its significance and consequences, and a greater willingness to accept responsibility for one's own feelings and actions.[19] Among Afro-Americans there is a higher probability that deficiencies in these areas will be due to some extent from feelings of powerlessness induced by the negative valuation experienced in the ethnosystem. Thus, in order for therapy to be effective, these points should be taken into consideration. Although particular techniques will be "therapy-specific," they should be directed toward empowerment. Empowerment has been defined as a process whereby the individual is assisted in utilizing interpersonal relationships effectively to enhance self-esteem and to obtain basic social supplies, such as health care, employment, or financial assistance. This is achieved by: (1) helping clients to perceive themselves as causal agents in reaching solutions to their problem or problems; (2) helping clients to perceive the practitioner as having knowledge and skills which they can use; (3) helping clients to perceive the practitioner as a peer and a collaborator in the problem-solving effort; and finally, (4) helping clients to perceive opportunities to change the responses from the wider society.[1]

Particular theories of practice hold particular dangers when the client is Afro-American and experiencing powerlessness from systemic sources. For example, a psycho-dynamically-oriented therapist was treating a 50-year-old Afro-American man for a depressive disorder after the death of his wife. His feelings of abandonment and hopelessness were so extreme that suicide was a distinct possibility. His therapist focused on his earlier relationship with caretakers as they related to his feelings about his wife, including his ambivalence over her death. The patient did not get better. After approximately three months of treatment he attempted suicide by carbon monoxide poisoning. Subsequently, he committed himself to a mental hospital where he was assigned to another psychodynamically-oriented therapist. However, this time the focus of treatment was expanded to include his experiences in the wider ethnosystem. Of particular interest was the fact that he had worked for the postal service for more than twenty years, although he had a college degree. He had been unable to obtain what he described as "more suitable" employment despite the fact that his wife had often urged him to "try harder." Now, at age 50, he thought his chances were finally erased for any other kind of employment. "No one wants to hire you when you're over 50, especially if you're black!" This was as large an element in his depressive reaction as his wife's death. Thus, as an adjunct to his regular therapy sessions, the patient was referred to a self-help group made up of persons interested in making "mid-life career changes." He remained in therapy and in the self-help group until he had successfully negotiated a franchise with a national auto-parts store as owner-manager. "I always wanted to have my own business," he stated as he and the therapist planned termination of his treatment. Thus, a tendency in the psychodynamically-oriented therapist to place too much emphasis on the effects of the patient's relationships within the family system and much less on relationships with the wider society, represents a risk for many Afro-American patients.

It is sometimes assumed that behavioral or social learning theories of practice eliminate the stigmatizing effect of having to define behavior as deviant or pathological in order to prescribe a "treatment." However, for persons with strong feelings of powerlessness, there is a heightened possibility that even successful modification of problem behaviors will be viewed as something that was done to or for them rather than something done by themselves. Thus, the behaviorally-oriented practitioner must take every opportunity to insure that clients perceive themselves as causal agents in producing the behavior change. Client-centered or humanistic approaches also have risks when attempting to engage Afro-American persons with emotional problems. These therapies have such objectives as fostering a positive self-image, facilitating self-understanding and the acceptance and full experience of one's own feelings, and personal growth, rather than the relief of illness or the reduction of symptoms. These would appear entirely consistent and even necessary goals when working with persons overwhelmed by feelings of low self-esteem and powerlessness. However, it is the extreme emphasis on self-understanding as the inevitable solution of problems that may be untenable. Furthermore, the emphasis on freedom to choose for persons whose life choices have been severely constrained, and on the uniqueness of the "self" for persons who have been perceived often only in terms of a stigmatized collective, also make these approaches alien ones for many Afro-Americans.

Clearly, empowerment strategies may be incorporated into the myriad theoretical approaches to treatment, and are not therefore identifiable with any one in particular. It is interesting to note that in Lerner's research study of the effectiveness of therapy in a low-income, predominantly Afro-American neighborhood, the single most striking relationship was found between democratic values or nonauthoritarianism on the part of the therapist and the client's improvement. Lerner speculates:

> Self-esteem is generally regarded as a necessary basis for adequate psychological functioning, and good therapy is generally expected to foster it, but exactly how it does this is far from clear. My own hunch is that . . . respect from others is an important source of self-esteem . . . for all adults, no matter how regressed or primitive they may appear. Democratic values on the part of a therapist imply a very healthy degree of respect for his clients, and thus, such values may have a very potent and beneficial effect on their self-esteem, an effect which fosters the display and development of real competence.[13,pp.141–142]

The scale devised by Lerner to operationalize the concept of democratic values in therapy, measured the extent to which the therapist was willing to have therapy be directed by the client, as well as the extent to which the therapist was willing to accept unorthodox or nontraditional approaches to mental health service delivery. Certainly, the empowerment process described earlier in this section would be facilitative of an infusion of democratic values into therapy. Thus, the end result would be an opportunity for any positive life changes experienced as a consequence of therapy to be attributed to the client's own efforts. In contrast to the humanistic approaches, however, the efforts are not merely in the direction of self-understanding, but in having an impact on the social environment as well.

IMPLICATIONS FOR FURTHER RESEARCH

The theoretical constructs of ethnosystem, negative valuation, powerlessness, and empowerment are loosely connected into propositions that are largely untested. They do, however, provide a framework for such testing in empirical research to be undertaken. For example, research is needed to determine the extent to which the unique aspects of the black experience influence the definition of mental health problems and entry into the mental health service delivery system. On the basis of the foregoing discussion, the following hypothesis can be proposed: Afro-American, low-income clients are less likely to drop out of treatment when personalistic approaches are utilized to establish the therapeutic relationship than when formal bureaucratic approaches are utilized.

Research is also needed to determine how important it is for the therapist to assess the extent to which exposure to negative valuation from representative social systems (e.g., schools, welfare department, probation department, etc.) contributes to problem behavior or provides direction to change efforts. The following hypothesis has been implied in our discussion:

Clinical judgments which include the assessment of person-system transactions are more likely to be accurate than when the assessment does not include person-system transactions.

Finally, research is needed to determine the relationship between specific aspects of mental health service delivery and the reduction of powerlessness for Afro-American clients. The following hypotheses appear supportable on the basis of existing evidence:

- The more egalitarian the client-practitioner relationship, the greater the reduction of the feeling of powerlessness.

- The more information provided the client by the practitioner for the client's use in his or her own problem-solving efforts, the greater the reduction of powerlessness.
- Those clients who are able to change some negative response to themselves from the wider social system to a more positive response will demonstrate greater reduction of powerlessness than will those clients who are unable to effect such change.
- At the end of treatment, clients who attribute positive change to the therapist alone will show less reduction in powerlessness than will those clients who attribute positive change to their joint efforts.

Thus, the real test of a new theoretical approach incorporating empowerment and its companion constructs in the treatment of Afro-Americans, must be whether it increases the effectiveness of that treatment as documented in rigorously designed empirical studies.

REFERENCES

1. Solomon BB: Black Empowerment: Social Work in Oppressed Comunities. New York, Columbia University Press, 1976
2. Thomas A, Sillen S: Racism and Psychiatry. New York, Brunner/Mazel, 1972
3. Cole J, Pilisuk M: Difference in the Provision of Mental Health Services by Race. Ortho-psychiatry 46:510–525, 1976
4. Sue S, McKinney H, Allen D, et al. Delivery of community mental health services to black and white clients. J Consulting Clin Psychol 42:794–801, 1974
5. Luborsky L, Chandler M, Averbach AH, et al. Factors influencing the outcome of psychotherapy: A review of quantitative research. Psychol Bull 75:145–165, 1971
6. Halpern F: Survival: Black/White. New York, Pergamon, 1973
7. Ullman M: A unifying concept linking therapeutic and community process, in Gray W, Duhl F, Rizzo N (Eds): General Systems Theory and Psychiatry. Boston, Little, Brown, 1969
8. Coleman J: Resources for Social Change: Race in the United States. New York, John Wiley & Sons, 1971
9. O'Malley M: Psychosis in the colored race. J of Insanity 71:309–36, 1914
10. Green EM: Psychoses among Negroes—A comparative study. J Nervous Mental Disor 41:697–708, 1914
11. Wilson DC, Lentz EM: The effect of culture change on the Negro race in Virginia as indicated by a study of state hospital admissions. Am J Psychiatry 113:25–32, 1957
12. Kramer M, Rosen B, Willie E: Definitions and distributions of mental disorders in a racist society, in Willie CV, Kramer B, Brown B (eds): Racism and Mental Health. Pittsburg, University of Pittsburg Press, 1973, pp. 353–462
13. Lerner B: Therapy in the Ghetto: Political Impotence and Personal Disintegration. Baltimore, Johns Hopkins University Press, 1972
14. Hernton C: Sex and Racism in America. New York, Grove Press, 1965
15. Eysenck HJ: Crime and Personality. London, Methuen, 1964
16. Gross HS, et al: The effect of race and sex on the variation of diagnosis and disposition in a psychiatric emergency room. J Nervous Mental Disor 67:123–128, 1969

17. Nathan PE, Harris S: Psychopathology and Society. New York, McGraw-Hill, 1980
18. Davis JM, Chang SS: A look at the data, in Brady JP, Brodie HK (eds): Controversy in Psychiatry. Philadelphia, Saunders, 1978
19. Kleinmutz B: Essentials of Abnormal Psychology (2nd ed). San Francisco, Harper and Row, 1980
20. Draper BJ: Black language as an adaptive response to a hostile environment, in Germaine CB (ed): Social Work Practice: People and Environments. New York, Columbia University Press, 1979
21. Pinderhughes C: Racism and Psychotherapy, in Willie, Kramer, Brown (eds): Racism and Mental Health. Pittsburgh, University of Pittsburgh Press, 1973

Ralph Greenson
Ellis Toney
Perry Lim
Annelisa Romero

11

Transference and Countertransference in Interracial Psychotherapy

EDITOR'S INTRODUCTION

In 1976, Dr. Ralph Greenson was invited to present a lecture on transference and countertransference in interracial psychotherapy to the UCLA seminar, "The Assessment and Treatment of Afro-American Families." While preparing the lecture, Dr Greenson suggested it would be more instructive and interesting to engage in a dialogue on these issues with the Afro-American psychoanalyst Dr. Ellis Toney, his personal friend and colleague. Their presentation was videotaped and has become a classic. To the best of our knowledge, this was the first time an analyst and an analysand openly and publicly discussed the influence of sociocultural issues as they interfered with or enhanced their therapeutic relationship. A transcript of the videotape is presented here, along with introductory remarks by Dr. Toney and comments from seminar participants during the discussion that followed the viewing of the videotape.

At the time the dialogue was videotaped, Dr. Greenson was a Clinical Professor of Psychiatry in the UCLA School of Medicine and active in private practice. He had authored numerous articles and a book, The Technique and Practice of Psychoanalysis,[1] *which is a primary text used in psychiatric training programs.*

This chapter presents the taped dialogue between Dr. Ralph Greenson and Dr. Ellis Toney, as transcribed by Perry Lim and edited by Annelisa Romero.

Dr. Toney is the first Afro-American psychiatrist to practice in Los Angeles and one of the world's first Afro-American psychoanalysts. In 1976, he was semiretired from private practice and involved in teaching in the Department of Psychiatry at the Martin Luther King Hospital of the Charles Drew Post-Graduate School of Medicine.

DR. TONEY'S INTRODUCTORY REMARKS

My analysis occurred between 1948 and 1954 and Dr. Greenson was my training analyst. There has been a considerable amount of change with the black individual in the 20 years following my analysis. In fact, I think that probably the greatest change has taken place in these 20 years. *Roots*[2] highlighted an aspect of black life that was strongly present in certain areas probably up to the fifties. And this aspect of it was, I think, the terror, the fear, because there was no such thing as the law being on your side. Not that it's there now. But, organizations such as the Ku Klux Klan were rampant during that time. I'll never forget my experience of having been stopped by a Ku Klux Klan member and being frightened when I was about 16 years old. The Klan did catch the person they were looking for and he was hanged. They justified it. I recall the editorial in our local paper. They justified it on the basis that people made the law—we, the people, made the laws—so, if the laws we make don't include everything, we can extend them. This is the way they justified the hanging.

When I say that things have changed, I mean that after the Congressional Act of 1954 concerning the school system when Eisenhower sent troops into Arkansas to show that there could be some law and order in the South, I think to a certain extent, there has been less flagrant use of any type of illegal activity various groups wanted to use. They could not just move in and take the law into their own hands. My period of analysis was prior to that period and there was the terror associated with going into the South, as far as I was concerned. Well, now I laugh at it with a few of my friends. While I don't visit the South that much now because my parents are deceased, I used to visit frequently. Prior to 1954, the restrooms were either for blacks or whites, and I had gone into this particular black restroom many times at the airport. Now that they changed it so that you can use either restroom, I have a difficult time going into the one that had been for whites only.

Well, my analysis took place in a different era, but there are many aspects of it that certainly relate to the blacks of today, of the 1970s, and probably will for many years, because I think black people unconsciously through their relationships with peers, family, and the like, have incorporated many of these ideas. These concepts still operate in relationships with whites to various degrees, but certainly, with sociological change, I think that psychological change within blacks, intrapsychic change, is taking place.

THE TAPE

Greenson: Dr. Toney and I did something very unique. I never heard of two people prominent in psychoanalytic and psychiatric circles expose themselves as we are about to do, psychologically. We're going to expose ourselves psychologically because we have to talk about transference and countertransference, which I will hope to define for you, and resistance. Toney was in training with me, which means he was a psychiatrist wanting to be trained in psychoanalysis, and part of that training means that you have to undergo analysis with a training analyst. I am a training analyst, in addition to my other defects. So he came to me . . . Actually, he didn't really come to me, I found him. I thought it was a secret, but he also found me. He was finally admitted to the training institute with great troubles. We didn't realize we were in over our heads because it had never really been done. What I have to tell you is not just to explain to you what goes on in transference, countertransference, and resistance with black and white training analysts, or patient and analyst. What I have to say is also in the nature of a confession, because we made so many mistakes, both of us, but primarily me. I should have known better. We both made many mistakes, as you will hear. I think we learned a lot. As usual, you learn more from your mistakes than from the things you think you do well. So we made lots of mistakes, but the mistakes managed to be very important turning points. Certainly, when Toney said to me that I was doing something wrong, and I had to say to myself, "Well, maybe he is right," the whole analysis changed.

I'll start with an example rather than go on to something else. I had my office in Beverly Hills, and Toney had an hour during the day, 2–3 o'clock in the afternoon. He said to me, "I hate coming on Friday's," so I immediately said, "Oh, I see you hate coming because it's the last hour of the day and you miss me, and you resent me," and all kinds of marvelous interpretations. He said, "No, that's not right. When I come to your office, and I drive away, the cops will stop me because when they see a black man driving a car, they'll stop me." And I said, "You know something, I think you're paranoid." Toney said "I'm not paranoid. The world is paranoid. Your white world is paranoid about us blacks." I couldn't believe it, but when incidents kept multiplying, then I began to believe it is really true. We live in two different worlds. I'm so sorry I was so ignorant when I began the treatment, but Toney educated me.

I couldn't believe if that was really a fact, or if he was paranoid. Even my landlord said, "Dr. Greenson, I understand you're seeing a black man during the day. Ordinarily, we see our black patients early in the morning or late at night." And I said, "Are you trying to force me to see my patient during the morning or during the night because he's black? I want to tell you something. This man is more educated than you. He's not only a doctor, but a psychiatrist. He can have you put away. I will put an ad in the paper saying you made me move because I see a black psychiatrist during the day." He said, "Oh, don't get upset! Don't get upset!" I said, "I'm not upset."

He never bothered me again, but that's the way it was. . . . You see, we didn't know what we were getting into. It was not only a myth that we were struggling within our own transference and countertransference and our own prejudice, but we were struggling with the prejudice of the outside world, which was even worse than ours. We had all of that to go through. And that was a tremendous resistance. We lived in two different worlds and we were trying to understand each other. It took an unusual amount of courage on Toney's part and on my part to admit that we were millions of miles apart in certain ways of thinking, values, and so forth. Nevertheless, he was a psychiatrist wanting to become an analyst; I was a psychiatrist wanting to train people. We had certain things in common which made it possible for us to work.

I must mention another fact. Not only was Toney the first black I ever tried to analyze, but he was also a Southerner, and I had a great aversion to Southerners, in particular, white Southerners. But I found out there's also a difference between blacks in the South and blacks in the North, although they originally came from the South. I was so ignorant. I must mention something else. My father is a doctor. I'm a doctor. My brother is a doctor . . . was a doctor, he died. And, my son is a doctor. I shared this with Toney. I think, Toney, you should say a little about your background, being the son of a doctor, and what that did in terms of giving you some peculiar kind of status and yet making it hard for you.

Toney: You mean my early background?

Greenson: Being a doctor's son in the South and a Negro doctor's son . . .

Toney: Of course, being the only doctor and a doctor's son, there was always jealousy, envy, difficulty, because we lived at a level that was above most of the community. I have a tendency, when I talk about that now, to say "Negro," so I'll probably vascillate between using "black" and "Negro" because when I go back to the past, it was always appropriate to say "Negro."

My father, as well as my uncle, was a doctor. I think that this, as with any group that was once singled out as being different, makes for difficulty in all situations but I think it was also helpful. I was accustomed to being different to a certain extent, and possibly looked for it. But in my particular area, being different brought about a number of conflicts. It brought me into contact with whites of the community even though it was a Southern community. In various ways, you come in contact with whites in the community if you have a certain status, so to speak, which makes it somewhat different from someone who's never interacted with whites. You interacted with them frequently in all areas, with the possible exception of the intimate social areas in that particular era. And here, there was a certain line that was drawn. On an intellectual and business level, interactions were possible.

The conflicts were also there with black jealousy, envy, put-downs and the like, which created some problems. I think coming from a family of doctors, in terms of transference and countertransference, would have meaning to a large extent because of the nature of what my father was like. I always felt, and probably still do to some extent, that in some ways Greenson resembled my father too much. My father was very ambitious and read a lot. At times, there was this close resemblance, except for color. This was a factor from the standpoint of transference.

Greenson: I think that's important and that we were lucky. Why did Ellis Toney want to become the first black analyst in the whole wide world? Number one: He was the son of a doctor and his uncle was a doctor. I came from a doctor's family.

By the way, black psychiatrists had tried before to become analysts, but either the candidates killed themselves or ended up in a state hospital. And he's managed to avoid both so far, and seems to be doing pretty well. One thing about any kind of uncovering therapy, psychoanalysis, psychotherapy, any kind of uncovering, is that you have to be able to deal with resistances. This means that as much as patients want to get well, from the time they walk into the office, there is a counterforce saying, "Please don't change me. For as miserable as I am, don't change me. Certainly, don't change something that I keep very hidden that I'm ashamed of." As much as patients want to change, there's a part of them that doesn't want to change. They like their familiarity with their own symptoms: "As much as I hate depression, I hate what's going to come up next because it's unconscious in me." So there's both conscious and unconscious resistance fighting you every step of the way. Now, this is magnified with prejudice. Prejudice magnifies both conscious resistance and unconscious resistance.

I thought I was a liberal. I came from a liberal family. I knew Paul Johnson when I was a kid. I knew Paul Robeson. I was supposed to be very liberal. Only then, in my work with Toney, did I become aware that I had certain resentments, certain put-downs of Toney, because he was black—even though my family was consciously liberal. Unconsciously, it's the same thing with the Gentiles. By the way, I'm Jewish. That's another problem, because I also have an antipathy to Gentiles, although not conscious. The Jews have a terrific antiGentile, antiGoyish complex. Those were odd things, those myths, and above all, the unconscious resistances that emerged with all those myths. It was a very stormy period.

I talked about resistances that oppose change, that oppose what comes to your mind spontaneously. You're afraid because there's mistrust. Everything that's new, we don't trust. And I'm working with someone who needs to trust me, or at least must have a balance in the mistrust–trust relationship on the side of more trust and less mistrust. I'm working with a patient who, in some ways, I wanted . . . I picked him out. Yet, in some ways, I had unconscious hostilities. I'm sure this was certainly true of Toney, in terms of the ratio of trust and mistrust.

Toney: I think that with the black person in American society, this is probably one of the major problem areas. Blacks, as you know, are not too far removed from slavery—only a little over 100 years. In my instance, at my age, it hasn't been that long. Blacks, practically every black individual today, has been traumatized, in some way, by the white person. If blacks have not been traumatized directly by whites, then through talk and hearsay, they have incorporated experiences that were traumatic. So you can say practically every black has been affected. If they have been traumatized by a situation, or by experience, vicarious or not, they are suspicious, they do mistrust. I think in the black–white relationship, one of the more difficult areas is the trust-mistrust factor. It's necessary to have a certain degree of trust for any therapeutic relationship. You could not have a patient–therapist relationship if there was not a certain degree of trust involved. With a black person and a white person, this is more difficult to achieve. It depends on . . . I don't like to use a generalized statement, but I think it varies with the individual. I think that some individuals can establish this more quickly, more easily, and with less difficulty than others. It depends on how severely individuals have been traumatized by society, by their early upbringings, and to some extent, on what sociological factors were operative at that particular time.

To work with this mistrust, from the standpoint of white or black therapists with black patients, requires certain skills and, to a large extent, white therapists' understanding of themselves and handling their own ambivalence, prejudices, or what not. Some people can handle this differently and more effectively than others. Establishing a therapeutic relationship depends largely on the therapist and how he or she can relate to a particular patient.

I was supervising a white therapist not too long ago. There were problems, not major problems, but those subtleties in terms of resistances which Greenson was bringing out. Resistances can be so subtle. This particular white therapist was treating a black woman. I thought therapy was progressing rather well; the patient had come out of her depression to a large extent, but her finances were at a rather low level, and her aunt asked her to move in with her. The patient was angry, resentful that she would have to move in with her aunt because the aunt lived in a black neighborhood. The patient thought that this would be awful, that the neighborhood would be dirty, and that they lived liked pigs. This conflict lasted for several sessions. She was depressed about it.

Now, on the surface of things, this doesn't appear to be very much. But, what happened was that the patient, who had not lived in that neighborhood—she was living in sort of a mixed neighborhood with whites—eventually found that the black neighborhood was far superior to the one she had been living in. The point about this conflict is that it lasted for a number of sessions. The problem here was with the black patient and white therapist. First, the therapist was not aware of the differences between the neighborhoods nor his own need to appear in a certain light to the patient. He did not inquire about the details of what was happening, or what the particular area was like. But above all, I think that his own idea of what "black" means interfered—when the patient said, "this black neighborhood is awful," it echoed the white therapist's own concept of all black areas being bad. All black areas are not bad. The patient had the need to identify with the therapist and be white. She wanted to stay in a white area like her therapist's, which was a denial of her own identity as a black.

There are many other ramifications, but all these resistances are there which emerge subtly and present problems in any type of therapy. I think the black person, myself included, uses various forms of resistances that may involve the black scene or what blackness is. This often presents a problem to white therapists because of their own needs to be omnipotent, or their own prejudices interfere with interpretations or get them bogged down in some way, or easily get them in a bind. There are many examples.

I think the resistances aspect that Greenson brought out is quite prominent.

Greenson: What Toney is saying is very important because resistance isn't always very obvious. A patient doesn't want to talk, doesn't want to come to therapy, doesn't want to say something—that's obvious. But other resistance, as in the example Toney described, is not so obvious. The patient didn't want to admit that she enjoyed being with blacks rather than being in a white community because she didn't want to offend her white therapist. And the therapist didn't have enough bigness or openness of heart to say, "Maybe a black community could be more enjoyable than a white community." This reminds me of something I learned from Eldridge Cleaver,[3] and by the way, I also learned tremendously from Brown's book, *Man-Child in the Promised Land*,[4] and from *Malcolm X*.[5] *Malcolm X* was a real education. When I read Cleaver, I could tell you from personal experience, there is an enormous amount of prejudice hidden by counter-transference feelings.

For example, when Toney told me about his early childhood sexual experiences, I was flabbergasted. I had never heard of such things. I was tempted to say, "It's all his fantasy," but I found out it wasn't fantasy. He was raised in a certain way. It was permissible to have a certain amount of sexual freedom. Later on, when he joined the Army and was in Europe, it was simple, you liked the European women, and the women liked you. I must tell you it brought about a certain kind of envy.

Well, this is very important. What seems to be contempt hides envy. For example, we often say, "Well, blacks are lazy, they're stupid." That hides something else. At the same time, it is hiding the fact that we envy the blacks' capacity to be physical, beautifully physical, the way that blacks move, the way blacks dance, the way blacks sing, and also the way blacks excell as athletes. Well, when Toney and I began analysis, there were only Jackie Robinson and Don Newcombe and a couple of other blacks, and that was something. I would ask Toney, "When you played games as a kid, and you pretended to be the Lone Ranger or God, was God black or white? Was the Lone Ranger black or white?" These things bothered me, puzzled me. But the point I want to make is that I envied the fact that Toney was more potentially sexually attractive than I was. Yes, you have to be open-minded and say, "I envy it" and not use envy as a put-down to say, "Well, they're lazy, that's why they're good with their bodies, but they have no brains." That's a lie. The same attitude is taken toward Jews: "The Jews are all money-conscious and are crazy to make a buck." What this hides underneath is that Jews are like everybody else—greedy. We're all full of greed, black, white, all of us, Gentile and Jew.

What it hides is an envy that Jews are smart with numbers and smart in school. It hides that. So, please, you have to be honest with yourself.

Did I envy my patient? In certain ways I envied him and he had to face the fact that in certain ways he envied me, and also hated me. At the same time, there was enough trust on both sides because we had good experiences. He had had some good experiences with white people before he came to me. I had had some good experiences with black people before I came to him. So we had a chance to work out a therapeutic alliance, a working alliance, which helped us get over our transference.

I must at this point define the concepts of transference and countertransference. The patient has a transference to the analyst. This means that the patient will sooner or later feel his or her analyst is omniscient, omnipotent, beautiful, marvelous, superb, hateful, bastardly, a devil, a witch. That's going to happen sooner or later. But this comes from one's past history. Toney said I reminded him of his father. I had certain qualities like his father. But, in addition to these certain qualities, being dependent on me reinforced negative feelings, and also positive feelings, because in basic ways, he loved me, hated me, and dreaded me. The appropriateness of it all comes from transference. When analysts react to their patients as though the patients were important people in their pasts, you call it countertransference.

I have reacted to my patients very often. I've always had countertransference reactions. Without it, you couldn't do analysis. But you must be aware of it when you're doing it. You can be off-target, you may be exaggerating. Many times, I found myself exaggerating things which made the analysis much more difficult. For example—I think this is worth telling—the whole business about the fee. We were working together and I said, "Listen, as hard as we work, we're not getting very far. We're in some kind of a stalemate." Toney said, "Yes, you're right." What was it all about? We started to talk and to analyze what it was all about. Why were we getting no place, although we both had good intentions? And then, Toney came up with an answer that startled me.

Toney: The issue was fees. At that particular time, I was paying an extremely low fee which was disproportionate, and I knew it . . .

Greenson: The fee was proportionate to your income, which was lousy, let's face it.

Toney: Disproportionate to the other candidates.

Greenson: Oh, to the other candidates.

Toney: That's right. We discussed this type of thing off and on.

Greenson: By the way, I want to tell you, that's a conflict. I was so afraid not to charge too high a fee, overly afraid, but he straightened me out. And I had to be honest.

Toney: It was from this standpoint that I had some qualms.

Greenson: Qualms! That's putting it mildly. Qualms.

Toney: As a result, it presented a problem in working this out in the analysis. I preferred not being involved in analysis rather than being involved and paying a different fee from other people, from other candidates. I suppose this was associated with many things. This only accentuated the differences I felt, as I pointed out earlier. It was this matter of being different, which I had learned to accept in one sense, but resented and rejected in another sense. The matter of being different is a most difficult thing . . . you're alone. Many blacks who have been the only one in a situation have experienced this. I was able to see this in several black athletes. One was very prominent, the only one at a particular time in his field. This created a number of problems for him, different problems from those of black athletes I had seen in sports when there was another black. Being different creates anxiety within itself—it's an aloneness. I think that many blacks who have pioneered, who were the first in anything, underwent considerable anxiety just based on being the only one. All these things were involved in my transference reaction to Greenson. It wasn't just the fee. It went back to my childhood, to being the only doctor's son.

Greenson: Toney said, "Look, I don't want to pay a smaller fee. That to me is a symbol of being a lesser person. I don't want to pay a black man's fee. I want to pay the average candidate's fee." I fought with him. I said, "You can't afford it." He said, "I'll come less often each week, but I want to pay the regular fee." I said, "It's going against the rules of Freud, you know." I knew I loved Freud, but I also knew I'd lose my patient if I charged him a fee he couldn't accept. I knew he couldn't accept that fee. Toney finally got it into me. He had to work hard to get me to accept this fact: "All the analysis in the world will not change the fact that I am alone in my fee. I can't stand it." So okay . . . I gave in. I said, "What do you want?" Toney picked the regular fee. He cut down the visits. Instead of four times a week, I think he came in twice a week. Sometimes he'd come in three times a week and then he paid a higher fee. It made a big difference. He was no longer alone when he paid the regular fee.

Who would have dreamt of this? But you see, in my countertransference, I wanted to be the good guy, the rescuer. I have always tended to feel I had to rescue people. I had always accepted it and I couldn't feel the aloneness that Toney must have felt with that peculiar little fee.

Remember, there were many analysts, in those "days of enlightenment," who had it in for Toney—training analysts, professors who couldn't wait for him to fail, couldn't wait for him to become absolutely, totally incompetent. And he knew it. I tried to keep it a secret. I fought about it, but he knew it. They actually—in fact, I think, at one time, in your presence . . .

Toney: Well, there were many analysts who felt a black could not be analyzed.

Greenson: And that made it doubly hard because again, I was so positively in a countertransference that I wanted to make sure he was going to do it. That doesn't make for good analysis. You have to be dispassionate, you have to inflict pain, you can't just be helpful. No, you can't do that in any kind of therapy. We had to go through these kinds of awarenesses of this transference, countertransference, and how that figured in with prejudice, unconscious and conscious prejudice, that magnified resistances.

Resistances are the whole of analysis. The basic part of analysis is to analyze resistances, particularly when they concern the therapist—resistances that therapists have to patients because they see patients in a distorted light. Freud was right. Every step of the way, you have to be aware that you are not giving in to some form of resistance. Toney mentioned obvious resistance and very subtle resistance. You have to become aware of this. Part of it has to do with myths that we take for granted, as though they were facts. You don't know that you're a party to mistaking a myth as a fact. I must say, the patient takes advantage of it by doing certain things which are to me, at times, incomprehensible.

Many times, when I talked with Toney, he had different kinds of languages that he spoke. First of all, he's a doctor who could always hide behind doctor talk. You know, one doctor to another. I remember he hurt his hand—he jammed his finger. I said, "What happened?" He said, "Oh well, I had some contusions, and lacerations," and so on and so forth. I said, "Look, what would you ordinarily say?" He said, "I mashed my finger." I said, "So why don't you say that to me?" See, in a way, that's a form of resistance Toney used at times to "build-me-up-and-make-me-a-fool" at the same time. For the most part, I would go along, but many times I would stop and say, "What did that mean?" Often, I didn't stop. Gradually, this changed and we began to speak a common language. In those days, Toney spoke a kind of jive. I don't know what it was. What was it?

Toney: Well, I had a Southern . . .

Greenson: A Southern version of jive. It was very difficult for me, a Jew from Brooklyn. But, Toney learned to translate and not only to translate, but he could afford to be honest. I think both of us tried and I think that was the saving grace—the fact that we both tried. Sometimes, Toney told me stories—one, in particular, about being in a car with two people when a relative of his was lynched. I was horrified . . . I couldn't believe it . . . I wanted to shrink. I was ashamed to be part of a people that would do this kind of thing, and it was true. I had to face up to it. It was not a fantasy. I must say, the Ku Klux Klan is white. They don't have black members. I'm sorry to say it. It's a horrible thing to recognize, but if you don't face it, you can't understand these kinds of problems.

Myths. How about myths? I'm sure that myths can be used as forms of resistances to hide certain things . . .

Toney: There's something I want to clarify in terms of comments made earlier because it relates to myths. There's a difference in blacks. I came from an almost rural-type Southern background. When you mentioned sexual activity, Northern blacks who have been isolated and more or less middle-class would not have had that type of experience. With a Southern background, sexual activity was . . . there was nothing else to play with or more enjoyable.

Greenson: How old were you when you started?

Toney: You started as soon as you were able to walk.

Greenson: Walk . . . But why is it a myth? What is a myth?

Toney: Well, I thought of that because of the myth of the black being more powerful and more sexual than the white. I don't think this is true at all. In terms of sexual experiences, I think that Southern blacks did have different rules and probably were sexually involved earlier because, as I said, they had to have something to play with. This myth of the blacks' sexual abilities being out of proportion to the whites' is often used.

Greenson: It may be out of proportion, but there is a certain amount of truth to it. I do think there is a certain amount of truth to it.

Toney: I don't know about that. I think that if you come from a certain area like I came from it may be true. But, I think to these blacks here in this room, it may be foreign to them because they didn't come from the area that I came from. I don't know. Blacks run the gamut of sexual problems, just like any other group. Sometimes, black women may have more hangups because there was a dichotomy, you see. There was a lower class, the class that was involved in all the destructiveness and sexual promiscuity, and then there was a sort of middle-class or religious upper-class. Frequently, these women, such as my sisters, had totally different sexual experiences from my experiences. They would act like Southern ladies in all respects—the Southern family demanded this. So, in that category, the black woman may have more hangups because of that strict training.

DISCUSSION

Toney: This is the first time I've seen the tape since we made it last year. If there are any questions, I'll be happy to answer them.

Comment: I haven't been in analysis, but Greenson seems to be an extremely vocal kind of person. My image of analysis has to do with a more passive kind of role. Is he an active kind of person in analysis as well?

Toney: That varies to a large extent. Greenson can be just the opposite, really: very passive and receptive and not showing that aggressive bombardment type of attitude. He's quite passive, really, in the analytic situation, or when you're discussing something with him privately, not necessarily just in the analytic situation. Just in talking with him. When he is speaking, he's sort of dramatic and aggressive. So I would say he's flexible to a large extent.

Comment: It's interesting to me that he subscribes to the things we talk about in class in terms of myths. He certainly buys the myth of black sexuality. It seems that when it comes to the bottom line, he readily accepts that as "given."

Toney: Well, that was somewhat of a surprise to me, too, at the time of the taping last year. Possibly, I could have really influenced his thinking there, without knowing it. You see, I would talk about sexuality rather freely and my background was different from most people's backgrounds. As I said there on the tape, we had a Southern rule—that was your activity. And then, of course, as he mentioned, I was in Europe during the war, and again I was in sort of a unique situation, different again from some of his experiences. I was in a top position and had men under me, so my activities, except for the battle, were enjoying Europe. Greenson, I think was somewhere over here during the war in some barracks. So both my Southern background and my going into the service provided different experiences.

Comment: If he had analyzed a white Southerner growing up in a rural area, he may have had the same misconceptions.

Toney: I agree with you there. I know that the white Southerner in a rural area participated in the same thing. In fact, as youths, we communicated with whites in these small Southern areas. We had contact with them. In fact, we were going to get together, and some of my friends did. It so happens that I was on my way to the place to get together with them for these little games we were going to play. My father stopped me along the way to have some conversation, so I didn't have a chance to participate in what was dangerous at that time. But we were going to do it. So what I'm saying is that I knew white kids engaged in the same type of activity.

Comment: What I don't see operating in his acceptance of the myth is the white man's fear of the black man raping his women. That's become the dominant theme behind the myth throughout the historical experience of this country.

Comment: What I'm wondering about, along with what this person just said, is if the analytical process can really be complete, would these kinds of thoughts and myths circulate in doctors' minds? I think the situation is still there, the problem still exists, there are still barriers, even though they recognize the problems. The question is that with those thoughts being in mind, such as black sexuality, can the analytic process really be complete, can it really provide an in-depth experience?

Toney: Regarding your comment about it being in-depth, I think it can be in-depth. But whether or not, at any point, one is able to change totally racial, ingrained concepts about certain things is a matter of degree. Some people are able to change these concepts more so than others. Certainly, having encountered so many situations might arouse me. Take "Roots,"[2] for example. Certainly, I would have more intense reactions than some other people. I mean, having encountered certain situations with whites up to this point, there would be some differences.

Comment: Yes, but can therapy situations be effective?

Toney: Not if you look at a therapeutic situation as just one total type of change. I think it would be better to look at any therapeutic situation as a matter of degree. Is this particular form of therapy more appropriate for this individual? Will this other individual reach a level where he or she can function? This other individual, to some extent, can function highly but another individual is just going to be able to remain out of the hospital. I don't think the total change type of situation we talked about at one time exists. I don't even think that the goal of psychotherapy should necessarily point itself in that direction for all people. I think we have to accept the fact that there are certain factors we haven't been able to pin down as yet. We don't know everything about the nature of the therapeutic process as yet. We only know certain things about it.

Comment: But doesn't the situation remain the same? I mean, we're talking about the problem of transference and counterference and if myths are allowed to still linger on in one's mind, doesn't the situation remain the same? Don't you still have the same kind of problem existing? Or am I crazy?

Comment: It seems we're picking up one myth Dr. Greenson had about black males and it sounds like that is going to affect the entire therapy or analysis with you or with any black patient.

Comment: We're assuming Greenson had other feelings like that.

Comment: Right, that's what I'm worried about—if it's not working from that standpoint. I was reading Greenson just a little bit racist. I mean, I'm sitting here thinking, "Hey, he's a charming man, but the man still has some problems that he needs to work out." That's what I was thinking just by looking at him on the film. I may be totally wrong.

Comment: Then we get into the issue of confusing the therapist with the client, and although Greenson's going through all that was a therapeutic process of a sort for him, at this certain level, he's not able to reach you, he's not able to reach you at this one point in this one encounter. At the first encounter, maybe he will reach that point, or maybe he won't. I think being aware of it and keeping it in mind when he goes into another therapeutic encounter with somebody may help him deal with that person. Greenson may say, "Hey, I have these ideas about black sexuality, and I have to watch out for this," whereas maybe before he wasn't aware of that. I think awareness is the issue.

Comment: Doesn't the therapeutic experience require that all those things be worked out on the part of the therapist? It probably never is, regardless of whether you have two black analysts working together or whether it's . . .

Comment: Please, pose that question in terms of yourself, analyzing psychiatrists in training. In relation to what that young man (above) was saying, what were some of the differences you experienced as a training analyst with black psychiatrists?

Toney: I'm not a training analyst, but I've analyzed black psychiatrists, and a number of black people in the field. I think the resistances and the defenses are not as prominent or utilized as much with the black therapist. I think they are used, but I think black itself—you see, black itself can be used so much as a resistance, as a defense, with the white therapist in particular, at least in those I've supervised. If this is what you mean, this would be one of the differences with me analyzing a black person—that there are certain defenses and certain resistances they might not use with me. But otherwise, I think there would be mostly similarities. It would just be in certain areas that the defenses and resistances would come up, where they would not come up with a white therapist. I feel that a white therapist can analyze a black person, but I think there may be more problems, from the standpoint of defenses and resistances.

Comment: I'd like to comment on the use of language, and perhaps you'd like to address yourself to this also. Dr. Greenson mentioned that at times you would speak to him in three different languages, or whatever. In "Roots,"[2] in terms of the slaves speaking to their masters, there were levels of language, and there were messages that always came through that weren't always picked up by the dominant culture. I was wondering about that relationship. Could you expand on that?

Toney: Oh yes, I was trying to think of examples, but there was a block for some reason or another. I had the typical Southern type of jargon, street jargon, because I had mixed a lot with the street people, too. It's been so long I can't think of some of the things I used to say. I can't recall them off-hand. Maybe things will come to me as we continue the discussion.

Comment: Would you consciously use phrases or jargon to deceive Greenson or, as he said, to make a fool of him, knowing he wouldn't understand?

Toney: I don't know whether that was conscious or not, but I'm sure I used some expressions that he couldn't understand. He was from a different area . . . From any area, there would be some different expressions that come out. You know, there are a lot of Southern expressions I would use, particularly street expressions. That was another difference with me. My father's office was located where all the prostitutes, gamblers, etc. were located. I knew them and their language and probably even used it from time to time.

Comment: Greenson said something on the videotape about how there hadn't been any black analysts because they had either committed suicide or been institutionalized. I wondered if that was before or during analysis by a white training analyst.

Toney: Well, you know that there are casualties in analysis, with people who have been strictly in analytic-type of therapy. I think most psychoanalysts today would change their course if they felt that the psychiatrist-in-training was regressing or decompensating. But there have been casualties in therapy.

Comment: I think that would be a very difficult time to have the white training therapists take out their aggressions or prejudices or whatever in the psychoanalytic process.

Comment: Do you mean designing it to fail?

Toney: There were several people in the country during that era who had been in psychoanalytic training and had dropped out for various reasons. Some of them have accused the therapist of this or that or the other. Yes, and certainly, some had gotten sick.

Comment: I was particularly interested in the fact that Greenson appeared to report it was a real learning experience for him. It was almost like a weekly seminar. That's the impression he gave; that each week there was more and more he was learning about, not just about you, but about life in general, black life in the South, etc. Sometimes, that has a tendency to make me feel uncomfortable in certain situations. I was wondering if during that time, that was how you felt? . . . Of course, you were there for your training and for your own personal enhancement, but perhaps there was an aspect of being almost a test case, or a case in which the therapist would extrapolate a lot of information from you.

Toney: I'm sure he did. Well, during that time, it was in 1948, there wasn't as much written about black life and I would relate black events to him. I was a little more active in the Urban League and the NAACP. I was involved a little with both of them and Greenson knew very little about them—or he knew about them, but the majority of people didn't. Blacks didn't know that much about the Urban League—a lot of them don't know about it. But I was active in the Urban League and the National Medical Association. I'm sure that most people here don't know that the NMA is a black medical association. So I had to enlighten a lot of people about a lot of things, including attitudes. Sometimes I didn't mind expanding on those things that Greenson didn't know about Afro-Americans. There were a lot of things. I'm sure he was educated.

Comment: At what point in treatment would you suggest to trainees to bring up the issue of race in interracial psychotherapy, or with blacks as to how they feel about being treated by a black therapist?

Toney: Well. I wouldn't suggest a certain point. It seldom, if ever, fails to come up when you're black. I mean, how would you . . . I can't think of any black that hasn't brought up being black . . .

Comment: Only in this recent period. I, unfortunately, go back a long way, too. The issue was avoidance of bringing it up at another point in time.

Toney: Avoidance of . . .

Comment: The racial issue.

Toney: You're right. Sometimes, blacks would avoid it, but sooner or later, it would come up . . . Well, most often it would come up. It's rare that it would not. The only times I think that racial factors would not come up would be sometimes with whites. But blacks would always emphasize black issues.

Comment: Are you talking about to a black therapist or a white therapist?

Toney: I mean to the black therapist. It's rare if black patients don't talk about black issues.

Comment: When would you bring it up with a white therapist, or does it matter?

Toney: I would bring it up. Sometimes, I would discuss it with patients in the initial interview. I went through a phase like that because, as I said, "Bring it up right away." But, I decided to let it come up when I felt that it was an issue, when I could detect it by certain resistances or certain statements. At one point, maybe for a couple of years, I would discuss it right away. I don't know which was best.

EDITOR'S NOTE

Many of the issues raised in this videotaped dialogue and subsequent discussion are highlighted in other chapters in this book. The reader is encouraged to read on in order to gain additional information about techniques that should be used or topics that should be discussed in psychotherapy.

We were most grateful to Drs. Greenson and Toney for their openness in discussing aspects of their therapeutic relationship that other therapists may encounter in interracial psychotherapy. By revealing their strengths as well as their weaknesses, we learn to appreciate the difficulties of self-disclosure in therapy when the therapist and patient may not have shared the same cultural or experiential background. We can also note the growth in sensitivity and understanding by both therapist and patient, resulting in an enhanced relationship that developed beyond the patient–student therapist relationship.

We deeply regret the death of Dr. Greenson in 1979. We feel he would have endorsed this book as a needed resource in the field of psychiatry. We would like to thank Dr. Toney for his help in transcribing sections of the tape and for offering his support to our endeavors.

REFERENCES

1. Greenson R: The Technique and Practice of Psychoanalysis (vol 1). New York, International University Press, 1967
2. Haley A: Roots, New York, Doubleday, 1976
3. Cleaver E: Soul on Ice. New York, Grove Press, 1964
4. Brown C: Manchild in the Promised Land. New York, Macmillan, 1965
5. Haley A, X M: The Autobiography of Malcolm X. New York, Grove Press, 1964

Helen A. Mendes

12

The Role of Religion in Psychotherapy With Afro-Americans

Afro-American churches have historically played major roles in the lives of many Afro-American families.

> The strong religious orientation of many black families has been a major sustaining element in the struggle to cope with social realities from the era of slavery to the present. Religion and the black church are adaptive mechanisms which historically have supported both social and psychological needs . . Religion and the social activities provided by the church were supportive features which gave hope for a better life.
>
> The black church continues its viability as a component of black American culture; it has the capacity to adapt to the changing needs of its members. The church has traditionally provided an outlet for the expression of musical talents and organizational skills and contemporary congregations offer day care centers, credit unions, housing developments, and senior citizen services. In the nurturing environment of the black church, a sense of belonging and fellowship is encouraged through shared value orientations and experiences.*

The religious value orientations of churches are founded upon a basic assumption that there is a supraempirical reality beyond this here-and-now world. This definition of reality is one that is fully accepted by the devoutly religious. The influence of the church, however, has not been confined to those who enter its buildings. Beliefs in God, spirits, a universal law, or some other spiritual entity are held by Afro-American

*From Anita J. Delaney (ed): Black Task Force Report. New York, Family Service Association of America, 1979, p. 11. Used with permission of the publisher.

families who rarely, if ever, attend church. Thus, in contemporary Afro-American communities, one finds myriad manifestations of religious beliefs. Among these families, and even within a single family, one may find those whose spiritual expressions take the forms of quiet meditation, genuflection, chants, whispered prayers to saints, or the forms of "shouts," spirit possession, and "holy dances" done to syncopated rhythms of trumpet, drums, and tambourines. Other manifest their beliefs by standing on street corners, or going from door-to-door exhorting "sinners to repent while there is yet time." Responding to a sense of urgency and fear, other Afro-Americans burn candles, purchase charms, and consult spiritists to conjure benign spirits or to ward off evil ones which they believe plague their lives. In many of these communities, it is not uncommon to see four or five storefront churches in a single city block. Religious orientations are found among Afro-Americans of lower, middle and upper classes. Although there are some social class variations in the specific dogmas and rituals adhered to by these families, the influences of religious paradigms cut across social classes.

RELIGION AS A PSYCHOSOCIAL DYNAMIC

The potent influences of religious beliefs lie not only in the definition of reality which underpins them, but also in the values which grow out of these beliefs. Values refer to the assumptions one makes about the intrinsic worth or utility of things or people. The religious values held by devout Afro-Americans help to shape their life-styles. These values also influence the socialization of children and adults, often prescribing how believers should think, feel, and behave. Such values become the conscious and unconscious standards by which adherents of the faith judge themselves and others.

The development of the believer's personality is, in part, shaped by the specific content of his or her faith. For example, devout Christians refer to themselves as "children of God." Such an identity conditions the behavior of believers and helps to determine not only what their superegoes judge to be right or wrong, but also helps to determine the contents of their ideal selves.

The religious faith of believers can promote or hinder their mental health. Religious beliefs may, for example, help the believer to deal with what O'Dea calls the fundamental characteristics of human existence. These characteristics are: (1) uncertainty—nothing in life is certain; (2) powerlessness—although human beings have increased their ability to control many things in this world, they do not have absolute control and are, therefore, ultimately powerless; (3) scarcity—all resources are finite, and because of social hierarchies these resources are unevenly distributed among people.[2] As a disadvantaged people, Afro-Americans keenly experience these existential characteristics. During times of severe crisis, people tend to search for meaningful answers to the poignant question, "Why me? Why is this happening to me?" The devout may find the answer within their religion. For such persons, religious formulations of meanings may make sense out of what, otherwise, would seem to be the meaninglessness of life. "If it wasn't for the Lord, I'da gone out of my mind!", is a commonly heard declaration of devout Afro-Americans. Even if they are members of a socially powerless group, Afro-Americans who believe that they are "children of God" have found a way to blunt the pain of their human condition by identifying with God and God's unlimited power.

If believers are actively involved with their church or religious community, their sense of connectedness or fellowship with other believers combats the commonly experienced maladies of isolation and anomie. Their sense of connection may be expanded to include adherants of the faith in other countries, as well as in other centuries. For people whose ethnic roots have been dislodged as radically as those of Afro-Americans, the sense of tradition and continuity which some find within their religious communities is restorative.

But just as a medicine may harm as well as cure, the religious faith of believers may be a help or a hazard to their mental health. The elastic nature of its orientation to a supraempirical reality—which cannot be verified by accepted scientific standards—makes religious faith especially vulnerable to neurotic and psychotic abuse. For example,

> Clara's mother died while giving birth to her. Clara's father, a Pentacostal preacher, devoted his life to rearing his only daughter. Now, at age 33, Clara is unemployed, phobic, and depressed. She explains her condition with assertions that she is "waiting for the Holy Spirit" to direct her life, as she has surrendered her will to God. She regards her severe bouts of depression as evidence that "God is purging her of imperfections," preparing her for a holy purpose.

Religious formulations of meanings are being used by Clara not only to structure her existence, but to severely restrict it, as well. She, like others, has a tyrannical superego which is buttressed by the belief that an all-seeing God may exact dire retribution for violations of some restriction. In its extreme form, such religious ideations become prominent in psychotic processes.

Because of the powerful influence religion exerts on the lives of many Afro-Americans, it is a factor which needs to be addressed in therapy with such clients.

THERAPEUTIC IMPLICATIONS

In order to effectively help any client, the mental health practitioner and the client need to share congruent realities. The incongruities between the worker's and client's respective realities may stem from differences in social class, ethnicity, age, sex, and value systems. When working with religious Afro-Americans, the incongruity may stem from the fundamental assumptions made by worker and client about the very nature of reality itself.

Most mental health practitioners operate from a naturalistic paradigm. Within this view of reality, all physical and social phenomena in the empirical world are explained and dealt with within the realm of natural causation and remedies. Humanity, not God or some other supraempirical reality, is at the center of life. This view asserts that people live only one life, and, therefore, this life is of utmost importance. The naturalistic perspective underlies the values of self-actualization and self-determination—values which guide much of the therapeutic process.

On the other hand, Afro-American clients who have religious paradigms have different definitions of reality. The religious definition of reality asserts that people have souls or some other spiritual quality; that there is a supraempirical reality in the form of a divine personality, power and/or law; and that there is a relationship between humanity and this supraempirical reality. The religious view of reality often asserts that there is a life after this here-and-now life. Thus, what one does in this life may well determine the conditions of the next or after-life. For the devout Afro-American, God-determination, rather than self-determination, is the highest value.

The clashes between the worker's naturalistic perspective and the client's religious paradigm can have serious consequences for the therapeutic process. For example, a worker's encouragement of a woman and her children to move toward self-actualization by expressing their angry feelings to their husband/father may contradict the family's interpretation of the Biblical injunctions for wives and children to be "obedient," "submissive," and "respectful" of the husband/father. The client may or may not openly share the reasons for her "resistance" to the therapeutic effort.

One practitioner found that when she met with her therapy group, two of the Afro-American women asked her if she was "saved." Rather than give a direct answer, the worker responded with questions designed to probe why they asked the question. They, in turn, did not give clear answers. Nevertheless, these questions arose with some regularity. After a few sessions, these women dropped out of the group, taking two other Afro-American Christians with them. This severely demoralized the therapy group.

In the above example, the clients' question, "Are you saved?" was an effort to find out if the worker was a "born-again" believer and follower of Jesus Christ. For these devout, "born-again" Christians, the answer to that question was important. If the worker was not—and her failure to give a clear "yes" to the question was, in their eyes, proof that she was not—they would be reluctant to allow her, as a nonbeliever, to influence them. To interpret their questions as mere therapeutic resistance is to miss the more fundamental issue stemming from their religious definition of reality; that is, they are answerable to God.

The clash between the naturalistic and religious perspectives can affect other aspects of treatment as well. For instance, a client may have a religious diagnosis of his or her problem which differs radically from the naturalistic diagnosis held by the worker. For example:

Mrs. R., a 48-year-old Afro-American woman, was referred to the worker by a guidance counselor at a local community college. Mrs. R. had given up her job to enter the nursing program at the college, but her acute anxiety was interfering with her learning.

The worker saw Mrs. R. for several sessions. In the first session, Mrs. R. mentioned that she was a Christian and attended a Pentacostal church. The worker, however, did not attach much importance to this. Instead, the worker focused on the apparent crisis which had been precipitated by Mrs. R.'s reentry into school.

One day, Mrs. R. telephoned the worker to thank her for the help she received, and to say that she would not be returning for therapy. "The Lord spoke to me," said Mrs.R., "and He told me that He would help me."

The worker heard Mrs. R.'s statement that "the Lord spoke to me" with mixed feelings. On the one hand, if she applied a naturalistic perspective to understanding this statement, she might have concluded that Mrs. R. had delusions or hallucinations. Thus, Mrs. R.'s diagnosis would have been more severe than the "Adjustment Reaction" which the worker had previously decided upon. On the other hand, the worker was familiar with the subculture of Mrs. R.'s religious group, and was aware that it was acceptable to speak of religious experiences or feelings in terms of personal encounters with the divine. "Jesus walked with me," "God spoke to me," "The Holy Spirit led me" are socially acceptable ways of communicating spiritual insights. By themselves, they do not indicate mental aberrations. Although the practitioner shared with Mrs. R. her understanding of the latter's religious belief, it was too late in the treatment process to be effective in keeping Mrs. R. in therapy. The worker had formulated a naturalistic diagnosis and had proceeded with treatment along naturalistic lines. On the other hand, Mrs. R. diagnosed her problem as lack of sufficient faith in God, and saw the remedy in spiritual terms, i.e., a reaffirmation of her faith and reliance upon Divine intervention.

One clear therapeutic implication of work with religious Afro-Americans is to be alert to determine the degree to which a religious paradigm is operating within the therapeutic experience. Sometimes, the practitioner must take an active role in ferreting it out and responding to it in a congruent manner. For example:

Mrs. W., a 38-year-old Afro-American woman, sought treatment because of depression and anxiety. For 15 years, Mrs. W. had been married to a man who was financially irresponsible and had had numerous affairs. In spite of her unhappiness, Mrs. W. was able to neither improve her marriage nor leave it. "I'm going 'round in circles," she said, "and it's driving me crazy."

During the first therapeutic session, Mrs. W. mentioned in passing that she was a practicing Catholic; that her sons attended parochial school; and that she and her sons went to mass every Sunday. During that first session, the worker tried to find out if Mrs. W. saw any connection between her religious beliefs and her problems. Mrs. W. denied that she saw any connection.

The worker, however, noted that Mrs. W., who had a strict Catholic upbringing, gave birth to her first son out-of-wedlock, and was pregnant with a second child when she married Mr. W. (Both children were his.) The worker's knowledge of Catholicism led her to suspect that, in spite of Mrs. W.'s denial, religious beliefs were potent influences in Mrs. W.'s marriage and self-identity. The worker suspected that Mrs. W. was, perhaps unconsciously, experiencing a great deal of guilt, and that this was behind her depression and anxiety.

After working with Mrs. W. for six months, the worker grew in her conviction about the significance of Mrs. W.'s religious beliefs. Trusting the strength of the good client–worker relationship, the worker, instead of asking, asserted that she believed that Mrs. W.'s religious beliefs greatly influenced how she functioned as a wife and mother. Mrs. W., who was normally a talkative woman, grew silent for some time as she reflected upon the worker's statement. Mrs. W. then began to recall her experiences with the nuns and priests during her youth. The theme of her recollections was that it was a mark of holiness to suffer, to endure pain. The worker was impressed with the fact that Mrs. W. had only extracted the "negatives," i.e., prohibitions and renunciations from her religion. Mrs. W. expressed none of the "positives," i.e., affirmations.

The worker, who was not Catholic, but was knowledgeable about Catholocism, challenged Mrs. W.'s understanding of the faith. In order to do this, the worker indicated an acceptance of Mrs. W.'s religious paradigm. Mrs. W. listened intently as the worker reminded Mrs. W. of the affirmations or "positives" of Christianity.

That session was a turning point in the treatment process, as it opened the discussion of sin, guilt, and suffering. The worker encouraged Mrs. W. to get in touch with her long-standing guilt about her sexual behavior and to avail herself of her religion's rituals of atonement and receiving of forgiveness. Mrs. W. did so, and began to make and sustain real gains in freeing herself from depression and anxiety. She also began to make demands upon her husband, and their relationship improved.

The above example illustrates two treatement issues. The first is that Mrs. W. had a spiritual diagnosis of which she was not conscious. Just as psychological theory helps a practitioner make inferences about some aspects of the client's unconscious psychodynamics, knowledge about the tenets and values of the client's particular religion can help the practitioner to infer some aspects of the influence of the religion upon the client's psychodynamics. The second treatment issue illustrated by the above example is that in order to deal effectively with the religious factor, the practitioner must convey respect for the client's basic religious paradigm. When the practitioner does this, the client is likely to be more receptive to a "yes, but . . . " discussion aimed at correcting misinformation or distortions. The client may not totally accept the worker's corrections, because the worker lacks the kind of "religious sanctions" which are conferred upon the clergy. In such cases, the client may need to be encouraged to consult with a minister, priest, rabbi, or some other persons clearly identified with the faith.

CONCLUSIONS

Religious beliefs may play important, but unconscious roles in the psychodynamics of the treatment process. Agencies with sizeable numbers of religious clients should enlist priests, ministers, and other religious specialists as consultants. These consultants can aid the staff in ascertaining the client's pathological or healthy uses of religion. In some instances, it may be appropriate for the religious specialist to be the primary treating person or a cotherapist. This is especially so, if the client and/or family have a consciously-held spiritual diagnosis. For example, Afro-Americans who believe that their problems stem from voodoo or some other form of "evil curse" are far more likely to respond to therapeutic efforts which take their basic paradigm into serious consideration than to those which do not. Such clients may respond to a treatment approach which calls upon the expertise of someone knowledgeable about the rituals for combating the "evil" influences which the clients believe are at the heart of their problems.

It would be important that the religious specialists, whether priests, ministers, herbalists, or excorsists, be accredited and respected by their respective communities of believers. These consultants should also agree with the general aims of the mental health profession. Mutual respect for professional competencies as they relate to naturalistic and religious skills are important, if collaborative efforts are to be effective.

Whether or not the agencies in which they practice have religious consultants, practitioners treating religious Afro-Americans should acquire a working knowledge of the basic tenets, values, and life-styles of their clients' religious groups. Such knowledge may be crucial to effective intervention. This is especially so when working with clients who are conflicted about their faith. Clients may be willing to frankly discuss with the worker questions and doubts which they may be reluctant to discuss with the clergy for fear that the latter may take a judgmental stance. Discussions with a nonjudgmental but informed therapist may be what the client needs in order to clarify and resolve his or her religious conflicts.

Clearly, not all practitioners can effectively help clients who have religious paradigms. The issue of countertransference is of paramount importance. Practitioners who are atheists, agnostics, or are themselves religiously ambivalent may find that their countertransferential responses to the client's beliefs create obstacles to the treatment process. Such practitioners may tend to dismiss the religious factor as unimportant or regard it as inherently pathological. On the other hand, devoutly religious therapists may abuse the treatment process by proselytizing their own beliefs. Or, if the client's beliefs seem similar to their own, therapists may fail to see the client's pathological use of the faith.

Religion is a highly emotionally charged issue. This is attested to by the difficulties of adequately dealing with it in the helping relationship. Nevertheless, the therapist who wants to help religious Afro-American families must face these difficulties head-on.

REFERENCES

1. Delaney AJ: Black Task Force Report. New York, Family Service Association of America, 1979, p. 38
2. O'Dea T: The Sociology of Religion. Englewood Cliffs, N.J., Prentice Hall, 1966

Yvonne B. Ferguson

13
Improving Intervention Strategies with Minority Group Adolescents

HISTORICAL NOTE

Heralded by the social unrest characterizing the late 1950s and early 1960s in the United States, psychiatry's "third revolution"[1] cut its legislative teeth with the passage of the Community Mental Health Centers Act in 1964. Coupled with the MediCare and MediCaid programs of 1965, which provided the currency of exchange for the medically indigent population, Afro-Americans and other minorities were able, for the first time, to purchase mental health services in mass volume. Thus, before American psychiatry had a chance to hone its skills for servicing a previously largely underserviced segment of society, minority patients were beating down the doors of these centers.

No small part of the problem has been the paucity of minority group mental health professionals. For example, as late as 1976, the total national statistic for Afro-American psychiatrists (not including trainees) was less than 500.[2] Assuming that not all of these psychiatrists have an exclusively Afro-American clientele, and assuming that Afro-American patients are being treated by white psychiatrists and by other mental health professionals as well, this paltry figure still serves to highlight the deficit of mental health services being delivered to this population. This form of what might be termed "institutional racism"—the failure to train adequate numbers of minority psychiatrists, whether from benign neglect or deliberate intention, is in part responsible for the failure of some minority group members to seek services from predominately white mental health facilities. For those who did find their way into such facilities, many unforeseen experiences awaited them.

CASE STUDIES

The following case studies were judged to be typical of minority adolescents and their families treated in a large urban psychiatric training center, located in an affluent area of the city and staffed by predominately white middle-class personnel. The adolescents were inpatients of the child division of the hospital during the period 1974 to 1978.

CASE STUDY 1

A 15-year-old Afro-American male was admitted to the pediatric inpatient service for a neurological work-up of a possible seizure disorder. A history of head injury 6 years prior to admission resulted in a comatose state of several days' duration followed by grand mal seizures. This provided the backdrop for the investigation of his present symptoms, consisting of erratic episodes of undirected aggression, with altered states of consciousness.

While a lumbar puncture was being attempted unsuccessfully by the pediatrician, the patient (hereafter referred to as John D.) who had been sedated and physically restrained, became delusional, perceiving that his leg had been amputated and that the physician was attempting to harm him. He grasped the pediatrician's necktie as he bent over. This act resulted in an immediate cessation of the work-up and an emergency psychiatric consultation, the purpose of which was to effect a transfer off the pediatric service. A transfer was accomplished in VIP haste through the administrative channels of both department chairpersons after the psychiatric consultant labeled the patient "homicidal" and "too dangerous" to be discharged into the community. The case was assigned to the only Afro-American psychiatrist on the adolescent psychiatric ward to which the patient had been admitted.

Of interest is the fact that the particular unit which received the request for immedate transfer was a unit for the mentally retarded, even though the patient was of low normal intelligence. The transfer bypassed the normal channels of a preadmission evaluation and was designated a "crisis case," with instructions from the ward psychiatrist to medicate the patient as quickly as possible, complete the neurological evaluation, perform a psychological assessment, and return him to the community. Of little concern was the need for a school evaluation, even though John D. evidenced academic retardation due to truancy, or the need for family assessment, even though the patient was a member of an extensively pathological family. Although the Afro-American therapist felt quite comfortable with her crisis intervention skills, the staff as a whole was inexperienced in this form of assessment and treatment, and no other patient on the unit at that time had been admitted as a "crisis case." This was a long-term treatment facility.

During hospitalization, there were no incidents of person-directed violence, except for one self-destructive act consisting of John thrusting his arm through a glass window. Several times, however, the staff would physically move in on John in anticipation of violence. For example, as John raised his hand to his head with an Afro pick, a staff member perceived him to be about to strike a patient, and rushed to him. This frequent misreading of the patient's behavior did not go unheeded by John, who sensed the staff's fear of him and would then play into it. He assumed a quasistaff position of authority and exercised his leadership abilities among his peers, often attempting to counsel them, and remained aloof during activities while being seductive with female staff and peers.

Individaul therapy revealed a terribly frightened and untrusting youth who was very verbal and therapeutically accessible. He astutely perceived the ward dynamics and admitted to his manipulation of staff. Artistic drawings and projective tests revealed an underlying thought disorder and homosexual conflict. With moderate dosages of psychotropic medication, complete restoration of impulse control early on in therapy brought all pseudoseizure activity under control and the completed neurological work-up was entirely normal. The mother expressed a desire for therapeutic work and the therapist capitalized upon her rapport with the family. Despite the therapist's plea for extended hospitalization, however, the treatment team pushed for discharge without contributing to any disposition planning. All disposition plans were made by the Afro-American therapist, who agreed to follow the patient and mother postdischarge. In addition, the therapist helped the patient obtain state funds for special education in a facility that offered art skill development and eventually orchestrated residential placement for John and treatment of a sibling. The unit was extremely resourceful and ordinarily these responsiblities were delegated to the social worker.

CASE STUDY 2

A 16-year-old Afro-American male was referred by the mother for problems of misconduct consisting of disruptive school behavior, lying, stealing from the mother, and running up large phone bills at home. More overt in this case were concerns about "homosexual tendencies." The mother voiced these at the time of admission. In this instance, a reverse of the former situation occurred. The patient (Joe S.) was admitted for a six- to eight-week evaluation but instead remained for seven months, even though at numerous points of evaluation of the case, many staff felt the patient was not therapeutically working and should not remain in the hospital. Indeed the case seemed to be one of Joe, who was very verbal, actively avoiding any meaningful therapeutic work while at the same time being charming, entertaining, and a decided leader among his peers. During his hospital course, he exhibited the same behavior he had at home and school—being disruptive, acting out, stealing from peers. At one point he was given a "therapeutic" temporary discharge for several days and at another time his sister was admitted to the unit on a crisis basis.

The family work with the mother and one sister was led by a social worker who was easily intimidated by the angry, loud-talking mother. Once, when the new ward psychiatrist attended one of these sessions, both the social worker and Joe's therapist were observed to be effectively silenced by the mother, who was literally running the session. The eventual discharge was decided upon by the new ward psychiatrist, an Afro-American woman, shortly after taking her job. By then the staff, for the most part, were angry and had given up on Joe. They were happy to be rid of the patient but unable to express these feelings to the ward psychiatrist. Joe's mother was infuriated by the fact that not only had Joe not improved, but in some ways he was "slicker," i.e., more manipulative than before. She also felt she had not been appraised of his deteriorating state and queried the staff as to why he was not discharged after the eight-week evaluation period if he could not be helped there. In her disappointment and rage she threatened to discuss the matter with her attorney.

CASE STUDY 3

A 13-year-old Hispanic female was admitted to the adolescent unit in a suicidal crisis. She had apparently overdosed in a culminative effort to get help following several previous incidents of self-injurious behavior including drug abuse and walking in front of cars. Sue J. was physically mature for her years, making it easy for one to forget her chronological or, worse yet, her developmental age. She lived with her siblings and mother who did not speak English. Formerly an excellent student and devoted daughter, for several months prior to admission Sue had begun to evidence declining academic performance and noncompliance at home. Paralleling Sue's behavior was an increasingly chaotic deterioration of the family, involving vicious verbal attacks (as well as a possible sexual assualt) by the mother's live-in boyfriend, the mother's discovery of her pregnancy by this man, and finally his separation from the family.

The staff was accepting of Sue's need for emergency hospitalization but felt that she was inappropriate for long-term therapy. They pointed to the fact that family therapy would be handicapped by utilization of an off-ward Spanish-speaking therapist and that Sue was extremely nonverbal, withholding, and repeatedly stated she didn't want to be in the hospital. Shortly after her discharge, Sue presented herself for application for a long-term bed having again threatened to kill herself. She had refused to keep her outpatient appointments and was not staying at her mother's house.

The perennial question of "Why are we keeping this girl when she's not therapeutically working?" was raised by staff who were unwilling or unable to look at their own behavior for possible clues to explain Sue's resistance. The issue of ethnic differences between this patient and the majority of the staff and peers was dismissed by the therapist as irrelevant even though Sue loathed going on outings where she might be seen by friends with her white peers. Sue also was noted to verbalize with the "tough" female staff, whom she respected, and presented only an angry, defiant posture towards "meek" or "ultrafeminine" female staff. At one point, she was assigned a new female staff member also of Hispanic origin, with whom she conversed in Spanish. This staff person was instructed by her immediate superior not to use Spanish when speaking to Sue because it set her apart from the other patients. The new staff member had come to the unit with a background in community work and was able to elicit a history of Sue's peripheral involvement with a gang. Sue's protest of wanting to leave, while making no effort to elope, expressed her ambivalence about wanting help while at the same time realizing that the help she was receiving would ill-equip her to survive in the barrio to which she would ultimately return.

DISCUSSION

These cases were selected to illustrate multiple examples of what might be considered "institutional racism" operative in an inpatient mental health facility. The findings are felt to be generalizable to other predominately white settings where delivery of human services takes place. The following areas cover only the more blatant manifestations of racism, the subtleties of which are almost too elusive to capture in writing, but nonetheless equally as destructive.

1. Inadequate or nonexistent recruitment of minority mental health workers.
2. Inadequate or non-existent in-service training of staff in the skills necessary to effectively treat minority patients.
3. Biases in minority patient admitting practices.
4. Biases in minority patient discharge practices.
5. Biases in minority patient diagnostic practices.
6. Blind spots of white staff in identifying staff dynamics and process which affect the course and outcome of treatment of minority patients.

A very elementary fact of staffing an inpatient service is the occurrence of non-deliberate role-modeling. Although this principle has begun to be applied in the elementary education arena as it relates to gender, little importance is placed upon insuring an optimal ethnic mix of staff unless minority administrators cognizant of this need are entrusted with the authority to do so. This is not to imply that only minorities can treat minorities. However, minority staff must be visible as role models and must be able and willing to prick the consciences of their white counterparts when that is in order.[3]

Very few training hospitals, much less proprietary hospitals, perceive the need for in-service training programs in minority patient treatment skills unless there is agitation for such by minority staff or trainees.[4] If, however, minority staff and trainees are not present in vocal numbers, few white staff are willing to seek outside workshops or literature on their own initiative. A training seminar was available in the facility from which the above cases were selected; however, it was neither incorporated as a mandatory component of the training program, nor attended by persons most in need of it.

Minority admissions on the above adolescent unit in Case Studies 2 and 3 never totalled more than one or two out of a total census of 16–18 patients at any point in time prior to the hiring of an Afro-American ward psychiatrist. The reputation of the ward prior to this therapist's arrival had been that of a long-term treatment unit which was very effective in treating middle- and upper-middle-class white-American adolescents of certain diagnostic categories. The staff was 92 percent middle- and upper-class white. Of those Afro-American adolescents who presented for admission, often ominous prognostic indicators should have served to screen them out. Instead, they would be admitted and a self-fulfilling prophecy would be realized, whereby the fantasy of the ward being an appropriate treatment setting only for white patients was perpetuated.

Another admitting practice which served to screen out appropriate Afro-American candidates for admission was the expectation that a good treatment case had to have an intact family for effective family therapy. Still another was that the prospective patient present him- or herself very verbally and ask to be admitted. The use of other than the traditional modality of "talking therapy," such as activities, art, writing, music, or even play therapy with nonverbal adolescents was not explored. Nor was the issue of the "lily-white ivory tower" image of the facility from a ghetto perspective explored when an applicant was not verbally requesting admission and yet obviously in need of it. This uncovering stance is entirely appropriate for younger adolescents of any ethnicity, but particularly for cautious, untrusting Afro-Americans.[5] While the mental retardation (MR) ward in Case Study 1 was more evenly mixed ethnically in terms of patient population, the staff mix was even less than that of the non-MR unit.

Discharge criteria should be as carefully thought out and planned as are admission criteria. In the cases cited, however, discharge was either inappropriately hasty or inappropriately prolonged. A patient admitted on an emergency basis can be converted to long-term status when the assessment points to the need for continued hospitalization. Such a change of status is merely an administrative manipulation. Although evidence of the need for long-term treatment was apparent in both Case Studies 1 and 3, the bed conversion was not effected until, as in the latter case, the patient acted out to get herself readmitted. Since there was no gatekeeping function of the ward with regard to emergency cases, which are likely to be minority patients because of their style of health service utilization,[6] rapid discharge was the only means at each unit's disposal for controlling ethnic proportions of the patient census. In Case Study 2, where the patient's discharge was long overdue, Afro-American staff on more than one occasion stated that had the patient been white he would have been discharged long before. The "temporary" discharge was an attempt to placate angry staff and salve the consciences of guilty staff.

As far as diagnostic bias is concerned, it is now well established that upper socioeconomic patients are more likely to receive a diagnosis of psychoneurosis, and lower socioeconomic patients one of psychosis or "psychopathic personality."[7] Up until 1962, it was reported that depression was rare in Afro-Americans,[8] and suicide supposedly rarer. Recent research is beginning to explode these myths, but in the meantime a diagnosis obviously determines treatment, and incorrect diagnostic assessment is not only responsible for patients not receiving appropriate treatment but no doubt is also responsible for iatrogenic suffering.

Between the point of entry and the point of departure for Afro-American adolescents on these inpatient units, a strange form of attrition occurs. It has to do with the psychodynamic processes taking place among the staff and the staff's inherent blind spots for collective introspection on their attitudes and behaviors. An institutional character pathology develops insidiously among staff. It reverberates among sophisticated Afro-American patients only to cause counterwaves whose amplitudes become additive as they return to the source of emission. Stereotypes representing the unacceptable impulses of the group in power (whites) are posited in the powerless group (Afro-Americans), and often precede the admission of a patient from the latter group. All therapists from the former group hold various of these false beliefs, of which they are largely unaware. In turn, they formulate diagnostic and dynamic questions in an attempt to validate these beliefs by eliciting information to support them.

Case Study 1 serves as an example of the stereotype of the Afro-American male being overly aggressive, resulting in his quickly being labeled "homicidal" for grabbing his doctor's necktie. Not only is homicidal potential difficult to assess because of the infrequency of its fulfillment,[9] but its capricious use is extremely dangerous in its stigmatizing effect and the potential for setting in motion a self-fulfilling prophecy. Hence, before Joe was transferred to the adolescent unit, the staff grapevine buzzed with descriptions of this "big, aggressive, dangerous Afro-American patient." Although muscular, in reality the patient was neither very tall nor heavy for his age. Other psychological stereotypes of Afro-Americans are that they are: "nonverbal, unmotivated for treatment, have primitive character structure, are impulse-ridden, and are not psychologically minded." Societal stereotypes upon which the former ones are laid are that Afro-Americans are: "lazy, unintelligent, unhealthy, criminal, dirty, and sexually promiscuous." Techniques which allow the patient to present his or her data unsolicited are more scientific than those which require responses to questions which represent the interviewer's bias. By using the former techniques, an interviewer sensitive to his or her own biases can avoid feeding these stereotypes.

Whenever visible differences between therapist and patient exist, they must be explored for the purpose of defusing countertransference and transference fantasies. The greater these differences, the more the therapist relies upon untested projection without realizing it.[10] The black-white pair serves as a symbolic expression of all the psychologically paired opposites—good versus bad; powerful versus powerless. Recognition of these differences will rarely be stated by the patient but must surface if in-depth therapy is to succeed. The therapist must pay special attention to the patient's responses following interpretations, suggestions, or advice, and each party may have to process messages twice before real communication takes place. Therapists must be sensitive to feedback and able to modify their initial appraisals, and be able to function beyond their own subcultures. A danger in this last guideline is for the therapist to attempt to slide over into the patient's subculture by artificially adopting the patient's lingo or to be so understanding as to "know what it must be like to be Afro-American." This latter attempt at empathizing is often committed by therapists who compare their oppressions, such as that of being a woman, a Jew, or a long-haired iconoclast, to that of the patient. This is inappropriate and likely to render a blow to the establishment of a therapeutic relationship.

The manipulation of staff by "street-wise" or "establishment-wise" Afro-American youths is a symptom of the parallel process alluded to above. Not only does this replicate what often occurs within other social service systems when guilt ridden white liberals attempt to work out their own conflicts through their clientele, but white psychiatric staff are equipped with skills to alter this type of behavior. Intimidation of staff, deceit, or verbal attacks on staff are forms of acting out for which simple behavioral limits are extremely effective. However, the staff in the above case studies inconsistently applied such limits, ignored those behaviors, or allowed them to escalate to the point where more radical interventions were necessitated. These circumstances prevailed in all three cases, especially so in Case Study 2, where limit-setting was indicated for both the patient and the family. Joe's mother and sister actually mocked the social worker but readily backed down when the Afro-American female ward chief entered a session. Neither special favors nor undue restrictiveness should result in Afro-American patients being treated differently, such as admitting a sibling where such practice would not prevail otherwise, or granting "temporary discharges."

The only way white staff can learn about Afro-American patients is by treating them. The presence of an Afro-American therapist in Case

Study 1 excused the white staff from becoming acquainted with Afro-American culture and from attempting to do some self-examination.

In Case Studies 1 and 2, the "double whamy" of being Afro-American and homosexual were therapeutic issues which were not opened and explored with the patients. Here were instances in which the sexual stereotype of the "black male stud" ill-served Joe and John, as they hid behind the fantasy and even acted upon it from time to time to keep the fires warm. The very thin "macho" veneer of both Joe and John needed to be gently but firmly eroded in order for them to accept themselves for what they were.

Finally, in all cases, staffs were permitted to escape their responsibilities by pleading ignorance or inexperience. Social workers were not aware of Afro-American family social structures and were not able to be confrontive, active, directive, or set limits with these mothers. They were not knowledgeable of Afro-American community resources, nor did they assist the primary therapists in disposition planning. Patients were discharged when long-term therapy was indicated and was a viable plan.

The lack of verbalization of some minority patients was not understood both in terms of its developmental appropriateness for a 13-year-old (Case Study 3) or in terms of its evidencing fear and distrust on the part of the patient generally. But when it became a form of acting out (Case Study 3), just as the superficial verbosity of Case Studies 1 and 2 was, it did not result in limits being set.

SUMMARY

Minority patients test the full repertoire of psychiatric skills of mental health deliverers. Social, economic, and educational sequalae of racism are ever-present, but must not serve to dilute efforts at unraveling intra- and interpsychic conflicts within the individual, within the family, and between the individual and family unit and the treatment staff.

Several strategic points offer themselves to intervention on various of these levels of conflict:

1. The staff's ethnic composition should provide numerically adequate role models for minority patients.
2. In-service training for the staff will undoubtedly have to be mandatory.
3. Admitting and discharge practices should be sensitive but fair to minority patients.
4. Diagnostic practices must reflect current, well-designed diagnostic research.

5. White staff must have consciousness-raising experiences to illuminate their biases and alter their behavior in the treatment process.

If these interventions are not applied systematically in inpatient treatment settings, the psychological attrition of Afro-American and other minority adolescents who are admitted to predominately white facilites will result in thwarted treatment efforts, and many such adolescents who need treatment will never get the chance to receive it.

REFERENCES

1. Bellack L: Handbook of Community Psychiatry and Community Mental Health. New York, Grune & Stratton, 1964
2. Black Psychiatrists of America, Directory. Boston, Solomon Fuller Institute, 1976
3. Jones A, Seagull AA: Dimensions of the relationship between the black client and the white therapist: A theoretical overview. Am Psychol 32:850–855, 1977
4. American Psychiatric Association (National Institute of Mental Health Minority Program). Anecdotal information from informal nationwide poll of minority psychiatric trainees, 1978
5. Blackwell JE, Sharpley RH, Hart PS: Health Needs of Urban Blacks. Boston, Solomon Fuller Institute, 1978
6. Schweitzer S: Incentives and the consumption of preventive care, in Mushkin S (ed): Consumer Incentives for Health Care. New York, Milbank Memorial Fund.
7. Hollingshead AG, and Redlich FC: Social Class and Mental Ilness: A Community Study. New York, Wiley. 1958
8. Prange AJ, Vitols MM: Pitfalls of Epidemiology, Racism and Psychiatry. New York, Brunner/Mazel, 1972, p.12
9. Kozel HL, Boucher RJ, Garofalo F: The diagnosis and treatment of dangerousness. Crime and Delinquency 18:371–392, 1972
10. Pinderhughes C: Racism and psychotherapy, in Brown B, Willie C, Kramer B, (eds): Racism and Mental Health. Pennsylvania, University of Pittsburgh Press, 1973, pp. 61–121

Lewis M. King

14

Suicide From a "Black Reality" Perspective

> *It would be a reactionary death to compromise with the system. Reactionary suicide means that the conditions, the reactionary conditions, would be the cause of our suicide. If we stand and do nothing, it would be self-murder. I would rather use the reverse, if it becomes necessary, and that is revolutionary suicide. That's suicide motivated by the desire to change the system or else die trying to change the reactionary conditions.*[1]

Newton's reference point is what is significant in the above quotation. He struggled to view suicide "with his own eyes" and there can be no more compelling reason for a re-examination of suicide from a black reality. What must enter into the scientific arena for the purpose of critical examination is the perspective of the oppressed group, a perspective which must challenge the hegemony of Eurocentric determination. For instance, some of the first recorded research on Afro-American people by white researchers is dated back to 1896. In that year, the American Economic Association published "Race Traits and Tendencies of the American Negro," a study by Hoffman,[2] a statistician and a member of the American Academy of Medicine, the American Statistical Association, and the Royal Statistical Society of London. His work reflected the thinking of these scientific communities about Afro-American groups. Hoffman found that there was a lack of suicides among Afro-Americans and he cited this as another instance of the inferior physiological and psychological organization. He went on to state that the Afro-American person committed suicide only in very rare cases "only in a fit of passion, during loss of self-control, or in most cases, to escape the consequence of his crimes." Hoffman viewed this tendency toward a lack of suicide as an absense of the traces of those "more subtle motives" which prompted "the more cultured and more advanced races".

Hoffman represented what appears to be some consensus in the reasoning that there was absense of anxiety in Afro-Americans, the tendency being for them to live wholly in the present, with the intellectual development of an inferior race. This type of thinking, research, and interpretation of data will not cease unless its deep structure is challenged by counter-theory, analysis, and interpretation for "our own eyes."

The 19th Century view of the black psyche would, one might assume, today be challenged by the fact that suicide is the fourth leading cause of death among Afro-American youth between ages of 15 and 24. This author suggests, however, the ideology espoused by Hoffman would not be changed: these data would simply be used in support of a new logic to derive the same ideology. There would be new explanations in the direction of negating the positive attributes of the group, explanations centered in the class-conditioned realities of the researcher, explanations which blame the victim and indict the Afro-American family or community.

This chapter will examine the data base on suicide among the Afro-American population especially over the last two decades, examine the limitations of existing theories in their explanation of the data, suggest the reformulation of a model for the generation of theory which may more adequately explain suicide among Afro-American groups, and finally conclude by suggesting alternative research issues to be examined.

The chapter will develop data primarily on young Afro-American adults aged 15 to 24 and 24 to 60. Only general comments will be made regarding other age and cultural groups. Obviously, the author's own deep structure ideology guides the discussion of this chapter. Frantz Fanon[3] best represents this position when he writes:

> If we want humanity to advance to a step further, if we want to bring it up to a different level than that which Europe has shown it, then we must . . . for Europe, for ourselves, and for humanity . . . turn over a new leaf . . . work out new concepts, and try to set afoot a new man.

Consequently, while the specific focus of this chapter is on suicide, we must bear in mind the parallel concerns of homocide and capital punishment. If we condone any one of these, then, as Kant says, we insult humanity. All human life is sacred and must be preserved at all costs. The prevention of suicide depends on the validity of this principle to both society and individual. We cannot separate the inhumanity of a body count in Viet Nam from the 20 million starving children in America or from the victim of suicide. They are ultimately linked to the moral and human credo of a nation and the honesty with which that nation believes in and acts upon it.[4]

DATA BASE

Man is condemned to narrowly delineated freedoms and the freedom to kill himself is not one of these. Apparently and unfortunately, among many Afro-American persons suicide seems to have been added as one of the choices. Support for this comes from the significant increase in the rate of suicide among Afro-Americans of almost all ages over the last decade. In some instances, especially in urban areas, rates have tripled over a 20-year period.

The average rate of suicide for all groups in the United States has shown little variance over the period 1970 to 1975 (11.8 to 12.4 per 100,000). While the average rate for Afro-American groups during the same period is lower (5.1 to 6.2 per 100,000), the significant rate of increase is alarming. This increase is particularly startling if one takes into consideration only urban areas or specific age groups.

In 1920, the rate of Afro-American suicide victims in Los Angeles County exceeded the overall national rate by 2.5 per 100,000. In 1980, the rate of victims in LA county is expected to exceed the over all national rate by 3.5 per 100,000.[5] When only age is taken into consideration, the United States census data indicate that suicide among Afro-Americans is primarily a youthful phenomenon[6] (see Table 14-1). The greatest percentage of suicides when both sexes are considered occurs between the ages of 20 and 34 (41 to 49 percent), with a 3:1 ratio of males to females. For Afro-American groups, suicide appears to decline after the age of 34. More recent data from urban areas also seem to point to a shift in the peak frequency age, which in 1975 was 25 to 29 years, to a younger age group (20 to 24 years) and also to a rapid increase in female suicide. Interestingly enough, the same directions and trends are found in data on drug abuse, alcoholism, smoking, and homicide.

The meaning of this statistical picture may not as yet have been brought home to the reality of the Afro-American community. In a 1975 survey by Reynolds and his colleagues of 102 Afro-Americans interviewed, fully 89 percent claimed that suicide was an "Anglo" phenomenon.[7]

Table 14-1
Suicide Rates per 100,000 United States Population by Race, Age, and Sex: 1970 and 1975

Age (in yrs)	Blacks						Whites					
	1970			1975			1970			1975		
	Both Sexes	Male	Female	Both Sexes	Male	Female	Both Sexes	Male	Female	Both Sexes	Male	Female
All Ages	5.1	8.1	2.5	6.2	10.2	2.7	12.4	18.0	7.1	13.6	20.1	7.4
5	—	—	—	—	—	—	—	—	—	—	—	—
5–9	—	—	—	—	—	—	—	—	—	—	—	—
10–14	0.4	0.3	0.4	0.2	0.2	0.3	0.7	1.1	0.3	0.9	1.4	0.4
15–19	3.8	4.8	2.9	3.9	6.4	1.6	6.2	9.4	2.9	8.1	13.0	3.1
20–24	11.7	20.5	4.8	13.6	23.6	5.3	12.3	19.3	5.7	16.9	26.3	6.9
25–29	12.0	19.7	5.8	16.3	27.9	6.6	14.1	19.8	8.6	16.6	25.1	8.0
30–34	11.8	19.7	5.5	12.0	21.5	4.3	14.7	20.0	9.5	16.7	23.5	10.0
35–39	8.7	14.5	4.0	9.9	17.3	4.0	16.9	21.9	12.2	17.0	22.8	11.4
40–44	7.1	11.4	3.5	9.0	15.2	3.8	19.1	24.6	13.8	19.9	26.1	13.9
45–49	9.2	15.9	3.5	7.9	13.7	2.9	20.6	28.2	13.5	21.4	29.1	14.0
50–54	7.3	11.3	3.9	6.0	10.4	5.3	21.9	30.9	13.5	21.6	20.2	13.6
55–59	6.9	12.9	1.7	7.2	11.7	3.3	23.5	34.9	13.1	21.9	32.0	12.7
60–64	4.7	7.7	2.2	6.5	9.8	3.8	22.5	35.0	11.5	20.7	32.3	10.6
65–69	5.9	9.7	2.7	5.1	8.5	2.5	21.9	37.4	9.4	20.9	35.	9.6
70–74	4.7	7.0	3.0	9.3	16.0	3.9	22.7	40.4	9.7	21.2	37.6	9.3
75–79	2.7	4.5	1.4	8.8	18.1	1.9	21.4	42.2	7.3	22.3	44.9	7.8
80–84	8.2	16.6	2.3	3.1	6.6	0.8	20.0	45.8	5.8	19.4	50.3	4.7
85+	5.8	10.2	3.1	1.3	3.8	—	20.0	45.8	5.8	19.4	50.3	4.7

Data from Vital Statistics of the U.S., 1970–1975 (vol 2, Mortality, Part A, Tables 1–26). Washington, D.C., U.S. Bureau of the Census, 1975, pp 23–28.

We now have three issues from the data that have traditionally been examined, first that rates have been on the increase over the last two decades; that these rates have particularly affected male youth between the ages of 20 and 34 years; and the incidence is very high in urban as opposed to nonurban areas.

In an attempt to offer further explanation, attention in the traditional literature has also been directed to another set of issues, that is, the characteristics of people who commit suicide and the method of injury. Among the early studies were those of Breed[8] who found that the most characteristic problems for Afro-American males seems to have been conflict with authority (particularly the police) and the burden of social regulation. He also found that while males committing suicide were downwardly mobile at the time. i.e., their occupations were lower than their fathers' or ones that they had previously maintained themselves. Afro-American males, who more frequently maintained employment with comparatively less salary and status at the time of suicide, were upwardly mobile: they were facing increased competition with its increased strains.[8] The implications for these findings are frightening. Breed goes on to state that the low suicide rates for Afro-Americans can be attributed in part to segregation, which has kept Afro-Americans from competing with their white counterparts while keeping goals low and lessening the strain.

For Afro-American females, the characteristic patterns suggested (in 1966) were loss of a mate, failure in the maternal role, or longstanding problems with family.

The reported patterns for males has remained largely unchanged over the last decade, although the issue of conflict with authority has taken on new meaning. Wolfgang formulated the concept of "victim precipitated homocide" in which he hypothesized that the developmental characteristic of Afro-Americans within the low socioeconomic stratum produced unconscious guilt and an orientation toward physical aggression and punishment from others.[9] Much of the police homicide over the last decade has been excused on this questionable premise. Very little attention is paid to the issue that a large percentage of the victims were low on finances. For women the pattern has shifted to family problems based on loss of emotional support, conflict with a mate, and finances. The use of firearms and drug overdose for injury has remained high, with men more inclined to use firearms, and women, drugs. The method is somewhat evenly distributed over all age groups.

Yet another data base that one finds in the literature is that most of the Afro-American victimes lived with a family or a spouse. They were not isolated or alone, although a large percentage of the victims (42 percent) were found to have traces of alcohol or drugs in their blood, liver, or stomachs, 14 percent were found to be seriously ill, and 17 percent had a prior psychiatric history.[9a]

The critical issue from an Afro-American perspective is not necessarily the validity of the data bases on the characteristics of suicide among Afro-Americans, but why particular variables were chosen to the exclusion of others. The data base search in suicide is guided by a concept called the psychological autopsy or biopsy. Implicit in this concept is a frame of reference with its own genetic epistemology and a search for causes in keeping with a deep structure of an orientation that views suicide as a disease, depsite early efforts to introduce into thinking a sociological[10] and cultural[11] orientation. Despite what appears to be a balance in the number of sociological perspectives as compared to those that are psychodynamic, the issue of suicide is still deeply embedded in the thinking that governs mental illness. This deep structure thinking generates a search for causes and indeed data within the person, with particular emphasis being given to suicide as a psychodynamic problem of dpression.[12] The following is a survey of the theories of suicide and an examination of the nature of their explanation of their epigenesis.

EXISTING THEORIES

Durkheim was among the first to address suicide from a sociological perspective, and he viewed suicide as a social phenomenon. His epigenetic principle centers on a person's relationship to society, i.e., whether the person is integrated into society, or feels a duty to his or her group.[10] Similar to Durkheim's anomie suicide is the theory of social disorganization in communities with high social conflict and lack of unity as a result of migration.[13] Gibbs and Martin suggest that the suicide rate of a population varies with the stability and durability of social relationship within the population. Their theory is based on the issues of status, role, and role conflict.[14] Here, as Davis explains, "the comprehensive sociological theory developed by Gibbs and Martin hinges partly upon the bittersweet realization that constructive social changes may in some ways have destructive consequences."[6] Henry and Short, in a similar social orientation, postulated that both suicide and homicide are a result of frustration growing out of economic forces.[15] Their epigentic principle rests on the strength of the relationship system. When external restraints are weak, direct aggression is unacceptable and the individual turns agression inward. However, the choice that a person makes between suicide and homicide depends on certain psychological as well as social variables.

In contrast to these theories are the psychodynamic theories represented in the works of Farber,[16] Schneidman et al.,[17] and Breed.[18] The central principle rests on viewing suicide as the combination of psychological vulnerability and certain deprivations. The suicidal person, it is postulated, possesses an inadequate psychological make-up, an impaired sense of competence, and an experience of loss. They perceive suicide to be acting-out behavior as a result of masochism, schizophrenia, ego weakness, alcoholism, or depression.

These two frames of reference, largely social, and the other, centrally psychodynamic, have been used to speculate on the nature of suicide among Afro-American populations. The speculative analysis, however, offered little toward understanding Afro-American culture or the concrete sociopolitical reality of Afro-American people in the United States. Interestingly, many of these speculative analyses were from Afro-American authors.

Proudhomme in 1938 was one of the first to address the issue of low suicide rates, and he developed an explanation from the role of the church.[19] He felt that religion, and particularly the spirituals sung in Afro-American churches, served as an emotional outlet. Poussaint supported this position and concluded furthermore that Afro-Americans have been able to adjust and adapt despite racial oppression because the Afro-American cultural experience fosters fortitude and endurance.[20] His analysis was developed through the exploration of Afro-American folklore and spirituals.

Numerous authors also assumed that few suicides among Afro-Americans were cause by economics or economic reversals because they were relatively insulated, by virture of their low status, from fluctuations in the economy.[8] It has been suggested that the reason young urban Afro-Americans had high suicide rates was that they felt the brunt of an economic change.[21,22]

From an economic perspective, the issue of class and status has been considered. The general trend in thinking was that absorption of Afro-Americans into middle class orientation increased their vulnerability to suicide.[19,23,24]

The Afro-American family has also been considered, and has been viewed as both a deterrant to and a contributing factor in suicide. Hendin views the Afro-American family as an influence because of the "rage and self-hatred that are an integral part of the black family situation" as an outgrowth of racial discrimination.[(25,26)] Breed assumes a similar position.[8] Both Wilkerson[27] and Poussaint[20] take issue with Hendin's position and suggest not only that Hendin's generalization cannot be inferred to the family or the larger Afro-American community, but that indeed the family and community have been the only real buffer against self-destruction.

Other variables studied in relation to suicide among Afro-Americans include research of the following: (1) geographic location—urban areas have higher rates than rural areas; (2) migration—the greater the migration, the greater the suicide rates[8]; and (3) black male–female relations—this is a modified deficit theory describing the stress and rage of Afro-American women as a function of the conflict with their mates that lead to suicide.[28]

In summary, from the growing body of literature we have two general frameworks to explain suicide: one sociological, the other psychodynamic. The tendency, however, is not to examine the concrete reality of the Afro-American experience but rather to emphaze the search for perceiving suicide as a psychodynamic problem of depression.[16,29] In the course of this search, some cultural issues germane to the "black reality" have been overlooked.

Four issues are critical. The first is that there has been a failure to focus on and understand the Afro-American cultural experience in relation to the historical experience of being in the United States. Instead, the emphasis has been on ethnicity, or treatment of Afro-Americans as a monoethnic group without regard to the complexities of the multiple cultural experiences within the black space and reality.[5] As part of this cultural exploration, one needs to understand the meaning of life and death, and the continuity of life and death in the cosmology of the Afro-American person. When Farbrow suggests that suicide (S) is a function of the reciprocal of hope (H), i.e., $S = f(1/H)$, by implication we are always suicidal, trapped in a death reality since S is always greater than zero.[30] From the Afro-American person and perspective, the will to live or to survive may have different meanings from the death wish so eloquently emphasized by Freud from the vantage point of his Eurocentric cosmology. The emphasis is on death rather than life.

The second issue is the equally significant failure to examine more critically the issues of reciprocity between the person and the socio-political environment. The key here is the failure of theories to examine in any real sense the concepts of the loss of political power and self-determination that genuinely threaten the feelings of personal freedom and worth. The issue of reciprocity in the relationship between person and the environment has been suggested, but in large measure ignored. What is sought, instead, is that element within the person, from the vantage point of pathology, that explains the wish to die. Theories conform to a sort of social physics in which the attempt to quantify suicide with exclusively individual personality variables ignores the social context of reality.

The third issue, closely connected with the failure to examine reciprocity and context, is the failure to examine by dialectual analysis the historical movement of the Afro-American person through social space, i.e., the social formation of the Afro-American person in the context of an American capitalistic experience. This social formation takes on different meanings and forms for differing historical experiences of black migrant groups—African, West Indian, Latin America—although they may have a common link in terms of sociopolitical exploitation.

Finally, there has been a failure to deal with historical oppression of black groups in America, oppression in the form of racism and social exploitation which has centrally characterized the relationship of the state to black peoples.

The net result overlooking these four critical issues is a failure to develop alternative integrated perspectives for the examination of black reality or the complexity of the behaving human organism in a social context. The following is an attempt to develop this alternative paridigm.

REFORMULATION

This chapter is not the first to attempt to develop alternatives. The most recent brief effort was by Davis in 1980. Davis tried to examine the relationship between the black community and the young black person. He indicated that one could begin to account for the increase in the frequency of suicide by an examination of the extent to which strong family and communal ties, as a protective and caring system, has become less available to an increasing proportion of young blacks. He writes:[6, p228]

> When young blacks begin to internalize personal failures and frustrations and no longer use the traditional institutional structures, relationships, and groups within the black community to shield them from full personal impact, alienation and anomie set in, increasing the liklihood of self-destruction.

Davis raises some central issues that must be at the core of any reformulation: one is explicit and centers on the issue of the strength of relationships—in this case between the Afro-American persons and their social space (family or community); the other is implicit and speaks to the issue of a black historical experience—family and communal ties.

In my alternative model these two issues are central, but there are others which, as orienting principals, are central to an alternative model:

1. The black reality is a cultural, sociopolitical, and personal experience that has been forged out of the history of and interaction with America. This experience at both objective and subjective levels can be scientifically studied. The black reality in America grows out of the social formation and is fundamentally tied to it, yet is simultaneously apart from it. This reality which has developed out of the social

formulation of America is characterized by its own values, life styles, meanings, and expectations. It grows out of racism and oppression, violence, and continuous attempts at prevention from "the trans-generational flow of human life."

Key to this principle is the concept of social formulation. What the Afro-American is in America is tied to what America is in a sociopolitical sense. One cannot remove oneself from this. In a racist society one is either racist or the victim of racism. To think otherwise is to be naive. In considering the issue of suicide one has to examine the tendency in the social formation to encourage, indeed promote, the actions of self-destruction. The massive distribution of both guns and drugs within the Afro-American community must be seen in the context of the social formation. When we point to an index on the characteristics of suicide and see that most of the victims use guns or drugs, we must begin to make the connection between the event and the social formation. Other events in this social formation may begin to explain not only the how but the why.

2. Closely tied with the issue of the black reality growing out of the social formation is the issue of the interaction between the person and the society. The society is only represented by significant others—parents, family, and authority figures—who have been formed out of the social formation. The process of this formation is reciprocal, i.e., the interaction produces changes in the other. It is not a linear interaction. This principle of reciprocity implies that the interaction between person and society (through its representatives) may not be equal and opposite in terms of impact: there is a real exchange. This exchange itself takes place in a context (political or social) and this relationship between the exchange (of person with society) and the context also has the essence of reciprocity

   Thus, when we examine the suicide of an Afro-American and we look at the exchange, we have to begin to understand the mutual promotion and at the same time to understand the relationship to context which promoted and facilitated the event. A good example of this is the evidence in the literature that a large percentage of suicide among Afro-Americans occurs among persons who have a family or a spouse. We need to understand the context of reality for these individuals and determine whether they could have exhibited alternative behaviors rather than those that led to suicide.

3. The third principle of our model centers on the issue of dialectical interactions. This is critical because it addresses the nature of relationships (see Principle 1) that will facilitate qualitative change. If

in the social formation the interaction simply produces more of the same, we have added quanity and not made changes in the structure of the relationship. Dialectical interactions are those which:

- Allow the interacting parties to fully represent themselves with all their contradiction; and
- Are based on the full consciousness of the contradictions, and seek solutions with which both parties can live. The solution contains the seed of its own contradictions and leads to the repetion of that which is called the dialectical process.

It is this process that is presented and/or blocked in the Afro-American person who contemplates suicide. The person is prevented from self-representation and transformation. The person simply gets "more of the same." There are no real structural changes in relationship or, therefore, in the quality of life. The context precludes resolution.

4. The fourth principle that is important in considering suicide among Afro-American populations is connected with the third and centers on the concept of power. Power defines the feelings real or imagined that one can create change. The basis of this power is economic but for the Afro-American is also related to family and the spiritual world. The principle holds that failure in attempts to resolve feelings of powerlessness leads to various forms of psychological vulnerability.

The society has its own power which it wields in its own way for or against the Afro-American community. This power emerges in the context of four subsystems of human action: physical health systems, cultural systems, social systems, and interpersonal relations. Any one of these may have its own external source of power to promote or restrain the well-being of the person. They may act individually, or in the case of Afro-Americans (historically), collectively. The person, over a history of relationships with representatives of these subsystems or combinations, develops (principle of social formation) internal sources of power or feelings of powerlessness. The various relationships of external restraint to internal are yet another context for psychological strength or vulnerability. Therefore, we have multiple outcomes—in this case, many potential types of suicide: for reasons associated with religion (cultural); those associated with health (physical health); those associated with employment (social); and those associated with loss of love (interpersonal).

What emerge from these principles are a series of interacting forms which are all part of the social formation moving from the macro event to the micro event of the individual behavioral choice. Three diagrams are used to represent this movement at three levels. However, each level is always in relation to the other. This analysis is taken from King,[5] who describes models of mental health.

The Level I relationships (Figure 14-1) are thoses that define the social formation, the society as a political reality, in relation to its level of organization. The society as a political process is represented on a continuum from open to closed. The levels of organization move from organized to disorganized. The relationships between these produce different social formations, systems, or arenas of sociopolitical action. Examples of social formation are represented in the Level 1 figure. Different social contexts tend to have different potential for producing different struggles in the will to live or die.

The Level II relationships (Figure 14-2) are those of the person with social formations which may be the community, the family, or the society. An example of social formation in the society is noted in the opening quotation from Newton.[1]

The social formations which emerge out of the relationships at Level I are now represented at Level II on a dimension of crisis, i.e., the extent to which the process is institutionalized and legitimized. The continuum is from high to low: high crisis, by implication, being situations where the process is the least institutionalized. The person is represented as a being with levels of consciousness of the process of self and social formation. The continuum ranges from high to low. Again, some possible outcomes in each quadrant are illustrated. Different interactions tend to have differing consequences for the person. The key issue here is the potential for transformation of both self and social formation process.

The Level III relationships (Figure 14-3) are those that are usually examined in the traditional literature, i.e., those of individuals in interaction with their personal world, variously called ego or self-formation (the intrapersonal). As a function of the person's relationship with the social formation (of which they are both a part and formed), they develop a feeling about their ability to bring about change (resources) and learn a process for participating in change (engagement). In the intrapersonal set of relationships, both parameters have a continuum from high to low. Some possible potential outcomes of the various relationships are illustrated. The final personal choice based on any of the relationships is a function of the multiple levels of relationships. What we have addressed is the point of greatest potential vulnerability.

These relationship levels allow an observer to see the act of suicide not as separate from but as part of the social formation, and as based on the particular psychopathology of the victim.

For Afro-Americans, the issues of racism, oppression, miseducation, unemployment, and a history of dehumanization are central to their social

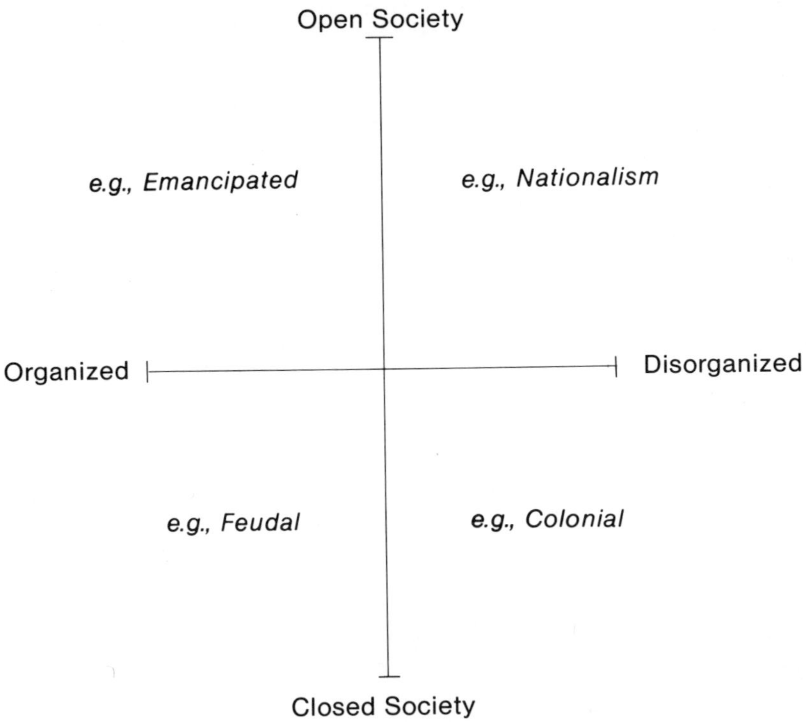

Figure 14-1. Level I, *The social formulation*: the society as political process in relation to its levels of organization.

formations. The will to live is clear among Afro-Americans. In the face of this single most critical strength of Afro-American people, what fosters the will not to live, and eventually the choice to die, is a significant question. Is the choice of death actually the will to live with greater dignity in a transcendant reality of another spiritual world?

CONCLUSIONS

This chapter presents recent statistics describing the increasing frequency of suicide among Afro-American groups. Research that explains this growing trend has been inadequate largely because of the limitations inherent in the deep structure of the theories that generate the research. The kinds of questions asked and data collected have largely

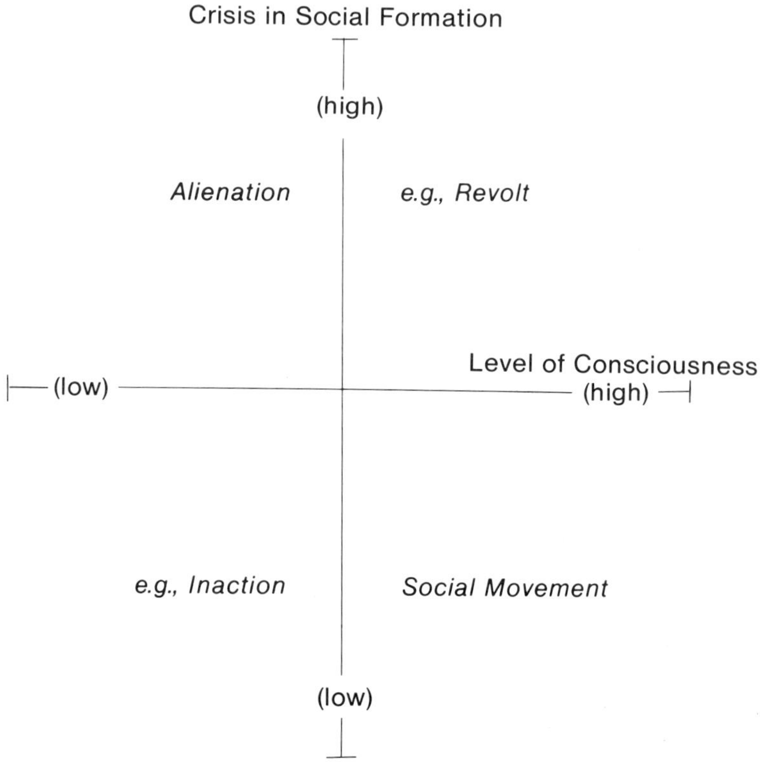

Figure 14-2. Level II, *The person–social formation interaction.*

been in the tradition of disease models, or have ignored the critical contribution of sociological frames of reference. An alternative model for research as been suggested. In this model the key issue is the examination of the various levels of relationships growing out of the historical social formation of the particular nation, state, community, family, and person. The task requires the vision from a black perspective. Without this perspective we, in fact, participate by default in a culture of silence to our scientific needs. Fannon warns us all—there comes a time when silence is dishonest: what matters is not know the world, but to change it.

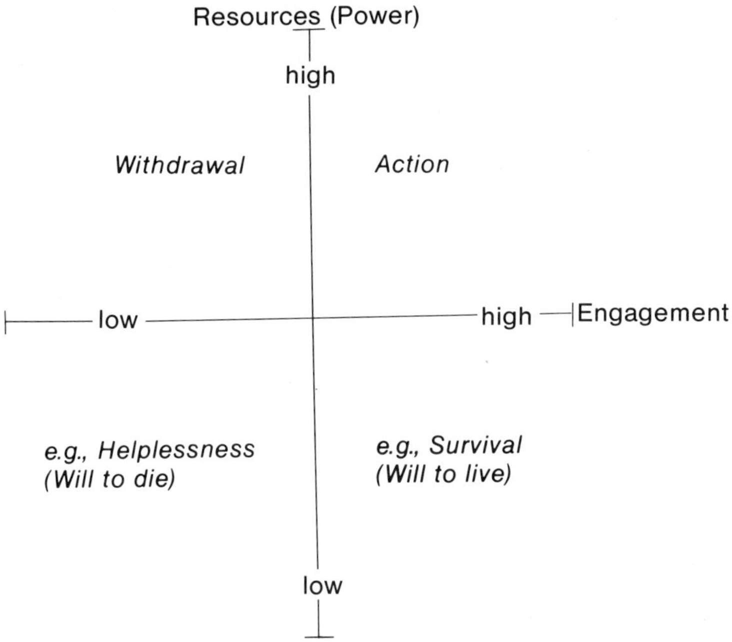

Figure 14-3. Level III, *The intra-personal relationships*.

REFERENCES

1. Newton HP: Revolutionary Suicide. New York, Morrow Publishers, 1975
2. Hoffman V: Race Traits and Tendencies of the American Negro. American Economic Association, 1896, p 140–42
3. Fanon F: Wretched of the Earth. New York, Grove Press, 1963
4. King LM: Suicide: A Social Analysis. Paper presented at Drew Medical School, April 1973
5. King LM: A Study of Black Suicide. Fanon Center, Drew Medical School, 1980
6. Davis D: Suicide among young blacks. Phylon 41:4, 1980
7. Reynolds: Some clinical consideration in the prevention of suicide. Am J Public Health 49:333–399, 1975
8. Breed W: Suicide, migration and race: A study of cases in New Orleans. J Soc Issues 22:30–43, 1966
9. Wolfgang ME: Suicide by means of victim-precipitated homicide. J Clin Exper Psychopathol 20:335–349, 1968

9a. Penderson A, Awad G, Kindler A: Epidemiological, differences between white and non-white suicide attempters. Am J Psy 130:1071–1076, 1973
10. Durkheim E: Suicide, in Simpson G (ed): translated by John A. Apaulding and George Simpson. New York, The Free Press, 1951
11. Farberow NL: Suicide in Different Cultures, Baltimore, University Park Press, 1975
12. Klein M: From Sad to Glad. New York, Blakiston, 1970
13. Cavan RS: Suicide. New York, Russell & Russell, 1965
14. Gibbs J, Martin WT: Status Integration and Suicide. University of Oregon, 1964
15. Henry AF, Short Jr JF: Suicide and homicide. New York, The Free Press of Glencoe, 1954
16. Farber ML: Theory of Suicide. New York, Funk and Wagnalls, 1968
17. Shneidman ES, Mandelkorn P: How to Prevent Suicide. The Psychology of Suicide. New York, Science House, p 138–139, 1970
18. Breed W: Five components of a basic suicide syndrome. Life Threatening Behavior 2:1, 1972
19. Prudomme C: The problems of suicide in the American Negro. Psychoanal Rev 25:374–391, 1938
20. Poussaint AF: Why Blacks Kill Blacks. New York, Emerson Hall Publishers, 1972
21. Seiden RH: We're driving young blacks to suicide. Psychol Today, August, 24–28 1970
22. Seiden RH; Why are suicides of young blacks increasing? HSMHA Health Reports 87:1, 1972
23. McLean HV: The emotional health of Negroes, in Grossack MM (ed): Mental Health and Segregation. New York, Springer, 1968
24. Woodford J: Why Negro suicides are increasing. Ebony 20:89–100, 1965
25. Hendin H: Black suicide. Arch Gen Psychiatry 21: 407–422, 1969
26. Hendin H: Suicide, in Freedman A, Kaplan H (eds) : Comprehensive Textbook of Psychology. Baltimore, Williams and Wilkins, 1972, p 1170–1179
27. Wilkerson CB: Review of Black suicide by Herbert Hendin 127:177–178, 1970
28. Maris RW: Social forces in urban suicide. Homewood, Ill, Dorsey Press, 1969
29. Shneidman ES (ed) : Essays in Self-destruction. New York, Science House, 1967
30. Farberow NL, Sheidman ES (ed) : Cry for Help. New York, McGraw-Hill, 1961

Kayvonne Wright

15 Sociocultural Factors in Child Abuse

Child-rearing and the mistreatment of children are complex and controversial issues that have been studied more intensely within the twentieth century than in the past, but are still not fully understood. Sociological, psychological, traditional, environmental, cultural, and religious factors are intricately woven into the practices of child-rearing.

Child-rearing has traditionally been a private, family matter. In our western culture, parents and other family members have cared for and disciplined their children within the religious and socioeconomic contraints sanctioned by the culture. Perceptions of what constitutes maltreatment in child-rearing have varied with time and culture. Practices that are now considered abusive have been accepted in the past as the normal exercise of parental rights, as culturally acceptable or expected, as economic necessity, or as appropriate disciplinary measures.[1]

Historically, society has not been concerned with the maltreatment of children. Ancient and contemporary literature and history, religious teachings, and widely accepted educational and child-rearing practices have all condoned and even encouraged the maltreatment of children under the rubric of discipline, education, and salvation.[2] When children were not wanted, mortality was high. In nineteenth century London, for example, 80 percent of illegitimate children who were raised by a "nurse" died; unscrupulous nurses often collected their fees and then promptly eliminated the babies.[3] When a profit could be made, adults sometimes sold children into slavery or used them as a source of cheap labor. This is not to say that individual parents did not care about their children; but pervasive values sanctioned many practices we now consider abusive. Infanticide was not only a threat to the infants of royal families, but in some cultures it had wide acceptance as a means of controlling population size and eliminating children with birth defects.[3]

Maltreatment of children has survived into the late twentieth century virtually unchallenged, because two beliefs remained strong: children were seen as their parents' property and it was assumed that parents had every right to treat their children as they deemed appropriate; furthermore, children were seen as their parents' responsibility and for many centuries harsh treatment was justified by the belief that severe punishment was necessary to maintain discipline, transmit educational decisions, and expel evil spirits.[3]

Standards of normal and acceptable child care vary in cultures and subcultures. Practices considered to be mildly abusive in some subcultures would be completely normal and desirable patterns of child-rearing in others.

As we begin to explore the considerable variation in child-rearing beliefs and behaviors cross-culturally or within subcultures, it becomes clear that there is not a universal standard for child-rearing, nor for child abuse. Before any judgments can be made about the cultural contributions in the occurrence of child abuse, considerably more needs to be known about culturally linked attitudes towards the acts of mistreatment or abuse.[4]

Careful attention must be paid to the levels at which cultural analysis is relevant to the assessment of child abuse. The cultural context of a behavior, however, must be viewed holistically. No single element of a cultural pattern can be removed from its context and examined in isolation of other integrated aspects of that culture.[5]

Psychological forces which shape individual behavior evolve out of the totality of life experiences in specific historical, cultural, social, economic, and political contexts. Individual motivation and behavior are thus always rooted in a societal force. Yet, societal forces are always expressed or mediated through the behavior of individuals.[6] Based on this reasoning, child-rearing and the mistreatment of children, at any level of manifestation, may be understood as acts or inactions of individuals whose behavior reflects societal and environmental forces mediated through their unique personalities.[6]

This chapter will attempt to explore historical perspectives, causative factors, involvement of the various social and legal systems, and treatment approaches as they impact Afro-American families where physical and sexual abuse has occurred.

DEFINING CHILD ABUSE

Not until 1961 was the long-standing abuse of children, both in the family and society in general, specifically identified clinically as the "battered child syndrome."[7] The Child Abuse Prevention and Treatment Act of 1973 defined abuse as "the physical treatment or maltreatment of a child under the age of eighteen by a person responsible for this child's welfare under circumstances which indicated that the child's health or welfare is harmed or threatened thereby." Abuse is generally associated with acts of commission that result in demonstrable external or internal physical injuries. The injuries are inflicted during extreme punishment, discipline, or physical assault on the child. They occur throughout childhood and adolescence, but the infant and young child are most vulnerable to irreversible damage.

Neglect, on the other hand, is usually associated with acts of omission, such as depriving the child of necessary food and emotional nurturing. These children are often underweight, have developmental lags, and frequently are apathetic. Neglect is most common among infants and the young child, but may also be seen in school-aged children.

Sexually abusive behaviors include intercourse, rape, incest, exposure, and fondling in which a child engages with an adult. It is estimated that 75 percent of the offenders, most of whom are males, are known to the victim and to the family. Approximately 90 percent of the victims are girls ranging from infancy through adolescence, with the greatest incidence occurring during prepubescence and adolescence.[8] In this chapter, the discussion of sexual abuse will be limited to those relationships that occur within the nuclear and extended families. These definitions are broad in scope and are meant to serve as guidelines. It can be argued that they do not delineate where discipline ends and abuse begins. In determining abuse, the norms of child-rearing within different cultures must be considered and judgments must be made based on a multitude of factors, including the future physical and emotional safety of the child.

In an effort to better understand child-rearing and the mistreatment of children in Afro-American families, the phenomenon of an individual's behavior reflecting societal and environmental forces should be examined in more depth. These forces have been prevalent from the beginning of slavery in this country through the socialization process that Afro-

Americans experienced as slaves. Though we lack empirical data to substantiate the extent of influence, this socialization process may have some influence upon some of the child-rearing practices of Afro-Americans today. We do know, however, that in African cultures child abuse and neglect were neither condoned nor a common feature.

PHYSICAL ABUSE

The History of Child Abuse during Slavery

The ultimate aim of the socialization process is social control. According to Dager, socialization is the most effective means of limiting deviant acts in society and to inculcate the young with values and attitudes that serve to perpetuate "those elements in the social system deemed important by its memebers."[9]

In view of the above, there is no question that the socialization process and outcomes were different for Afro-Americans and the majority culture.[10] In his autobiography, Frederick Douglass chronicles the extreme adjustments he made to live in a dominant white society. He states:

> Of my father I know nothing. Slavery had no recognition of fathers, as none of families. That the mother was a slave was enough for its deadly purpose. By its law the child followed the condition of its mother. The father might be a free man and a the child a slave. The father might be a white man, glorying in the purity of his Anglo-Saxon blood and the child ranked with the blackest slaves. Father he might be, but not be husband, and could sell his own child without incurring reproach, if in his veins coursed one drop of African blood.
>
> The practice of separating mothers from their children and hiring them out at distances too great to admit their meeting, save at long intervals, was a marked feature of the cruelty and barbarity of the slave system; *but it was in harmony with the* grand aim of that system, which always and everywhere sought to reduce man to a level with the brute.[11 pp. 2–3]

From the beginning of their enslavement, all slaves had been confronted with the option to "submit or die," and obviously those who survived to rear children had chosen to live and therefore to submit. Once a mother opted for her child's life, she assumed the task of conveying to the child the nature of the world and how to survive in it. In some instances, she had to assume a role much like that of the slave master, sometimes treating the child with capricious cruelty, including hurting the child physically and emotionally, and demanding an obsequious response in a manner she knew would enhance the chances of survival. Particular pains had to be taken to crush any defiant or aggressive responses to certain situations. In order to survive as a slave, the child often had to learn to abandon the usual narcissistic investment of self, at least as it was expressed in the presence of the slave master.[12]

A mother dared not allow the child to grow up expecting love and loving concern from every source. She had to demand that the child always show the parents the greatest respect, whether they seemed to earn it or not. This conditioning would serve as the basis for the later relationship with the slave master, and the less conflict experienced in connection with obedience, the greater the likelihood of survival.

Child-rearing among the slaves was infrequently allowed to develop beyond the crucial techniques for survival. At all times, slaves were in danger of their lives, and their thorough knowledge of slavehood was considered an asset. Whatever else was taught the child, it was taught in the context of survival instructions. Mothers would say as they punished rebellious sons: "I'd rather kill him myself than let those white folks get him. He's got to learn."[12]

In many respects, Afro-American children have to learn even in the twentieth century to "submit" to aspects of the dominant culture. We've progressed from legal slavery to an informal system of quasislavery.[12] Some of the child-rearing practices may be slow to change. The vigorous psychological trends evoked by slavery, their contradictions and confluence, are impressive even when, at this distance in time, we attempt a reconstruction.[12]

Child-rearing is a delicate process, bound irrevocably to the reality of the society. However, Afro-American parents have been placed in a double bind. Child-rearing practices that were instituted to teach responsibility and a means of survival in a hostile environment, are now considered unduly harsh and abusive. Yet, who would argue that the environmental conditions are so very different now. The environment continues to inflict Afro-Americans with inequities, but many parents are being told that their methods of child-rearing and discipline are inappropriate, and that they need to incorporate others that are now sanctioned by society.

To compound the problem, Afro-Americans have been misrepresented in the national statistics of child abuse. Researchers have documented figures that parents who abuse and neglect their children are from lower socioeconomic levels, and are from poorly educated minority families. For example, in 1968, the nationwide reporting rate of child abuse was 6.7 per 100,000 for white children, to 21.0 per 100,000 for non-whites.[13] The accumulated facts do indicate that among reported cases of mistreatment, families at the lower end of the socioeconomic spectrum are overrepresented.

In estimating over- or underrepresentation of any segment of the population in a problem-identified group, a major methodological hazard is the selection of inappropriate comparison statistics. Afro-Americans, for example, may constitute 20 percent of the total population. However, in some cities they may constitute 40 percent. Thus a national statistic cannot validly serve as a basis for selected parts of the country. Further, Afro-Americans are overrepresented in the lower socioeconomic strata. In making comparisons with the general population on a problem known already to draw disproportionately from the lower economic strata, their differences must be controlled for in making estimates of disproportionate representation. None of the studies cited controlled for the comparison of the problem group with the proportion of low-income Afro-Americans in the population where the study took place. For example, in Green's 1974 study, research was conducted at an outpatient clinic at the Kings County Hospital Center in New York. The majority (62.5 percent) of the cases studied were Afro-American subjects with only 12.5 percent white-American subjects.[14]

Another study conducted in 1971 from case reports gathered from a Welfare Department in the Boston area presented data on cases that were from four inner-city hospitals. The families reported were from the lower socioeconomic class and were predominantly Afro-American.[15]

These and other studies used different definitions of the kinds of mistreatment under scrutiny, and varying indices of social status. Hence they do not constitute a body of work with comparable findings. Yet the consistency of the findings lends some support to the popular notion that the incidence of various kinds of mistreatment is greater among the less affluent lower classes.[4]

Lower socioeconomic and non-white families are also reported more frequently for child abuse than middle to upper middle class white families. Additionally, members of lower socioeconomic groups are more frequently the clients of social agencies, municipal hospitals, and public health clinics. Compared to middle- and upper-class families, they not only have more contact with many different types of professionals, but their home lives and problems are also more open to professional scrutiny.[8]

The middle and upper classes are said to be shielded from public intrusion by the biases in the reporting mechanisms as well as other factors, including the reluctance of private physicians (with higher frequencies of affluent clientele) to report cases of abuse among their patients. Futhermore, the more isolated single-family dwelling patterns of the middle and upper classes have been thought to decrease the potential for detection of abuse by friends and neighbors. It is further speculated that community agencies may be more reluctant to intervene into the lives of such families.[4,16]

It can be further noted that professionals in social work and medical fields may find it more difficult to report a family with whom they can identify: white-Americans may have more difficulty reporting other whites and Afro-Americans may experience more difficulty in reporting their Afro-American peers; those of the middle class find it more difficult to report a middle-class family; and so on. It is interesting to observe the relationship between these two findings: most professionals are middle- and upper-class white-Americans, and poor non-white families tend to account for the greatest proportion of reports.[8]

Children are abused in families from all socioeconomic levels, races, nationalities, and religious groups. The National Center on Child Abuse and Neglect estimates that from 100,000 to 200,000 American children are battered and beaten by adults each year. About 700,000 to 800,000 are deprived of food, clothing or shelter. Some 200,000 to 300,000 children are sexually abused each year, and 75 percent of the children know their abusers.[8] Estimates of actual incidence vary; most, in fact, are inconsistent. But all suggest a far more massive problem than that which is reported.

Based upon a recent article from the Los Angeles Times, child abuse is reported to be on the rise. Figures go up every year, and depending upon what estimate is read, the numbers range from 1 million to more than 4 million children under the age of 18 in the United States who are physically abused, neglected or sexually molested every year.[17]

Local figures from large metropolitan cities like Los Angeles are concurrent with those on a national level. There has been a steady increase in child abuse over the last five years. In 1975, the Los Angeles County Department of Public Social Service (DPSS) referrals numbered 19,000 families. In 1979, more than 27,000 families (more than 53,000 children) were referred because of suspected child abuse and neglect. During the first six months of 1980, the Department of Public Social Services for Children had received 14,329 family referrals, which were above the 1979 figures.[17] An examination of some of the causes of child abuse will more specifically explain its prevalence in abusive Afro-American families.

Causative Factors of Child Abuse

Fundamentally, causal factors of child abuse consist of a cluster of interacting elements. However, in the final analysis, it is the philosophy and value premises of a society, the nature of its major institutions, and the quality of its human relations that determine whether or not individual members of that society will develop freely and fully in accordance with their inherent potentials.[6]

Another causal dimension of child abuse relates to how a society views its children. Presently, in our society, social policies sustain different levels of rights for children depending upon such factors as race, sex, and social and economic backgrounds. These different levels of rights are a major, direct cause of many forms of child abuse on the societal and institutional levels, and an indirect cause of abuse on the family level.[6]

A further causal dimension of child abuse is a society's attitude toward the use of force as a legitimate means for attaining ends, especially in imbalanced interpersonal relationships such as those of the master–slave, male–female, and adult–child. The tendency to resort to force to deal with conflicts, and the readiness to use physical force for disciplinary objectives is certainly endemic in our society.[6] Whenever corporal punishment in child-rearing is sanctioned, and even subtly encouraged by a society, incidents of serious abuse and injury are inevitable, either as a result of deliberate, systematic, and conscious action on the part of perpetrators, or under conditions of loss of self-control.

The next dimension may be referred to as "triggering contexts."[6] These contexts operate jointly with the societal sanction of the use of physical force in adult–child relations. Adults who use force toward children do not do so all the time, but only under specific circumstances which serve as triggers for their abusive behavior. In general, abusive attacks tend to be triggered by stress and frustration which may cause reduction or loss of self-control. Stress and frustration may facilitate abusive attacks even without causing a reduction or loss of self-control, as long as the appropriateness of the use of force in child-rearing is accepted.[6] This should be a major consideration when assessing whether or not a disciplinary action is abusive in an Afro-American family. The society and its socialization process has systematically sanctioned the use of corporal punishment, which many families are continuing to utilize.

Some of the major sources of stress and frustration for adults, in our society are the multifaceted deprivations of poverty and its correlates: living in areas of high density in dilapidated, inadequately served neighborhoods; having large numbers of children, especially in one-parent, mainly female-headed households, and with the absence of good child care alternatives. Decreased parental capacity for child care might be due to a loss or diminution of support from a spouse or key family member previously involved in sharing parental functions, from physical or emotional illness of the parent, or from pregnancy. Having identified poverty and its correlates as an important triggering context of child abuse in the home, it may now be inferred that social policies which sanction and perpetuate the existence of poverty among large segments of the population, and especially in our Afro-American communities, can be considered as indirect sources of child abuse in the home.[6].

Reports of child abuse may be increasing because more persons are likely to report abuse as it is discussed more openly. However, another explanation given in a recent Los Angeles Times article, is that stress related to the increase of unemployment, economic instability, and inflation has directly influenced family functioning.[17] More lower socioeconomic families suffer because of increased financial difficulties and an inability to make "ends meet."

It should be emphasized, though, that poverty and economic instability, per se, are not direct causes of child abuse in the home, but operate through an intervening variable, namely, concrete and psychological stress and frustration experienced by an individual within the context of the culturally and socially sanctioned use of physical force in child-rearing.

The final causal dimension of child abuse is on the interpersonal level in the family and is made up of intrapsychic conflicts and various forms of psychopathology on the part of perpetrators. The child abuse literature mainly focuses on this dimension.[6]

The wide variety of behavior and personality traits observed in parents who have been abusive suggests that a specific "abusive" personality does not exist; rather, individuals with a certain psychological makeup, operating in combination with a painfully perceived childhood and environmental stress, might be likely to abuse their offspring. A review of the literature indicates that the majority of abusive parents were raised in a similar style which they have recreated in the pattern of rearing their own children.[18] Abusive parents who were themselves abused is the most consistently reported factor in the work which deals with the etiology of child abuse.[16,18,20–22] Solomon notes that between 30 and 60 percent of abused parents reported abuse in their own childhoods.[19] Gil's survey found that 11 percent of parents who abuse their children were victims of abuse during childhood.[20] An individual who was raised by parents who used physical force to train children, and who grew up in a violent household, has had a role model of force and violence as means of family problem solving.[22]

Generational abuse may be well exemplified in a family of a well-known Afro-American. In his book *A Lonely Rage*, Bobby Seale describes in detail how his paternal grandfather used "physical force" and "whippings" to discipline his father. He wrote: . . . "And you know Arch

Seale (Bobby Seale's grandfather) wouldn't pay George (Bobby Seale's father) and George went and asked the white man, old man Seale, how come he couldn't get paid like everybody else: Arch found out about it and took a tree limb and beat George. George finally run off because Arch Seale would beat him and cuss him so bad and still wouldn't pay him half the time. Arch just drove them childrens of his 'way from 'round him."[22, p.16] Bobby Seale's father, George, in turn whipped him many years of his early life out of frustration and displaced anger. However, his rationale was to discipline and teach Bobby "better ways." This generational pattern in abuse in his family was compounded by unstable employment, poverty, and a fragmented family.[22]

At an early age, Bobby Seale was given the message he was "not good enough," and "bad." He soon incorporated these messages and also perceived himself as such. His emotionally and physically chaotic childhood predisposed him to the violence and aggression that has permeated much of his adult life. Many maltreated persons pattern their adult lives on their past, abusing their own children and sometimes others as well. Among the more infamous adults who were maltreated as children are Arthur Bremmer, Sirhan Sirhan, James Earl Ray, Lee Harvey Oswald, and John Wilkes Booth.[8]

Poor self-concept and a lack of self-confidence are other inherent psychological components in the personality makeup of persons who abuse their children. Both the environment and the family are integral parts of the frame of reference that influence one's self-concept.

Outside the family, experiences and identification with the dominant society are equally important in determining one's perception of self-worth. For Afro-Americans, their aspirational level, good conscience, and adequate performance are often irrelevant in the face of the glaring fact that Afro-Americans obtain a poor reflection of self in the behavior of white Americans in the dominant society, regardless of the behavior or the merits exhibited. In the past it has been thought that Afro-Americans often have less potential for healthy self-concepts and many incentives for self-hatred.[24] Since that time, however, such theories have been challenged.[25]

When parents are frustrated, they have a way of transferring their poor self-concept, and possibly their self-hatred, to their children, from whom they expect achievement and productivity as adults. If the child does not attain these goals, parents heap on the child an ill-concealed disappointment that the child interprets as dislike or even hatred.

Child abuse has also been related to the decline of the extended family. An extended family is best described as that in which a sizable number of immediate relatives reside in the same household or in close proximity, and are readily available in times of need. In the "nuclear" family, more prevalent in today's transient society, we find a family that generally consists of mother, father, and child or children with few relatives close enough to provide immediate supports. There are fewer sympathetic listeners helping with frustrations, and fewer potential baby-sitters or persons who may assist parents with child-rearing. Mobility and the degree of transiency, characteristic of the nuclear family, also results in parents having fewer close friends upon whom to depend. This pattern tends to increase the social and emotional isolation that abusing families already experience.

Another contributing factor to child abuse is a lack of knowledge about normal child development.[16,18,26] There is a general confusion about proper parenting techniques that is borne out by the proliferation of books offering advice and strategies for child-rearing when parents themselves have little experience in caring for infants and young children.

Child abuse is seldom the result of any single factor. Rather, it is a combination of circumstances as well as personality types which precipitate the abusive acts. When parents or caretakers are under emotional or environmental stresses such as marital problems or joblessness; when they have a predisposition toward maltreatment perhaps because they were abused children themselves or because they firmly believe in corporal punishment due to cultural sanctions; when children happen to trigger their contempt for whatever reason; and when parents or caretakers have no other outlet for tension, anger, or aggression and have little impulse control, abuse may occur. Psychological disturbances and their manner of expression are not independent factors but are deeply rooted in, and constantly interact with forces in the social environment. Given the necessary combination of circumstances, anyone could physically abuse or neglect a child.

Prevention and Treatment

Child abuse is a prevailing problem, but not a hopeless one. The majority of abusive parents are not monsters, but anxious, unhappy people who care deeply about their success as parents and feel great guilt about the damage they do in moments of uncontrollable rage. There are reports that approximately 10 percent of abusive parents are not treatable because of long-term emotional problems. However, the remaining 90 percent can potentially be helped.[3]

While law enforcement is usually involved in the initial response and investigation of child abuse whether or not criminal action is instituted, it should be remembered that it may not always be appropriate to respond to the suspected parent with traditional crime and punishment approaches to the solution. Fines or prison sentences alone are unlikely to rehabilitate the child-abusing parents. Since the abused tend to grow up to abuse others, the intervention and treatment offered should not only serve to protect children at present; they should help to break the chains that bind future generations. If professionals intervene early, families can obtain the help that is needed before a child suffers extreme physical and emotional damage.

Abused children not only must cope with the effects of physical attacks and injuries, but they must also cope with parents and a home environment in which the abuse occurred. This means coping with rejection, emotional disturbance in parents, and other distorted and disturbed parent–child interactions.[27] Psychological trauma of the child is one aspect that may not be given adequate attention by authorities and personnel working with the family.

The child needs to process the guilt, fears, conflicts, rage, and depression that usually occurs after the abuse has been revealed. The child also has to cope with the stresses of becoming involved in the various social systems which include hospitals, court, foster placement, and visitation rights of parents. Long range adverse psychological effects can be minimized if psychotherapeutic support is given to the child.[27] This support may be a therapeutic day care center or preschool placement, and individual and group therapy. Psychiatric hospitalization may also have to be utilized for some children.

In considering the appropriate therapeutic intervention for the abusive family, the treatment of the parent is of primary importance. Many disturbed parents cannot cope with the idea of their child receiving help while they do not. These parents are immensely sensitive to rejection and desperately need a long-term relationship with an accepting, gratifying and uncritical adult.[5] The treatment of abusive families poses special difficulties beyond those encountered in traditional psychotherapeutic models. However, therapists who have a minimal understanding of and experience working with Afro-American families, may also encounter difficulties. The suspiciousness and basic mistrust of authority figures exhibited by the parents may interfere with the formation of a trusting relationship with the therapist. This is sometimes a result of life-long experiences of humiliation and criticism at the hands of their own parents and others in positions of authority and control. These feelings are intensified with experiences with the legal system, social service caseworkers, and probation officers.

When Afro-American families have had disturbing and unsatisfactory experiences with these specific systems, they may be reluctant to accept more intrusion in their lives. Based upon cases at the Family Support Program at the Neuropsychiatric Institute, UCLA, the involvement of Afro-American families with the court and social service systems takes place for longer periods of time than for some white families for the same charges. In several instances, the children are removed from the parents' custody and placed in foster homes or residential placements much more quickly than when white children are in similar circumstances. More intervention, coordination, and general involvement is required when working with these families. This may include being available on an emergency basis, making home visits, securing medical services for the family, and establishing a liaison with the school and numerous social agencies as an advocate of the parents.

Treatment for abusive parents is primarily a process of reparenting. This area of therapeutic focus must be approached gradually and with caution, as the parents may feel threatened by a change in their special relationship with their child. Exploring the possible involvement of extended family members, especially in Afro-American families, can be a productive intervention when parenting issues and caretaking alternatives are dealt with, because members of the family may be more likely to come to the aid of a troubled member. It may be preferable to remove Afro-American children, when possible, from an explosive home situation, lodging them temporarily with a relative, thus minimizing the utilization of social service alternatives, in light of the discrepancies noted in these agencies' involvement with Afro-American families.[12]

BARRIERS TO TREATMENT

The phenomenon of negative countertransference is an obstacle in the treatment of child abuse cases. This involves the tendency of the therapist to condemn and dislike a parent who would cruelly subject an innocent infant or child to physical abuse.[14] These feelings may be combined with other assumptions or stereotypes when a therapist is working with a family who is from another ethnic, religious, or racial group. A greater understanding of cross-cultural issues and differences is an important area for training professionals who work with minority families. Additionally, since much of the existing literature and research over-represents minority families as abusive and distorts the full scope of the problems involved, negative countertransference is more likely to be an obstacle in treatment.

In addition to psychotherapy, alternative therapeutic modalities such as parent self-help groups, Parents Anonymous and Parents United, have been successful treatment programs. Parents who have either physically abused or sexually abused their children band together in the self-help groups and offer a tremendous amount of support, understanding, and incentive to reorganize their lives after the abuse has been revealed. Some treatment programs also emphasize "play therapy" and other "activity-oriented" therapy groups for both parents and children.

In general, long- and short-term approaches in therapy are undertaken to help establish, strengthen, and maintain emotional and physical coexistence between parents and their children. In the short-term therapy process, it is important to intervene in the immediate situation, but the key is in the long-term approach. Although the physical and sexual abuse has been discovered and terminated, emotional abuse is a more long-term problem that usually occurs along with the physical and sexual abuse, and can most effectively be dealt with within the context of a trusting long-term therapeutic relationship.

SEXUAL ABUSE

Another aspect of child abuse that is of increasing concern to mental health professionals is sexual abuse. The remaining portion of this chapter will focus on the history, incidence, causative factors, and treatment issues related to this area.

Incest is a phenomenon that has interested scholars and practitioners in psychology, psychiatry, anthropology, sociology, and biology for decades. According to Webster's dictionary, incest has been defined as sexual intercourse between persons so closely related that they are forbidden by law to marry.[28] Many authorities now consider incest to include any sexual activity between parent and child or brother and sister. Most also consider sexual activity between stepparent and stepchild as incest.[29]

The National Center on Child Abuse and Neglect uses the term "intrafamily sexual abuse" for incest, and defines abuse as that "which is perpetrated on a child by a member of that child's family" and includes not only sexual intercourse, but also any act designated to stimulate a child sexually, or to use a child for the sexual stimulation either of the perpetrator, or of another person.[29]

A discussion of incest and other forms of sexual abuse of children is likely to bring forth strong feelings of revulsion or disbelief among readers. However, these are the same feelings that have caused professionals to shy away from the problem of sexual abuse and to underestimate its severity and extent.[3]

History of Cross-Cultural Incest Taboos

Incest is a taboo in all cultures: even the discussion of incest is avoided. Yet keeping incest a forbidden subject has not prevented intrafamilial sex.

Theoreticians have focused their attention upon the incest taboo: its origins, implementation, and consequences. This prohibition is one of the few that appears to be universally cross-cultural. One theorist, Murdock, thought that an adequate explanation of the incest taboo required a multidisciplinary approach utilizing ideas drawn from psychoanalysis, sociology, and behavioristic and cultural psychology.[30]

Freud's theory of universally repressed desire for incestuous relationships could account for the intensity of incest horror through the ego defense mechanism of reaction formation—the strong condemnation in others of ideas or behaviors that one is struggling to keep repressed in oneself. On a sociological level, the incest taboo would serve the function of preventing sexual competition and jealousy within the family—an extremely important function, since societies depend on families that are adequate for their primary role of socialization of children.[31] Also, along the lines suggested by White, the incest taboo would increase "internal diffusion," the process by which customs and inventions are spread throughout the culture, and promote cooperative, peaceful ties between family groups.[32] In turn, behavioristic psychology explains incest through its concept of "stimulus generalization." Relatives who are seen as being very similar to nuclear family members would tend to become taboo as sexual partners whether or not they were related by blood. Cultural anthropology, with its knowledge of the structure of kinship systems, by providing information regarding which relatives will be seen as very similar to nuclear family members, explains how stimulus generalization is channeled in various cultures. Murdock believed that in this way one could account for the confusing variability in application of the incest taboo to extended family members.[30] Murdock's multidisciplinary approach, and his rejection of any one theory as an explanation for the complex nature of the incest taboo continues to be widely favored by incest theorists.[31]

Once established, the incest taboo and resultant exogamous marriage customs have the advantage of forging links of cooperation and shared knowledge between family units that would have survival value for the larger group. The extension of the incest taboo is almost as universal as its existence, and some of the most extreme forms of exogamy are found in very primitive cultures, such as the Australian aborigines, where individuals do not seek marital partners within their tribe but rather select partners from neighboring groups to insure intertribal cooperation and survival.[31]

Incest Taboo During Slavery

During slavery, despite the fact that many relatives were on the same plantation, the strength and pervasiveness of slave exogamous beliefs persisted from their African marriage patterns. In West Africa, marriage between "relatives of legally established affiliation" was "forbidden as incestuous," and affiliation stood "in the way" of marriage. A detailed study of African marriage patterns shows that an individual is limited by prohibitions against marriage with related persons, the extent of which varies from tribe to tribe but is nearly always much wider than in the Western world.[33].

These African marriage patterns and exogamous beliefs persisted and can be exemplified in examples from the time of slavery. A secular work song recollected by an exslave is explicit in its meaning:

Sally's in de garden siftin' sand,
And all she want is a honey man.
De reason why I wouldn't marry,
Because she was my cousin.

O, row de boat ashore, hey, hey
Sally's in de garden siftin' sand.[33 p. 88]

A more emphatic example was related in a story about:

> a man who "married a woman after freedom and found out she was his mother." He had been sold from her during his infancy. "They quit, and he married ag'in. He had a scar on this thigh the mother had recollected. The scar was there when he was grown. That brought up more talk and they traced him up to be her own boy."[33,pp 89–90]

Taboos rooted in exogamous beliefs had traveled with slaves in the forced migration that carried hundred of thousands of Afro-Americans from the upper to the lower South.[33]

Incidence of Sexual Abuse

For many years the known cases of incest were cited as 1–2 per million population in this country. The highest for any state was 1–9 per million in Washington. On both a metropolitan area and state level, 50 to 500 percent increases in confirmed cases of incest are being reported each year.[29]

One study[29] cites the reported incidence of incest as increasing from 1 in a million in 1940, to 1 in 100 in 1950, to 1 in 20 in 1970. Reported incidents of incest now reach 200 per million population per year, but underreporting is massive.

Father–daughter incest accounts for approximately 75 percent of the incest cases. Girls involved with fathers or stepfathers are often the first daughters in preadolescence or early adolescence. Sister–brother is the next most common occurrence of incest cases, followed by grandfather–granddaughter, uncle–niece, father–son, mother–son, and the least common dyad, mother–daughter.[3]

It is believed that sexual abuse of children by immediate family members and other relatives is rising in epidemic proportion, and that when more programs are developed throughout the country to provide the kind of intervention that stresses rebuilding family relationships rather than punishing and separating them, more families will be seen seeking help.[34]

Similar to the studies cited in physical child abuse cases, the lower socioeconomic minority families have been overrepresented in research. Studies of incest behavior involve the use of skewed nonrepresentative samples, since the most frequently utilized approach for collecting data has been from the legal, social, or clinical agencies.[31]

A court- or prison-collected sample tends to be skewed toward a lower socioeconomic level, with minorities representing the larger ethnic backgrounds. Lower class minority males are actually more likely to go to jail for the offense given their lack of financial and legal resources, their lack of sophistication when coping with the legal system, and the unusually harsh and punitive sanctions that are ordered by the court.[34]

Collecting cases through social agencies also tends to limit sampling to the lower socioeconomic, minority groups, since middle- and upper-class white-American families are more likely to seek aid from a variety of private practitioners. In Tormes' 1977 article, her subjects studied were from a Brooklyn, New York social service department, with the Afro-Americans represented as the majority group of incest offenders. Puerto Rican families were the group of next largest representation, followed by white-Americans, who were the least represented.[35] However, in a study conducted in a Los Angeles psychiatric clinic from 1973–1976, it was found that of the 100 cases studied, 66 percent of the participants were white-Americans, 14 percent were Afro-Americans, 16 percent Hispanics, and 2 percent Asian. [31] These statistics are concurrent with those from 1978–1980 for the UCLA Family Support Program which treats victims of sexual abuse. Out of 104 cases, 39.4 percent were white Americans, 24 percent Afro-Americans, and 6.7 percent Hispanics.

Many studies that have focused on the lower socioeconomic minority families in this society have highlighted those on public assistance, with children born out of wedlock, and with a high degree of drug and chemical dependency, wife-beating, violent behavior, physical child abuse and neglect, promiscuity, and crowded living conditions. All of these behaviors have been viewed as corresponding to the incidence of incestuous abuse within these families, and many as having contributed to the assault.[34] It has become increasingly difficult to continue to ascribe the difficult conditions of lower socioeconomic life as the source of incestuous assault. Such a simplistic, culture-bound analysis cannot hold up in the face of the growing number of aggressors whose singular characteristic in common is that they sexually assault their children.[34] Factors relating to incest in families have little to do with class, race, economic status, or social background: It is a personal and a social problem. By taking incest out of the category of a dreaded curse or unthinkable abomination and placing it in the context of child abuse, more public attention and action on the problem are likely. Understanding how and why it occurs with such discomforting frequency will facilitate the development of programs and alternatives, rather than the ineffective and often contradictory approaches presently taken in most communities.[3]

Causative Factors

Freud saw sex, including incestuous wishes, as the basic determinant in human behavior. But the central issue of incest goes beyond sex. As Eric Fromm has noted, there is a nonsexual 'incestuous striving inherent in man's nature" based on deep needs for roots, belonging, warmth, and protection.[36] Frightened and insecure in the world outside, people turn to the family to have their needs met. The more stressful people find the world, the more likely they will turn inside the family. The fusion that develops between parent and child is almost invariably damaging. The child fails to get basic emotional needs met and is prevented from establishing ties with the world outside that are necessary for growth and experience in relating to others.

As it has been noted, incest involves intimate physical contact of some kind. Children need to be hugged, kissed, and held. Their feelings of self-esteem depend on receiving a great deal of affection. There has to be a distinction between physical affection needed by a child and physical contact that is incestuous or sexual.

"Sexual misuse" has been described as exposing a child to sexual stimulation inappropriate to the child's age, development, and role in the family. It is believed what is inappropriate may also be determined by parents asking themselves whether they are giving physical affection to the child to meet their own need for sex, stimulation, love, and nurturing. A mother without a partner who is lonely and isolated may try to satisfy her need for love and warmth through intimate contact with a young son: sleeping with him, fondling or caressing him. A husband whose marriage has deteriorated may let passion and need enter into his relationship with his daughter, kissing, embracing, and touching her as a lover, not as a father.

Incest and sexual misuse or abuse within a family involves the whole family and not just the person who initiates the activity. The total environment of the family is involved in terms of contributing to the conditions under which incest or sexual abuse occurs.

It is believed that incest has been increasing in the United States in recent years, perhaps because of the great changes in family life: rising divorce rates, and a more tolerant view of sexual acts between nonrelated household members who come from divorced or previously separated homes. This is particularly true of brother–sister incest between stepchildren who are living as a family but are not related.[3]

In the transition from the extended family of our recent past to more insulated and isolated nuclear family units in which we now live, several problems have surfaced. While family members are very dependent upon one another to satisfy the emotional, physical, and social needs, the nuclear family alone cannot provide all of these resources, and thus forces many persons into social and emotional isolation.

Furthermore, this is a period when the significance of the family and the role it is expected to play are no longer clear. In moving away from a time when rigid societal attitudes dictated the roles of men and women and their responsibilities as parents, there is uncertainty and confusion about how these new roles relate to the family structure.[34] Other dynamics that may occur in a family where incest has occurred include:

1. Poor communication patterns between the parents and the children that also protect the continuation of sexual abuse through secrecy.
2. A poor or deteriorating sexual relationship between the parents. The most common event preceding the onset of incest is sexual estrangement between the father and mother. The mother may refuse sexual relations with the father, she may have an aversion to sex, or simply may be unresponsive because of an unsatisfactory sexual relationship. The sexual relationship may also be decreasing or absent because of illness and/or sexual dysfunction.[29,31]
3. Role reversal. The daughter (who usually becomes the incest victim) begins to assume many of the responsibilities of the mother. Gradually the mother relinquishes her responsibilities of the household

tasks, the care of younger siblings, and allows the daughter to play the role of "little mother" in the family. This role reversal implies a special, wife-like relationship with the father. Although encouragement of incest is not on a conscious level, the mother is asumed to have relinquished her sexual role in the marriage, and may be relieved when the husband directs his sexual attention to the daughter.[29,31]

Some, perhaps many, mothers whose husbands and daughters engage in incest are depressed. The depression may have begun before the onset of the incestuous relationship and played a part in the mother's withdrawing sexually from her husband and delegating responsibilities to the daughter.[29] The mother may also work long hours outside the home and want help from the daughter with the household responsibilities. This also generates more time for the father to be alone with the daughter.

4. Social Isolation. One of the most prominent characteristics that has been observed in the family is the tendency to limit the social contacts with members of the family. The isolation is often encouraged by the father, and contact with others outside of the family is either cut off or quite minimal.[29,31] Most activities are conducted with only nuclear family members.

   For example, a family in the Family Support Program would not allow any of its members to be without any or all of the other family members outside of the home. The incest in this particular family continued for approximately 10 years in secrecy.

5. Lack of impulse control may be the result of excessive physical or emotional stress. Some people experience a heart attack, acquire some form of cancer, ulcers, or colitis, have headaches or hypertension. Others may become depressed, suffer from chronic anxiety, hostility, guilt, or shame. Still others cope with the excessive stress by acting out in such ways as committing incest or physical abuse, becoming alcoholic and assaultive, or battering spouses.[29]
6. Incest as a generational occurrence. There is much evidence from cases reported in the literature that incest is passed from one generation to the next.[3,29,31] There is also another way in which the future generations can be affected by incest. Parents who were sexually abused as children are more likely to be physically, sexually, and emotionally abusive to their children.[29] In the Family Support Program, approximately 80 percent of the mothers whose children have been sexually abused had themselves been incest victims as children.

Why should a woman who had been sexually abused as a child select a mate who would abuse her children? Several factors play a part in this selection. To some extent, most individuals use the parenting received as children as a model for parenting their children. If that model was abusive, the possibilities increase for that parent to become abusive.

Additionally, people are more likely to choose a partner who has a similar view of parenting and of how husbands and wives should relate. Most people pick someone who perceives the world much the same way as they do. Consequently, a women who has a parenting model and view of the world that includes a father turning to his child for sex may marry a man with a similar inclination. Another factor that contributes to the occurrence of incest being perpetuated through the generations is the struggle to be cared for. The daughter who is used sexually by her father loses the battle with her parents in the competition for nurturing. The parents may have their needs met, but she does not. She grows up thinking that, "I'll marry someone who will love and take care of me." Unfortunately, she usually chooses someone who is also looking to be cared for and who shares her confusion about sex and love. When the mates fail to meet each other's expectations, they both may turn to the child for nurturing, and the cycle repeats itself.[29]

There are additional characteristics of the family members to those that have been described, and the literature contains numerous case reports and theoretical assumptions that tend to support these findings.[6,22,29,31,37] Only a few of the general family dynamics could be presented here. However, there is a scarcity of studies or empirical data that can be generalized to identify specific characteristics that may be found in Afro-American parents who abuse their children. More research is needed to identify the sociocultural aspects in the lives of these Afro-American parents and their families, and the antecedents which led to sexual abuse.

Treatment Issues

Once incest has occurred, the probability that anyone in authority will gain knowledge of it during or immediately after the incest is rather slim. The adults in the family have a realistic fear of social shame and legal sanctions, while the child involved often feels too fearful of family dissolution or retaliation by the parents to risk disclosure to outside authorities. For these reasons, most current incest cases will continue to go undetected no matter how well informed and well intentioned authority figures may be. Nevertheless, the rate of incest detection can be improved and, more importantly, the response of society to detected incest cases can be much more humane and effective in preventing these incidents than is currently the case.[31]

When incest is reported to some authority outside the family, the report should generally be accepted as true. Believing reports of incest not only facilitates the treatment process but also is in accord with the best evidence currently available on the veracity of such reports.[31]

When a current or recent case of incest has been reported, the incest victim should be assured that he or she will be protected against any further incestuous incidents, and the responsible authority should take whatever steps necessary to guarantee the security of the child.

The severity of laws against incest and the possible long prison sentences that can be meted out to incest offenders have probably served to increase the ambivalence and fearfulness of the family members. Anticipation of punitive treatment has made it more difficult for incest victims to seek help outside of the family and for the family to fully cooperate with authorities once incest has been disclosed. Harsh penalties are intended to deter people from a repetition of such crimes, but in practice, they often backfire. With pressure from the mother or other family members, victims may retract their accusations when the harshness of the penalty is realized. It is often the case that because of the victim's inability to withstand the judicial procedure of questioning, testifying, and direct confrontation with the perpetrator, the case may be overthrown in court.

The intention of the Juvenile Court to protect the child with the involvement of the Department of Public Social Services (DPSS) also may frustrate and alienate the family to such a degree that cooperation is deterred. This has been quite a problem with a majority of the Afro-American cases that have been seen through the Family Support Program at UCLA. More often than not, these children are immediately removed from the home by DPSS, stay out of the home for a long period of time, have more difficulty with the judicial system, and feel more victimized after having reported the incestuous incident. The following case illustrates these trends:

Ms. B. had five children, four daughters and one son. Her live-in boyfriend sexually abused the four daughters (two of whom were his biological daughters) over a period of approximately ten years, and physically abused the son. After the oldest daughter disclosed the incest, all the children were removed from home. After several court appearances, her daughters were returned home; however, the son has not been returned and is currently in a residential placement. The many stipulations ordered by DPSS have made it tremendously difficult for Ms. B to satisfactorily comply to each. At each court appearance, the return of her son has been delayed another 6 to 12 months. The disruption of the family has created several problems in the therapeutic process, and necessitates more of the clinician's involvement, understanding, and advocacy on the part of the family. Many letters to both the DPSS and the court have been needed to mediate further disruption of the family. This process has continued for 1–1½ years, and the family has yet to be reunited.

Another problem that seemingly besets Afro-American families is the inconsistent and generally longer prison sentences received for incest assault. In our Family Support Program, the majority of the Afro-American fathers have received prison sentences, whereas the majority of the white-American fathers have not. Of the 29 white fathers and stepfathers who sexually abused their children, five of them were incarcerated and 24 were not. Of the 12 Afro-American fathers and stepfathers who sexually abused their children, 7 of them were incarcerated, and 5 were not. Although this may not be statistically significant in terms of hard research, it is interesting and may be reflective of what may occur in the larger society. This may also be a result of ineffective legal representation.

As with families who physically abuse their children, more involvement and case coordination are required to work with families where incest has occurred. On several occasions, a clinician may be subpoened in court to testify on the behalf of the child. Individual, group, marital, and family therapy are the modalities most often incorporated in the treatment process for these families. Crisis intervention is utilized a great deal, especially when the incest is initially revealed, and when the families have to cope with the different legal and social systems.

Parents United, the self-help group for families in which incest has occurred, also provides an additional supportive mechanism for the families outside of the conventional therapy milieu.

Understanding the complexities involved in working therapeutically with families where physical abuse and incest have occurred—especially in cases where there has been incestuous involvement—clinicians should anticipate an increased involvement, coordination, consultation, and advocacy with Afro-American families. Because of the discrepancies in the delivery of services in the legal system and the inconsistent penalties involved when Afro-American parents are identified as sexually abusive, mental health professionals need to be aware of potential as well as existing support systems that are available. These may be within the extended families, in community organizations, and possibly in the church.

In Maya Angelou's authobiography, *I Know Why the Caged Bird Sings*, an explicit example is described where the extended family provided an effective support system following an occurrence of incest. After being sexually abused by her stepfather, Ms. Angelou was involved in a traumatic court experience, and later felt totally responsible for the subsequent events that occurred in the family. As a result, Ms. Angelou became electively mute. She and her brother were then sent to live with relatives in Arkansas. There, with family and friends, she received the kind of emotional support, understanding, encouragement, and "permission" that enabled her to begin talking once again.[38]

Treatment will hopefully be identified as a positive intervention that will assist the family in coping with the problems, crises, and frustrations that result from the disruption of the family unit. It is possible that this therapeutic invervention will also help reconstitute the family or, if necessary, assist the family in making decisions that will enable the family members to cope with a different living situation.

REFERENCES

1. Taylor, L, Newberger EH: Child abuse in the international year of the child. The N Eng J Med 301:1205–1212, 1979
2. Johnson SH: High Risk Parenting. Philadelphia, J.B. Lippincott, 1979
3. Kempe R, Kempe CH: Child Abuse. Massachusetts, Harvard University Press, 1978
4. Giovannoni JM, Becerra R: Defining Child Abuse. New York, Free Press, 1979
5. Korbin JE: The cultural context of child abuse and neglect. Child Abuse and Neglect 4:3–13, 1980
6. Gil DG: Unraveling child abuse. Am J Orthopsychiatry 45:346–356, 1975
7. Kempe CH, Silverman FN, Steele BF, et al: The battered child syndrome. JAMA 181:17–24, 1962
8. U.S. Department of Health, Education, and Welfare: Child abuse and neglect: The problem and its management, 1, OHD, 75-30073, 4–13, 1975
9. Dager EZ: Socialization Process. Product and Change. Chicago, University of Maryland Publishing, 1971
10. Swinger HK: Black perspectives on child abuse and neglect. Paper presented at the Ninth Annual Child Abuse and Neglect Symposium, Keystone, Colorado, 1979
11. Douglass F: The Life and Times of Frederick Douglass. New York, Crowell Publishing, 1966
12. Grier WH, Cobb PM: Black Rage. New York, Bantam Books, 1968
13. Mayer J: Today's Education: The abused child. Today's Education 63:40–43, 1974
14. Green AH: A psychodynamic approach to the study and treatment of child-abusing parents. J Am Acad Child Psychiatry 15:414–429, 1976
15. Newberger EH, Hyde JN: Child abuse: Principles and implications of current pediatric practice. Ped Clinics N Am 22:695–715, 1975
16. Kempe CH, Helfer RE: Helping the Battered Child and His Family. Philadelphia, J.B. Lippincott 1972
17. Los Angeles Times: Child abuse on the rise in today's economic bad times. Part V, August 18, 1980

18. Steele B, Pollack C: A psychiatric study of parents who abuse infants and small children, in Helfer R, Kempe CH (Eds): The Battered Child. Chicago, University of Chicago Press, 1968.
19. Solomon T: History and demography of child abuse. Pediatrics 51:773–776, 1973
20. Gil D: Violence against children. J Marriage and Family 33:637–657, 1971
21. Gil D: Violence against children: Physical child abuse in the United States. Cambridge, Harvard University Press, 1970.
22. Gelles RJ: Child abuse as psychopathology: A sociological critique and reformulation. Am J Orthopsychiatry 43:611–621, 1973
23. Seale B: A Lonely Rage. The Autobiography of Bobby Seale. New York, New York Times Book, 1978
24. Kardiner A, Ovesey L: The Mark of Oppression: Explorations in the Personality of the America Negro. Cleveland, World Publishing, 1951
25. Powell G: Coping with Adversity: The Development of the Afro-American Child. Bruner/Mazel, (in press)
26. Korbin J: Anthropological contributions to the study of child abuse. Child Abuse and Neglect 1:7–24, 1977
27. Martin HP: The abused child: A multidisciplinary approach to developmental issues and treatment. Cambridge, Bullinger, 1976
28. Webster: Webster's New Collegiate Dictionary. Massachusetts, G. & C. Merriam, 1973
29. Justice B, Justice R: The Broken Taboo: Sex in the Family. New York, Human Sciences, 1979
30. Murdock GP: Social Structure. New York, Macmillan, 1949
31. Meiselman KC: Incest: A Psychological Study of Causes and Effects with Treatment Recommendations. San Francisco, Jossey-Bass, 1979
32. White LA: The definition and prohibition of incest. Am Anthropologist 50:416–435, 1948
33. Gutman H: The Black Family in Slavery and Freedom. New York, Pantheon, 1976
34. Butler S: Conspiracy of Silence: The Trauma of Incest. New York, Bantam, 1978
35. Tormes YM: Child victims of incest. The American Humane Association Children's Division, 1–39, 1977
36. Fromm E: The Sane Society. London, Routledge and Kegan Paul Ltd, 1956
37. Finkelhor D: Sexually Victimized Children. New York, Free Press, 1979
38. Angelou M: I Know Why the Caged Bird Sings. New York, Random House, 1969, pp 71–99

PART IV

Special Issues

Editors' Introduction

This final section of the book examines self-concept of Afro-American children and aspects of male/female relationships, issues in which an understanding of sociocultural variables is critical. These issues receive attention from the media, yet are ones about which little is written and researched. They are intensely relevant to the lifestyles of Afro-Americans today.

Gloria Johnson Powell

16

Six-City Study of School Desegregation and Self-concept among Afro-American Junior High School Students: A Preliminary Study with Implications for Mental Health

Between 1968 and 1972, a study of the effects of school desegregation on the self-concept of Afro-American children was conducted in three southern and three northern cities. Although the results of the southern cities have been published, as well as the results of one of the northern cities, this is the first report of the data of the entire six cities.[1–4] There have been many studies to date on the effects of school desegregation on self-concept: there have been few studies using the same research paradigm involving six school systems, and few comparing northern cities with southern cities.

Before the 1954 Supreme Court decision on school desegregation, seventeen southern and border states and the District of Columbia operated completely separate schools for whites and Negroes. On May 17 1954, the Supreme Court held that such separate schools were inherently unequal. This decision ushered in an era of American social revolution. About fifteen years later with the survey of equality of educational opportunities,[5] the great majority of American children still attended schools that were defined as segregated, i.e., schools where almost all of the students were of the same racial background. However in October 1969, the Burger Court declared that the "all deliberate speed" for desegregation was no longer permissible and that every school district north and south was obligated to terminate dual schools systems at once. The scramble to desegregate schools began, and the controversy over the logistics of how to desegregate schools continues to increase.

In the original Brown versus Topeka Board of Education filed in the U.S. District Court for Kansas in 1951, although the court ruled against the plaintiffs, the court felt compelled, so it would seem, to speak out on the effects of segregation upon the plaintiffs:

> Segregation of white and colored children in public schools has a detrimental effect upon the colored children. The impact is greater when it has the sanction of the law; for the policy of separating the races is usually interpreted as denoting the inferiority of the Negro group. A sense of inferiority affects the motivation of a child to learn. Segregation with the sanction of law, therefore, has a tendency to retard the educational and mental development of Negro children and to deprive them of some of the benefits they would receive in a racially integrated school system.[6,p.49]

Indeed, the lawyers for the plaintiffs used this argument when the case was presented before the U.S. Supreme Court, and their brief had an appendix of more than one hundred social scientists presenting evidence regarding the psychological problems for Afro-American children caused by segregation and prejudice. The hypothesis for this study was based on that premise: namely that if segregation of Afro-American children into separate schools was detrimental to their self-perceptions, then the desegregation of the nation's school would see an enhancement in the self-perceptions of Afro-American children.

The purpose of this study was twofold: (1) to compare the effects of school desegregation on self-concept of Afro-American children in segregated schools to those in desegregated schools; (2) to identify the variables involved in the postive or negative self-concepts of Afro-American children involved in school desegregation.

It must be stated at the outset, however, that although this study was mounted to focus on the effects of school desegregation on the self-concept development in the process of school desegregation, the implications from the findings of this research have broader implications than the school desegregation process per se, as we shall see. The long term significance of this study lies in the information it provides about what fosters optimal psychosocial development for Afro-American children, for other minority group children, and nonminority group children as well.

PROCEDURES

I have often said that I could write a book just about the responses I received from more than 100 school districts in cities with populations over 500,000. From a southern school district came a letter briefly, and, I presumed, alarmedly written: "Dear Dr. Powell: Please do not test our students. Please do not come to our city." An equally frightened letter came from a school district in a northern city that had a reputation of liberal race relations until school desegregation began. Indeed, Pettigrew has rightly noted: "The failure of private and public funding agencies to support systematic, widespread and overtime research of the racial desegregation process as it occurred is undoubtedly one of the most tragic setbacks the study of race relations has experienced"[7,p.14]

Students from at least two segregated schools and three desegregated schools in each city were given the Tennessee Self Concept Scale (T.S.C.S.), which is simple for the subject, widely applicable, and multi-dimensional in its description of the self-concept.[8] The standardization group from which the norms were developed was a broad sample of people from various parts of the country, ranging in age from 12 to 68, with equal numbers of both sexes, and including both Afro-American and white subjects. The scale was devised on a phenomenological system, and the subject is asked to rate him- or her-self in terms of (1) what he or she is (identity), (2) how he or she feels about self (self-satisfaction) and (3) what he or she does (behavior). Within these dimensions the subjects also rate their physical selves, moral-ethical selves, personal selves, family selves, and social selves. These self-descriptions coincide with Allport's seven aspects of self-hood which together comprise the self as felt and known, i.e., sense of bodily self, sense of continuing self identity, self-esteem and pride, the extension of the self, the self image, the self as a rational coper, and the self as a propiate striver.[9]

In addition to the T.S.C.S., the students were also given the Powell-Fuller Socio-Familial Questionnaire, which asked specific questions regarding the aspirational level and self-attitudes of the student.[4] There were no questions regarding race or racial attitudes on the self-concept scale or the questionnaire. The students were told that the investigators were interested in how young people thought and felt about themselves.

Self-Concept Scale

In this report of the data, the scores of the T.S.C.S. which will be discussed are: (1) Total Positive Score (TP) (Mean norm=345.37); (2) the Self-Criticism Score (mean norm =35.54); (3) the Variability Score (V) (mean norm =48.53); and (4) the Distribution Score (D) (mean norm =120.44).

A high Total Positive score (above the mean of 345.57) indicates that the individual feels positive about himself, and conversely a low score indicates a negative self-picture.

The Self-Criticism Score (SC) is composed of 10 items from the L-Scale of the M.M.P.I., which are all mildly derogatory statements that most people admit as being true for themselves. A high SC score indicates that the invididual can accept negative statements about him- or herself, is very self-critical, but has a healthy openness. A low SC score indicates defensiveness and an inability to accept negative concepts about the self.

The Distribution Score is a summary score of the way the individual distributes his or her answers across the five available choices and thus measures the certainty about the way the individual perceives him- or herself. A high D score indictes definiteness about the self-picture; a low D score indicates that the individual is indefinite and noncommittal, answering 3's (partly true, partly false) on most items.

The Variability Score measures the amount of consistency for the entire test. Well integrated people generally score below the mean (48.53) but above the first percentile, i.e., above a score of 26.

It was decided to limit the study of self-concept to those students in junior high schools and/or in early adolescence, the reasons for which will be enumerated in the discussion section of this report. The three southern cities studied were Nashville, New Orleans, and Greensboro,[4] and the three northern cities (or cities outside of the southeast South) were Minneapolis, New York, and Los Angeles (See Table 16-1).

In addition, there are three Total Positive Scores for Identity, Self-Satisfaction, and Behavior. There are also separate scores for Physical Self (Ph Score), Moral-Ethical Self (M-E Score), Personal Self (P Score), Family Self (F Score), and Social Self (S Score).

Sample

SOUTHERN CITIES

There were 1,720 students from three southern cities, 775 were Afro-American and 945 were white. There were 11 segregated schools, 5 of which were white and 6 of which were Afro-American. Of the 775 Afro-American students, 455 were attending segregated schools and 320 were attending desegregated schools. Among the 945 white students, there were 370 students attending segregated schools and 575 students attending desegregated schools.

In the three southern cities, 21 schools participated, 15 of which were public schools and 6 of which were parochial. The parochial schools were included to insure a higher participation of middle-class Afro-American students in the study. There were 10 desegregated schools, 8 public and 2

Table 16–1
TSCS Profiles of White and Afro-American Southern Junior High School Students

TSCS Scores		Black n = 775	White n = 945	Significance (%)
TP	Mean	344.85	333.10	1
	SD*	41.46	42.57	
SC	Mean	35.21	36.18	N.S.
	SD	6.34	6.61	
V	Mean	58.48	53.37	5
	SD	13.75	13.33	
D	Mean	133.63	123.54	1
	SD	27.36	27.84	
Identity	Mean	117.20	115.22	N.S.
	SD	15.26	26.21	
Self-Satisfaction	Mean	110.29	105.34	5
	SD	18.27	18.78	
Behavior	Mean	117.40	114.76	N.S.
	SD	15.41	23.40	
Physical Self	Mean	73.09	71.48	N.S.
	SD	9.40	28.53	
Moral-Ethical Self	Mean	66.84	66.49	N.S.
	SD	10.40	19.28	
Personal Self	Mean	63.87	61.47	N.S.
	SD	11.67	18.68	
Family Self	Mean	74.27	71.55	5
	SD	12.02	24.95	
Social Self	Mean	66.88	66.38	N.S.
	SD	10.53	10.45	

*SD means standard deviation

parochial. Of the 11 segregated schools in the three cities, 5 were white segregated schools (or predominantly white with less than 5 percent Afro-American students attending) and 6 schools were Afro-American segregated. Four segregated parochial schools participated, 2 for white students and 2 for Afro-American students. In all there were 800 students in segregated schools (320 Afro-American and 575 white students) and 920 students in desegregated schools (455 Afro-American and 370 white students).

In regard to educational attainment of fathers, 55.6 percent of the students indicated that their fathers had completed high school, compared with 54.3 percent of the white students; 16.6 percent of the Afro-American students and 16.6 percent of the white students indicated that their fathers had completed college; and 9.6 percent of the Afro-American students and 10 percent of the white students indicated that their fathers had had some college, but had not completed college. Only in Nashville was there a decided difference in educational attainment of Afro-American and white fathers, with more Afro-American fathers completing high school and college.

It should be noted that in Nashville the percentage of Afro-American fathers in professions is higher than that for whites. In Greensboro and New Orleans, the reverse is true. In the entire sample, 14.6 percent of the Afro-American students report that their fathers are in professions, while 22 percent of the white students do; 54.3 percent of Afro-American fathers and 47 percent of white fathers are reported to be in the technician-trade category; and 12 percent of Afro-American fathers and 13.6 percent of white students have fathers working as laborers.

In comparing educational and occupational status of mothers in the three cities, the Afro-American students' mothers had more education, were in more professional jobs, and more often worked than did the mothers of white students. Among the total sample from the three cities, 63.3 percent of Afro-American mothers and 59.3 percent of white mothers were reported to have finished high school; 14.6 percent of Afro-American mothers and 10.3 percent of white mothers had finished college; 7.3 percent of Afro-American mothers and 12 percent of white mothers had had some college. Afro-American students reported 57.6 percent of their mothers working, and 45 percent of white students reported that mothers were working.

In New Orleans more parents were reported to be separated or divorced than in the other two cities. Also, the families in New Orleans tended to be larger than in the other two cities. No students in Greensboro or Nashville reported having more than six children in the family. In the entire sample, 75 percent of the Afro-American students reported their parents living together and 78.6 percent of the white students reported the same. The percentage of white parents separated or divorced was 20 percent, and of Afro-American parents, 20.3 percent.

NORTHERN CITIES

There were 2,368 students from the three northern cities who participated; 1,236 were Afro-American and 1,132 were white. The number of girls and boys were evenly distributed amongst each group. There were 524 Afro-American students who were in 5 segregated schools and 712 who were in 9 segregated schools. By the same token there were 680 white students in 10 desegregated northern schools and 388 northern white students who were attending desegregated or predominantly white (less than 5 percent Afro-American enrollment) schools. The socioeconomic staus, educational and occupational attainment of parents, and family stability did not differ significantly from that of New Orleans. However, in the three segregated Afro-American schools in Los Angeles and New York, the schools were located in high crime areas, and were racially isolated minority schools (RIM) with very low achievement scores, and high drop out rates. These schools were significantly different from the segregated Afro-American schools in Minneapolis and very different from any segregated Afro-American schools in the South.

In Los Angeles, however, with the exception of the RIM schools, the socioeconomic status (SES) of both Afro-American and whites were 55 percent middle-class and 30 percent upper class. Indeed the 25 Afro-American students at the predominantly white private school had average family incomes of $50,000.

Results

SOUTHERN CITIES

In Nashville, the 616 students tested obtained a TP mean score of 340.43 below the normative mean and in the 40th percentile. Sixteen percent of the students scored below the 7th percentile (300), and 8 percent scored above the 97th percentile. Forty-five percent obtained a score of 350 or above. Thus, it would seem that at least 53 percent of the Nashville students have adequate-to-high self-concepts and score equal to or above the normative mean. The V mean score of 53.8, and D mean score of 126.9 are above the normative means, but the mean SC score of 34.6 is below the normative mean.

The TSCS mean scores of the 634 students tested in New Orleans are similar in some respects to those of Nashville. The New Orleans students obtained a TP mean score of 340.3, below the normative mean and in the 40th percentile. Sixteen percent scored below 300, 6 percent scored above 400, and 43 percent obtained a score of 350 or above. At least 49 percent of the New Orleans students have adequate or high self-concepts and score above the normative mean. The mean SC score of 36.1, the mean V score of 56.1, and the mean D score of 132.2 are all above the normative mean and higher than those scores in Nashville.

Greensboro's 470 students do not score as high as the Nashville and New Orleans students on the TP mean score. Their TP mean score of 335.54 is below the normative mean and in the 30th percentile. Nineteen percent of the students score below 300, 6 percent score above 400, and only 28 percent obtained a score of 350 or above. Thus, the majority (about 60 percent) of the Greensboro students have low self-concepts or score below the normative mean. The mean SC score of 36.3 is higher than in Nashville, the same as in New Orleans, and above the normative mean; the mean V score of 54.72 is above the normative mean, higher than in Nashville but lower than in New Orleans; the mean D score of 126.42 is above the normative mean, similar to that in Nashville, but lower than that in New Orleans.

In comparing the TSCS scores of the 775 Afro-American students with those of the 945 white students, some significant differences can be noted. (See Table 16-1) First of all, the Afro-American students score higher on the TP mean score (344.85) than the white students (333.13), and the difference is significant at the 1 percent level (See Table 16-1). The Afro-American students score lower (35.21) than the whites (36.18) on the SC score, but the difference is not significant. On the V and D scores (58.48 and 133.63, respectively), Afro-Americans score significantly higher than whites (53.37 and 123.54); and the differences in the means are significant at the 5 percent and 1 percent levels, respectively. The Afro-American students also score significantly higher than the white students on self-satisfaction (110.29 and 105.34 respectively), as well as on family self (74.27 and 71.55 respectively), with a significance at the 5 percent level for both scores.

The Afro-American girls score significantly higher than the white girls on TP mean score, mean D score, mean self-satisfaction score, mean behavior score, mean personal-self score, and the mean family-self score.[4]

The Afro-American boys score significantly higher than the white boys on TP mean score, mean V score, mean D score, and mean identity score.

The segregated Afro-American students score higher on identity, self-satisfaction, and behavior than the Afro-American desegregated students, but none of the differences was statistically significant. Likewise on the five subprofile scores, the segregated Afro-American students score higher than the desegregated students, but the differences are not statistically significant (See Tables 16-2, 16-3, and 16-4).

Within each of the three cities, although the Afro-American segregated students score higher than the Afro-American desegregated students, the statistical significance for any one score is not consistent.

For instance, in Greensboro, Nashville, and New Orleans, the segregated Afro-American students score higher than the desegregated Afro-American students, and in Greensboro and New Orleans, the difference was significant at the 5 percent level for each (both had $p < 0.02$). In Nashville, however, there was no significant difference be-

Table 16–2
TSCS Profiles of Afro-American Students in Segregated and Desegregated Schools in the Southern Cities

TSCS Scores		Segregated n = 437	Desegregated n = 314	Significance
TP	Mean	349.65	337.81	P<0.04
	SD*	40.27	42.83	
SC	Mean	34.78	35.80	N.S.
	SD	6.48	5.90	
V	Mean	56.04	57.36	N.S.
	SD	13.40	14.21	
D	Mean	133.74	133.50	N.S.
	SD	27.08	28.33	
Identity	Mean	118.84	115.19	N.S.
	SD	15.20	16.25	
Self-	Mean	111.64	107.57	N.S.
Satisfaction	SD	16.34	13.48	
Behavior	Mean	118.66	115.07	N.S.
	SD	22.63	13.09	
Physical Self	Mean	73.57	72.17	N.S.
	SD	7.34	8.33	
Moral-	Mean	67.52	65.89	N.S.
Ethical Self	SD	9.07	9.85	
Personal Self	Mean	67.86	64.44	N.S.
	SD	9.13	10.36	
Family Self	Mean	75.35	72.20	N.S.
	SD	9.95	10.96	
Social Self	Mean	67.59	65.78	N.S.
	SD	9.04	9.50	

*SD means standard deviation

tween mean TP scores of the two groups. (See Tables 16-3, 16-4, and 16-5.)

In Greensboro, not only is there a significant difference betweeen the segregated and desegregated Afro-American students on mean TP scores, but also on mean SC scores, the desegregated group scoring higher with a significance at the 1 percent level. On Identity and Family-Self mean scores, the segregated Afro-American students score higher with a significance at the 5 percent and 1 percent levels, respectively. (See Table 16-3.)

In New Orleans, not only do the segregated Afro-American students

Table 16–3
TSCS Profiles of Afro-American Students in Segregated and Desegregated Schools in Greensboro

TSCS Scores		Segregated n = 94	Desegregated n = 66	Significance
TP	Mean	343.93	327.55	P<0.02
	SD*	45.22	45.14	
SC	Mean	33.81	37.29	P<0.001
	SD	6.53	5.86	
V	Mean	55.42	59.12	N.S.
	SD	13.29	13.35	
D	Mean	132.06	129.38	N.S.
	SD	26.26	25.28	
Identity	Mean	117.56	112.09	P<0.03
	SD	15.48	15.55	
Self-	Mean	108.65	102.53	N.S.
Satisfaction	SD	21.94	21.37	
Behavior	Mean	117.44	113.01	N.S.
	SD	15.54	14.73	
Physical Self	Mean	72.78	70.87	N.S.
	SD	8.47	11.16	
Moral-	Mean	65.05	62.47	N.S.
Ethical Self	SD	11.61	11.02	
Personal Self	Mean	63.12	60.70	N.S.
	SD	12.18	11.90	
Family Self	Mean	75.12	69.43	P<0.005
	SD	12.27	12.90	
Social Self	Mean	67.62	64.40	N.S.
	SD	10.91	10.85	

*SD means standard deviation

score significantly higher on the mean TP scores, but also on the mean Behavior and mean Moral-Ethical Self scores, with a significance at the 5 percent and 1 percent levels, respectively. (See Table 16-4.)

In Nashville, the segregated Afro-American students score significantly higher on the mean Self-Satisfaction and mean Personal-Self scores with a significance at the 5 percent level for each. (Table 16-5.)

The Afro-American girls in segregated schools scored significantly higher than the Afro-American girls in desegregated schools on mean TP score (with a significance at the 5 percent level) (See Tables 16-6.) In addition, the Afro-American segregated girls scored significantly higher on Self-Satisfaction, Moral-Ethical Self, and Family Self (with a signifi-

Table 16–4
TSCS Profiles of Students in Segregated and Desegregated Afro-American Schools in New Orleans

TSCS Scores		Segregated n = 137	Desegregated n = 155	Significance
TP	Mean	353.74	344.08	P<0.02
	SD*	36.59	39.47	
SC	Mean	35.94	36.31	N.S.
	SD	6.72	6.46	
V	Mean	58.20	58.46	N.S.
	SD	13.73	14.39	
D	Mean	139.96	140.43	N.S.
	SD	26.49	27.20	
Identity	Mean	118.36	116.70	N.S.
	SD	14.02	14.71	
Self-Satisfaction	Mean	115.07	112.88	N.S.
	SD	16.58	17.67	
Behavior	Mean	119.48	115.62	P<0.03
	SD	16.35	15.26	
Physical Self	Mean	75.33	74.14	N.S.
	SD	8.75	9.04	
Moral Ethical Self	Mean	71.03	67.80	P<0.005
	SD	9.70	10.44	
Personal Self	Mean	64.25	63.33	N.S.
	SD	10.34	12.53	
Family Self	Mean	75.74	73.99	N.S.
	SD	11.19	12.29	
Social Self	Mean	66.77	65.84	N.S.
	SD	11.03	10.07	

*SD means standard deviation

cance at the 5 percent level for each mean score) than the desegregated girls.

In Greensboro, the Afro-American segregated girls scored significantly higher than the Afro-American desegregated girls on Total Positive, Identity, Self-Satisfaction, Behavior, Moral-Ethical Self, Social Self, and Family Self; the difference is significant at the 5 percent level for each mean score with the exception of Family Self, which is significant at the 1 percent level. (See Table 16-7.)

In Nashville, the Afro-American segregated girls scored significantly higher than the Afro-American desegregated girls on Self-Satisfaction,

Table 16–5
TSCS Profiles of Afro-American Students in Segregated and Desegregated Schools in Nashville

TSCS Scores		Segregated n = 206	Desegregated n = 93	Significance
TP	Mean	351.33	341.86	P<0.02
	SD*	39.04	43.91	
SC	Mean	34.62	33.81	N.S.
	SD	6.28	5.42	
V	Mean	54.51	54.54	N.S.
	SD	13.28	14.96	
D	Mean	120.62	117.82	N.S.
	SD	16.23	18.52	
Identity	Mean	120.64	117.83	P<0.03
	SD	16.22	18.59	
Self-Satisfaction	Mean	111.28	107.34	N.S.
	SD	10.53	11.42	
Behavior	Mean	119.12	116.61	N.S.
	SD	36.01	9.32	
Physical Self	Mean	72.62	71.54	N.S.
	SD	4.83	4.80	
Moral-Ethical Self	Mean	66.52	67.43	
	SD	5.91	8.13	
Personal Self	Mean	67.53	63.22	P<0.02
	SD	6.10	6.33	
Family Self	Mean	75.21	73.22	N.S.
	SD	6.43	7.71	
Social Self	Mean	68.40	67.11	N.S.
	SD	5.21	7.61	

*SD means standard deviation

Physical Self, and Personal Self, with a significance at the 5 percent level for each. (See Table 16-8.)

In New Orleans, the Afro-American segregated girls scored significantly higher than the Afro-American desegregated girls on Moral-Ethical Self, with a significance at the 5 percent level. (See Table 16-9.)

There is no significant difference on any TSCS scores between the Afro-American boys in segregated schools and the Afro-American boys in desegregated schools in Nashville, New Orleans, or Greensboro.

Table 16–6
TSCS Profiles of Afro-American Girls in Segregated and Desegregated Schools in Southern Cities

TSCS Scores		Segregated n = 253	Desegregated n = 184	Significance
TP	Mean	353.94	337.66	P<0.02
	SD*	40.32	41.81	
SC	Mean	34.29	36.27	N.S.
	SD	6.76	6.03	
V	Mean	55.56	56.36	N.S.
	SD	13.72	13.70	
D	Mean	135.79	131.59	N.S.
	SD	26.50	27.68	
Identity	Mean	120.02	116.10	N.S.
	SD	15.19	16.63	
Self-Satisfaction	Mean	113.30	106.30	5%
	SD	16.94	16.10	
Behavior	Mean	120.08	115.33	N.S.
	SD	16.76	12.12	
Physical Self	Mean	73.78	71.83	N.S.
	SD	7.04	8.09	
Moral-Ethical Self	Mean	69.19	66.45	N.S.
	SD	8.66	9.69	
Personal Self	Mean	65.93	62.11	N.S.
	SD	9.92	9.69	
Family Self	Mean	75.95	71.72	N.S.
	SD	9.93	8.81	
Social Self	Mean	68.45	65.65	N.S.
	SD	9.58	9.18	

*SD means standard deviation

NORTHERN CITIES

There were less than 10 percent of all northern students scoring above the norm mean for the TSCS. There were 40 percent of the students scoring below 300, and 1 percent scoring above a TP mean of 400. Most of the students had TP mean scores between the 20th to the 30th percentile for the scale.

In Minneapolis, the TP mean score for the 615 students was 330.25. There was only onc significant difference between the mean D score, with

Table 16–7
TSCS Profile of Afro-American Girls in Segregated and Desegregated Schools in Greensboro

TSCS Scores		Segregated n = 48	Desegregated n = 37	Significance
TP	Mean	351.93	326.41	P<0.01
	SD*	46.47	46.56	
SC	Mean	32.35	38.16	P<0.001
	SD	7.22	6.19	
V	Mean	54.89	59.33	N.S.
	SD	14.54	12.56	
D	Mean	138.10	131.33	N.S.
	SD	27.05	23.52	
Identity	Mean	120.41	112.88	P<0.04
	SD	15.72	17.14	
Self-Satisfaction	Mean	110.75	100.08	P<0.03
	SD	24.18	20.12	
Behavior	Mean	120.77	113.50	P<0.02
	SD	13.84	14.93	
Physical Self	Mean	73.41	71.13	N.S.
	SD	7.88	10.85	
Moral-Ethical Self	Mean	68.18	62.16	P<0.01
	SD	11.08	11.57	
Personal Self	Mean	64.41	60.94	N.S.
	SD	13.34	11.24	
Family Self	Mean	76.16	68.66	P<0.008
	SD	12.31	12.74	
Social Self	Mean	69.58	63.83	P<0.02
	SD	11.19	11.57	

*SD means standard deviation

the Afro-Americans scoring significant ($p < 0.05$) (See Table 16-10). Although the 130 Afro-American students in the 3 desegregated schools had a TP score of 327.41 compared to 333.20 for the 168 Afro-American students in the two predominantly segregated schools, the differences were not significant, and indeed, the differences between the other mean scores were not significant (See Table 16-11). The Afro-American students in Minneapolis had higher TP mean scores overall, as well as in desegregated and segregated schools, than those of Afro-Americans in the other two northern cities.

Among the New York students, the white students had significantly higher mean scores for Identity and Behavior. In general, the Afro-

Table 16–8
Comparison of Black Girls in Segregated and Desegregated Schools in Nashville

TSCS Scores		Segregated n = 113	Desegregated n = 57	Significance
TP	Mean	351.7	339.2	P<0.008
	SD*	37.1	39.9	
SC	Mean	34.1	34.1	N.S.
	SD	6.1	5.6	
V	Mean	54.2	50.8	N.S.
	SD	13.1	14.4	
D	Mean	130.4	124.0	N.S.
	SD	25.8	32.6	
Identity	Mean	120.8	118.4	N.S.
	SD	16.1	17.9	
Self-Satisfaction	Mean	111.3	104.6	P<0.01
	SD	10.9	10.4	
Behavior	Mean	119.4	116.2	N.S.
	SD	17.7	7.5	
Physical Self	Mean	72.6	69.9	N.S.
	SD	4.6	4.6	
Moral-Ethical Self	Mean	66.7	67.6	N.S.
	SD	5.9	7.0	
Personal Self	Mean	67.5	62.3	P<0.03
	SD	6.3	5.8	
Family Self	Mean	75.2	72.0	N.S.
	SD	6.1	6.5	
Social Self	Mean	69.0	67.4	N.S.
	SD	5.1	6.3	

*SD means standard deviation

American mean scores were lower than those of white students, with only two significant differences. (See Table 16-12.) The Afro-American students in the two segregated schools scored significantly lower than the Afro-American students in the desegregated schools (See Table 16-13). There were significant differences between TP, Identity, Behavior, and Moral-Ethical mean scores.

The Los Angeles situation proved to be unique. Although there were no significant differences between the TSCS Profiles of 462 Afro-American students and 379 white students, there were significant differences between the 326 Afro-American students in desegregated

Table 16–9
TSCS Profiles of Afro-American Girls in Segregated and Desegregated Schools in New Orleans

TSCS Scores		Segregated n = 92	Desegregated n = 90	Significance
TP	Mean	358.11	347.38	P<0.05
	SD*	37.41	38.97	
SC	Mean	36.43	36.67	N.S.
	SD	6.98	6.31	
V	Mean	57.71	58.96	N.S.
	SD	13.53	14.14	
D	Mean	138.87	139.46	N.S.
	SD	26.67	26.94	
Identity	Mean	118.87	117.04	N.S.
	SD	13.75	14.85	
Self-Satisfaction	Mean	117.85	114.24	N.S.
	SD	15.75	17.78	
Behavior	Mean	120.08	116.31	N.S.
	SD	18.75	13.93	
Physical Self	Mean	75.33	74.48	N.S.
	SD	8.65	8.82	
Moral-Ethical Self	Mean	72.69	69.61	P<0.03
	SD	9.01	10.51	
Personal Self	Mean	65.88	63.09	N.S.
	SD	10.12	12.04	
Family Self	Mean	76.50	74.52	N.S.
	SD	11.39	13.04	
Social Self	Mean	66.78	65.72	N.S.
	SD	12.47	9.97	

*SD means standard deviation

schools and the 136 Afro-American students in the racially isolated minority (RIM) school (See Tables 16-14 and 16-15). Desegregated students scored significantly higher on TP, Self-Satisfaction, Behavior, Family Self, and Social Self. Curiously, the segregated Afro-American students scored significanlty higher on the mean Identity score than the desegregated students.

There were 25 Afro-American students at a predominantly white (less than 5 percent Afro-American enrollment) private school. Their TSCS Profile is decidedly lower than the TSCS Norm group of other junior high TSCS samples, particularly on TP, Identity, Moral-Ethical Self, Personal Self, and Social Self mean scores. (See Table 16-16.)

Table 16–10
TSCS Profiles of Afro-American and White Students in Minneapolis

		Afro-American	White	
TSCS Scores	n = 298	n = 317	Significance	
TP	Mean	329.34	331.42	N.S.
	SD*	39.82	41.82	
SC	Mean	37.13	36.71	N.S.
	SD	6.14	6.21	
V	Mean	45.18	46.80	N.S.
	SD	7.42	8.92	
D	Mean	123.51	119.23	N.S.
	SD	25.01	24.81	
Identity	Mean	112.48	113.23	N.S.
	SD	23.61	24.21	
Self-Satisfaction	Mean	104.87	104.11	N.S.
	SD	17.01	16.87	
Behavior	Mean	111.96	113.11	N.S.
	SD	19.84	23.01	
Physical Self	Mean	71.32	72.01	N.S.
	SD	12.01	13.14	
Moral-Ethical Self	Mean	63.89	64.23	N.S.
	SD	9.01	10.14	
Personal Self	Mean	60.18	60.92	N.S.
	SD	10.29	14.38	
Family Self	Mean	69.19	70.25	N.S.
	SD	12.90	8.39	
Social Self	Mean	64.75	65.19	N.S.
	SD	9.98	11.00	

*SD means standard deviation

Discussion

It is ironical, indeed, that twenty years after the Brown decision and the pronouncement of Chief Justice Earl Warren on May 17, 1954 that "to separate (Afro-American children) from others of similar age and qualifications soley because of race generates a feeling of inferiority as to their status in the community that may effect their hearts and minds in a way unlikely ever to be undone"[5] that those children who have the most adequate self-concepts are southern Afro-American children and particularly those southern Afro-Americans in segregated schools, the children for

Table 16–11
TSCS Profiles of Afro-American Students in Predominantly Segregated and Desegregated Schools in Minneapolis

TSCS Scores		Desegregated n = 130	Predominantly Segregated n = 168	Significance
TP	Mean	327.41	333.20	N.S.
	SD*	46.39	32.71	
SC	Mean	37.13	37.38	N.S.
	SD	5.14	6.28	
V	Mean	50.81	52.03	N.S.
	SD	4.29	3.89	
D	Mean	122.82	124.04	N.S.
	SD	22.81	25.31	
Identity	Mean	112.40	114.98	N.S.
	SD	15.40	16.03	
Self-Satisfaction	Mean	103.32	105.18	N.S.
	SD	21.45	17.22	
Behavior	Mean	112.08	113.02	N.S.
	SD	26.71	13.16	
Physical Self	Mean	68.52	70.46	N.S.
	SD	12.84	16.25	
Moral-Ethical Self	Mean	64.02	66.21	N.S.
	SD	10.68	19.03	
Personal Self	Mean	61.02	61.22	N.S.
	SD	14.38	10.94	
Family Self	Mean	68.18	70.59	N.S.
	SD	14.01	12.84	
Social Self	Mean	65.46	66.20	N.S.
	SD	10.01	9.70	

*SD means standard deviation

whom the decree was pronounced. The second most important finding is that desegregation in the South is particularly noxious to the self-concept of the Afro-American girl. The third most important finding is that, Afro-American children in the North, as well as northern and southern white children, show no difference in self-percept. Finally and most importantly, the lowest self-concept profiles were found among Afro-American students in racially isolated minority (RIM) schools and neighborhoods in Los Angelés and New York.

In rank-ordering the groups of students in the South and the North according to self-concept scores, the following emerges:

Rank No.	Student Group	TP Mean Score
1	Southern Afro-American students in segregated schools	349.65
2	Southern Afro-American students in segregated and desegregated schools	344.85
3	Southern Afro-American students in desegregated schools	337.66
4	Northern Afro-American and white children in segregated and desegregated schools	325.16

(It is interesting to note that the group of southern students with the lowest Tennessee Self Concept Scores (TSCS) were the Afro-American girls in desegregated schools in Greensboro, N.C., with TP mean score of 326.41). (See Table 16-7.)

Among the northern cities, Afro-American and white children score the same in terms of mean TP scores, 322.82 and 327.49, respectively. However, the Afro-American children in the desegregated Afro-American schools in Minneapolis (TP mean 327.41) do not score as low as their cohort groups in New York (TP mean 311.16) and Los Angeles (TP mean 316.92). (See Tables 16-11, 16-13, and 16-15.)

What is ultimately clear, however, is that southern Afro-American children have a way of overcoming racism, family pressures, puberty changes, and social changes, and maintain their self-esteem in a way that is seemingly not available to the other groups of children studied. The desegregation process puts the healthy self-concept development process attained by a southern Afro-American adolescent at risk, but RIM school and community in the North places self-concept development at higher risk, making a healthy self-concept less attainable for the Afro-American adolescent. How can a segregated community and school enhance self-concept in one instance in the South, and deter it in another in a large urban northern city? Perhaps a closer look at the two environments, as well as an assessment of the variables of self-concept, will provide some much needed clues.

Table 16–12
TSCS Profiles of Afro-American and White Junior High Schools Students in New York City

TSCS Scores		Afro-American n = 476	White Students n = 438	Significance
TP	Mean	316.99	322.82	N.S.
	SD*	43.91	42.57	
SC	Mean	36.14	36.70	N.S.
	SD	6.34	6.45	
V	Mean	51.43	51.32	N.S.
	SD	13.62	13.46	
D	Mean	116.83	115.08	N.S.
	SD	24.45	24.49	
Identity	Mean	108.23	111.06	P<0.05
	SD	15.42	15.48	
Self-Satisfaction	Mean	100.70	101.40	N.S.
	SD	17.91	18.66	
Behavior	Mean	107.68	110.40	P<0.05
	SD	16.41	15.07	
Physical Self	Mean	66.88	67.70	N.S.
	SD	10.60	10.24	
Moral-Ethical Self	Mean	62.91	65.31	N.S.
	SD	12.23	11.16	
Personal Self	Mean	56.34	57.24	N.S.
	SD	10.81	11.63	
Family Self	Mean	66.81	67.56	N.S.
	SD	11.52	11.50	
Social Self	Mean	63.62	64.83	N.S.
	SD	7.69	8.74	

*SD means standard deviation

AGE AND SELF-CONCEPT

When this study was originally undertaken, it was decided not to include younger students because of their age. Allport has given considerable attention to the formulation, theory, and development stages of self-concept.[9] The first stage of self-concept development is the sense of bodily self,occurring during the first year of life. The second stage, the sense of continuing identity, follows during the second year of life. The third stage, the development of self-esteem and pride, occurs primarily during the third

Table 16–13
TSCS Profiles of Afro-American Students in Desegregated and Segregated Schools in New York City

TSCS Scores		Segregated n = 258	Desegregated n = 218	Significance
TP	Mean	311.16	322.82	P<0.04
	SD*	42.85	45.57	
SC	Mean	35.58	36.70	N.S.
	SD	6.25	6.45	
V	Mean	51.54	51.32	N.S.
	SD	13.87	13.46	
D	Mean	118.58	115.08	N.S.
	SD	25.02	24.49	
Identity	Mean	105.39	111.06	P<0.04
	SD	15.87	15.48	
Self-Satisfaction	Mean	100.31	101.40	N.S.
	SD	17.76	18.66	
Behavior	Mean	105.81	110.40	P<0.02
	SD	17.05	15.07	
Physical Self	Mean	66.36	67.70	N.S.
	SD	11.42	10.24	
Moral-Ethical Self	Mean	60.52	65.31	P<0.05
	SD	12.78	11.16	
Personal Self	Mean	55.44	57.24	N.S.
	SD	10.57	11.63	
Family Self	Mean	66.44	67.56	N.S.
	SD	11.54	11.50	
Social Self	Mean	62.19	64.83	N.S.
	SD	6.69	8.74	

*SD means standard deviation

year, and the fourth year sees the development of the extension of the self. The fifth developmental stage is that of self-image, first created by the child's parents. At the entrance into school the teacher supplants the parents, and peer rules become binding. The process of self-image continues throughout latency and elementary school and into adolescence. Following the self-image stage is the sixth stage of the self as a rational coper. The child's cognitive development proceeds through the concrete operations stage into a cognitive stage characterized by reflective, conscious rational thought. With the process of the self as a rational coper, which begins during early adolescence, is the renewed search for self-

Table 16–14
TSCS Profiles of Afro-American and White Students in Los Angeles Junior High Schools

TSCS Scores		Afro-American n = 462	White Students n = 379	Significance
TP	Mean	323.11	328.23	N.S.
	SD*	37.81	45.14	
SC	Mean	36.09	35.44	N.S.
	SD	6.42	6.42	
V	Mean	56.05	53.47	N.S.
	SD	14.41	12.51	
D	Mean	127.75	125.21	N.S.
	SD	29.31	36.38	
Identity	Mean	113.26	112.15	N.S.
	SD	14.89	16.30	
Self-Satisfaction	Mean	106.90	103.84	N.S.
	SD	13.68	18.11	
Behavior	Mean	102.95	101.38	N.S.
	SD	12.42	9.32	
Physical Self	Mean	68.89	69.00	N.S.
	SD	10.02	10.82	
Moral-Ethical Self	Mean	62.01	62.23	N.S.
	SD	10.43	10.79	
Personal Self	Mean	62.02	63.32	N.S.
	SD	10.06	11.05	
Family Self	Mean	65.26	67.73	N.S.
	SD	10.88	14.58	
Social Self	Mean	63.71	65.53	N.S.
	SD	8.68	11.03	

*SD means standard deviation

identity. This stage of self-concept development, which is called by Allport "propiate striving," is the time the individual begins to integrate the bodily sense, the self-identity, self-esteem, self-image, self-extension and propiate striving into a continuing self-concept. Self-concept is a part of the organization and adaptation of the cognitive process. Every act of intelligence involves an interpretation of external reality, an assimilation of that event into some kind of meaning system in the subject's cognitive organization. The process of integrating the various stages of self-concept development seemed crucial to capture in this stage of early adolescence,

Table 16–15
TSCS Profiles of Afro-American Students in Desegregated and Segregated Schools in Los Angeles

TSCS Scores		Segregated n = 136	Desegregated n = 326	Significance
TP	Mean	316.92	329.30	P<0.02
	SD*	31.35	45.21	
SC	Mean	36.44	35.73	N.S.
	SD	5.79	7.27	
V	Mean	57.48	54.62	N.S.
	SD	14.38	14.68	
D	Mean	126.24	129.27	N.S.
	SD	28.22	30.69	
Identity	Mean	116.17	110.34	P<0.05
	SD	13.23	16.57	
Self-Satisfaction	Mean	98.56	107.34	P<0.02
	SD	13.43	18.79	
Behavior	Mean	102.16	111.64	P<0.01
	SD	11.49	15.84	
Physical Self	Mean	68.30	69.15	N.S.
	SD	9.04	11.12	
Moral-Ethical Self	Mean	60.38	63.91	N.S.
	SD	8.43	12.39	
Personal Self	Mean	63.22	61.35	N.S.
	SD	8.02	12.17	
Family Self	Mean	63.16	68.36	P<0.05
	SD	8.58	13.90	
Social Self	Mean	61.82	65.61	P<0.05
	SD	7.94	9.51	

*SD means standard deviation

when the perceptions of the outside world are impinging on the young adolescent's self-percept, and when social changes are being experienced, perceived, and reflected upon in relation to the self.

According to Lipsett the major tasks of early adolescence are identity and self-esteem.[10] Thus, crucial to psychosocial development is the continuing task of identity formation which is always challenged by the "vagaries," as it were, of self-esteem. Likewise, according to Elkind, research in the area of cognitive development in adolescence has identified five areas for continuing research: (1) the self-concept, (2) the generality of formal operation, (3) conceptual orientation shifts, (4) ethnic differences in cognitive ability, and (5) moral judgment and behavior.[11]

Table 16–16
TSCS Profiles of Middle Class/Affluent Afro-American Junior High School Students in Los Angeles and Other Junior High School Samples and TSCS Norm Groups

TSCS Scores		Los Angeles n = 25	TSCS Norm Group	Other Junior High Samples (N = 1918)
TP	Mean	310.51	345.57	325.45
	SD*	42.85	3	
SC	Mean	35.58	35.54	36.31
	SD	6.27		
V	Mean	52.54	48.53	54.70
	SD	13.87		
D	Mean	117.58	120.10	114.23
	SD	25.02		
Identity	Mean	104.39	127.10	122.21
	SD	15.87		
Self-Satisfaction	Mean	100.31	103.67	97.87
	SD	17.76		
Behavior	Mean	105.81	115.01	105.38
	SD	17.05		
Physical Self	Mean	68.36	71.78	69.07
	SD	11.42		
Moral-Ethical Self	Mean	60.52	70.33	63.74
	SD	12.78		
Personal Self	Mean	55.44	64.55	62.58
	SD	10.57		
Family Self	Mean	65.44	70.83	65.71
	SD	11.54		
Social Self	Mean	61.19	68.14	64.30
	SD	6.69		

*SD means standard deviation

During adolescence, a qualitative change in thought processes takes place. There is a shift in thinking from "logical" inference as a "set of concrete operation," to an ability to "combine combinations" and "relate relationships."[10,11] The adolescent can create thought systems, or theories: he or she is aware of "the observed as only a subset of what may be logically possible."

In an attempt to combine the process of self-concept development with that of cognitive development, Elkind proposes that the onset of formal operations makes it possible for the young adolescent to see himself as others see him, and reveals to him "the privateness of his thoughts and the social isolation of his reflective self."[11] Elkind poses such questions as "How does the adolescent handle these new discoveries? How does he deal with them while coping with physical and social changes?"[11]

These processes and changes in the development of cognitive and self-concept seemed crucial in understanding the effects of school desegregation on self-concept in Afro-American youth. A cross-sectional study of Afro-American youth who are developmentally in the process of a reflective, hypodeductive self-examination of themselves and the social order would more nearly reflect on the changes in self-concept that might occur because of social changes such as school desegregation. Although younger children are affected by school desegregation, their hypodeductive reflective reasoning is less well-developed, and may more closely mirror the opinions of their significant others, particularly their parents and teachers. The adolescent is entering a much wider world, and is synthesizing inputs from all directions.

It is important to recognize that self-concept changes with age. There are numerous studies to date which indicate self-esteem increases with age. Wylie's reviews of this subject cites Jerseld's study of fourth- and sixth-grade children in which sixth-grade children demonstrated greater self-ideal congruence than fourth-grade children.[12] Two interpretations of such results are presented as possible interpretations: (1) that there are developmental changes in self-ideal congruence, and (2) that with an increase in age comes a greater reliability in sorting, because of more familiarity with tests and improved reading skills. For children, these two issues are particularly germane.

The Wylie review cites those studies no age trends as well as those showing decreasing self-regard with age.[12] The explanation offered for the diversity of such findings are worth reviewing. However, for the sake of time the remainder of the discussion on age and self-concept will focus on those using the Tennessee Self Concept Scale (T.S.C.S.). In summarizing the data on age as a factor in self-concept using the T.S.C.S., Thompson concludes that TP score profiles indicate that self-esteem increases with age.[13] The elderly subjects who earn the higher level of T.S.C.S. scores may do so because of more defensiveness and a disinclination to make negative statements about themselves. Older subjects have a tendency towards more denial but also show more certainty about their self-perceptions than younger subjects.

Eight studies of self-concept among junior high school students are reveiwed by Thompson with the following conclusions:[13]

1. Junior high school students show considerable consistency in their self-reports.

2. TP mean scores are generally below the norm for the scale.
3. Behavior is consistently lower than identity and self-satisfaction.
4. Among the column scores, Physical Self and Personal Self are elevated, but Moral-Ethical Self and Family Self are lowered.
5. The pattern of column scores bears some resemblance to the delinquency profile described by Fitts and Hammer.[14]

Among the high school students, the TSCS scores are similar to those of junior high school students, with TP scores one std below the mean and the level and patterning of the row and column scores similar to the junior high school students. The Distribution and Variability Scores are usually within normal limits. "Although the profiles of normal nondelinquent high school and junior high school students show many deviant aspects, the profiles of delinquents show greater deviancy than their normal peers."[14]

The profiles of college students studied closely resemble the T.S.C.S. norm group but a relatively high level of self-acceptance is reported. Likewise the adult samples resemble the TSCS norm groups with the exception that lower variability scores are reported.

Interestingly, Thompson concludes:

> Why should adolescents have lower self concepts than adults? . . . Is this true in other cultures also? . . . Is the low self-esteem of our teenagers a reflection of child-rearing practices, of the ways they are treated in school, of over-permissiveness or over-control, of their lack of responsibilities, of their necessary dependence upon parents, of their search for roles, identity and purpose in life, or of the fact that they still have to prove themselves?[13,p.28]

Segregated Southern Afro-American Schools

The TP mean scores of the junior high school students included in the studies received by Thompson range between the mid 330s and low 320s, which fall between 20th and 30th of the percentile scores for the TSCS (See Table 16-16). The TP mean scores for the southern white students, and all the northern white and Afro-American students fall within this range (See Tables 16-1, 16-10, 16-12, and 16-14). Only the Afro-American students in the South, particularly those in segregated schools, had mean TP scores resembling the norm group (See Table 16-2). What is it about southern segregated schools for Afro-American youth that fostered self-concept development, given the difficulties of living in a racist society and the changing social values and family stability?

The picture often conjured up when Afro-American schools in the South were mentioned was that of one-room school houses, with children from the cotton fields who attended sporadically depending on the needs of their share cropper families, and a teacher who had little education herself. Although that image was not completely untrue, it was not the whole truth. It naturally became assumed that any Afro-American school in the South was naturally inferior than any public school anywhere else in the country. It was also assumed that since southern Afro-American students came from such inferior schools, they must of course view themselves as inferior.

Having myself gone to northern schools where, most often, I was the only Afro-American or one of the few Afro-Americans, I was particularly struck by the Afro-American schools that I visited in the South. When I walked into the hallways, auditoriums, and classrooms, all the Afro-Americn heroes were on the walls—Frederick Douglas, Harriet Tubman, Mary McLeod Bethune, William DuBois, Lanston Hughes, Charles Drew—and on and on. When I sat in on the American History course, I heard the students talk about George Washington in one breath and George Washington Carver in the next. The subject was American History, and the role of Afro-Americans in the history of this country was an integral part of the curriculum. There was no need for a separate Black Studies course so that an Afro-American student could learn about the role his ancestors had in shaping this country. Such material was part of American history and so it was in English, and the sciences and art and music! So very different form my own school experiences in Boston.

At Boston Girl's Latin School, where I had attended junior and senior high school, the first day of school the teacher commented on what a little United Nations the class represented. She then asked each of us to stand, give our names and some data about our ethnic background and how our families came to this country. There were two Afro-American students in our class, and I sat in the fifth seat in the first row, and my chest swelled with pride as my turn grew closer and I could tell about my great-great-grandparents, runaway slaves with Harriet Tubman, who settled in Canada until after the war and then returned to upper New York State. My mother had told us this story many times and about the hardships they had endured. She had also taken us to see the Underground Railroad in Boston so we would know that our courageous ancestors had passed the same streets we crossed. It had been a great source of inspiration and pride for me and I was anxious to tell it. The teacher ignored me, passing over me and the other Afro-American girl, assuming that Afro-Americans would have nothing of significance to tell of their families or heritages.

In the South during the testing, the students were usually excited when the research team would appear, and there would be the usual giggling and whispers. One teacher called one young boy and reprimanded him and reminded him that if he did not behave she would tell his mother at bridge club that evening. When did my mother and white teacher ever sit down at any table together in my Boston community? We lived worlds apart and my teacher never understood my world, nor cared to understand it.

Many of the teachers in the southern Afro-American schools approach me about some of their students, who were only reading at sixth-grade level but whose reading comprehension seemed to be improving with the tutoring the teachers provided on their own time. One particular teacher was tutoring a student in her English class three times a week after school, and the student was now reading at grade level. Another teacher had an after school tutoring program that she ran with a group of parents in her home. The teachers knew all of their students and their families, and cared about them, encouraged, and chastised them as needed. In many instances the teachers went to the same churches and taught some of their same students in Sunday schools. They belonged to the same social and civic organizations as their students' parents. These cohesive communities were such that if Johnny dared to steal a piece of candy from Mr. Jones' store, Mr. Jones would whip him and call his parents who would whip him again—one for stealing and two, for embarrassing the family. It wasn't child abuse, it was child caring and consistent rearing.

Erik Erikson has said that in order for a young person to reach that inner core of unity in his or her identity process, the mores and values of the home must be reinforced in the immediate community, and that there must be readily identifiable adult models that the growing person can incorporate into his sense of self.[15] In short, the young adolescents need models and heroes.

We have described the cohesive communities from whence these Afro-American southern youths came. Their teachers, parents, tradesmen, ministers, and civic leaders all lived in the same community and expected the same prescribed behaviors of all children. Young persons in such communities knew the value of education, for there were only two options: (1) work in Miss Annie's kitchen or as Mr. Smith's sharecropper farmer, or (2) get an education and be a teacher, doctor, lawyer, minister, and "further your race"—a motto that was always stressed and repeated. You were part of a common cause and struggle.

Such school environments also stimulated academic achievement, contrary to the prevailing theme of the underachieving Afro-American student. Most certainly the high academic achievements of Afro-Americans who attended segregated Afro-American school is a case in point. By the early 1960s more than 50 percent of all Afro-Americans with advanced degrees had been educated at 11 Afro-American High Schools in this country, 9 of them located in the central South.[16] In a well researched and well documented study, Sowell notes the achievements of the Afro-American students from one of these 11 Afro-American high schools, Dunbar High School, Washington, D.C., as "one of the most remarkable Afro-American educational success stories."[17,18] Dunbar students scored the highest in tests given to both Afro-Americans and whites throughout the city. Of the 34 Dunbar students admitted to Amherst College between 1892 and 1954, more than 25 percent were Phi Beta Kappas. Dunbar graduates include Benjamin Davis, the first Afro-American general; William H. Hostie, the first Afro-American judge; Rober C. Weaver, the first Afro-American cabinet member; Charles Drew, the discoverer of blood plasma; and Edmund W. Brooks, the first Afro-American Senator since the Reconstruction. However, as Sowell notes, the "ignoring of Dunbar's achievement is most remarkable considering the voluminous outpouring on black educational pathology."[18]

The Dunbar experience can be contrasted with and supported by the report of the National Scholarship and Service Fund for Negro students, which from 1948 to 1963 helped over 9,000 Afro-American students to enroll in interracial colleges situated mostly in the North.[19] The record of college success was far above that of the national average percent, with 5.6 percent having an average of A or A−, 50.3 percent with a B average, 32.4 percent with a C average, and 0.7 percent with D averages or below.[19] Additional material on these students suggests that academic success was associated with social acceptance on the campus. It is significant to note that there have been other studies which indicate that successful school desegregation cannot occur without significant modification of white prejudice.[17]

The teachers, parents, tradesmen, ministers, and civic leaders of these communities were the civil rights leaders of the sixties. It was the adults in such southern communities across the nation who sounded the trumpet heard round the world. Segregation must go: freedom now! It was in such a community that the Rev. Martin Luther King, Jr. was born and became heir to the same trumpet call for freedom. Indeed, his captivating theme was "We shall overcome! The Bible, the Supreme Court, truth, justice, and the Lord are on our side. It is our Christian duty to show the white man the error of his sinful ways." He appealed to the masses from the model of ultimate self-esteem and pride—a nonviolent Christian and American struggle for freedom and the American creed.

The parents, college students, and even the high school and junior high school students from these communities were the foot soldiers in the struggle for this new call for freedom and recognition of the American creed. The parents, teachers, and other adults in these communities became the heroes for these youngsters, the models that they could incorporate into their sense of self and forge an identity that gave them purpose and direction. And, although the Afro-American students in the desegregated schools had a hard time maintaining their self-esteem in schools that did not want them, their self-esteem scores were rarely as low as the northern students because of the families, communities, and social causes sustaining their beliefs in themselves.

If I could bottle it all up, I would give two tablespoons a day to the lost, depressed young adolescents that I see every day in my clinics. "Here, have a taste of hope, and courage, and believing, and belonging, and a fight for freedom and dignity!"

As one examines the TSCS profiles of the southern Afro-American students, not only do the Afro-American students score significantly higher than the white students on mean TP scores, but also on mean scores for D in Self-Certainty, Self-Satisfaction, and Family Self. Indeed, this is a consistent finding among Afro-American students in each of the three southern cities. Another significant finding is that they also scored significantly higher than white southern youth on Moral-Ethical Self.

These findings are particularly noteworthy in view of the prevailing theme of the damaged self-percept of the Afro-American child, and the prevailing theme of the disorganized chaotic Afro-American family life, as well as the over-reporting of delinquency and antisocial behavior among Afro-American youth. The profiles of these southern Afro-American youngsters are not similar to the delinquent profiles reported by Fitts and Hammer.[14]

Martin and Martin note the pathology-disorganization perspective of Afro-American families from the early 30s to the mid 60s.[20] After the Moynihan report in 1965 which described the Afro-American family as "a tangle of pathologies,"[21] the strength-resiliency perspective with Billingsley, Ladner, and Hill as the chief exponents began to emerge. Billingsley's view is that the Afro-American family "in the theoretical perspective of a subsystem of the larger society,[22–25]" is an absorbing, adaptive, and amazingly resilient mechanism for the socialization of its children and the civilization of its society. Most certainly the southern Afro-American children which we tested viewed their families as nurturant, expressive, and supportive. The southern Afro-American children know what ethical values and morals they believe and why, and they seem certain about why they believe. Perhaps this is due to the high religious orientation which Hill has discussed in his *Strengths of Black Families*.[25]

Certainly the cohesive southern Afro-American communities, their churches, schools, and civil rights activities, their leaders, and their fervent belief in freedom, human dignity, and "overcoming" have resulted in a kind of resiliency in self-concept that is unique to them. However, even in the South, school desegregation threatens that resiliency in self-esteem in many instances. For instance, in New Orleans and Greensboro, the TSCS scores of Afro-American girls in desegregated schools decline significantly, for "Black is not beautiful" in a newly desegregated school in the South. The boys scores are not as high as those in the segregated schools but they do not decline as much as the girls do. But boys sublimate through sports.

The Dissonant and Consonant School Setting

One of the most thorough studies to date on self-concept and school desegregation is the 1972 Rosenberg-Simmons study in Baltimore involving more than 1,900 white and black children in grades 3–12.[26] Among the Baltimore students, 12 percent of the Afro-American students went to desegregated schools, and only 30 percent lived in desegregated neighborhoods. Afro-American students had higher self-esteem than white students. At the junior high school level Afro-American children in desegregated schools had somewhat lower self-esteem than Afro-Americans attending predominantly Afro-American schools, and the difference was even greater at the senior high school level.

Social comparisons remain a fundamentally basic principle in determining self-concept effects, and the differences in the comparisons that result reflect the consonance or dissonance of the individual's environment. For instance a study in New York found that Catholics raised in non-Catholic neighborhoods had lower self-esteem than Catholics raised in Catholic or mixed neighborhoods.[27] The same study found that Jews raised in non-Jewish neighborhoods had lower self-esteem than Jews raised in Jewish or mixed neighborhoods, and likewise for Protestants.

Attitudes, values, or competency levels may also affect the contextual environment and thus mediate the various attitudes towards the child and how he or she is evaluated. These attitudes and evaluations will affect the child's own self-perceptions and self-esteem.

Family structure was found to be an important variable in mediating self-esteem in the Baltimore study.[26] However, the effects of family structure depended on the racial context in which the family structure occurred. Thirty percent of the Afro-American children came from separated or never-married families, compared to 6 percent of the white children. The intact nuclear family is the most desirable family structure in American society and the least desirable is the unmarried or abandoned mother and child family. It could be assumed that children from these stigmatized family structures would have lower self-esteem. According to the Baltimore study these consequences depended on the racial context in which the family structure occurred. In predominantly Afro-American schools there was no difference in self-esteem levels of Afro-American children from separated or never-married families and those from other family structures. However, Afro-American children from separated or never-married families in predominantly white schools had lower self-esteem than Afro-Americn students from other family structures, with 42 percent of those from separated or never-married families showing low self-esteem compared wth 19 percent of the other Afro-American children with different family structures.[26]

It must be remembered that in a consonant segregated environment where the child is surrounded by others like him, he may have very limited day-to-day interpersonal experience with discrimmination and the child is less likely to be exposed to the negative attitudes about his racial group and more likely to hear positive statements about people of his own racial group. Among the Baltimore junior and senior high school Afro-American students the more racially dissonant the student's neighborhood or school, the greater the chances that he or she had been teased, laughed at, or left out of things because of race. The greater self-concept instability of Afro-American children and teachers in these settings do not provide sufficient confirmation for the Afro-American child's self-concept. In such school environments the minority child is more likely to hear depreciatory, and fewer laudatory things about himself as a group member. One could understand then how such communications could contribute to the decreased self-esteem and the increased awareness of the low esteem in which one's group is generally held in the society. These kinds of awareness often bring weakening of group pride and identification. The instability of the self-concept in group disidentification then is related to the dissonant communicaiton within the dissonant environment. Rosenberg and Simmons, however, stress that in spite of the dissonant setting, "Only in the rarest of instances do we find the kind of strong racial disidentification implied by Gardiner and Ovessey, 1951; Erikson, 1966; Lewen, 1948, and others."[26,p.111] In the South, in spite of the overt discrimmination, children were taught the rules about to where to go and where not to go, but also received the nurturance and praise within their own communities.

A Review of the Correlates of Self-Esteem

A recent review of the literature on the positive self-concept of Afro-Americans examines several new findings and theories:

1. Many studies now show that Afro-Americans do not believe the negative stereotypes about themselves or that they are inferior to whites.[28,41]

2. Recent exhaustive literature reviews based on Wylie[12] and Weinberg[29] reveal that there is little or no difference in self-concept between white or Afro-American children, and that in most instances the Afro-American children have higher self-esteem than white children.
3. Large sample studies do not support the damaged self-percept of the Afro-American child.[4,26]

The significant others in the Afro-American child's life, as Norton[30] points out, are not the majority group or society as a whole, but primarily the family and then those significant others in his immediate community or world.

There are many correlates of self-concept—age, sex, intelligence, achievement, race, socioeconomic status, peer relationships, and parental attitudes—and many more recent studies have demonstrated the importance of controlling for these variables. Although Rosenberg[31] and Coopersmith[32] have found that higher social class is directly related to favorableness of self-concept, the study of Soares and Soares[33] shows that disadvantaged children do not necessarily reflect more negative self-perceptions or lower self-esteem than advantaged children.

A comparison of the self-perceptions of disadvantaged children with those of advantaged children in grades 4 through 8 in a public school of a New England city indicated more positive self-images on all measures (self-concept, ideal concept, reflected-self-classmates, reflected-self-teacher, reflected-self-parent) for disadvantaged children over advantaged children.[33] The disadvantaged children lived in low-rent tenements or subsidized housing. The ethnic composition was about two-thirds Afro-American and Puerto Rican and one-third white. The family incomes were less than $4000 per year and many families received state aid or welfare funds. The children who were not disadvantaged came from a middle-class neighborhood in the same city. There was usually at least one adult working in a steady job or profession with an income of over $7,000 per year. The families of these students tended to live in one-family homes which they themselves owned. The ethnic makeup was about 90 percent white and 10 percent various minority groups.

Early Adolescence Among Northern Afro-American Young Adolescents

In comparing TSCS profile means for 1918 junior high school students with those for the original TSCS norm group, the same significant differences were noted. Thompson suggests that the low self-concept profiles of young adolescents may be due to child-rearing practices, such as overpermissiveness or over-control, the ways in which young people are treated in school; or their intense search for roles, identity, and life purpose, three identity problems which are just as prominent among their parents and other adults.[13] The Group for the Advancement on Psychiatry (GAP) Committee on adolescence suggests that rapid social change has been a problem for adolescents.

> Surely the future has never been truly certain for any society at any time, and there have been other historical instances of cultural despair. But if one may take evidence from the recorded attitudes of earlier periods in our culture, there usually has been a prevailing generally accepted fantasy that the future was predictable and secure . . . Today there is no such preponderance of widely accepted prophet of security.[34,p.49]

The committee cautions against the proliferation of skepticism and anxiety and reminds us that puberty is as universal as it is biological. The adaptations to puberty occur against a backdrop of a particular culture, and only by understanding the culture which surrounds the adolescent process can one understand the adolescent.

A review of the self-concept profiles of the southern white students might also prove helpful in understanding the low self-concept profiles of the northern students. As striking as the finding that Afro-American students in southern urban communities have higher self-concepts than whites is the finding that southern white students score extremely low on the total positive mean score, indicating very low or negative self-concepts. They score in the 30th percentile for the scale, well below the normative mean (see Table 16-1). Although there is a tendency for the 1,720 southern students tested to score below the normative mean on Identity, Moral-Ethical Self, and Social Self, in many instances the white students score significantly lower on these items than Afro-American students. Thus, although the adolescents in general have some conflicts in the area of Identity, Moral-ethical Self, and Social Self, the southern white students also score very low on the Personal-Self score. In general, the southern white students score slightly higher on the Self-Criticism score than the Afro-American students, but the difference is not significant. However, the southern white students have a tendency to be a little more critical about themselves in the various areas of self-perception (which is generally more negative), and demonstrate less certainty in how they think and feel about themselves.

In considering the variables for positive self-concept for southern white students, it would appear that the most important variables are family stability, college education of the father, and, to a lesser degree, college education of the mother. For southern white boys the most important variable is occupation of parents; segregation plays a minor role, but is the next important variable. For southern white girls family stability and size of family are the two most important variables. College education of the father and segregation have less importance.

In Greensboro, for white boys the most important variables are family income, working mother, and college eduction of the father; for white girls, high school education of the mother and segregation have the highest correlation with positive self-concept. The most important correlate of self-concept for all the white students in Greensboro is working mother; income of family and college education of father have less importance.

In Nashville the most significant correlates of self-concept for white students are family stability, college education of the father, and income of the family. College education of the mother and family size are also important, but not as significant. The most significant correlates for the white girls are college education of the father, family size, and family stability. For white boys the most important variable is family stability; occupation and income of family are less important.

So, it would seem that the correlates of high self-concept for southern white students follow the usual ones reported in the literature, but those for Afro-American students are very different, with segregation and sex being the most significant. It would also seem that there are more alienating forces affecting southern white adolescents than southern Afro-American adolescents, unless the assumption can be made that there were more sampling errors in the selection of white students than in the selecton of Afro-American students. It might seem that Nashville is more atypical for Afro-Americans, which could account for the Afro-Americans excelling in self-concept, but New Orleans and Greensboro cannot be considered atypical in that respect. However, regardless of the differences or similarities among cities, the southern white students score the same in each city Let us look beyond the cities to explain the phenomenon of low self-concepts of white students. It should be stressed that the importance of this finding lies not in the fact that southern Afro-Americans excel in self-concept when compared with southern whites, but that southern white students score so much lower.

What meaning did "Black Monday" May 17, 1954 have for southern white children in spite of the resistance, violence, and noncompliance? It said to the white community, "You are immoral, inhumane, illegal, and unconstitutional. Because of you, our reputation abroad as a democratic nation has been seriously damaged. You have violated the very principle on which this country was founded. You have made a hypocrisy of the American Creed and the American Dream."

As schools begin to desegregate, sometimes with violence, some conflicts regarding identity models (some of these poignant stories have been told in *Black Monday's Children*[4]) presented themselves for white adolescents. Basically believing in human decency and the American ideal, can one really identify with the cruel "red necks" abusing passive nonviolent children? To have federal troops in one's city (because of your racist parents) to enforce the law of the land and the American Creed on which one was reared, raises some puzzling questions. And, then, the final compliance and desegregation proceeds; does that not mean the white adults have admitted that they were wrong, that they were illegal and immoral? On the one hand, one is taught the American Creed and all men are created equal, and on the other hand, that Afro-Americans are inferior and whites superior. But then the Afro-Americans, with dignity and strength, with courage and determination, one by one destroy all the symbols that stood for white superiority and supremacy and Afro-American inferiority, and the nation and indeed the world applauds. In such a changing, inconsistent, hypocritical system one asks "Who am I?" and "Where do I belong?" Afro-American leaders talk about the injustices whites have imposed upon Afro-Americans, and many white people agree. White adults who at first clung to segregation are confused and do not know what to do. They say they believe in liberty and justice for all, but they resent Afro-Americans coming to their white schools. And, white America knows that even though these students are "only" Afro-American, they are proud to be. They believe in what they are fighting for. There is courage and strength among them and even power, "Black Power." Are whites really superior to them?

That southern white adolescents have low self-concepts should not be surprising in the face of the social revolution of the 1960s, the inequities, and inconsistencies. First of all, a system of self-esteem based on the degradation of other human beings is bound to collapse. Secondly, following the Afro-American student movement in the South, there was the white student movement in the North with the same theme—liberty and justice for all, as well as an attack on the military–industrial power structure. The white student movement augmented the civil rights movement in the South, but then moved north to concentrate on major issues there. Many adults called it an antiestablishment movement, but more exactly it was and still remains an antihypocrisy movement. The hippie phenomenon was an attempt on the part of white youth to reject the hypocrisy and materialistic values of the adult white world of their parents. The Vietnam War further demonstrated the hypocrisy and racism in this country, and students began to raise their voices in protest. The response to their protest can be witnessed by the events at Kent State and in Jackson, Mississippi.

Then the drug scene which had started with LSD in the late 1950s began to reach alarming proportions—at first the hallucinogenics, then the uppers and downers, the cocktails, and then the "hard stuff," which previously was a phenomenon prevalent only in the poor northern Afro-American ghetto subcultures. Now it reached into the very homes and lives of the great silent white majority. It represented alienation, hopelessness, aimlessness, depression, and the ultimate of rebellion and rejection of the "white way of life" with its power and corruption. And, then came Watergate and the theories were now a reality.

It was a curious sight indeed to see throngs of white students waiting to hear Eldridge Cleaver or Bobby Seale. How many Afro-American students go to hear Senator Eastland, or George Wallace, or John Casper? It is a curious sight indeed to walk through a Western college town and see the Afros on white students and the dashikis. For the white students the world today holds no place for them. They see a third world order of peace, sharing, and kinship; they wander about the country and the world looking for places to set up communes and a new way of life.

The phenomenon of low self-concepts among southern white students extends to the North also. As a matter of fact, northern white students score lower than southern white students with white southerners in the 30th percentile, white northerners in the 20th to 25th percentile. The phenomenon extends to white students in upper, middle, and lower social classes, those with high academic achievement, and those with low academic achievement.

For a long while we have focused attention on the effects of white racism on Afro-American children; perhaps we need to take a closer look at the effects on white children as well. It would seem that the sins of the white fathers have been visited upon their white children.[4] Gordon Allport summarizes it in *The Nature of Prejudice*:

> In short, America cannot escape the values represented by democratic and Christian teaching. Under this aegis, many habits and beliefs are learned by subsidiation. But at the same time there are opposing postures engendered by infantile egoism, needs for status and security, material and sexual advantage, and even conformity—all leading to subsidiary learning of many contrary habits and beliefs. The average American, therefore, experiences moral uneasiness and a feeling of individual and collective guilt. He lives in a state of conflict.[35,p330]

In short, Allport is inferring that racism has implications for mental health not only from the standpoint of the victim but especially from the viewpoint of the perpetrator.

In addition to the racial changes within our society that may make it difficult for young adolescents to foster a stable self-concept, the discontinuity of race-concept from childhood to adulthood stands out as one of our society's contradictions in childrearing, particularly when some cultural institutions begin to lose meaning and force for the adults who continue to uphold them. In observing these discontinuity's the GAP Report on adolescence noted:

> The adolescent is a particularly sharp observer of adult culture, and even the most casual observation reveals a decreasing adherence to the Judaeo-Christian ethic, which is still the official ethic of our culture . . . there is an important difference between an adult society that as a whole believes in and tries to live by its own moral values and one that does not. There is often little consonance between the expressed middle-class values and actual adult behavior. Caught in their own confusion, adults may be at a loss to demonstrate to adolescents any consistent rewards in their own lives which derive from accepting the "official" ethic. The adult world therefore often appears to adolescent eyes to operate upon principle contrary to honesty and other espoused cultural values.[34,p.53]

One of the most striking significant differences in scores between southern Afro-American youngsters and southern white youngsters, and indeed northern youngsters regardless of race, was the mean scores of the Moral-Ethical Self, which were higher than all groups. The mean scores on Self-Satisfaction and Behavior of the southern Afro-Americans were higher than those for other junior high school students in this study, as well as those for other junior high school samples reviewed by Thompson[13] and the original TSCS norm scores. The maintenance of ethical family values that brings with it self-satisfaction and self-esteem still abide for southern Afro-American youngsters, but in important ways it is lacking for the other adolescents in this study. Simmons and Rosenberg have indicated particular difficulties for the adolescent child in the level of self-consciousness, the level of self-esteem, and the degree of instability of the self-picture.[36] It is stressed that self-consciousness is such that the self becomes so primary in the adolescent's concern and he becomes so aware of what others are thinking of him, that interactions with others become very difficult. On the other hand, if the adolescent is uncertain of what he is actually like, than he does not have enough security to act or to make decisions for himself. Self-esteem, however, is crucial because it is an indication of emotional disturbance or mental health.

In reviewing the sex differences in self-image, Simmons and Rosenberg have noted the following:

1. There are few self-image differences among boys and girls from age 8 to 11.
2. By early adolescence both sexes show an increase in self-image disturbance, which is greater for girls.

3. Between 12–14 years of age, girls show greater self-consciousness, higher unstable self-image, and lower self-esteem than the boys.
4. The differences between white males and females in adolescence is greater than the differences between Afro-American males and females, although in early adolescence Afro-American girls will have more disturbances in self-image than boys.[36]

The Simmons-Rosenberg review concludes that different aspects of the self-concept will be affected differently by the socialization process. The family is the chief agent of the socialization process for the child and the school is the second. Both, however, have fallen upon hard times—role confusion and economic survival being two of the most crucial for the family. As for the public schools, their lists of problems become longer and longer. One, most eloquently stated by Fantini, underscores the issue of identity and self-concept:

> The school has devised an educational process which necessitates everyone's being treated with a sense of sameness. This adjustment to sameness has come into direct conflict with the basic reality of human and group differences. Consequently, conflicts between the uniqueness of the individual and cultural pluralism and community style, have come into direct conflict with the established mores of the school.[37,p.xiv]

The contrast between southern Afro-American young adolescents and northern Afro-American young adolescents in regard to school and family is quite striking. It would seem that assimilation, amalgamation, and desegregation of the family and the school bring with it uncertainty and lowered self-esteem. It would seem that for Afro-American adolescents a large urban industrialized sophisticated milieu transfers the same difficulties in formulating the self that confronts young white adolescents. The Baltimore study[26] indicates that the process increases from latency through junior high school and high school, especially in the desegregated schools for Afro-American students, for the reasons given by Fantini.

Erik Erickson, in describing adolescence, speaks of a technological process that increases the time between the world of school and the world of work.[15] Thus, "the stage of adolescing" becomes a more conspicuous and self-conscious process, "a way of life between childhood and adulthood." During this process the adolescent may become preoccupied with how others think and feel about her rather than who she thinks she is. She gropes "to connect the roles and skills" cultivated earlier and she searches out a process of becoming that connects with the continuity and sameness of the earlier childhood years. "They need" says Erikson, "a moratorium for the integration of the identity elements" before "the larger unit, society, replaces the childhood milieu."[16] What kinds of environments and socialization processes allow this process to evolve for the growing person? For our southern Afro-American students they may have evolved in such a milieu. However, because it was "black" and thought to be inferior, we destroyed it before we could fully understand it.

Interestingly enough there are no significant differences in self concept scores between (1) segregated and desegregated Afro-American and white students in Minneapolis, and (2) white segregated and desegregated students in Los Angeles. However, the segregated Afro-American students in New York and Los Angeles have the lowest TSCS profiles and the desegregated (N=25) affluent Afro-American students in Los Angeles score even lower. The same kinds of processes which affect the self-concept of other junior high school students can presume to be operating in these instances. However, there is no data from our northern cities that white girls are more affected than white boys.

With continued white flight, there has arisen great concern about the racially isolated schools in the large urban centers in Los Angeles and New York. A predominantly Afro-American community and school in the South produces "patterns of black excellence" and youth who are evolving for themselves a healthy psychosocial identity. However, a similiar environment outside of the South does not yield similiar results.

Glasgow in a chapter on "Failure of Schools" in his book has presented some of the most salient and perceptive analyses of the problems of the racially isolated schools.[38] He begins by declaring that the educational system provides a very basic paradox for Afro-Americans. It masquerades as the way possible for upward mobility, "yet black youth's encouters with it have resulted too often in destroyed aspirations and failure." He goes beyond the rhetoric, which he articulates so well, to examine the root causes of the statements he makes. His study of typical high school and junior high school students in Watts is very telling.

For Glasgow, the failures of the school system were many. First of all the schools failed in their mandate of the socialization of its students. The primary goal of school is to instruct students in the ways of acquiring success in their culture. This process is accomplished by providing students the knowledge and skills to meet the demands of their social environment, to understand and assume the roles expected of them to meet the goals society expects them to have acquired, to learn and understand the history, mores, and values and beliefs of their society.

According to Glasgow, the schools failed to perform for the following reasons:

1. They attempted to make Afro-American students accomodate to the mainstream society.

2. They attempted to deny and omit the "positive relevancies" of the Afro-American students' environment.
3. Their teachers taught them to adopt "paths to success and forms of behavior" unknown to them and unconnected with their lives, their families, and communities.
4. Because of misdirected and poor counseling, the schools were unable to move young Afro-Americans into the opportunity system.
5. The educational system tried to involve their Afro-American students in racially isolated and ghetto areas like Watts in a change process that coincided with their own intense identity search of adolescence at the same time "the message of cultural inferiority" was conveyed in myriad ways, from outright speech corrections to the ommission of every day Afro-American referrants and the absence of Afro-American history in the curriculum."[38]

Glasgow's point is well made in his summarizing statement that Afro-American life "had a different pace, style, and requirements for survival," factors that were not considered necessary in class materials.

While these factors have been prevalent in the racially isolated Afro-American schools, they are probably more prevalent in the desegregated junior high schools, who often feel that by having accomplished the logistics of bussing and school desegregation they have fulfilled their responsibility, and little responsibility is taken to integrate the Afro-American student into the life of the school. The Afro-American girls remain more uncomfortable and more uncertain. In one northern high school the Afro-American girls formed a drill team which excluded white girls as their way of making a place for themselves in the life of the school, having been denied participation in the cheer leader program, the May Queen Festival, and the Drama Program. The only time available for the drill team was during the advanced academic classes, which was another systematic way of reinforcing the tracking of Afro-American students in the noncollege preparatory classes, and avoiding the issue of integrating a resegregated school.

The respondents from Watts that Glasgow interviewed were explicit in describing the cultural-ideological conflict they experienced in school:

> the proselytizing of a strange model of life by both white teachers and integrationists Black instructors, engendered some discomfort and alienation. However, what really made these men angry was the implicit and explicit put down of these things that were the core of their lives. For example, Black dance, music, and modes of communication were viewed negatively and characterized as improper. Additionally, their whole living environment—their parents and community people in general; 103rd Street and the other ghetto streets with the mom-and-pop stores, small

Black-owned shops, and hangouts; their homes, furnishings, food, and social codes—was assigned a negative value or at best not given appropriate respect.[38]

This kind of phenomenon may account in part for the lower self-concept scores among the northern Afro-American students. Socioeconomic status, in addition, may account for the lowered scores among the students in the racially isolated minority schools. These schools are located in ghettos populated by a trapped, hopeless group of the Afro-American underclass. Their communities have been deserted by the working lower class, middle class, and upper class Afro-Americans who have escaped the ghetto and do not return as participants except as professionals who earn their living there. If the world of the Afro-American underclass is isolated from mainstream middle class American, it is also isolated from mainstream Afro-American middle class America and those who have the aspirations and means to reach it. They have been abandoned by the Federal Government and the white and Afro-Americans who "have" and can no longer relate to those who "have not." Williams[39] and Wilson[40] both address these issues, as well as others posed by Glasgow, such as the social and economic failure that entraps Afro-American youth in the growing Afro-American underclass and how the Afro-American male trapped within the underclass can not break free from the socially dysfunctional survival tactics acquired as a reaction to an institutional vacuum. As mental health professionals and social scientists, can we counter the failure of the educational system to produce the social mobility which was its mandate, and turn around the process in which our social institutions and programs have been co-oped to unwittingly promote the entrapment?

The Affluent Afro-American Young Adolescent and His School Setting

In Los Angeles, there were 25 Afro-Americans in predominantly white private schools (less than 5 percent of the Afro-American student body) whose TSCS profile scores resemble those of Afro-Americans in the racially isolated minority schools in the poverty neighborhoods of Los Angeles and New York. Although socioeconomic status, family stability, educational, and vocational attainment of the parents, as well as size of family, are correlated highly with self-esteem among white adolescents, they have not been found to be as significant for Afro-American students.[28,31,32] However, it would seem reasonable that given those attributes as described by Coopersmith[32] as significant to self-esteem, such factors would be important in acquiring self-esteem in any ethnic group of adolescents.

Although there have been some studies among Afro-American adults which indicate that self-esteem varies with economic status,[42] such consistent findings have not been reported for Afro-American children. Indeed, Soares and Soares found that disadvantaged children had higher self-concept than advantaged children.[33] Some have postulated that such findings may be due to the fact that disadvanteged children are less self-critical about themselves and thus more defensive in admitting negative concepts about themselves.

However, it would seem that Afro-American children from affluent homes (annual income $45,000), with educated professional parents, high family stability (less than 2 percent divorced or separated), with high IQ and academic achievement scores, would represent the "secure of the most secure" about what they think and feel about themelves, their families, their friends, their way of life. Yet their TSCS profiles were as low as those for the Afro-American students in the ghetto racially isolated minority schools (See Table 16–16).

In a reanalysis of the midtown Manhattan data, Conger and Coie found that emotional symptoms were more prevalent among middle class Afro-American children than among those living in public housing.[43] The stresses and strains of Afro-American families are well known. It takes two parents working with the free services and contribution of relatives for a middle-class Afro-American family to maintain the same status as a white family. What was also interesting about the Conger and Coie reanalysis was that there were more college educated Afro-American fathers among the lower socioeconomic status group than the white middle and upper class fathers.[43]

In some respects our middle class and affluent Los Angeles sample is the same and different from those studied in the midtown Manhattan study. The differences lie primarily in the special social milieu of Los Angeles and what it breeds—it breeds isolation of social groups, a major factor in the Watts riot, as well as a view of the opulent affluent life which breeds dissatisfaction for those who have no way of attaining it.

There were several parochial schools in the southern cities in which the Afro-American students' families were comparable in terms of family stability, educational, and vocational attainment, although salaries were not as high as those in Nashville.

One such school was a 100 percent parochial Afro-American school in Nashville that had many students whose parents were physicians and professors at the local Afro-American universities. There were 36 girls and 31 boys; both groups had mean TP scores of 355 with SC mean scores of 35, V mean scores of about 52, and mean D scores of 130 for girls and 135 for boys.[4] Less than 5 percent of the students scored below

TP of 300; 60 percent scored more than a TP of 350, and 12 percent scored higher than 12 percent. Clearly these middle class children with well educated, professional families felt good about themselves, which was revealed in their TSCS profiles with additional higher scores than their comparable white students in white parochial schools in Self-Satisfaction, Moral-Ethical Self, and Family Self.

However, inasmuch as the affluent Afro-American students were in less than 5 percent Afro-American schools, a more favorable comparison with Afro-American students in predominantly white schools would be more appropriate. In Nashville, there are 26 Afro-American students in a 10 percent Afro-American school. Their mean TP score was 344, with 11 percent scoring below 300, 40 percent scoring above 350 and 12 percent scoring above 400. The mean SC, V, and D scores were 34, 52 and 125 respectively. The 12 Afro-American students in the 10 percent Afro-American parochial school in Nashville had a TP mean score of 339, with 46 percent scoring above 350.

Likewise, comparable Afro-American students in 50 percent and 100 percent Afro-American parochial schools in New Orleans achieve mean TP scores of 347 and 346.8, respectively.

All 25 students were girls (although the school was co-ed) who had attended desegregated schools all of their lives, and 60 percent had always been in private schools. No student achieved a TP mean score above 350 and certainly none scored above 400. Sixty percent achieved TP mean scores below 300, which falls within the 10th percentile for the scale. The TSCS profiles of these girls in no way are comparable to those of middle-class Afro-American students in the South or their middle-class Afro-American and white peers in Los Angeles.

They have significantly lower scores than other Afro-American students in desegregated schools on the following mean scores: TP, D, Identity, Self-Satisfaction, Behavior, Personal Self, and Social Self. They also have significantly lower TSCS mean norms when compared to the entire sample of Afro-American students on the same mean, with the exception of Social Self. What is very striking about the TSCS profiles of these young girls is that in comparison with the TSCS norm group, Thompson's group of junior high school students, and their Los Angeles cohorts, they have strikingly low scores on identity.

If the desegregated school, even if private with high academic standards, omits, ignores, and demeans a child's ethnic group, it is difficult to forge an identity that is self-sustaining. If wealth and affluence separate a child from cultural ties, extended kinship networks, the folklore of his or her ethnic culture, and these are not replaced with something of equal psychological value; if acceptance at school is dependent upon how white-like the child, then education becomes a giving up of who you are and an attempt to blindly find a new self or identity. Sometimes Afro-American parents who have acquired the economic security they never had as children are eager to provide the extras. The private school with the affluent families, a door that was closed several decades ago, makes them feel they have provided the best for their children, and they no longer participate in the life of the school as they used to do. They don't look at the curriculum to see if it is culturally inclusive. Will your child have an opportunity to read James Baldwin or Langston Hughes? A multiethnic curriculum at the crucial time when a young person is trying to establish a self-concept is important. If a child's cultural group is ignored, the child assumes that there is nothing of value within his or her ethnic group.

It would seem, then, that middle-upper class status in a desegregated, private school mitigates against adequate self-esteem in Afro-American adolescents who are from educated, professional, achieving families and who do well in school, i.e., average IQ 120. Less tangible and obvious factors may be operating. Sixty percent of the Afro-American students lived in the affluent Afro-American neighborhoods, and so still had daily contacts with Afro-Americans, but the extent and quality of contacts is not known.

However, there are aspects of the Afro-American bourgeoisie life which are antithetical to the development of that inner core of unification which Erikson has stressed.[15] E. Franklin Frazier was less than complimentary about the "Black Bourgeoisie," and one of his major criticisms was the overindulgence of the children and the failure to inculcate a striving for Afro-American nationhood—a commitment to the goals of advancing Afro-American culture, art, and life.[42] Conspicuous consumption is an obvious aspect of the lifestyle described by Frazier, with an emphasis on "keeping up with the Joneses," the latest cocktail party, and social gathering with the "in-group" consuming most of the leisure time.

In Los Angeles, however, there is the tinsel world of Hollywood which competes for the adolescent's attention, and this is particularly available when one attends schools with the children of Hollywood stars. The emphasis on Afro-American culture, art, and history is not present at home and not included in the curriculum at school. The moral-ethical religious values of the conservative middle class family are discarded and replaced with the values of the peer culture. More often than not, parents are proud that their children have assimilated and have been accepted in the affluent, wealthy white world. It represents some measure of accomplishment for them, for whom the kind of car, neighborhood, and amenities of one's home are important.

Sometimes lost are the traditional values of the Afro-American survival strategies—extended family kinships, reversal of family roles, strong work ethic, strong achievement motivation, pride in one's ancestry, and participation in the civic and political life of Afro-Americans. It was interesting that not one of the Afro-Americans attending this school had an "Afro" at a time when Afros were very prominent. In a real sense, in spite of their skin color, they were not Afro-American. They were amalgamated, assimilated youngsters, and they preferred being that way, either because of peer or parental approval. Although there was no obvious race misidentification, there was no interest in anything Afro-American.

The most salient arguments to explain this similar process in two such divergent groups are offered by Webster and Sobiezek.[43] They assert that others are essential to the growth and form of the resulting personality: their theory is one of the social self. "The end product, the visible personality and the self that is produced is at least as dependent on this biological inheritance as it is on the social influence impinging on the individual and the interactions and experiences that he has."[43,p.2] The theory of the social self proposes that there is no existential process of discussing the existence of a person or of his personality without reference to the way in which others mold that person and his self. Those who adhere to this theory are called environmentalists; they stress that contact with others is important to the development of personality. These social influences determine the self. These arguments are not too far from those proposed by Camus and Sartre.

While self-concept theory has focused on the significant others in shaping the self-percept, significant others may shift for various groups. Clearly, the significant others for the affluent Afro-American adolescent are not other Afro-Americans. They are white school peers whom they try to emulate in dress, manner, and social norms. The importance of family and ethnic background have receded to a less important level of significance for the self.

For the lower socioeconomic youth in the racially isolated minority school, there is a trap. To give up their lifestyle without guaranteed entry into the other American lifestyle is risky. The path to selfhood is not certain; self-hatred and degradation of the self do not prevail. There is only disdain of the system and the processes which propel and maintain it.

SUMMARY

In examining the self-concepts of Afro-American students from six cities, some interesting patterns emerge—patterns which have implications for the rearing of Afro-American children. Clearly, a cohesive Afro-

American school and community: (1) with maximal participation of parents and teachers; (2) where the mores and norms of the home are reinforced in the immediate community; (3) where Afro-American culture and lifestyles are presented as important aspects of the school curriculum; (4) where children are accepted by peers and teachers; (5) where adequate counseling and career options and choices are presented to the children; (6) where the principal of the school provides clear educational leadership; (7) where academic achievement is encouraged regardless of family background; and (8) where there are readily identifiable adult models for the youth to incorporate into their sense of self; the self-concept process proceeds in an orderly, coherent, and definitive pattern. The segregated schools in the South provided such environments in many instances, but we destroyed them before we really understood what they provided. The emphasis was on academic excellence, and no Afro-American school could provide it. We swallowed the stereotypes. There are many paths to excellence, as Afro-American history has shown—e.g., Harriet Tubman, Frederick Douglas, Mary McLeod Bethune. The roll call from Dunbar High School in Washington, D. C., during the 30s and 40s continues the honor roll.

Our desegregated schools fail to provide such milieux because they are not integrated schools. Not all students, especially minority students, are accepted by their peers and teachers. They, especially Afro-American girls, have no real part in the life of the school. The conflicting views of the home and the school, the conflicting norms and mores of the various ethnic and socioeconomic groups, prove to be confusing, especially if the school teachers feel no need to incorporate the multiethnic cultures represented in the school into the curriculum. To place lower achieving minority group children in remedial classes begins the resegregation in the newly desegregated school, which effectively precludes integration of that school.

It has been noted that social comparisons affect the self-esteem of Afro-American children; however, in most instances, the Afro-American child compares himself with other Afro-Americans and not with whites. However, Powell has cautioned that the Afro-American child's comparisons are done on the basis of the actual structure of the environment in which the child lives.[44] For affluent Afro-American adolescents, their community may not constitute the significant others in their lives. The assimilation process may portray the affluent white world of their peers as more significant in formulating the self-percept.

However, the Afro-American underclass youth are trapped in the ghetto and in their racially isolated schools. In Glasgow's interviews with the young men of Watts, many of whom had been disillusioned and pushed out of school, he notes:

Thus, the majority of the men generally supported the federal push for integrated education, yet with mixed feelings. They had positive memories of belonging in southern all-Black schools. Despite the material inadequacies of those institutions, the teachers showed concern, taught them appropriate Black customs, provided real and consistent models to emulate, and most of all were socially available. Despite the reality of second-class status held in broader southern life, they were educated in Black schools with first-class respect because they were to become the future leaders of Blacks. But all-Black education in Watts, with its emphasis on negative differences and unnatural separation, was worse than segregated education in the South.[38,p.62]

Twenty years after Brown, the survivors are the Afro-American students in segregated schools in the South. At the bottom of the list are the Afro-American students of Los Angeles and New York City, in the racially isolated minority schools in the ghetto, who feel that the educational process in the ghetto succeeded in its real purpose, which is to deter Afro-Americans from reaching the mainstream, and to create an underclass of underachieving, immobilized, obsolete Afro-American youth.

As Glasgow has articulated the needs and frustrations of the young Afro-American adolescents trapped within the confines of the underclass, the GAP Report on Normal Adolescents does shed some light on the problems and conflicts of the affluent Afro-American young adolescents. In order to understand them, we need to understand adolescents in the white mainstream American middle class. There are distinct qualities and features of the American middle class adolescence period. The mass media focus on this particular group which makes "being a teenager" an influential and important status group. Middle class adolescents have a distinct, separate group to whom they give intense and exclusive allegiance (group peers). The peer group sets the guidelines in everything from fashions and recreation to vocabulary and dating practices. The peer group, it should be remembered, has little or no adult influence. The peer group, and not the family, becomes the major support system for the teenager.

The "hiatus status" process which emerges for the American middle class adolescent has its pluses and minuses. On the one hand, because they are not considered adults, adolescents are not required to assume full responsibility. For instance, even though an adolescent may receive enough of an allowance to meet nominal expenses, most often his or her parents will continue to pay his bills. The GAP report notes:

> Adolescents may even succumb to the seductive and persuasive temptation to remain adolescent, enjoying the measure of adult status and provilege while avoiding the responsibilities implied in acceptance of the adult role . . . The acceleration of the granting of privileges to young people has the effect of

telescoping the generations and obscuring adult-child differences . . . A primary determinant to middle class adolescence is the fact that middle class society is organized so exclusively around the nuclear family as opposed to the extended family.[34,p.41]

These observations are particularly germane to the middle-class Afro-American family whose family network and kinship ties are broader and cross age lines. Socialization with elders and relatives is the norm rather than the exception. As Afro-American middle-class families move up the status ladder, their lifestyles will change. The challenge will be to help their children understand the changes and maintain a sense of self and stability with it.

In Galbraith's final chapter in *The Affluent Society*, which is entitled "On Security and Survival," he wisely notes:

"The pursuit of happiness is admirable as a social goal. But the notion of happiness lacks philosophical *exactitude*; there is agreement neither on its substance nor its source. We know that it is "a profound *instinctive* union with the stream of life" (as noted by Bertrand Russell) but we do not know what is united."[46,p.349]

REFERENCES

1. Powell GJ, Fuller M: School Desegregation and Self-Concept: A Pilot Study on the Psychosocial Impact on School Desegregation on 7th, 8th, and 9th Graders in a Southern City
2. Powell GJ, Fuller M: The Variables for Positive Self-Concept Among Young Southern Black Adolescents. J Nat Med Assoc:1972
3. Powell GJ: Self-Concept in White and Black Children, in Willie CV, Kramer B, Brown B (Eds): Racism and Mental Health, Pittsburgh, University of Pittsburgh Press, 1973
4. Powell GJ: Black Monday's Children: The Effects of School Desegregation on Southern School Children. New York, Appleton-Century-Crofts, 1973
5. Coleman J: The Equality of Educational Opportunity. HEW Office of Education, U.S. Government Printing Office, 1966
6. Blaustein A, Ferguson CC: Desegregation and the Law: The Meaning and Effect of the School Segregation Cases. New York, Vintage, 1962
7. Pettigrew TF: Trends in Research on Racial Discrimmination, in Pettigrew TF (Ed): Racial Discrimmination in the United States. New York, Harper & Row, 1975
8. Fitts W: Tennessee Self-Concept Scale Measure. Counselor Recordings and Tests, Box 6184, Acklen Station, Nashville, 1965
9. Allport GW: Pattern and Growth in Personality. New York, Holt, Rinehart, and Winston, 1963
10. Lipsett J: Growing Up Forgotten: A Review of Research Concerning Early Adolescence. Lexington, Lexington Press, 1978
11. Elkind D: Egocentrism in Adolescence. Child Devel 38:1025–1034, 1967

12. Wylie R: The Self-Concept: Revised Edition (Vol. 2: Theory and Research on Selected Topics). Lincoln, Neb., University of Nebraska Press, 1978
13. Thompson W: Correlates of Self-Concept. Dede Wallace Center, Monograph VI. Nashville, Counselor Recordings and Tests, 1972
14. Fitts WH, Hammer WT: The Self-Concept and Delinquency, Research Monograph No. 1. Nashville, Nashville Mental Health Center, July 1969
15. Erikson, E: Identity, Youth, and Crisis. New York, W.W. Morton, 1968
16. Witty PA, Theman VA: A Followup Study of the Educational Attainment of Gifted Negroes. J Ed Psychology 34:43–49, 1943
17. Hundley MG: The Dunbar Story (1870–1955). New York, Vantage Press, 1965
18. Sowell T: Black Excellence: The Case of Dunbar High School. The Public Interest 4:11–18, 1973
19. National Scholarship and Service Fund for Negro Students: Annual Report 1962–1963. New York, NSSFMS, 1978
20. Martin, EP, Martin JM: The Black Extended Family. Chicago, University of Chicago Press, 1978
21. Rainwater L, Yancey WL: The Moynihan Report and The Politics of Controversy (Including the Test of Daniel Patrick Moynihan's The Negro Family: The Case for National Action). Cambridge, MIT Press, 1967
22. Billinglsey A: Black Families and White Social Science, in Ladner J (Ed): The Death of White Sociology. Vintage Books, New York, 1973
23. Billingsley A: Black Families in White America. Englewood Cliffs, N.J., Prentice-Hall, 1968
24. Ladner JA: The Death of White Sociology. New York, Vintage Books, 1973
25. Hill R: The Strengths of Black Families: A National Urban League Research Study. New York, Emerson Hall, 1972
26. Rosenberg M, Simmons RG: Black and White Self-Esteem: The Urban School Shild. Rose Monograph Series. Washington, D.C., American Sociological Association, 1972
27. Rosenberg M: The dissonant religious Context and emotional disturbance. Am J Sociol 68:1–10, 1962
28. Rosenberg M: Conceiving the Self. New York, Basic Books, 1979
29. Weinberg M: Minority Students: A Research Appraisal. U.S. D.H.E.W. National Institute of Education, Washington, D.C. Government Printing Office, 1977
30. Norton, D: Black Family Life Pattern: The Development of Self and Cognitive Development of Black Children, In Powell GJ, Morales A, Yamamoto J (Eds): The Psycho-Social Development of the Minority Group Child. New York, Brunner/Mazal (in press)
31. Rosenberg M: Society and the Adolescent Self-Image. Princeton, Princeton University Press, 1965
32. Coopersmith S: The Antecedents of Self-Esteem. San Francisco, Freeman, 1967
33. Soares AT, Soares LM: Self-perception of culturally disadvantaged children. Am Ed Res J 6:31–45, 1969
34. Group for the Advancement of Psychiatry: Normal Adolescence: Its Dynamic and Impact. New York, Charles Scribner's Sons
35. Allport GW: The Nature of Prejudice. Addison-Wesley, 1979
36. Simmons RG, Rosenberg F: Sex, sex roles, and self-image. J. of Youth and Adol. 4:229–257, 1975
37. Fantini MD: Forward, in Haskins J (Ed): Black Manifesto for Education. New York, Williams Morrow, 1973
38. Glasgow DG: The Black Underclass: Poverty, Unemployment and Entrapment of Ghetto Youth. San Francisco, Jossey-Bass, 1980

39. Williams JD (Ed): The State of Black America 1979. New York, National Urban League, 1979
40. Wilson WJ: The Declining Significance of Race: Blacks and Changing American Institutions. Chicago, University of Chicago Press, 1978
41. Cole B: Self-Esteem Among Adult Afro-American Men and Women. Doctoral dissertation, Department of Sociology, 1978
42. Frazier FE: Black Bourgeoisie: The Rise of New Middle Class. New York, Free Press, 1956
43. Webster J, Sobieszek B: Sources of Self-Evaluation: A Formal Theory of Significant Others and Social Influence. New York, John Wiley, 1974
44. Conger AJ, Coie JD: Who's crazy in Manhattan: A re-examination of treatment of psychological disorders among urban children. J. Consul and Clin Psych 43:179–182, 1975
45. Powell GP: Coping with adversity: The psychologic development of the Afro-American child, in Powell GJ, Morales A, Yamamoto J (Eds): The Psycho-Social Development of the Minority Group Child. New York: Brunner/Mazel, 1982
46. Galbraith JK: The Affluent Society. Boston, Houghton Mifflin, 1958

LIST OF TABLES

Gordon L. Berry

17

Television, Self-esteem, and the Afro-American Child: Some Implications for Mental Health Professionals

MASS COMMUNICATION AS A CULTURAL FORCE IN THE LIFE OF THE AFRO-AMERICAN CHILD

Mass media in today's society is not only part of the total culture, but it has a subculture of its own with an organized set of beliefs, values, and traditions that predisposes children and adults to a way of thinking about the world and indeed, about themselves. The mass communication system, to include newspapers, magazines, books, radio, film, and television, all have a way of providing us with subtle and overt messages, which help shape for us a set of mores and codes of behavior. This audio-visual information base reaches us from within this country and from countries throughout the world. Through these print and electronic communication media, we are bombarded with rational and irrational ideas of people and places, many of whom we have never seen and often have never heard of in any formal sense. This panorama of the rituals, life-styles, and values indigenous to our small communities, our ghettoes, our barrios, the Little Tokyos, the Chinatowns, the Indian reservations, and even a glimpse at the hill folk of Appalachia, is all accomplished through the rich communication subculture with its special media language and images.

We are, in contemporary society, like it or not, ready or not, faced with various forms of mass communication with its media components which all play a role in what we learn and the way we learn it. The dynamic impact associated with learning through various forms of mass communication is often so complex that it is difficult to identify. The complicated nature of the power associated with communications has led some authorities to explain the phenomenon in terms of it being a "process." This process, according to Hiebert, Ungurait, and Bohn, suggests that communication is a series of actions or operations which are always in motion, directed toward a particular goal. It is not a static entity fixed in time and space, but rather a dynamic process used to transfer meaning, transmit social values, and share experiences.[1]

The most powerful medium within the mass media family is that of television. As Nicholas Johnson observed:

> Television is more than just another great public resource—like air and water—ruined by private greed and public inattention. It is the greatest communications mechanism ever designed and operated by man. It pumps into the human brain an unendng stream of information, opinion, moral values, and esthetic taste. It cannot be a neutral influence. Every minute of television programming—commercials, entertainment, news—teaches us something.[2,p.31]

Television, as an actual and potentially powerful teacher, is indeed meaningful, given the extent of its use and availability in the United States. Hiebert, Ungurait, and Bohn, commenting on the scope of television in this country, observed "that over 66 million homes (95 percent of all U.S. households) are equipped with television sets." More than 60 percent of the people own two sets, and Hiebert and his colleagues reported that the A. C. Nielson Company data show that the average TV household uses its sets more than 44.5 hours per week.[1]

Professor Alberta Siegel, writing in the foreword of a book by Liebert, Neale, and Davidson, pointed out that more American homes have television sets than any other electrical appliance; many more homes have TV than indoor plumbing. These same researchers, looking at the consumption of television by children, noted that it is estimated that a child born today will, by the age of 18, have spent more time watching television than in any other single activity, with the exception of sleep.[3]

The messages of television pervade our lives daily and establish profound mental sets which consciously or unconsciously influence our behavior. As Richard Adler pointed out:

> television is not simply a "medium" but a "mediator"—between fact and fantasy; between our desires to escape and our need to deal with real problems; between our old values and new ideas; between our individual lives and the life of a nation and world. Seen from this perspective, television becomes much more interesting and much less simple than before.*

*Reprinted from Adler R: Introduction: A Context for criticism, in Adler R, Cater D (eds): Television as a cultural force. New York, © Praeger, 1976, p. 13. With permission of the publisher.

Any medium that is potentially present in the daily lives of more than 95 percent of American households; carries words, images, music, and pictures depicting a multiplicity of life-styles; and through its script mechanisms can communicate time, mood, place, language, dress, and racial characterizations, has the potential to develop value situations from which children can compare themselves and learn. Such a medium must be understood as a potential shaper of attitudes and molder of a child's behavior. Yet there is still so much about television that we do not understand. Evelyn Kaye in her book, *The Family Guide to Children's Television*, cited a statement from Professor John Condry which brings home the gap in our knowledge about this medium and its potential in terms of power. According to Professor Condry:

> Our understanding of the impact of this medium has lagged far behind its commercial success. We have only recently become aware of the changes it has brought about in the nature of politics, the entertainment industry, and the dissemination of news. Whether these changes will be, in the long run, good or bad is still to be determined. Yet the changes television brings to these and other areas of American life may prove trivial compared to its potential effect upon the lives of children.[5,p.3]

As we consider both the potential positives and negatives of television in our society, we must be aware of how it influences the lives of children. While those of us in the helping professions must clearly be concerned with the welfare of all children, nowhere is the challenge of understanding television's potency more acute than in the pyschological impact it can have on Afro-American and other minority children. This position becomes abundantly clear when we observe that for Afro-Americans, social injustice is still the order of the day and racial prejudice is still a way of life. Given that Afro-American children, through their parents and sometimes directly, must come to grips with the race question in a country that is almost "phobic" on the biological condition of skin color, no emerging medium should, through its programming, add to the psychological stress of the child's growth and development.

Concern about the medium and its impact on Afro-American children and adolescents becomes especially striking when the literature tends to support the notion of a differing pattern of television viewing among Afro-Americans as opposed to whites. This pattern suggests that children from lower socioeconomic families and Afro-American children devote more time to television and tend to feel that television accurately portrays real life situations.[6] Other studies related to viewing patterns generally report the same heavy viewing patterns found among Afro-American adolescents. In one study, the researchers pointed out that low income Afro-American teenagers watched over 6 hours of television a day, while low income white teenagers watched 4½ hours. While there are a few explanations for the viewing patterns of Afro-American children, not all of which are negative, most of the research still shows that these children are heavy television viewers, and that television appears to play an important role in their lives.[7]

While much of the research to date has attempted to compare differences in viewing patterns between Afro-American and white children, or the causal link between viewing violence and acting out aggression, it is clear that the issue of television's impact on American society and social life go beyond these questions. As it relates to Afro-American children, there is a need to consider other aspects of the medium's messages, especially those factors which relate to the socialization functions of television, broadly conceived, including television's impact on personal identity, cognitive development, moral development, cultural awareness, and finally the interrelated core of all of these issues—self-concept and self-esteem formation. These individual personal and self-esteem attitudes do not emerge as discrete entities but are integrated into a holistic development pattern. It is likely, therefore, that one cannot separate viewing and aggressive patterns of behavior from what individuals are learning about themselves and others. In addition, one cannot separate other psychological characteristics of the individual as if these learned behaviors emerged discretely within the psychosocial development of the individual.[8]

It is within the psychosocial development of Afro-American children that the messages, images, sights, sounds, and racial portrayals of their ethnic group on television may begin to reinforce a sense of positive self-worth and pride. One can also speculate that faulty depictions and portrayals on television can build up negative feelings about an individual's culture and racial group. Regardless of the open question as to the degree of television's influence on children's feelings about themselves and their racial group, television does serve as a type of auditory and visual feedback mechanism for reinforcing and shaping those negative or positive perceptions about ethnicity that constantly come to the child from the broader community.

A significant observation was made by Alvin Poussaint in suggesting that television offers an influential challenge to the guidance in the home environment, which may be particularly acute in the case of the minority child. He noted:

> . . . a child's sense of self is affected by how he views his environment both through direct involvement and through various media presentations. The powerful influence of television and films often challenges parental guidance. Even a child in a strong family may develop self-doubt if he lives in the midst of poverty

and social disorder. A poor young black viewing television may see no representation of his community or life style and get the impression that he does not count in this society . . .[9,p.142]

While Poussaint's position is sound, a related issue is that Afro-American children may also see misrepresentations of their communities and misrepresentations of their life styles. In this case, the sin of omission, in terms of negative portrayals, can be as personally destructive as that of commission, in terms of a minority child's self-concept and self-esteem attitudes. It is to this issue of television portrayal and self-concept that the author next turns his attention.

SELF-CONCEPT THEORY, THE TELEVISION MEDIUM, AND THE AFRO-AMERICAN CHILD

The major theoretical positions associated with self-concept and self-esteem cover volumes of works. These theories range from Freudian views, which suggest that self-concept is closely tied to body-image and sex role development; to Eriksonian views which place more stress on the social aspects of self-esteem; to the views of Lewin, Werner, and Piaget who focus on showing the consequences of cognitive development on self-concept.[10] A corollary to the problem of having a number of theoretical positions is that one finds it difficult to develop a definition because of the lack of precision and degree of variability in what comprises an individual's "self-concept." Vinacke does describe self-concept as a cognitive system that represents people's views of themselves, or the pattern of traits by which they describe themselves.[11] In an attempt to construct a working definition consistent with current research and which can be used to begin to integrate empirical evidence, Shavelson et al.[12] describe self-concept as people's perceptions of themselves, and point out that these perceptions are formed through experience with the environment, perhaps in the manner suggested by Kelly,[13] and are influenced especially by environmental reinforcements and significant others. Rogers reminds us that children develop a concept of self early in life, and they tend to behave or want to behave in a manner that is consistent with their self-concepts at that time, and their perceptions of what is happening to them in the environment.[14]

There is a tendency to use the terms "self-concept" and "self-esteem" interchangably in this chapter and in other writings. While both terms refer broadly to the same constructs this chapter will focus on self-esteem within Coopersmith's framework. Coopersmith identified self-esteem as the evaluation which individuals make and tend to maintain with regard to themselves: it expresses an attitude of approval or disapproval and indicates the degree to which individuals believe themelves to be capable, significant, successful, and worthy.[15] The Coopersmith notions of self-esteem become important here because they place emphasis on what the author perceives as an evaluative process on the part of individuals in comparison to factors both inside and outside of their environments. There is, within the self-esteem construct, a real element of self-acceptance on the part of the individual. Wells and Marwell noted that in self-acceptance descriptions, there is also an evaluation activity going on with respect to some ideal or standard, and the important aspect of the process is the feeling attached to the individual's evaluation.[16] Self-esteem is, therefore, an evaluation that one makes of oneself, and high feelings of self-esteem mean that individuals feel good about themselves, while low self-esteem can mean some dissatisfaction with themselves.[17] Thus, each position is important to the thesis of this chapter because each places self-concept and self-esteem notions into a cognitive, affective, environmental, and developmental or nonstatic frame of reference.

The components of the Coopersmith self-esteem definition which relate to the "degree to which individuals believe themselves to be capable, significant, successful, and worthy," and the other concepts related to self-evaluation, take on special significance when we consider Afro-American children. These are children from families, especially those from the underclass, where societal racial attitudes can affect them in such a way as to provide negative feedback as to their worth, and economic and educational forces can work against these families in terms of their potential for upward mobility. While some social scientists working in the area of self-concept theory might suggest that these negative forces are not felt by the children because they are aimed at the adults, it must be noted that the feeling of powerlessness within a family unit can quickly become part of the perceptual framework of a child. In the final analysis, we take our attitudinal cues about self from internal (family and friends) and external (school, church, and media institutions) groups which are present in our lives, and those who make up a broad spectrum of significant others. "What an individual thinks and feels about himself is mediated through his perception of what others think and feel about him," Powell wrote in 1973.[18] She continued, "within a given culture and society, an individual's self-perception is mediated via his status and role, which are acquired or assigned to him by the dominant members of that society."[18,p.28] For Powell, the dominant group is white-American. It stands to reason, therefore, that the decision-making power of what Afro-American children will see on television and how they are portrayed will grow out of views that whites hold of them and promulgate through their control of media in general, and the medium of television in particular.

The assumption is that television is now firmly rooted in our culture, and is now a dynamic part of the experiential environment of Afro-American children. Its program content aids in the socialization process by instructing and helping these young people gain impressions and ask questions such as: "Who am I?"; "Who are they?"; "Am I as good as they are?"; and "How do my home, school, community, and racial group measure up to the portrayals I see on televison?" These issues are at the very heart of self-esteem constructs, and the presentations and portrayals that Afro-American children see daily must surely be considered as we work with and interact with them in our attempts to understand at least one of the outside factors influencing their socialization—television.

There can be little doubt that contained within the content of some television comedies and dramas are messages with both subtle and overt judgemental values about people and places. When minority young people utilize program content as a source of information, their new knowledge may well become a way of reinforcing views about themselves, their families and races. Concern about the impact of television, and its ability to influence the attitudes of children, was expressed by Leifer and others in an article on this subject. Writing in the *Harvard Educational Review*, these researchers noted that children often change their attitudes about people and activities to reflect those encountered in television programs. Their work led them to conclude that television is not only entertainment for children, it is also an important socializer.[19] Himmelweit et al, in a significant study, concluded that almost imperceptibly, television entertainment brings about changes in children's outlooks and values, even though the programs that achieve this may not deliberately set out to so influence.[20]

The discriminating Afro-American child could, of course, have a background and set of social experiences which would place distorted racial and cultural information in the context of a creative or entertaining story. On the other hand, it is possible that less sophisticated children may believe that the negative or inadequate portrayals of the Afro-American community; the stereotyped behaviors of the characters; the levels of occupations and aspirations of the Afro-American performers; and the interpersonal male and female relationships are representative of people like themselves, and are worthy of internalizing as an adequate set of truths. When one adds to these presentations or portrayals the potential impact on Afro-American children of accepting the characters as role models, and the community depictions as being correct, it raises further issues about television's place in influencing their present and future behaviors.

To the extent that television exposes children to accurate and positive representations of the "black experience," the self-evaluation and comparisons with the child's ethnic group are potentially helpful to the development of personal pride and self-esteem. To the extent that Afro-American children see a disproportionate number of weak, violent, corrupt, and powerless Afro-American men and women, their personal frames of reference may be negatively skewed in terms of identifying with an appropriate comparison group. Shaver touched on a phase of this self-perception by pointing out that individuals learn about and judge their opinions and abilitites by explicit references to the opinions and abilities of others.[21] Shaver's position is consistent with what we know about the socialization process in that all children have, as a principal source of information, the behavior of others inside and outside of their immediate environments. While the family unit is one of the most powerful influences on the child's beliefs and behavior, television is also part of the child's environment, and can become a meaningful reference point for some minority children whose family structures and social conditions leave them searching for a measure of self-esteem in their lives.

PAST AND PRESENT PORTRAYALS: THE NEED FOR A NEW PERSPECTIVE

If the portrayals are important and if the program content reflects the black experience as negative, then what have we seen and are we seeing that might affect self-esteem? These questions can be best answered by a brief analysis of past and present portrayals of Afro-Americans in various types of media.

Historically, the portrayals of Afro-Americans in various types of media have reflected the perceptions that whites had of them. These perceptions were developed from early teachings in the home, school, and a media system, especially film, which exposed whites and Afro-Americans to an entire set of stereotypes. Noble, drawing on the work of Reddick brought this point home vividly when he described the principle stereotypes associated with Afro-Americans the American public had gained from early movies and other media.[22] Some of these were:

1. the savage African
2. the happy slave
3. the devoted servant

4. the petty thief
5. the social delinquent
6. the sexual superman
7. the superior athlete
8. the natural born cook
9. the perfect entertainer
10. the mental inferior[22,p.12]

Thus, television, as a cousin to the movies, the press, and radio, has brought some traces of the same representations from the past. As the Kerner Commission observed about the depiction of Afro-Americans in media:

> Not only was visibility of blacks generally low, particularly in regard to their routine portrayal as part of the society, but when blacks did appear on the screen they were presented as whites saw them, not as they saw themselves.[23,p.383]

There has been some improvement in the numbers of Afro-Americans on television, and in some cases, in their general portrayal. There is, however, still the tendency to reach back for old stereotypes and perceptions from the past. For example, many of the so-called "black" situation comedies and dramatic presentations seem to be preoccupied with:

- Portraying Afro-Americans as coming from a single parent home, with usually only the mother present.
- Portraying the Afro-American woman as an overly aggressive, dominant person able to intimidate men through physical action as well as by loud words.
- Utilizing nonstandard English with Afro-Americans, regardless of their educational backgrounds and social experiences. (Note that while Afro-American dialect has structure, form, and linguistic soundness, it is often utilized to distinguish the "bad" characters from the "good." Thus, the creators often do not show the beauty of the language, but utilize it as a vehicle to highlight a special type of a character.)
- Portraying the "black" community as a weak and destructive place, and playing down its strengths and positive characteristics.
- Portraying the pimp, drug pusher, and similar characters as individuals prized and even respected by the Afro-American community.
- Portraying Afro-Americans as a homogeneous group (a form of stereotyping) and failing to identify the heterogeneity of their culture and life style.[24]

It is necessary at this point to pause long enough to note that not only are Afro-Americans still cast in certain types of stereotypic roles, so also are minority groups in general. For example, minority men and women are most often typecast in ghetto roles and appear primarily in programs set in ethnic locales; minority characters tend to appear as tokens in otherwise all-white shows, and a disproportionate number of minority women are portrayed as victims of violence.[25]

Mental health professionals must particularly appreciate the fact that a positive self-concept is directly related to a feeling of competence, and depends to a large degree on how one comes to view the world around one and one's ability to deal with this world.[26] Since feelings of competence, success, and worthiness are at the very core of self-esteem, it might be reasonable to raise some questions as to what the Afro-American child perceives and learns from present day television series which show a tricky junkman who has the seeking of pleasure as his only activity; a consistently single-parent Afro-American mother with a small daughter who learns very early how to intimidate Afro-American males; and a constant preoccupation of showing Afro-American communities as destructive, poverty ridden places, as if Afro-American people had no other life style.

Regardless of the one-to-one psychological impact on the Afro-American child gained from the previously mentioned portrayals, it is fair to assume that certain television presentations can convey a time, place, and social role to the Afro-American child-viewer concerning his or her racial group and then have these elements validated by this powerful medium. Moreover, the predominance of minority characters in heavily or totally minority casts suggests that minorities should remain within, or are only important within, the context of their own minority groups. Perhaps you belong if you are poor, part of a fatherless family, servile, or living in an ethnic ghetto, but you are not very likely to belong if you are rich, strong, or successfully bicultural.[27] This statement presents some clear issues to consider when we think of the possible impressions to be gained by the young Afro-American who may watch the so-called "black oriented show."

Another equally powerful notion was advanced by Dorr when she observed the type of perceptions television can provide minority children in terms of their role and power in our society. When minorities are presented on television, their occupational roles, actions within these roles, and lack of power in integrated settings suggest that in the larger American society "White is still right." Whites have power and are likely to keep it by virtue of both their own and minority characters' attributes. Our current social order is one which everyone seeks to maintain, even those who as a group suffer most within it. It is a natural right or at least inevitable order. If minority children see this place for themselves repeatedly on television and take it seriously, imagine the chilling effect it must have on their self-concepts and aspirations.[27,p.30]

The author is aware that one runs a special risk in criticizing some of the characteristics that emerge from Afro-American-oriented programs, because it can be deomonstrated statistically that large numbers of Afro-Amercans from all social classes view and enjoy them. We also must recognize that many Afro-American viewers are poor, and often their communities do indeed reflect the disorder which accompanies social condtions associated with poverty and discrimination. It is also true that these same communities have a great many strengths, which are seldom tapped by television material or lobbied for by minority people themselves. What is needed for the Afro-American child's attitudinal development is a more balanced and accurate picture of Afro-American life in America. This call for a sense of balance was articulated in a piece written by A. S. Doc Young. He stated:

> There are many black-based stories, which could be produced on television, which would win mass approval and, hence, high ratings. But blacks and whites alike approach black subjects from a negative angle; they're always concerned about problems; they're always trying to glorify poverty and the ghettos, if not slavery. True black heroes, the great achievers, the larger-than-life characters, always were ignored.[28]

Psychologists and sociologists have, for a number of years, suggested the "looking glass" concept in connection with self-construct. While this concept did not have television in mind, it may well be that for Afro-American and other minority children (especially the underclass) it is a type of looking glass from which they can compare their life-styles with the "significant others" so prominent on television. Although white Americans portray a variety of different roles on television, it becomes clear, because of sheer numbers, that they represent patterns and behaviors that introduce them to the Afro-American child as significant others, validated by this powerful medium. It is not inconsistent, therefore, to suggest that Afro-American children may face some conflict when the most prominent models are not consistent with their race and class. This feeling, if and when it does exist, presents personal conflicts because the most prominent models are distinctive and have little in common with their immediate environments. Indeed, from the looking glass of television, the Afro-American child does not see many portrayals of other Afro-Americans as productive and dynamic people who might serve as role models from whom the child can draw inspiration. This absence of appropriate role models can once again reinforce the concept that individuals from their racial group are not part of any educated and power base class beyond that of the ghetto. It becomes crucial, therefore, for Afro-American children and other minorities to see diversified roles which can assist them in placing into perspective the variety of characterizations and possibilities available to Afro-American people within the context of the broader society.

Clearly, this author's attempt to establish a relationship between the Afro-American child's development of self-esteem and television program content is done with a recognition of the psychological and methodological problems inherent in such a linkage. In addition, it is important that the reader not assume that the author's position infers that Afro-Americans inherently have low self-esteem. However, the quality of life many have been forced to live might well support the early findings of low self-esteem among Afro-Americans, advanced by Stevenson and Stewart,[29] Goodman,[30] as well as the opposite concepts of Arnez[31] and Nobles.[32] Whatever the gaps in these difficult issues of the effects of this medium on the Afro-American child, and its relationship to the complicated constructs of self-concept, the essential idea of the need to consider television's attitudinal influences on self-esteem, as we work with Afro-American children, is still a basic premise.

There have, of course, been many positive aspects of present programs on television. But it is important that Afro- and white Americans not be seduced into believing that they are getting a true sample of the culture and life style of Afro-Americans, and therefore that these programs are serving a "social good." To assume that pimps who report all community activities to the police, down-and-out business people who are ready to make a fast buck, loud-talking emasculating women, wealthy but bigoted uptown folk, and a group of hip-talking and finger-popping adolescents around a soda shop, are portraying the experience of all Afro-Americans, is inconsistent just on the face of things. Indeed, many of these characters present types of images that only increase stereotyped thinking in whites and further demonstrate to Afro-Americans that their communities and life styles are devalued and disorganized.

CONCLUSION: TELEVISION, THE AFRO-AMERICAN CHILD, AND MENTAL HEALTH PROFESSIONALS

The complete verdict on the effects of television on the self-concept of Afro-American and other minority children is not in. As a researcher who works with children, however, it is clear to the author from clinical judgments and some empirical data that television programs and characters can play a role in the cognitive aspects of a child's informational base as well as influence the affective base, through raising issues about self and others. The potential for this medium to permeate the very psychological structures of children raises significant questions, issues, and responsibilitie for mental health professionals. Thus, it might well be important for mental health professionals to focus on the following issues and questions when attempting to understand and work with Afro-American children and adolescents:

1. The development of a child's self-concept is to a large degree dependent on the influences of the people and experiences in his or her environment. To what extent does television, with its images, messages, and portrayals, and as part of the environment, develop positive and negative self-esteem views in the child?
2. Television is an audio-visual medium that relies on pictures and words. To what extent do the pictures and language reflect the broad multicultural as well as innercultural experiences of Afro-American children?
3. Television is a communicator of the society and its values. To what extent does television communicate society's racial stereotypes to Afro-American children, which confuse them about the value of their racial identity and the strength of their culture?
4. Television advances notions related to sex roles and the structure of the family. To what extent does television perpetuate the notion that the Afro-American family is weak, the Afro-American man is powerless, and that there is conflict between the Afro-American man and woman?
5. Television depicts levels of academic and occupational attainment. To what extent does television convey to Afro-American children the concept that they can be successful only in an Afro-American environment, and to what extent must aspirations for broader occupational and academic positions in a multiracial world be limited?
6. Television occupies a prestige position in our society, and for some minority young people, it tends to validate and add glamour to the roles being portrayed. To what extent are children patterning their behaviors and establishing personal attitudes from television characters who may not be wholesome role models for their present and future psychosocial growth?
7. Television communicates concepts concerning intergroup and intragroup relationships. To what extent does television portray, through violent and aggressive action and formats, that wholesome relationships between various racial groups, and within one's own group are difficult to obtain?

These issues are crucial for mental health professionals because the developers of program materials simply do not have the luxury of not showing Afro-American children destructive adult and/or child models who will reinforce old sterotypes concerning the image of Afro-Americans. Afro-American children need programs that are bold enough to show the strengths of their history and a cross-section of their culture and life styles. They need programming aimed at showing adult and child models who have human foibles, but who are also fully capable, humane, and cognitively functioning individuals. The Afro-American child needs to learn that this is a pluralistic country which has no "model American." They need to understand from television that to be racially, religiously, or ethnically different does not make you "disadvantaged," "deprived," or "inferior," and that it is important to take pride in unique customs, skin color, language, and life styles.[33]

Clearly, one can argue that the development of faulty self-esteem attitudes among minority children in general, and Afro-Americans in particular, does indeed retard psychosocial progress. In the final analysis, however, damage is done to white children as well. They also must learn not to develop stereotyped attitudes toward children of different racial groups. While this chapter has focused on the Afro-American child, the core of the author's concern, and the concern of all of us in the helping professions, is to foster good mental health among all children everywhere.

REFERENCES

1. Hiebert RE, Ungurait D, Bohn TW: Mass media: An Introduction to Modern Communication. New York, McKay, 1974, p. 6
2. Johnson N: What can we do about television? In Emery MC, Smythe TC (Eds): Readings in Mass Communication: Concepts and Issues in the Mass Media. Dubuque, Iowa, William C. Brown, 1977, p. 31
3. Liebert RM, Neale, JM, Davidson ES: The Early Window: Effects of TV on Children and Youth. New York, Pergamon, 1973, p. ix
4. Adler R: Introduction: A context for citicism, in Adler R, Cater D, (Eds): Television as a Cultural Force. New York, Praeger, 1976
5. Kaye E: The Family Guide to Children's Television: What to Watch, What to Miss, What to Change and How to Do It. New York, ©Pantheon Books (a Division of Random House, Inc), 1974, p. 3
6. Greenberg B, Dervin B: Mass communications among the urban poor. Public Opinion Quarterly, 1970, 34:224–235
7. Comstock G: Television and Human Behavior: The Key Studies. Santa Monica, Cal., RAND, 1975, p. 23

8. Berry G, Mitchell-Kernan C: Toward a Conceptual Focus for the Study of Television and Ethnicity. Unpublished manuscript, Center for Afro-American Studies, University of California, Los Angeles, 1976
9. Poussaint AF: Building a strong self-image in the black child. Ebony, 29:138–143, 1974
10. Sutton-Smith B: Child Psychology. New York, Appleton-Century-Crofts, 1973, p. 486
11. Vinacke WE: Foundations of Psychology. New York, Van Nostrand Reinhold, 1968, p. 818
12. Shavelson RJ, Hubner, JJ, Stanton, GC: Self-concept: Validation of construct interpretations. Rev Ed Res 46:407–441, 1976
13. Kelly HH: The process of causal attribution. Am Psychologists 107–128, 1973
14. Rogers C: Client Centered Therapy. Boston, Houghton Mifflin, 1965, p. 498
15. Coopersmith S: The Antecedents of Self-Esteem. San Francisco, W. H. Freeman, 1967, pp. 4–5
16. Wells LE, Marwell G: Self-Esteem: Its Conceptualization and Measurement. Beverly Hills, Cal., Sage, 1976, p. 62
17. Rosenberg M: Society and the Adolescent Self-Image. Princeton, N.J., Princeton University Press, 1965, p. 67
18. Powell GJ: Black Monday's Children: A Study of the Effects of School Desegregation on Self-Concepts of Southern Children. New York: Appleton-Century-Crofts, 1973, p. 28
19. Leifer, AD, Gordon NJ, Graves SB: Children's Television—More than Mere Entertainment. Harvard Ed Rev 44:213–245, 1974
20. Himmelweit HT, Oppenheim AN, Vince P: Television and the Child: An Empirical Study of the Effects of Television on the Young. London, Oxford University Press, 1966, p. 3
21. Shaver KG: Principles of Social Psychology. Cambridge, Mass., Winthrop, 1977, p. 325
22. Noble P: The Negro in Films. Port Washington, N.Y., Kennikat Press, 1969, p. 12
23. Report of the National Advisory Commission on Civil Disorders. New York, Bantam, 1968, p. 383
24. Berry GL: Television and Afro-Americans: Past legacy and present portrayals, in Withey SB, Abeles FP (Eds): Television and Social Behavior. New York, Social Science Research Council, 1977, p. 20
25. U.S. Commission of Civil Rights: Window Dressing on the Set: Women and Minorities in Television. Washington, D.C., U.S. Government Printing Office, 1977, p. 148.
26. Banks J, Grambs J: Black Self-Concept: Implications for Education and Social Science. New York, McGraw-Hill, 1972, p. 185
27. Dorr A: Television and the socialization of the minority child, Paper presented at conference sponsored by the Center for Afro-American Studies and the National Institute of Mental Health, University of California, Los Angeles, 1978
28. Los Angeles Times, September 21, 1978, part 4, p. 25
29. Stevenson HW, Stewart EC: A developmental study of racial awareness in young children. Child Devel 29:399–410, 1958
30. Goodman, ME: Evidence concerning the genesis of interracial attitudes. Am Anthropologist 48:624–630, 1946
31. Arnez NL: Enhancing the black self-concept through literature, in Banks JA, Grambs JD (Eds): Black Self-Concept: Implications for Education and Social Science. New York, McGraw-Hill, 1972, p. 112.

32. Nobles WW: Psychological research and black self-concept: A critical review. J Soc Issues 29:11–31, 1973
33. Berry GL: Television and the black child: Some psychological imperatives, in Smith WD, Burlew KH, Mosley MH, et al (eds): Reflections on Black Psychology. Washington, D.C. University Press of America, 1978, p. 115

Gail Elizabeth Wyatt

18 Identifying Stereotypes of Afro-American Sexuality and Their Impact upon Sexual Behavior

The expression of sexuality is but one aspect of an individual's makeup and one dimension of the personality. However, interest in the sexual behaviors of Afro-Americans has ranged from one of piqued curiosity to concern and fear, and consequently has sometimes excluded Afro-Americans from the mainstream of society. Much of what we know about sexuality is derived from sex research literature which describes sexual behaviors in America. But, Afro-American populations have either been excluded from these studies, or the samples utilized were highly stratified, about which few, if any, generalizations could be made to larger populations.[2,3]

Other studies of attitudes of sexual permissiveness and social codes have included Afro-American samples, though they tend to be equally as select and are usually representative of only indigent populations.[4,5] These studies describe Afro-Americans as generally more sexually permissive than their white peers and as having social codes that adhere to a single rather than a double standard of sexual behavior for men and women. In other words, virginity would be no more expected for an Afro-American woman than it would be for an Afro-American man. More recently, pregnant Afro-American teenagers and women have been the focus of research in order to better understand the reportedly earlier onset of sexual activity, the increase in teenage pregnancies, and the general increase in unwed pregnant women.[6–10]

One study by Bell took advantage of the large population of men in the armed services to gather data on the differences in penis size of white and Afro-American men. While Afro-American men were found to have longer penises in the flaccid state, there were no significant differences in the length of the erect penis between the two ethnic groups.[12] There is less empirical data regarding Afro-American men than women, but it is not difficult to speculate why this particular study was conducted. Penis length must have been of great concern to men who reinforced their sense of masculinity based upon the size ot their genitalia.

Consequently, much of what has been written about Afro-American sexuality has been criticized because of the sampling biases, the tendency to report data on sexual attitudes, and the tendency to assume that these attitudes are an accurate gauge of sexual behaviors.[14] There are few descriptions of the sexual attitudes and behavior of the Afro-American adults from middle and upper economic backgrounds.[15] Essence magazine has conducted a nationwide survey of the sexual behaviors of 25,000 college educated middle income Afro-American women.[16] However, this information is of limited value because the data was collected through mail correspondence, and suffers from problems of accuracy and generalizability. Probably one of the favorite pasttimes of children and adults of all ages and sexes is to fill out questionnaires sent through the mail. Undoubtedly, a sex questionnaire offers endless possibilites for fulfilling one's fantasies, especially when the respondent does not have to take responsibility for the accuracy of his or her responses. There may also be differences in sexual behavior according to region of the country in which the subjects are reared as well as according to economic background and family values. Few researchers have attempted to utilize a model which accounts for these differences with any ethnic group.

In the face of limited empirical descriptive data on samples from which generalizations can be made, we can only assume that there may be some sociocultural factors influencing the sexuality of Afro-Americans that have yet to be identified. On the other hand, stereotypes of Afro-American sexuality are still perpetuated in jokes, social conversations, and in the written and visual media, as well as through research.

The socialization experiences that took place during slavery with its history of sexual exploitation has contributed to this society's preoccupation with the sexual mores of Afro-Americans. There has been no other ethnic group in America, and indeed in many parts of western civilization, whose existence was dependent upon their ability to reproduce other "saleable" human beings for the economic gain of their owners. Thus, there are several hundreds of years worth of attitudes, assumptions, and generalizations about Afro-American sexuality that have managed to survive the span of time and to manifest themselves in stereotypes or myths about the sexuality of Afro-American people. These generalizations characterize Afro-Americans in much the same way as some of the literature: sexy, hypersexual, permissive people, who have few morals about sexual promiscuity in or out of marriage.

This chapter will explore the genesis of some of the statements, explore the variety of sterotypes that appear to be prevalent, and examine their impact upon Afro-American sexuality.

THE GENESIS OF STEREOTYPES OF AFRO-AMERICAN SEXUALITY

There are a variety of sources that first observed the African culture and compared it to Western standards. As early as 1550, African religion, skin color, and behavior were perceived as inferior to that of white-Americans.[17] Missionaries who first traveled to Africa to convert "heathens" to Christianity were shocked by the "polygamy and diversity of sexual relationships" that they observed.[18] The religious belief that sexual mores were incorporated into the total concept of Christianity contrasted greatly with the African concept of sexuality. Many African nations followed a religious standard which did not include sexual morality as it is incorporated in Christian doctrine. The violation of laws was perceived as an offense against a person and not against God.[19] Nevertheless, assumptions about the innate sexual immorality of black people grew from these early observations.

Social scientists adhered to the biologically-determined immorality of Afro-Americans as a function of their adaptation to the hot climate of Africa. The climate was thought to preserve more intense sexual passions and to increase fertility.[20] An example of this kind of thinking was illustrated in the following: "Soberly speaking, Negro nature is so craven and sensuous in every fiber of its being . . . so deeply rooted in immorality are our Negro people that they turn in aversion from any sexual relation which does not invite sensuous embraces".[21] The stereotypes and myths which developed as a consequence of slavery were legitimized by literature describing slaves in the new world. As early as the 16th century, accounts describing the sexual prowess of Africans can be found. For example, African women brought to the new world on slave ships were described as "hot, unconstitutioned ladies". There was also great interest in the size and use of African male genitalia dating back almost four hundred years.[22]

Decker described many of the sexual stereotypes about women which developed with American slavery before the Civil War.[23] According to the southern image of the white-American woman was a perfect lady, delicate in looks and manner, and submissive to her husband. These stereotypes glorified motherhood but in reality, for many of the white women, there were endless pregnancies and deaths in childbirth as well as numerous children to care for. The circumstances around the lack of available contraceptives to control the number of births in this country's early history may have contributed to the stereotype of white women as disinterested in sex or asexual. These stereotypes of the womens' roles as homemakers were perpetuated into the 1950s and 60s, and were more the rule than the exception. The assertive womens' rights movement of the 60s and 70s served to change the image of the white-American woman and to equalize acceptance of their role and status within the home and in interpersonal relationships. However, these changes and stereotypes have not necessarily generalized to Afro-American women and the images that society has about them.

There are a number of vivid descriptions of the treatment of African slaves and their Afro-American descendents by slave masters in the South beginning in 1690 which served to perpetuate myths.[24,25] The breeding of slaves to swell the working force, and the subjugation of the female slaves to their slave masters, was best described in this passage: "Sexual intercourse between blacks and whites seems to have begun as soon as the former were introduced into America. Many white men and women came to think of black women as basically immoral, "loose and easy," deliberately enticive of white men. Some whites still believe this."[25,p.342]

The following quote describes how stereotypes of the white-American women as sexually chaste individuals and the Afro-American women as sexually available developed. "The cultural belief about the black female's sexuality emerged out of the experience of slavery. Sexual availability of slave women allowed white men to put white women on a pedestal, and to be perceived as goddesses of virtue. In a way, this became a self-fulfilling phophecy . . . white women were held aloof from the world of lust and passion and in many cases became more inhibited emotionally, sexually, and intellectually because of the oppressive impressions of slavery".[14,p.40)]

The reported hypersexuality of Afro-Americans was also equated with their potential to be savage and bestial with their partners.[22] Credibility was added to these accounts by physicians who, fearing attacks on white women, warned of Afro-American males' dangerous sexual potential.[22] Physicians were a major source supporting the scientific argument for racial separation. One physician who was concerned about limiting the sexual expression of Afro-American males, suggested that, "a few emasculated (by castration) Negroes scattered around and through the thickly settled Negro communities would really prove [insure] the conservation of energy, as far as the repression of sexual crimes is concerned".[26] Symbols of sexuality were increasingly manipulated to justify oppression and to increase fear and hatred between the races.

The period of reconstruction did not offer Afro-American men and women any greater rights to sexual integrity. For example, many women were still forced to submit to the sexual advances of white men often as a contingency for seeking and maintaining employment.[6] During this time, until the 1960s, Afro-American men were frequently lynched or almost assuredly convicted of rape or assault due to their suspected interests and relationships with white women.

The early scientific literature did not shed any insight upon the true nature of Afro-American sexuality, and instead tended to perpetuate stereotypes of its own. Some descriptions identified the Afro-American culture as one that tolerated promiscuity and readily accepted illegitimacy due to traditions that grew out of slavery.[11,28] Another example of the perpetuation of stereotypes in social science research was found in the study of the sexual patterns of three lower socioeconomic ethnic groups of adolescent males. Of the Afro-American youth, Rosenberg and Bensman state that "The Washington, DC Negro meets his date at school functions, has some sex instruction and knows some terminology (which is not always correct). He feels no obligation to marry a girl whom he impregnates".[30,p.26]

More recently since the wake of the Civil Rights movement, attempts by Afro-Americans to obtain more dominant roles in media than the images portrayed in the early years of film-making created a surge of black exploitation movies focusing on the hypersexuality of Afro-American men and women. The following quote encapsulates this new image: "Negative black stereotypes were more subtle and neatly camouflaged than they were in films of yesteryear, but the same insidious message is there; blacks are violent, criminal, sexy savages who imitate the white man's ways as best they can from their disadvantaged sanctuary in the ghetto".[30,p.26]

Poussaint expressed concern that Afro-Americans had incorporated these negative and destructive images and stereotypes and tended to develop a self-hatred that has made them easy victims for oppression.[30] King writes that the image of black women as depreciated sex objects also serves the function of rendering psychological damage upon black women as suitable marital partners of black men, and white men as well.[31]

In the popular press there seems to be a mixed message about Afro-American sexual behavior. One popular magazine exclusively written for Afro-American women described them as more sexually inhibited and aggressive than white women.[32] In another publication during that same year, Afro-American women were described as more sexually restrained and traditional in their sexual expression than white women, particularly in wife swapping and group sex.[33]

As recently as the summer of 1978, a top selling album recorded by an English group, "The Rolling Stones", included a song regarding the behavior of women of various ethnic group affiliations. In the song "Some Girls", they sing:

> White girls are pretty funny, sometimes they drive me mad; black girls just want to get f_______ all night. I just don't have that much jam. Chinese girls are so gentle they are really such a tease, you never know what they're cooking, inside those silky sleeves".[34]

This is a dramatic illustration that the stereotype of the "sexually uninhibited Afro-American woman" is still being perpetuated even in contemporary music, written and recorded by an English rock group, and serves to demonstrate how that stereotype has been accepted around the world.

Although Afro-American males have also been reported to be undersexed and unconcerned with their partner's sexual gratification, experiencing a decrease in masculinity, and having poor relations with females, the myth of black hypersexuality is still the most widespread today.[27] Currently, Afro-American men are being described as "super-studs" with unique retention powers and movements. Our society continues to perpetuate this image through media and other forms of communication. In spite of the limited study of black females hyposexual behavior by Kardiner and Ovesey,[27] the majority of stereotypes regarding Afro-American women described them as highly sexual and desirous of sex. The inconsistency in the messages communicated throughout the media are striking, and yet they have persisted throughout several centuries of this country's history.

DEFINING AND IDENTIFYING SEXUAL STEREOTYPES

Stereotypes have been described as preconceived notions regarding various groups and are often a component of prejudical beliefs towards groups or individuals.[35] Stereotypes cannot be defined as roles that individuals assume. Roles are learned and organized actions and attitudes which are covert or overt, and they are performed by a person within social interactions. However, sometimes stereotypes assume role properties, especially when the expectations of the role are favorable ones. For example, one sexual stereotype regarding Afro-American men that continues to be perpetuated in media is that they are super-studs or sexual "over-achievers."[30] This stereotype demonstrates the impact of favorable expectations regarding the extraordinary prowess of Afro-American men that some enjoy because the stereotype increases curiosity about Afro-American men's sexual behavior. However, there are few if any stereotypes which create favorable role expectations regarding the sexuality of Afro-American women.

Generally, stereotypes categorize people, tend to overlook individual differences and other influential factors which may explain behaviors, and may more frequently convey negative expectations. To quote Allport, Pettigrew, and Williams, "Life is simplified when stereotyped rejections are used. With the aid of aversive categories I avoid the painful task of dealing with individuals as individuals. It appears to be economically feasible as a mode of thought to use stereotypes".[36,p.518] Sexual sterotypes have often been used in order to understand Afro-American sexuality, rather than to examine individual behaviors, attitudes and to seek a dynamic approach to understanding these behaviors.

There is considerable evidence to substantiate that the stereotyping of minority group members has been shown to be important in understanding how people think they are expected to behave with others and what they think of themselves.[37] Concomitantly, there is documentation that some professional groups have images and stereotypes about Afro-Americans that tend to focus around their intelligence, impulsivity, and social desirability.[38–40] It is not surprising to note that Afro-Americans have been attributed the most undesirable of these traits. Other than the trait "pleasure loving," studies identifying stereotypes regarding Afro-Americans have excluded those directly related to sexual behavior. Thus, information is needed about the nature of stereotypes regarding Afro-American sexual behavior that are being perpetuated, as well as an assessment of Afro-American's awareness of these stereotypes and their influence upon sexual behavior.

In an attempt to identify stereotypes regarding Afro-American behavior, the following have been collected over the past 5 years, from a range of lay and professional people ranging in age and ethnic group origin. The purpose was to collect stereotypes and to note the range and diversity of their content.

Sexual Anatomy

AFRO-AMERICANS

- Have large buttocks and big legs (women)
- Have larger, longer genitalia (men)
- Have sexual anatomy which is located lower on the male anatomy

Sexual Behavior

AFRO-AMERICANS

- Are superstuds (hypersexual), i.e., frequently desire sex; are animalistic (highly physical and aggressive) (men).
- Are more sensuous, permissive, promiscuous (women).
- Have unusually long latencies to ejaculation (men).
- Make more noise during sexual intercourse (both sexes).
- Engage in premarital sex at early ages (both sexes).
- Are more sexually experienced and learn about sex at an early age (both sexes).
- Middle income women tend to be frigid and uninterested in sex.
- Seldom have difficulty becoming pregnant when they want to (women).
- Seldom require or desire foreplay before intercourse (both sexes).
- Are more fertile, and are rarely childless and have to adopt children (both sexes).
- Always have girlfriends even though they may be married (men).
- Lust after white women (men).
- Prefer to rape white women (men).
- Perspire more during sexual intercourse (both sexes).
- Willingly have babies outside of marriage (women).
- Are more sexually provocative and seductive than their other peers (women).
- Mature faster physically than their peers (both sexes).
- Don't engage in wife-swapping, group sex, or swinging (both sexes).

Attitudes and Values

AFRO-AMERICANS

- Are more clearly attached to their mothers than their husbands (women).
- Devalue sex for pleasure and emphasize sexual performance (both sexes).
- Use sex to gain material possessions (women).
- Do not perceive an illegitimate birth as immoral or sinful in the Afro-American family (both sexes).
- Believe that oral sex is not acceptable as a sexual behavior in the Afro-American community and is seen as degrading (both sexes).
- Believe that marriage is not as important to cement relationships as it is for other groups (both sexes).

THE IMPACT OF SEXUAL STEREOTYPES ON SEXUAL BEHAVIORS

Documenting sexual stereotypes has been difficult because of limited research in this area, and because the stereotypes themselves are so frequently controversial and inflammatory that they often generate heated discussions. In a recent study of sexual stereotypes, their sources, and ethnic group reference, Wyatt collected sexual sterotypes from a variety of lay and professional groups as well as from historical and social science literature. Fifty Afro- and white-American women from 20 to 35 years of age were asked if they had heard 13 of the most frequently listed statements. The majority of the women had heard statements describing sexual attitudes and values, descriptions of anatomy, male-female sexual relationships and sexual behaviors. However, for four of the statements, the Afro-American women had heard them significantly more than a similar group of their white-American peers.[13]

This study was the first to identify sexual stereotypes and to validate that these statements were somewhat familiar to women in general, and specifically to Afro-American women. The next question asked was, "Are these statements more frequently made in regard to women of one ethnic group?" The review of the history and social science research appears to single out Afro-American women more often as those with questionable morals regarding sex. Wyatt posed this question to the 50 subjects in her study and found that both ethnic groups of women more frequently ascribed statements regarding sexual attitudes and values, descriptions of anatomy and sexual behavior, both liberal and conservative, to Afro-American women. However, the Afro-American women tended to agree more with stereotypes regarding conservative sexual behaviors and positive aspects of their sexual performance.

They disagreed with statements describing liberal sexual behaviors which often duplicated the same messages conveyed by some social science research and media: Afro-American women are sexually promiscuous. In terms of the sources of these statements, both groups of women most frequently listed social interactions, peer groups, and general conversation with people as the sources of these sexual stereotypes.

This study offered some empirical support to the existence of these sexual stereotypes as they relate to Afro-American women. These stereotypic statements do raise questions about the expectations that Afro-American couples have about their sexual abilities, and the possibility of performance anxiety that stereotypes can create. In one study, a case history of a sexually dysfunctional Afro-American couple was described with a particular focus upon the stereotypes and expectations that both partners had internalized about their anatomy and sexual behaviors.[15] The following case study also illustrates the impact of expectations on sexual behaviors.

Ann, a 23-year-old, slightly overweight Afro-American woman, came for sex therapy with John, her tall and thin 27-year-old Afro-American husband of six years. They had two small children, and were both employed on different shifts, one during the day and the other one at night. They were renting a home while saving for one of their own. Ann was extremely shy and let John explain their reason for seeking therapy: Ann was "frigid" and had been uninterested in sex all during their marriage, but particularly after the children were born. John, on the other hand, was very adamant about their having intercourse every night. While he carefully described the conflicts that they were having about the differences in their sexual interests, he brushed a badge sewn on his jeans which read, "super-stud." John expected Ann to perform sexually during the two hours in which they were at home together, which also included dinner with their children, before he left for work. Ann experienced great guilt in admitting that she did not live up to the image of the "sexy black woman," both pysically and mentally, while John clearly perceived himself as "taking care of business," as was expected of a black man. In actuality, John failed to spend an adequate amount of time allowing Ann to become lubricated prior to intercourse, which became painful for her and increased her sense of failure when she failed to reach orgasm. Repeated failures lessened her desire to engage in sexual relations with her husband, thus diminishing her interest in sex. The responsibilities of parenting in their already busy and conflicting schedules only made matters worse.

It became clear that both partners were attempting to emulate sterotypes characterizing sexually uninhibited black couples, when in fact, their schedules and individual needs often did not necessarily fit these expectations.

This case illustrated the impact of performance anxiety upon sexual behaviors due to stereotypes about Afro-American sexuality. There are often stereotypes assigned to Afro-American sex therapists which can also influence the treatment process, as the following case study illustrates:

A middle-aged white couple sought sex therapy because their sexual contact had diminished greatly during the 29 years of their marriage. Initially, when greeted by a male and female Afro-American cotherapy team, they were skeptical about their therapists' competence. A brief verbal biography from each therapist assured the couple of their credibility, and subsequent conversations put the couple more at ease. In an individual history taking session with the male client, the Afro-American male therapist was assured that he would probably be a good teacher because if anyone knew how to "do it," this black therapist would, and therapy should be "exotic" with black male and female co-therapists.

The stereotypes of Afro-American males as exceedingly knowledgeable about sex and the sensual animalism of Afro-Americans became quite apparent in the conversation. Sexual stereotypes can influence the expectations of individuals and those that confront sex therapists. Optimally, once these stereotypes are identified, the couples or the therapist should be confronted as to their difficulty in accepting individual needs and situations presented in each therapy case.

AFRO-AMERICAN SEXUALITY AND TREATMENT ISSUES

Traditional psychoanalytic literature has not been helpful in understanding the relationship between sexuality and racism. The conflicts around Afro-American sexuality have been found to provide the basic motive of racism. In the past, according to one anonymous analyst, "The black man has been hated in the unconcious of most whites because he is believed to possess superior attributes for the act of copulation."

Current formulations focus upon the concept of infantile sexuality. A theory by Abrahamson states that the anxiety and hatred a white-American may feel toward Afro-Americans are really emotions that are displaced from early sexual feelings and conflicts toward the parents. This line of thought communicates the message that, unless an individual grows up free of the oedipal conflict, there can be no eradication of racism. Thus, liberation from sexual stereotypes are contingent upon the emancipation of the id. It also implies that there is nothing that we as behavioral scientists can do about racism, except to refer racist people to analysts. Yet, there are no systematic studies with adequate controls to support the broad speculations about the sexual basis of racism. More than likely, if the racial situation were absent, there would still be individuals with the same sexual problems, though the problems might assume different forms. Therapists have the responsibility to clarify racial issues that arise and to define and modify their own racial attitudes, as well as those of their clients.

IMPLICATIONS FOR FUTURE SEX EDUCATION TREATMENT AND RESEARCH

Treatment programs for sexual dysfunctions have largely been staffed by white therapists, and attract a white-American, affluent population. Recently, in many urban cities, Afro-American couples are increasingly seeking therapy for a variety of sexual problems, partly because sex therapy clinics are more readily available, and because our society generally has become more tolerant of sexual adjustment as an aspect of adult life. However, sex education should also be more readily available in order to raise the consciousness of those who are less willing to identify their sexual problems or lack of information as a problem requiring "therapy." Additionally, with increasing education regarding human sexuality, those who may be less likely to seek therapy may gain additional information on their own, and attempt to resolve problems which may be easily remediable with more educational information. Those who cannot resolve problems with more education may at least have the information available in terms of where they can seek sex therapy should it be needed.

There are several implications for future treatment and research which emerge from the review of the literature and examples of the impact of sexual stereotypes upon sexual behavior.

First, the therapist's receptivity to working with individuals whose sexual behavior is influenced by their cultural background is essential to treatment success. It is difficult, if not impossible, to maintain an objective approach to the treatment of anyone, and specifically Afro-American couples or individuals, without the therapist's committment to accepting aspects of the client's experience which might be expressed in forms of sexual behavior different from their own. It is helpful to understand sexuality, or the expression of sexuality, as one dimension of a socialization experience in which we all participate as individuals. Information conveyed, or the lack of it, as well as the expectations that others have, communicate educational messages which can, in fact, influence the expression of sexuality.

Secondly, it is the therapist's responsibility to obtain information regarding sexual stereotypes which permeate the greater community, and to identify stereotypes to which the client adheres. Prior to therapy, it is also important to examine whether sexual stereotypes, culture, and ethnicity tend to influence the therapist's attitude toward the clients. This kind of self-examination might lessen the likelihood of these variables interfering with the development of the therapeutic relationships.

Afro-American clients may enter treatment with feelings of discomfort, distrust, and resentment toward white therapists, especially where sexual behavior is the focus. As Bernard has cautioned, these feelings may produce counter-feelings in the therapist which could seriously jeopardize the treatment outcome.[41] Clients resent a therapist assuming the role of expert in discussions of sex, when, according to the stereotype, the "client" is supposed to be the "expert". The therapist needs to facilitate an open exploration of this possibility. The use of self-disclosure by therapists revealing their resistance to acknowledging and discussing their own problems can often allay the client's apprehensions about revealing their feelings in sex therapy.[42] Therapist's self-disclosures legitimize the client's expressions of discomfort when it becomes apparent that they are shared by more than one individual in the client–therapist relationship. In addition, interracial tensions can be minimized by assuring the clients that they can set their own goals, and that they will be enlisted as "therapeutic colleagues" in the treatment process.

This chapter elucidates several issues involved in treating Afro-American couples in sex therapy. It also exposes the critical need for additional descriptive research regarding Afro-American sexuality. Of particular importance are normative data, beyond that collected by Kinsey[1] and others,[3] which would illustrate similarities and differences within as well as between ethnic groups. Additional studies are needed to examine whether there are differences in the quantity of sexual contact and forms of sexual expression, as well as the incidence and prevalence of sexual dysfunctions. Research of this type would be a valuable asset to therapists and lay persons in validating or dispelling the sexual stereotypes regarding Afro-American sexual behavior.

REFERENCES

1 Kinsey A, Pomeroy W, Martin C, et al: Sexual Behavior in the Human Female. Philadelphia, W.B. Sanuders, 1953

2 Gebhard PH, Pomeroy WB, Martin GE, et al: Pregnancy, Birth and Abortion. New York, Wiley, 1958

3 Hunt M: Sexual Behaviors of the 1970's. Chicago, Playboy Press, 1974

4 Reiss I: The Sexual Context of Premarital Sexual Permissiveness. New York, Holt, Rinehart and Winston, 1967

5 Rainwater L: Some aspects of lower class sexual behavior. J Soc Issues 22:96–108, 1966

6 Castadot RG: Need for, difficulties and experiences with sexual behavior questionnaires among teenagers. Maryland St Med J 24:40–44, 1975

7 Kantner JF, Zelnick M: Sexual experiences of young unmarried women in the United States. Fam Planning Persp 4:9–18, 1972

8 Brunswick A: Adolescent, health, sex and fertility. Am J Pub Health 61:711–729, 1971

9 Delcampo R, Sporakowski M, Delcampo D: Premarital sex and permissiveness and contraceptive knowledge: A racial comparison of college students. J Sex Res 180–192, 1976

10 Youth Values Project. The Youth Values Report. The Experiment, Brattlesboro, Vt., 1978

11 Liben F: Minority group clinic patients pregnant out of wedlock. Amer J Pub Health 2:485–505, 1961

12 Bell A: Black sexuality: Fact and fancy, in Staples R, (ed): The Black Family: Essays and Studies. Belmont, Wadsworth, 1970, p. 77–80
13 Wyatt GE: Sexual stereotypes of Afro-American women: Their source and ethnic group reference. A paper presented at the American PsychologicalAssociation Convention, 1981
14 Staples R: The Black Woman in America. Chicago, Nelson Hall, 1973
15 Wyatt GE, Bass BA, Powell GJ: A survey of ethnic and socio-cultural issues in medical school education. J Med Educ 53:627–632, 1978
16 What does sex mean to you? Essence Magazine, January, 1979, p.50–68
17 Vontress C: The black male personality. Blk Scholar 2:10–16, 1971
18 Goldstein M: The roots of prejudice against the Negro in the United States. Boston, Boston University Press, 1948
19 Staples R: Sex behavior of lower income Negroes. Sexology October, 34:52–55, 1967
20 Dow GS: Society and its Problems. New York, Crowell, 1922
21 Thomas WH: The American Negro: What He Has, What He Is and What He May Become. New York, Macmillan, 1910
22 Thomas A, Sillen S: Racism and Psychiatry. New York, Bruner/Mazel, 1972
23 Deckard BS: The Women's Movement: Political, Socio-economic and Psychological Issues. New York, Harper and Row, 1975
24 Walker E: The black woman, in Smythe M, (ed): The Black American Reference Book. Englewood Cliffs, N.J., Prentice-Hall, 1976
25 Williams M, Newman P: Black Women's Liberation. New York, Pathfinder Press, 1970
26 Haller J. The physician versus the Negro: Medical and anthropological concepts of race in the late nineteenth century. Bull of the History of Med 44:154–167, 1970
27 Kardiner A, Ovesey L: The Mark of Oppression. Cleveland, World, 1951
28 Myrdal G: An American Dilemma. New York, Harper and Row, 1944
29 Rosenberg B, Bensman J: Sexual patterns of three ethnic subcultures of an American underclass. The Annals of the American Academy of Social Science: Sex and the Contemporary American Scene 376:61–75, 1968
30 Poussaint A: Cheap thrills that degrade blacks. Psychology Today, February, 1974, p.22-23
31 King MC: The politics of sexual stereotypes. The Blk Scholar 4:12–23, 1973
32 Young LC: Are black women taking care of business? Essence, May, 1974, p. 58
33 Staples R: Is the sexual revolution by-passing blacks? Ebony, March, 1974, pp.111–114
34 Rolling Stones Records. Some Girls. New York, Warner Communications, 1978
35 Baron B, Byrne D: Social Psychology: Understanding Human Interaction. Boston, Allyn and Bacon, 1977
36 Allport G, Pettigrew T, Williams R, Jr: Prejudice: A symposium, in Smythe M (ed): The Black American Reference Book. Englewood Cliffs, N.J., Prentice-Hall, 1976, pp.515–536
37 Sue S, Kitano H: Stereotypes as a measure of success. J Soc Issues 29:83–98, 1973
38 Zimet C, Zimet S: Educators view people: Ethnic group stereotyping. J Comm Psych 6:189–193, 1978
39 Maykovich MK: Changes in racial stereotypes among college students. Human Rel 25:101–120, 1972
40 Katz D, Braly K: Racial stereotypes of one hundred college students. J Abnorm Soc Psychol 28:280–290, 1933
41 Bernard VW: Psychoanalysis and members of minority groups. Am J Psych 1:256–267, 1953
42 Jourard SM: The Transparent Self. Princeton, N.J., D. Van Nostrand, 1964

Barbara Ann Bass

19

Interracial Dating and Marital Relationships: A Lecture

Interracial dating and marriage have always been touchy, explosive issues for both Afro- and white-Americans. Gunnar Myrdal, a Swedish social scientist, was invited to come to the United States and conduct a study of the race problem in America, the most thorough yet undertaken. One of the most interesting aspects of the race problem as formulated by Myrdal in his monumental work, *The American Dilemma*, is a schema he calls "The Rank Order of Discrimination." When white Southerners were asked what they thought blacks wanted most, they responded as follows:

1. intermarriage and sexual intercourse with whites
2. social equality and etiquette
3. desegregation of public facilities
4. political enfranchisement
5. fair treatment in the law courts

The curious thing about this rank order was that when Myrdal approached Afro-Americans, they listed exactly the same items as white-Americans, with one major difference: they listed them in exactly the reverse order. Today, the same reverse positions continue to be maintained with equal vigor by both white- and Afro-Americans.

Hernton asserts that neither whites nor blacks are being completely honest with themselves: "Of the various facets of the race problem in America, there is no doubt that the sexual aspect is as much a thorn in the side to blacks as it is to whites."[2] For their own special reasons, both groups are enormously concerned about this "thorn." In the North, the Midwest, and West, where there are few legal barriers against racial mixing, many Afro- and white-Americans suffer social ostracism and castigation for engaging in interracial sexual relations. The sexualization of the race problem is a reality affecting the sexual behavior of whites and blacks towards one another.

This American sexual nightmare began during slavery, when the first light-skinned Negro infant was born to a white woman; when the first black man was hunted down by a mob of jealousy-ridden white men; when the black man's genitals were torn off for "raping" a "chaste" white woman—the myth of sacred white womanhood became a reality.

One fact is certain: this myth was not created by the Southern white woman, and it was not propounded by the black woman nor the black man. It was, as it could only have been, the Southern white man who invented it to salve his own guilt. The white man's fear and guilt grew, as time went on, to an intensity that made him look around for even more stringent devices to ensure the "chastity" of his woman and to absolve himself from further guilt feelings toward his wife.[3] There were two psychological processes going on in the Southerner's mind: One was the deep sense of guilt arising from his cohabitation with black slave women: the second was his sense of immorality about a society founded and maintained on the principles of human slavery. Somehow, the entire "Southern way of life," sexual and otherwise, had to be justified. Sacred white womanhood emerged in the South as an immaculate mythology to glorify an otherwise indecent society.

As time went on, the Southern white woman accepted the sterile role her husband insisted she play; she became a doll, an ornament, a beautiful painting on a wall that is admired and given lip service by everyone but which is respected by no one.[4]

It was in this way, out of sheer necessity for sexual release and expression, that the Southern white woman focused her fantasies upon the most feared sexual symbol of her times—the black male. Her preoccupation with rape was not only a grotesque fantasy, but also an accurate index of her sexual deprivation. The black male became the scapegoat of the ideology of sex and racism as it was accepted by the white woman in Southern culture. While she did not actually lynch and castrate blacks herself, she permitted her men to do so in her name. The black male became the object of mutilation in and through which white women as well as white men could drain themselves of guilt, fear, and inadequacy. The black male became the living embodiment of not only the white woman's unconscious sense of sexual poverty, but of everything that was wrong with her life and her society. Just as it became necessary for the white man to protect the image of the black man as a savage rapist to soothe his guilt, it was equally imperative that the white woman accept this image as a means of proving to herself that she was sexually attractive, if not to white men, then at least to black "savages."[2]

For the white woman, "fighting the feeling of attraction" is an unconscious or a built-in process. Segregation and the myth of sacred white womanhood, combined with all the other ingredients that comprise the American brand of sex and racism, have distorted and vulgarized her perception of black men as sexual beings.[5] The thought of having relations with a black may be a revolting or an exciting thing. In either case, however, it is a vulgar thing, a perverse thing. Against the backdrop of taboo, of lies and stereotypes about the sexuality of blacks, theoretically the black man becomes the most powerful sex attraction in the life of the white woman. And this is largely due to the sexual myth that white men have created about black men.

Just as these sexual stereotypes may stimulate the curiosity of the white woman, the black male may be equally attracted by the concept of sacred white womanhood. It could only add to the natural attraction that most men feel toward the opposite sex.

Beth Day points out that, by contrast, the French, despite some early colonial laws against intermarriage with slaves that were as stringent as British law, have always held very different attitudes toward blacks from the British: "To begin with, no self-respecting Frenchman considered the black male—or any male—as a sexual threat, because in his heart he knew without a doubt that he was the greatest lover in the world."[6]

In a culture with the most sexual self-confidence, the least prejudice seems to exist. French sexual security was sufficiently strong that it did not demand the degradation of the conquered, as did the British, Dutch, German, and Belgian. The French dealt with the black man as a man, a potential equal.

The misuse of the sexual issue to obscure the problem of racial prejudice and oppression is most apparent in relation to the subject of marriage between black and white persons. The question, "Would you want your sister to marry one?" is one of the stalest chestnuts in the repertoire of racism. Nowhere else in the world is the question of one's potential brother-in-law considered a fitting retort to the demands for equal pay, decent housing, or the vote. This old retort may not be used as openly nowadays, but variations on the same theme are often sounded by people who are convinced that they really mean well.

Objections to Afro/white relationships are often couched in terms of the difficulty that the partners will face. Whenever people openly challenge deeply ingrained prejudices, they will meet with hostile responses.

Intermarriage poses an intense challenge. It says in the clearest possible way through a commitment of joining lives that the conventional wisdom is being discarded. Without a doubt, such a commitment will mean special stresses that will have to be coped with, but there are enough examples of successful interracial marriages to make it clear that such stresses are not necessarily overpowering.[7] As a matter of fact, when a husband and wife meet special problems and stresses of whatever kind, it can bring them closer if they cope with the problem cooperatively.

Another rationalization of those who oppose intermarriage is that such marriages are made for neurotic reasons. The marriage may be described as a gesture of defiance, usually toward the parents, an act of masochism, or a symptom of exhibitionism.[2] It is interesting that the emphasis on the neurotic basis for intermarriage is usually directed toward the white partner. Presumably, it is understandable why a black should want to marry a white, but the reverse must be due to some irrational motivation on the part of the white person. Since a substantial number of all marriages have neurotic bases, certainly many Afro/white marriages may have unsound bases. But such sweeping judgments do serious injustice to the healthy, normal individuals who have entered into such marriages manifesting the strength to withstand social disfavor and the courage to remain faithful to their own feelings. The "neurotic" theory feeds the racist concept that blacks and whites cannot live together on an equal basis.

Another racist argument related to intermarriage is that children of such marriages will be handicapped. One of the most tenacious myths of racism is that persons of mixed parentage are more vulnerable to mental disease than those of pure stock. In fact, it has been said that the "mixed blood" suffers from a disharmony and self-division that ultimately generate a mental breakdown.[6] The woebegone and psychologically torn mulatto, a perennial stereotype since the days of slavery, is proof that amalgamation of the races can lead only to disaster.

Robert Staples discussed the fact that because there are social taboos on any intimate association between members of different races, there may be different motives for the people who establish such relationships. First, he states, we must assume that blacks and whites may be equally attracted to each other as sexual partners.[9] Too often it is believed that the Afro-American partner is most desirous of the white-American partner because of higher social status of whites in this society. Yet the taboo on Afro-Americans as sexual mates may give them a certain mysterious quality which also stimulates the sexual appetite of white-Americans.

Whatever the reason, Staples shows that interracial dating appears most often in certain situations and among certain types of people;

especially in cities and among university students and professional people, where racial equality and integration are widely supported. Among these groups, interracial dating occurs with increasing frequency, and interracial marriage becomes increasingly likely.[9] There are white-Americans, mostly in the North, who do not make deliberate efforts to exclude Afro-Americans from the possibility of sexual intimacy. Such people usually come from radical or liberal family backgrounds and they themselves are often dedicated to liberal causes.[6,7]

Where interracial sex relations occur, problems can arise that are unique to this type of relationship. Especially in interracial sexual activity among unmarried couples, the possibility of an illegitimate child poses special problems. If the mother is white and unmarried, she may be reluctant to have what is socially considered a black child which she must raise by herself. This means that she must have an illegal or legal abortion or give birth to the baby and then put it up for adoption. A unique situation emerged in the state of Minnesota where the majority of black babies put up for adoption were children of white mothers.[6] In such cases, it was very difficult to find prospective adoptive parents for children who were products of such an illicit interracial sexual union. Many people of both races felt that any white female who has sex relations with a black male may be of low moral character or mentally deficient. As a result they were reluctant to adopt the children of such unions because they feared that the child may have inherited some of its mother's bad genes or traits.

Despite the problems inherent in interracial marriages, such unions appear to be increasing. The United States Supreme Court Ruling of 1967, making all laws prohibiting marriage between members of different races unconstitutional, along with the status gains for Afro-Americans in the 60s, also influenced this increase, yet black/white marriages are still less than 1 percent of all marriages in the United States.[10,11] Staples notes that most spouses in this type of marriage are in the same educational bracket,[9] and authorities who have studied the subject generally have concluded that these marriages have a fairly good chance of survival. The external pressures faced by the interracial couples are often great, but do not appear to be overwhelming. Staples points out that there is little research available on the success of interracial marriages.[9]

Day found that partners in interracial marriages are apt to be older than those who marry within their own race and that they are likely to be second marriages for one or both. She feels the implication is that the spouses may try even harder based on their first bad marriage or that, being older, they are now more mature. Reference is also made to the Burma study of marriages from 1948 to 1959 in Los Angeles, California, in which the white males who married black women were among the oldest group of males who married (median age of 36.7). Afro-American men who married white-American women, and Afro-American women who married outside of their group were also older than those who married inside their group.[6] The Golden study looked at 50 interracial marriages in Philadelphia; one-third of the spouses had been previously married to members of their own race.[8] In Day's sampling of 23 couples in California, the 4 oldest husbands (3 black, 1 white) and two of the black wives had been previously married. In the group of 5 couples who were still in their early 20s, it was a first marriage for both partners.[6] Four of this group were white husbands with black wives, which may indicate that white male partners are beginning to out-marry at an earlier age than they were at the time the Burma study was concluded.

Anticipating that they are likely to be discouraged by family and friends, interracial courtship is frequently characterized by concealment and secrecy. Sometimes the secrecy results from the fact that the home is unavailable to the mixed couple. White-American girls of high school and college age especially report that their parents do not allow their Afro-American boyfriends inside the house, that doors were slammed in their faces, and so on. There are cases where white parents have sent their daughters to psychiatrists, turned them over to a juvenile court, or sent police to see the Afro-American boyfriend in the hope of destroying the relationship.[8]

Mixed couples are usually correct in assuming that both sets of parents will be upset by the news. Although Afro-American parents are less likely to disown their child or attempt to separate the couple, and are more inclined to judge the in-law on individual merit later, Afro- and white-American parents appear to be equally distressed by the initial news.[12] In a study made of 721 black families in the Chicago area in 1964, nearly one-half said they strongly opposed interracial marriages and would try to prevent them.[13] Despite whites' fears of blacks' desires for intermarriage, only 3 percent of blacks of all classes said they would encourage such a marriage. The majority of Afro-American parents indicated, however, that they would put up with such a marriage, especially if it was already a fait accompli. Several of the black partners felt there was more real hostility from the black community today than from the white.

In Day's study of college students at Berkeley, among the militants, black women students were apt to hold the racial line more tightly than the men.[6] It is not unusual for the black coed who is committed to the black movement to say, in effect, that she wouldn't be caught dead with a white date, although males seem to feel that one can be politically committed and still date the partner of one's choosing. Some black militant men have been accused of persuading their white girlfriends to wear Afro hair styles and suntan make-up so that they can pass for black at black gatherings and not destroy the black man's credibility as a leader in the cause for black freedom. Campus dating and marrige appeared to be two very separate things, however. In a poll of white college students, five times as many students stated that they would date a black partner as would marry one; less than one-third, or 29 percent would consider marrying one.[13] Among Afro-American students, the order of preference in dating was first for members of their own group, followed by Northern whites of the same class; third for Africans of the same class; next for lower class American blacks, and last for white South Africans and lower class whites.

The Virginia Slims survey, "Women and Their Changing Values," was a massive study of the opinions of American women, including the issue of interracial marriage. Participants were asked a series of questions designed to determine how parents would react if their daughters married someone of another religion, used marijuana, had a homosexual relationship, etc. The results were broken down into a number of categories: males, females, black, white, various age groups, and so forth. The breakdown of the results from the question concerning interracial marriage was as follows: 14 percent of white women would accept it where 33 percent of the black women would; 38 percent of white women would accept it but would disapprove, as compared to 29 percent of the black women; 44 percent of the white women would both disapprove and not accept it, as compared to only 16 percent of the blacks; 5 percent of white women said that they did not know how they would react as compared to 21 percent of the black women. Male responses, on a racial basis, were consistent with female responses.[14] It is suggested that acceptance is more important than approval. It must be remembered that when people give responses to polls they tend to give more liberal answers, and they respond in a way that they figure is proper or expected when asked about controversial issues such as interracial marriage. In particular, it would be appropriate to presume that when confronted with such issues on a very personal level, their responses are likely to be quite different.

Golden's study of the patterns of interracial marriage was organized into different categories, one of which was the public symbolization of the marriage. He found the following:[8]

1. Relatives and friends discourage the marriage, and pressure is exerted to discontinue the relationship.
2. The couples find little opportunity for participation in larger groups unless they have previously moved in interracial groupings.
3. Each spouse is an outsider to the racial group of the other. The white

partners tend to become black oriented, and their social life is primarily with other interracial couples. However, there are contradictory findings in this area.[2,10,11]

4. A tendency of most mixed couples to carry on a sub-rosa courtship. Unless the black partner is passable, many couples frequent black places of public entertainment. Those who have little regard for public disapproval or who take delight in shocking respectable circles of society attend white resorts and public gatherings.
5. Many couples are isolated from their families—their parents are either dead or reside in another community. Since they have no strong ties to the community, group pressure has relatively little effect on them.

With regard to family relationships, Golden found that after the wedding, the pattern of concealment continued. The parents and siblings frequently were not notified about the marriage, especially when they were not told about the courtship. In some cases, the white spouse informed his or her parents in the hope that they would become reconciled; and sometimes the white spouse would avoid contact with his or her parents. While in many instances the white spouse's family refused to have any contact with the Afro-American spouse, the Afro-American family usually was willing to meet the white spouse. Their treatment of the white spouse depended on their judgment of the spouse as a person, rather than as a violator of mores. Couples whose marriages stood the test of time came to feel more comfortable in the black community. Many of the white spouses developed warm relationships with their wife's or husband's relatives, and in some cases, white in-laws became friendly with the black kinship group. A genuine liking of the black spouse developed in some cases, usually when the white parents were foreign-born. Sometimes the parent's affection for their child was great enough to overcome their feelings about interracial marriage. Lastly, there was no case in which the couple was completely ostracized by both white and black relatives.[8]

With regard to residence, Golden found that the couples tended to reside near other interracial couples. The tendency was to reside where Afro-Americans formed a small proportion of the population. In fact, a number of the families lived in peripheral areas, on the border between white and black residential areas.[8]

Golden also discussed briefly the children of such relationships. The child production record was small and may be accounted for partly by the high age at marriage—the median age was 28.3 for the entire group—and the possibility that these families feel insecure enough in their married lives not to invite the additional hazard of children. Many of the spouses had children from previous marriages.

Concerning the couples' relations with the community and their occupational adjustment, Golden found no instance of a white spouse with a prominent position in the community. Several of the black spouses were persons well-known in the black community, and their prestige seemed not to be injured by their intermarriage. Those couples who had associations with radical or Bohemian groups before marriage experienced no perceptible effect on their social positions. Some couples were sought after more, either from curiosity or admiration. A more common experience was for the white spouse to be avoided by former friends and acquaintances. Many white spouses admitted that they had not retained membership in their clubs, fraternal organizations, and other groups. A number of white wives joined black churches; others attended white churches without their spouses. It was further reported that relations with neighbors were cordial but not intimate, and that like the children, the white spouses became black socially.

Several white spouses reported that they had lost their jobs when their intermarriages were discovered. Others were careful not to let the fact of their marriages become known at their places of employment. Afro-American spouses seemed less subject to economic sanctions. The investigator was told of a few black professional men whose white wives were "passing" as black in order to avoid possible economic sanctions by the black community.[8] A sizeable proportion of both black and white husbands were self-employed and, therefore, less subject to economic reprisals. The black professionals interviewed had made a successful economic adjustment with a large clientele and high income.

Day, whose research took place eighteen years after Golden's, presents the opposite view in many respects.[6] However, as reported in a recent article by Maye, biracial couples still face widespread discrimination,[15] although some say bias has subsided. Housing problems and fears of violence are cited. The climate surrounding interracial relationships is much calmer than it was 10 or 15 years ago, particularly in the major cities. At the same time, however, some attitudes have not changed greatly. The shooting of Vernon E. Jordan, Jr., Executive Director of the National Urban League, while he was in the company of a white woman, has made many biracial couples fearful. Mixed couples might feel comfortable when seen in commerical areas of large cities, but in small towns in the North and South they still attract a great deal of attention. While some things may have changed, many people's tolerance or acceptance of interracial dating and marriage has not.

REFERENCES

1. Myrdal G: An American Dilemma. New York, Harper, 1944, pp. 60–61
2. Hernton CC: Sex and Racism in America. New York, Grove Press, 1966, p. 4
3. Smith C: Negro-white intermarriage—Forbidden sexual union. J Sex Res 2:169–178, 1966
4. Smith L: Killers of the Dream. New York, Doubleday, 1963, p. 79
5. Grier WH, Cobbs PM: Black Rage. New York, Grove Press, 1969, p. 92
6. Day B: Sexual Life between Blacks and Whites: The Roots of Racism. New York, Thomas Y. Cromwell, 1972, p. 121
7. Golden J: Facilitating factors in Negro-white intermarriage. Phylon 20, Fall 1959, p. 132
8. Golden J: Patterns of Negro-white intermarriage. Am Soc Rev 19:144–147, 1954
9. Staples R: Negro-white sex: Fact and fiction. Sexology 35:49–58, 1968
10. Heer DM: Negro-white marraige in the United States. J Marriage and the Fam 28:262–273, 1966
11. Heer DM: The prevalence of black-white marriage in the United States, 1960–1970. J Marriage and the Fam 36(2):246–258, May 1974
12. Washington JR: Marriage in Black and White. Boston, Beacon Press, 1970, p. 305
13. Gordon A: Intermarriage: Interfaith, Interracial, Interethnic. Boston, Beacon Press, 1964, p. 265
14. Bontemps A: National poll reveals startling new attitudes on interracial marriage. Ebony, 144–151, Sept 1975
15. Maye JD: Biracial couples still face widespread discrimination. Los Angeles Times, Part I-A, p.1, Sept 13, 1980

Index